A COLLEGE OF HER OWN

A COLLEGE OF HER OWN

THE HISTORY OF BARNARD

ROBERT McCAUGHEY

Columbia University Press
New York

COLUMBIA
UNIVERSITY
PRESS

Columbia University Press gratefully acknowledges the generous support
for this book provided by a Publisher's Circle member.

Columbia University Press wishes to express its appreciation for assistance
given by the Pushkin Fund in the publication of this book.

Columbia University Press
Publishers Since 1893
New York   Chichester, West Sussex
cup.columbia.edu
Copyright © 2020 Columbia University Press

Library of Congress Cataloging-in-Publication Data
Names: McCaughey, Robert A., author.
Title: A college of her own : the history of Barnard / Robert McCaughey.
Other titles: History of Barnard
Description: First Edition. | New York : Columbia University Press, 2020. |
Includes bibliographical references and index.
Identifiers: LCCN 2019059107 (print) | LCCN 2019059108 (ebook) |
ISBN 9780231178006 (Cloth) | ISBN 9780231552004 (eBook)
Subjects: LCSH: Barnard College—History.
Classification: LCC LD7033 .M34 2020 (print) | LCC LD7033 (ebook) |
DDC 378.747/1—dc23
LC record available at https://lccn.loc.gov/2019059107
LC ebook record available at https://lccn.loc.gov/2019059108

Cover design: Noah Arlow
Cover image: ©Barnard College

For Hannah, BC '89 and Stephen, John and Sarah

River and Bode, Wyatt and Fiona, BC 2030,

And, as Always, *Con Molto Amore*, Ann.

And for Colleagues Who Died in The Service
of Barnard College

Annette Baxter, BC '47
Bernice Segal
Sally Chapman
Les Lessinger
Barbara Miller, BC '61
Bill Mcneil
Irene Bloom
Natalie Kampen
Alan Segal
Cathy Nepomnaschy

CONTENTS

PREFACE

A COLLEGE OF HER OWN: THE HISTORY OF BARNARD

What follows in this book is a comprehensive history of Barnard College. It tells the story of an educational institution, from its founding in 1889 to the outset of its current presidency in 2019. Like others, past and present, Barnard is an academically rigorous, private, liberal arts college for women that, beginning in the 1920s, numbered among the prestigious Seven Sister colleges and, with five of them, has retained its original single-sex status. However, its affiliation with Columbia University and its location in New York City set Barnard apart.

While my history considers a variety of institutional characteristics, I am unevenly equipped to give each equal justice. Barnard's private status, its curriculum, and its place among other women's colleges all fall within the workaday concerns of historians of American higher education, which for my sins I am so classified. The college's other defining characteristics are more problematic. In my favor is that I have written a history of Columbia University and another on Columbia's engineering school, I have been a member of the Columbia History Department for most of my Barnard-based career, and I have served for seven years as Barnard Dean of the Faculty; with these credentials, I hope I am able to shed new light on the ups and downs of the Barnard-Columbia relationship.

I also acknowledge that I may be less able to appreciate the essence of Barnard as a women's college than others who have studied and written about the college's history. These include departmental colleagues Rosalind Rosenberg and Nancy Woloch; Barnard alumna and historian Lynn Gordon, class of 1962; and the Wellesley-based historian Helen Lefkowitz Horowitz. Also included in this group are Barnard alumnae of an earlier generation who wrote official histories of Barnard: Alice Duer Miller, class of 1899; Susan Myers, class of 1898; Marian White Churchill, class of 1929; and Marjorie Housepian Dobkin, class of 1944. I allow also that in reading the accounts of Barnard's history by Annie Nathan Meyer and Virginia C. Gildersleeve, I may have missed some gender-related nuances, but not for lack of trying. Nor can I bring to the task direct knowledge of the college as an undergraduate, however much my daughter Hannah, class of 1989, has tried to communicate her experience intergenerationally.

To my surprise, it was Barnard's continuous New York City locale that has most captured my attention in the course of researching and writing *A College of Her Own*. Barnard is a longtime resident in two New York City neighborhoods, and I have spent an occupational lifetime on its snug four-and-a half-acre campus. Both facts produced a belated appreciation in me of the role of geographical propinquity and setting in the lives of both individuals and institutions.

Let me provide two preemptive comments for interpretive approaches that violate instructions received in graduate school. The first was to avoid what Herbert Butterfield disparaged as the "Whig interpretation of history," writing history as an inevitable march of progress, with the present always an improvement on the past. The narrative that follows, while not one of uniform upward movement, does takes us to higher ground as the college approaches the present. It also gives hope—if not assurance—of still further progress. We can call it neo-whiggish, if you like.

The second preemptive comment concerns avoiding the "presidential synthesis," by which Thomas Cochran warned political historians against structuring their national narratives around the presidents of the moment. Here, too, the following narrative is unapologetically old-fashioned. I assign the college's female administrative leaders a substantial measure of responsibility and agency for what occurs on their respective watches. And if, on balance, and clearly of late, doing so involves giving more credit to recent leaders, it aligns Barnard's trajectory with a larger vision subscribed to here, as expressed by Theodore Parker, by way of Martin Luther King Jr. and more recently Barack Obama: "The arc of the moral universe is long, but it bends toward justice."

ACKNOWLEDGMENTS

My first acknowledgments are to Barnard administrators who helped make this book project possible. They include Joanne Kwong, in 2014 the college's communications director, who at the time of Barnard's 125th anniversary first encouraged me to undertake such a book. Former resident Debra Spar, President Sian Leah Beilock, and Provost Linda A. Bell provided encouragement and support. Several Barnard trustees, past and present, have taken a lively interest in its progress: Anna Quindlen, class of 1974; Jolyne Caruso-Fitzgerald, class of 1981; Cheryl Milstein, class of 1982; Mary Ann Lufromento, class of 1977; and the late Gedale Horowitz.

Next come the Barnard students in my seminar, Making Barnard History, and in my senior thesis seminar, and who have provided research assistance over the past five years. Special thanks go to Mollie Galchus, class of 2015; Elizabeth Moye, class of 2015; Jenna Davis, class of 2015; Loren Gorab, class of 2016; Emma Jones, class of 2017; Maya Garfinkel, class of 2019; Allison Stewart, class of 2020; Peter Richards, Columbia class of 2018; and Ganesh Ravichandran, SEAS class of 2019.

Crucial help during the research phase was provided by Barnard archivists Shannon O'Neill and Martha Tenney, as well as by Jocelyn Wilk, the curator of the Columbia University Archives. Technical support also came from Alyssa Rod; Anna Carlson, class of 2018; and Izy Sibbers, class of 2019, and of the Barnard Empirical Reasoning Center; and Marko Krkejias, of the Barnard Digital Instruction Center.

I wish to acknowledge the support throughout of Columbia University Press, in the persons of Director Jennifer Crewe and Senior Editor Philip Leventhal. Philip Leventhal worked with me on my last two books, improving both with his incisive suggestions. (He bears no responsibility for those I have not followed.)

To several departmental colleagues, I owe much thanks. As successive department chairs, Lisa Tiersten and Dorothy Ko have been supportive and forbearing. Herb Sloan, Rosalind Rosenberg, and Nancy Woloch merit recognition for their close readings, critical analysis, and knowledgeable support at all stages of this project and projects past.

A COLLEGE OF HER OWN

1

"WHAT'S A NEW YORK GIRL TO DO?"

I had the shrewd theory that to put any radical idea across, it must be in the most conservative manner possible.

—ANNIE NATHAN MEYER, *IT'S BEEN FUN*[1]

I t is in the nature of origin stories that they aspire to the mythic. Should Barnard's beginnings be so rendered, the story would properly begin with the college's two prime movers, the admirable Frederick A. P. Barnard, who tried in 1879, at the age of seventy, to open the male-only Columbia College to women, and the estimable Annie Nathan Meyer, who, a decade later, at the age of twenty, succeeded in creating a college for women in New York City and assured Barnard a measure of immortality by naming "her college" after him.

The more prosaic approach begins with an account of women's higher education before Barnard College to understand the particular challenges Barnard and Meyer took on. When Barnard opened in 1889, some fifty institutions spread across twenty-five states already provided collegiate instruction to women. Among the women's colleges that later came to be known as the Seven Sisters, Barnard College was the last to open. Barnard and Meyer's claim to our attention is their taking up the more localized challenge of introducing collegiate education to the young women of New York City. The history of Barnard is very much a Gotham tale.

BEFORE BARNARD: WOMEN'S HIGHER EDUCATION IN THE GILDED AGE

Historians of American higher education for women typically begin their account in the 1830s, two centuries after the founding of male-only Harvard College in 1636. Georgia Female College (later Wesleyan College) in Macon, Georgia, was chartered in 1836 and opened shortly thereafter as a women's college under the auspices of the Methodist-Episcopal Church. Oberlin College, in northeastern Ohio, founded in 1833 by Presbyterian ministers, admitted women along with men upon its opening in 1837. That same year, Mary Lyon founded Mount Holyoke Female Seminary in South Hadley, Massachusetts. Chartered as a seminary and focused on preparing women for careers in the foreign missions, Mount Holyoke most closely approximated in its setting, curriculum, and ambitions the leading men's colleges of the antebellum period.[2]

Other women's colleges followed, including Mills College (1852) in northern California and Elmira College (1855) in upstate New York. The 1860s witnessed a second surge in educational opportunities for women. The decision of the brewer Matthew Vassar to commit his fortune to establishing a women's college in his hometown of Poughkeepsie, New York, led in 1861 to the chartering of Vassar College and its opening four years later. The college's substantial financial backing, spacious campus, architecturally distinctive buildings, and impressively credentialed faculty promptly put Vassar at the forefront of women's colleges and on an academic par with all but a half dozen of the two-hundred-plus men's colleges then operating.[3]

The passage by Congress of the Land-Grant College Act (also known as the Morrill Act) in 1862 advanced the cause of state-funded higher education by allotting federal lands to the sixteen states of the Union for the support of colleges focused on agriculture and technology. Among the states that moved aggressively to do so, Michigan, Wisconsin, Illinois, and California all admitted women to their newly established land-grant universities, in some cases to achieve enrollment levels sufficient to satisfy state taxpayers. Cornell University was a hybrid: it was founded in Ithaca, New York, as a private institution by telegraphy magnate Ezra Cornell in 1865 but was also a recipient of New York's land-grant funding; it also admitted women upon its opening in 1868.[4]

In 1875, two more women's colleges in Massachusetts opened their doors. Smith College, in Northampton, was founded with funds from the local estate of Sophia Smith (1796–1870) for "the establishment and maintenance of an Institution for the higher education of young women . . . to furnish for my own sex means and facilities for education equal to those which are afforded now in our Colleges to young men." That same year, Wellesley College, situated in the Boston suburb for which it was named, admitted its first class of women thanks to the support of founders Henry and Pauline Durant. Four years later, agitation by Arthur Gilman and prominent Cambridge women, among them Elizabeth Agassiz, the widow of Harvard scientist Louis Agassiz, persuaded Harvard's President Charles W. Eliot to open an "Annex," where local young women could receive instruction similar to but separate from that offered the men of nearby Harvard.[5]

In 1885, Bryn Mawr College opened in the Philadelphia suburb of the same name, thanks to the benefaction of Joseph W. Taylor (1810–1880), a wealthy Quaker physician. His reasons for doing so mirrored those of Sophia Smith: "I have been impressed with the need of such a place for the advanced education of our young female Friends, and to have all the advantages of a College education which are so freely offered to young men." In 1887, after five decades as a seminary, Mount Holyoke Female Seminary altered its charter name by adding "and College."[6]

In addition to these six colleges, by the late 1880s, women had access to a dozen other women's colleges. While most were clustered in the Northeast, coeducational institutions, which enrolled a majority of the 50,000 women attending college, represented the norm in other regions. In New York State alone, colleges open to women included the aforementioned Vassar College, Elmira College, and Cornell University, but also the women-only Wells College in upstate Aurora, and the coeducational Colgate University and Syracuse University.[7]

What then of opportunities for the higher education of women in New York City? By the 1880s, New York City had been the nation's largest city for seven decades, with a population approaching 2,000,000 and with contiguous Brooklyn home to another 1,000,000. The city boasted five colleges, the oldest of which, Columbia College, was founded in 1754 by the city's Anglicans as King's College. The University of the City of New York (later New York University) came next, privately founded in 1831 by Presbyterians, to be followed by St. John's (later Fordham), founded in 1841 by the Catholic archdiocese and located in the Bronx; the Free Academy (later City College of New York), founded in 1847, located on Twenty-Third Street and supported by city taxpayers; and Cooper Union, in the East Village, founded in 1859 by the manufacturer and philanthropist Peter Cooper. All were men-only and in the late 1880s collectively enrolled almost one thousand young men.[8]

The sole local option for New York City's women in search of higher education was the Female Normal and High School, which opened in 1870 in lower Manhattan just east of Astor Place. Its purpose was preparing young women for teaching positions in the city's primary and secondary schools. Like the Free Academy and Cooper Union, the Normal School was tuition free, but unlike its male counterparts, which offered four-year programs and an AB degree, it had a two-year program and provided only a certificate upon completion.[9]

This paucity of educational opportunity had not gone unnoticed by New York's women. In 1869, thirty-six-year-old Lillie Devereux Blake, a widow, mother of two, feminist, and journalist, launched a campaign to open Columbia College to women. Her point of attack was the college's law school, founded in 1857, where she proposed enrolling her older daughter. She later sought permission for women to attend lectures (and tacitly received it from two accommodating instructors) at the college's School of Mines, which opened in 1864. In 1873, she presented a half dozen young women for admission to the college. All these efforts were thwarted by the Columbia board of trustees, although one of its members, the lawyer and diarist George Templeton Strong, while finding the prospect of mixing Blake's "pretty little daughters" among freshmen to be a "shock [to] all my conservative instincts," did not dismiss the idea that "strong-minded womankind" had a right to a collegiate education.[10]

Three years later, in 1876, a second petition calling for the admission of women into Columbia College was directed at its trustees. It came from Sorosis, a network of women's clubs with a chapter in New York City under the leadership of suffragist and activist Elizabeth Cady Stanton. This, too, was summarily rejected by the Columbia board. Although there is no evidence that Columbia's president Frederick A. P. Barnard dissented from the board's action, it may have been the occasion for him to question the conventional wisdom as to the deleterious impact serious study had on women's reproductive functions, to which his colleagues on the board faithfully adhered. Columbia's tenth president was by constitution and habit a contrarian and, with his wife's urging, something of a feminist.[11]

THE ADMIRABLE FREDERICK

In the spring of 1879, during the fifteenth year of his presidency, the seventy-year-old Frederick A. P. Barnard publicly launched his campaign to open the 125-year-old Columbia College to women. He could not have known then or in the decade before his death in 1889 that the failure of this quixotic effort would nonetheless gain him a place in posterity as the namesake of a women's college whose gender-exclusiveness was precisely what he had faulted the all-male Columbia of his day.

Barnard was one of those rare people who grew more progressive with age. Born in 1809 in the southwest corner of Massachusetts to Episcopalian parents, he entered the Calvinist-infused Yale College in 1824. In his senior year, Yale's president Jeremiah Day, joined by his faculty, published a spirited defense of the college's prescribed classical curriculum, to which most other colleges of the day and for the next generation faithfully subscribed. Barnard, however, in his subsequent academic career favored the free-elective system championed by Harvard presidents Josiah Quincy and Charles W. Eliot. Further evidence of Barnard's openness to progressive ideas were his evolving views on race. As a professor at the University of Alabama and president of the University of Mississippi in the 1850s, he owned at least one slave, but as the tenth president of Columbia College (1864–1889), he urged the Columbia board to open the college to "every religious creed and race—and sex."[12]

Although Barnard's championing of women's higher education came late, he readily acknowledged the outsized role women had played in his life, including his mother, Augusta, and his older sister, Sally. Another was Catherine Beecher, the feminist educator and founder of the Hartford Female Seminary, who hired Barnard after Yale dropped him (either because of his Episcopalian faith or his deafness). Beecher also secured Barnard his next position at the coeducational New York Institution for

FIGURE 1.1 Frederick A. P. Barnard (1809–1889), tenth president of Columbia College (1864–1889), and namesake of Barnard College. Portrait in oil by Eastman Johnson, 1886. Art Properties, Avery Architectural & Fine Arts Library, Columbia University, Commissioned by the Trustees (C00.110).

the Instruction of the Deaf and Dumb. In 1838, intent on landing a collegiate position and finding none in the Northeast, Barnard accepted a mathematics professorship at the new and decidedly raw University of Alabama in Tuscaloosa. There he achieved modest success as a popularizer of astronomy and physics.

In 1849, after several years as a bachelor and an acquired reputation as a drinker, the forty-year-old Frederick married the twenty-four-year-old, Ohio-born Margaret McMurray. The drinking stopped, and thereafter

Margaret never left his side, helping him revive his stalled academic career even as his deafness became nearly total. After he secured ordination as an Episcopalian minister, Barnard and his wife departed Tuscaloosa for Oxford in 1854 when he accepted the presidency of the University of Mississippi. When the Civil War broke out seven years later, the Barnards quietly planned their escape from the Confederacy with their two young sons in tow. They managed to flee in 1862 on a diversionary visit to Norfolk, Virginia. Once behind Union lines, they declared themselves admirers of President Lincoln and were welcomed to Washington, DC, by Frederick's younger brother, John, a Union general charged with the defense of the nation's capital.[13]

Barnard's election as the tenth president of Columbia College in 1864 was a fluke. Shortly after his arrival in Washington, Columbia announced a faculty opening in physics (the incumbent had defected to the Confederacy) and Barnard's scientific friends, who had seen to his election to the newly created National Academy of Science, submitted his name. While too late for the physics job, his application was passed to the trustee committee charged with finding Columbia's next president. Anxious to fill the post and impressed with Barnard's credentials as an Episcopalian and ardent Unionist at a time when the Columbia board was under suspicion of harboring Confederate sympathizers, the board elected him president sight unseen.[14]

It took the fifty-five-year-old Barnard little time to make clear his presidential agenda. His first act was to champion the newly opened School of Mines by enrolling his two sons there rather than in the School of Arts, the classics-oriented college to which five generations of New York Knickerbockers had sent their sons. In identifying with Columbia's brand-new School of Mines—and with its seven-year-old law school—Barnard aligned himself with the handful of faculty members and trustees who saw Columbia's future as a multischooled university, not just another undergraduate college in a region overrun with them. His university-making efforts were unceasing. In 1875, he oversaw the School of Mines when it awarded Columbia's first PhDs; a year later he helped hire John W. Burgess away from Amherst College for the purpose of transforming Columbia into a university along the lines that Burgess had encountered during studies in Germany and that the Amherst trustees had summarily rejected.[15]

Both Barnard and Burgess were New York outsiders who identified with Columbia's university future, not its church-college past. Both expressed doubts about whether Columbia should maintain an undergraduate program. Might it not cede undergraduate instruction of adolescents to the multitude of country colleges, letting Columbia focus on advanced instruction to older and more professionally focused students then available at only a handful of true American universities? Where they differed, however, was that Burgess was an elitist, a male supremacist, a racist, and an anti-Semite, whereas Barnard was none of these. Instead, he sought to bring collegiate education to a broader section of the population.

Barnard's open skepticism about the ongoing utility of Columbia as an undergraduate institution put his trustees, most of them loyal graduates of the college, on critical alert. But what drove a majority into open opposition was Barnard's conclusion that if Columbia were to continue providing undergraduate instruction for the children of the families of New York City's upper class, it ought not limit such instruction to their sons. Fifteen years into his presidency, Barnard declared himself in the most public way available to him as favoring the admission of women into Columbia College. As the Columbia trustee Rev. Morgan Dix concluded, Barnard had joined forces with the city's "little knot of persevering women."[16]

However late to coeducation, Barnard brought personal experiences in support of the cause. As a Yale undergraduate, he had observed the calming effect the presence of women at Professor Silliman's public lectures on astronomy had on his rowdy male classmates. While teaching at the Hartford Female Seminary, he was impressed by the academic seriousness young women brought to their studies, and his stint at the New York Institution for the Deaf and Dumb exposed him directly to coeducation. During his years teaching in Tuscaloosa and Oxford, he allowed women to audit his public lectures, to the same good effect that Silliman experienced back in New Haven. Once at Columbia, he permitted two instructors in the School of Mines to allow women to audit classes until the trustees objected. In 1879, he aligned himself with New Yorkers of both genders who had for more than a decade been calling on Columbia to open its doors to academically prepared and intellectually ambitious young women.[17]

Barnard joined the cause for higher education for women at the urging of his wife, whom some trustees believed exercised an undue influence

on him. But the timing of his intervention suggests another factor: attentiveness to the competition. Although a son of Yale, he saw Harvard as
Columbia's principal rival. In an earlier presidential report to his trustees,
Barnard applauded President Eliot's reintroduction of the elective system while dismissing President Noah Porter's defense of Yale's prescribed
curriculum. His efforts to displace the required classical curriculum he
inherited only partly overcame trustee resistance. But it was almost certainly Eliot's response in 1879 to calls upon Harvard to open its doors to
women by creating a separate Annex that moved Barnard to call upon
Columbia to do what Harvard would not: award women degrees. The
opportunity for stodgy Columbia to upstage the ever-reforming Harvard
must have been irresistible.[18]

Barnard chose as his bully pulpit his annual *President's Report*; while
addressed to the college's twenty-four trustees, it was circulated widely.
His 1866 report, which made the case against the continued proliferation of undercapitalized colleges in the Northeast in the face of declining
enrollments, had attracted national attention. His 1879 *President's Report*
joined the issue in its opening sentence: "The condition of the College is
now such as to justify the suggestion of the question whether its advantages should not be open to young women as well as to young men." (The
referred-to limitation was spatial, which with the completion of Hamilton
Hall in 1878 had been eliminated.) He then launched into a comprehensive overview of the educational institutions in the United Kingdom and
the United States that offered women instruction at the collegiate level.
This was immediately followed by his recommendation that Columbia
join them. But when, as he later put it, "the question failed to attract the
serious attention of the Trustees, but it is believed that it did not fail to
excite interest," he doubled down.[19]

Barnard used his next two annual reports to delineate the three institutional arrangements where advanced instruction of women existed
in the United States. The first was at private women's colleges, among
them Vassar, Smith, and Wellesley. The second was an Annex, or coordinated education, the best-known instance of which was in Cambridge,
Massachusetts, where, beginning in 1879, Harvard instructors provided
instruction to women two blocks from Harvard Yard. Finally, Barnard
described the handful of denominationally controlled private colleges,
such as Oberlin, Grinnell, and Carleton in the Midwest, where men and

women were enrolled on equal terms and instruction was provided to both sexes simultaneously. In New York State, the nonsectarian Cornell and the Methodist-controlled Syracuse University already operated on this coeducational basis, as did Boston University and Wesleyan University in New England. Among state institutions outside the East and South, especially those receiving support from the Land-Grant College Act of 1862, such as the University of Michigan and the University of California (1870), coeducation had become the norm.[20]

Barnard made clear that it was the third arrangement—full coeducation—that he favored. In support of this choice, he described his own exposure to coeducation with positive outcomes for both men and women. As for the latter, he preemptively assured his readers, coeducation would not turn "the girl who enters college a modestly shrinking maiden" into "a romping hoyden, or a self-asserting dogmatist."[21]

Barnard's 1880 *President's Report* also included a discussion of recent developments at Oxford and Cambridge, suggestive of the increased attention male-only British institutions were now paying to the instruction of women. His 1881 *Report* began with a description of the mail his previous reports had generated. "From many quarters, during the past few years, the anxious inquiry has been coming in upon the undersigned: Will not Columbia College do something for the higher education of our girls?" Barnard then tried appealing to his trustees' ever-present financial concerns:

> Opening the College to women would be an early and very material increase in the number of our students, which would be attended by an augmentation of the revenue from tuition fees, amounting, in the course of about four years, to not less than $10,000 per annum and probably more than $15,000 per annum.[22]

All to no avail. With the publication in 1881 of Barnard's third annual *President's Report*, the Columbia trustees promptly retaliated by slashing the president's budget line for publishing to limit its dissemination. A majority of Columbia faculty members and students (including the college junior Nicholas Murray Butler) similarly rejected the president's call for coeducation. Professor of political science John W. Burgess led the faculty opposition. Fifty years later, Burgess still thought well enough of his clinching argument to repeat it in his autobiography: "I suggested that New York parents preferred to keep their girls in school in the city, the tendency would be, in case coeducation were adopted in Columbia, to make the college a female seminary, and a Hebrew female seminary, in the character of the student body, at that."[23]

Barnard stayed on as president for another seven years, but his call for coeducation cost him whatever capacity he earlier had to move Columbia away from its sleepy past and embrace the future. His announced resignation in 1888, after twenty-four years as president, was met with universal relief. He died six months later. A coda he attached to his 1881 report attests to both his steadfastness and his prescience: "Columbia College may not, in our own day, be opened to the admission of women; but that it will be so in that better coming time which awaits another generation appears to the undersigned to be as certain as anything yet beneath the veil of the future can be."[24]

However unpopular on his own campus, Barnard's campaign for coeducation attracted a wide audience among New Yorkers sympathetic to the local cause of women's higher education, if not necessarily to coeducation. A gathering of like-minded New Yorkers assembled at the Union League Club on April 22, 1882, to form the Association for Promoting the Higher Education of Women. Its organizers included Sorosis veterans Caroline Dutcher Choate, the wife of New York attorney Joseph H. Choate; the Rev. Henry C. Potter, rector of the Church of the Incarnation; the Rev. Arthur Brooks; and the editor of the New York Evening Post, Parke Godwin. A petition calling on Columbia to admit women secured 1,352 signatures, among them those of President Chester A. Arthur and ex-president Ulysses S. Grant, and the wives of Cornelius Vanderbilt and J. Pierpont Morgan. Barnard's wife, Margaret, was also a signatory.[25]

Receipt of what he called "this monster petition" found the chair of the education committee of Columbia's board of trustees, Rev. Morgan Dix, rector of Trinity Church, in a decidedly unreceptive mood. "The thing seems to have been engineered from the beginning by a little knot of persevering women, most of whom are Unitarians of the Boston type." He must also have chafed at seeing two fellow Episcopalian clerics among the signatories. Nor did it put him in a more placatory state when his annual Lenten lectures, "The Calling of a Christian Woman," delivered at Episcopal churches throughout Manhattan, were roundly criticized as being patronizing to women. Undeterred, Dix used the Columbia board's meeting of March 5, 1883, to urge his colleagues to reject the petition. They did so unanimously but for Barnard's lone dissent.[26]

Persistent public criticism likely kept Dix from objecting when Dr. Cornelius Agnew introduced at the next board meeting, on June 8, 1883, a conciliatory proposal whereby Columbia would entertain the idea of a "collegiate course" for women along the lines of Harvard's Annex should a reputable group come forward to propose it.[27]

In the fall of 1884, the Columbia board rolled out its own Collegiate Course for Women, which was intended to quell charges of misogyny. Women admitted to the Collegiate Course by examination would be allowed to sit for the same examinations taken by Columbia College men, but the exams would be administered separately. The women would not be allowed to attend classes. Should a woman pass enough of these examinations, she was to receive a Columbia degree. In the summer of 1885 six women took the entrance exam and enrolled that fall. The following year, a second batch of homebound but academically ambitious young women signed up, among them eighteen-year-old Annie Florence Nathan.[28]

"THERE'S THAT CHILD AGAIN"

Annie Nathan's experience in the Collegiate Course was brief and dispiriting. While enrolled, she complained of faculty openly hostile to women and of exam questions not covered in the assigned texts but discussed in classes from which women were excluded. She dropped out in February 1887 after one semester upon her marriage to thirty-five-year-old Dr. Alfred Meyer, a distant cousin. However unedifying, the experience instilled in Annie Nathan Meyer a lifelong, proprietary, and sometimes off-putting commitment to the general cause of higher education for women and specifically to the women's college she, more than anyone else, was to bring into being.[29]

The Nathans came originally from the Caribbean in the 1650s and numbered among the first Jewish families to settle in New York City following their move there from Portugal, when the town was still under Dutch rule. By the time of the American Revolution, the Nathans had

FIGURE 1.2 Photo of the young Annie Nathan Meyer (1877–1951), prime mover behind the founding of Barnard College. Barnard Archives.

been in America for four generations, a fact that Annie made known to genealogically focused New Yorkers inclined to flaunt their own less lengthy American lineage. Both she and her daughter Margaret belonged to the New York chapter of the Daughters of the American Revolution. Nathan's ancestors included Gerson Mendes Seixas (1745–1816), the first rabbi of Congregation Shearith Israel, an outspoken patriot during the Revolutionary War and trustee of Columbia College from its rechartering in 1787 until his death in 1816. (He was to be the only Jew to serve as a trustee of Columbia until the election of Annie's cousin, jurist Benjamin Cardozo, in 1928.)[30]

The Nathans were part of a tight network of Sephardic Jewish families, including the Cardozos and the Lazuruses, who conceded nothing to the city's more numerous Knickerbocker families in terms of ancestry or social standing. Meyer once referred to New York's Sephardim as "the nearest approach to royalty in the United States." Stephen Birmingham, a chronicler of Jewish life in New York, calls them "The Grandees."[31]

The Grandees differed from New York's later-arriving and often wealthier German Jews, those Birmingham refers to as "Our Crowd." The latter included the Altschuls, Guggenheims, Lehmans, Lewisohns, Schiffs, Seligmans, Strauses, and Warburgs, all of whom moved to New York City in the second half of the nineteenth century, some after stopovers elsewhere in the United States. These families lived on Manhattan's East Side; attended Temple Emanu-El on Fifth Avenue; and sent their children to the Sacks School, conveniently located at East Thirty-Ninth Street. But not the Nathans. "I do not like the atmosphere of the Sacks School," Annie Nathan Meyer told Barnard's second dean, Laura Drake Gill, in 1902, who in her innocence of the city's intratribal matters suggested it for Meyer's ten-year-old daughter Margaret, "simply because the girls there come almost exclusively from a wealthy class—one which has not had the stability of generations of wealth—and which is unfortunately an intensely materialistic class. Margaret comes from a family in America since the 17th century."[32]

Annie's distinguished lineage did not spare her a traumatic childhood. Her father Robert was profligate, a philanderer, and regularly absent. In 1875, having squandered the family's fortune on Wall Street, he fled New York just ahead of his creditors, relocating his family in Green Bay, Wisconsin. Annie's mother suffered from depression and drug addiction and died in 1880. Two years earlier she had attempted suicide, only to have eleven-year-old Annie intervene. About that time Annie developed a sibling rivalry with her older sister Maud, and they later found themselves on opposite sides of many of the issues of their day, most famously women's suffrage, which Maud actively campaigned for and Annie, seeing it as antimale, actively campaigned against.[33]

For two years, Annie and her brother Harry lived with maternal grandparents. "I remember only," she later recalled, "that Harry and I never felt at home. We were conscious in some way that Papa had made a failure of his life and that Grandpa felt . . . that he had to look after his daughter's children." The sharpest memory she had of those days, recalled a half century later, was of her grandfather complaining about her, "There's that child again!" In 1882, a small, inexpensive apartment was found for them on Third Avenue, and it was there that Annie, whose schooling to that point was virtually nonexistent, became an inveterate reader.[34]

Annie's father returned to New York City and Wall Street in 1882. He managed to come up with the funds to send Annie's older brother Robert to Columbia, but he showed no interest in Annie's education. He specifically objected to her going off to college, arguing that doing so would make her unfit for marriage. That Annie, not quite twenty during her only semester in Columbia's Collegiate Course for Women, proceeded to meet and marry a cousin fifteen years her senior after "a courtship of less than a fortnight" allows the inference she did so in some measure to prove Papa wrong.[35]

Marriage to Alfred Meyer, a respected physician and medical researcher, provided Annie's subsequent life with previously absent security and companionship. But no measure of domestic harmony eliminated her acute sensitivity to social affronts, real or imagined, especially if she suspected an anti-Semitic dimension to them. She was equally alert to any account of Barnard during her sixty-two years as a trustee that slighted her role in its founding.[36]

Meyer, in *Barnard Beginnings*, shared credit for the idea of founding a college for women in New York City with Melvil Dewey, who came to New York in 1883 from Wellesley College as director of Columbia's new library. They met when the teenage Annie, a regular user of the library (to which she had access as sister of an alumnus), asked Dewey for a reading regimen to compensate for her spotty schooling. After enrolling in the Collegiate Course, she found Dewey receptive to her complaints. He had his own problems with Columbia, especially trustee opposition to his plan for a school of library science, which would have been certain to attract women. For their part, the trustees viewed the soon-to-be-gone young librarian and his Wellesley-trained wife much as they viewed their aged president and his wife: as co-conspirators in a feminist plot to hand over Columbia to the "women of the Boston type."[37]

As she recounts the story, Annie informed Dewey in early 1887 that she had withdrawn from the Collegiate Course and despaired of the prospects for New York women like herself to secure a proper college education. Dewey was more hopeful: "Of course there should be a college for women in New York; there must be! We must obtain one!" "To all of this I whole-heartedly agreed," Annie responded. "But what was to be done about it? What could I do about it?" To which she answered: "Why, start a college for women myself. That was all." Dewey soon thereafter decamped from Columbia; he and his library school idea were dispatched to Albany in 1888, to the relief of Columbia's trustees. But for Annie Nathan Meyer, their discussions led directly to the great sustaining cause of her life.[38]

GETTING TO YES

A key to Annie Nathan Meyer's success in implementing the idea for a women's college in New York City was that she understood why others had earlier failed. From their mistakes she derived three "lessons":

I: Contra Lillie Devereux Blake—do not promote the cause of women's higher education as part of a larger radical feminist agenda identified with "wild women" and men-haters.

II: Contra Frederick A. P. Barnard—do not insist on coeducation as the only acceptable way of achieving women's access to higher education.

III: Contra the Union League petitioners—do not try to intimidate the Columbia trustees with sheer numbers but instead respectfully win them over to your cause for their own reasons.

Meyer on her strategy: "I had the shrewd theory that to put any radical idea across," she explained seven decades later in her autobiography, *It's Been Fun*, "it must be done in the most conservative manner possible."[39]

Meyer began learning all she could about women's colleges by seeking out those with relevant experience, including Arthur Gilman, the prime mover behind the Harvard Annex. He advised her against starting a col-lege in the absence of a major benefactor. Closer to home, she picked the brains of Thomas Hunter, the president of the Female Normal and High School, plus the heads of several New York private girls' schools, including Ella Weed, the headmistress of Miss Annie Brown's School. She also met with President Barnard, but privately, to avoid being identified with his single-minded commitment to coeducation. Writing to Columbia President Nicholas Murray Butler more than two decades later, she explained her reasoning: "I never considered coeducation for a moment. And in that lay my strength with the trustees of the University."[40]

On January 21, 1888, Meyer launched her campaign with a 4,500-word letter published in *The Nation* under the title, "The Higher Education for Women in New York." She began by identifying four already existing clienteles for a women's college in New York City. The first were New York women currently attending colleges outside the city. If these sixty-seven young women (by her count) were prepared "to leave their homes and encounter the discomfits of an independent life for the sake of pursuing a collegiate education," she reasoned, would not even more like-minded young women "attend college gladly, enthusiastically, were it not necessary to face the obstacle of leaving home?"[41]

Her second prospects were the sixty-nine New York women currently enrolled, "for lack of better," in local correspondence programs. The third were the twenty-eight women attending what she dismissed as "an apology for a collegiate course for women held out by Columbia College."[42]

Her fourth and last set of prospects were a select portion of the 1,600 girls currently attending the city's tuition-free Female Normal and High School (later Hunter College), which offered a two-year curriculum designed to turn out teachers for the city's public schools. "It is commonly supposed that only parents who could not afford to pay tuition fees send their children to Normal College," Meyer wrote. "On the contrary," citing the Normal School's President Thomas Hunter as her authority, "a very large percentage of the parents could easily afford it, and would gladly send their daughters to a private college where a higher curriculum and degrees could be procured." Everywhere she looked, Meyer found local instances of an unmet and growing demand for a New York–based women's college.[43]

The letter included an upbeat rendering of the prospects for the trustees of Columbia College approving a variation of the Harvard Annex model. But lest her New York City readers think she was merely proposing to copy the arrangement in Cambridge, she pointed out that, whereas women completing the Harvard Annex course of studies received only a certificate, not a Harvard degree, the Columbia trustees had agreed to award those completing its Collegiate Course a Columbia degree. "In Cambridge, they have an Annex and are praying for certain conditions that will insure its permanent existence and success. In New York we have the conditions that would bring permanent existence and success, *but we have no Annex.*" She closed with another bit of hometown bravado, quoting Longfellow: "In this 'dark, gray city,' this huge, growing, starving, ambitious city with its many means of satisfying life's demands, there is one lack—the lack of a college where women may attain a complete education without leaving their homes and families." "Ought we not, therefore, to begin at once to organize an association for the collegiate instruction of women by the professors and other instructors of Columbia College?"[44]

Already under way was the drafting of a memorial to Columbia's trustees seeking an annex arrangement. In the writing thereof, Meyer again acknowledged the role of Melvil Dewey, along with that of Mary Maples Dodge, editor of the popular children's magazine *St. Nicholas*. The selection of the memorial's fifty signatories, however, she reserved for herself. The target number followed on an exploratory visit with Columbia board chair Hamilton Fish, arranged by her uncle Jonathan Nathan, a onetime political associate of the retired Republican senator and former secretary of state. Fish, who had supported Agnew's 1883 resolution allowing for a separate collegiate course for women, urged Meyer to seek quality over quantity in signatories, and Annie took his advice to heart. Hers, she proudly recalled a half century on, included:

> thirteen ministers, four lawyers, an ex-Judge of the State Supreme Court, five doctors, five educators, including the presidents of the two City Colleges, four editors, four men of importance in the world of finance, the president of the Board Of Education, one representative of an old, distinguished New York family, one railroad president, two women who led in important philanthropic work, four literary women, and three women who were important as being the wives of influential men.[45]

Among those intentionally missing from the memorialists were Lillie Devereux Blake and any of New York's other feminist firebrands and assorted "wild women" who would have set the likes of Dr. Morgan Dix against it. This also involved rejecting the "excellent sister of President Cleveland," who wore her hair too short to be countenanced. Board chairman Fish, upon receiving the memorial, complimented Meyer, calling her list of signatories "the best he had ever seen for its intended purpose."[46]

Meyer spent the six weeks between her letter in *The Nation* and the submission of the memorial in March lobbying the twenty-four members of the Columbia board. She saved her visit with Dix for last, given his reputation as an outspoken opponent of women's higher education and the recent object of Lillie Devereux Blake's ridicule.

On February 9, 1888, she was received at the Trinity Church rectory by the sixty-year-old Dix, who immediately put her at her ease by warmly mentioning her cousins, the Harmon Nathans, as his summer neighbors at Rye Beach. When she broached her plan for a women's college affiliated with Columbia, Dix quickly gave it his support and told her how to proceed. "Somewhere among the Minutes of our Board," he assured her, "you will find a resolution to the effect that if an appeal comes to us for a separately financed College for Women, manned by the instructors of Columbia College, and with proper safeguards as to the dignity and responsibility of its sponsors, it would be approved." This was the resolution that Agnew had secured following the board's repudiation of the Union League petition. On leaving rectory, Meyer allowed: "I knew the battle was won."[47]

At its March 5, 1888, meeting, the Columbia board took up the Meyer-engineered memorial, referring it to a select committee that included Dix and Agnew. At its May 7 meeting, the whole board, on the recommendation of the select committee, voted to give the memorial provisional approval, conditioned on their receiving "reasonable security that, once established, the institution will be permanent." This meant the memorialists could proceed to put together their own board of trustees to take full fiduciary responsibility for the college. Unfortunately, the absence of a board clerk at the May 7 meeting kept the resolution from being communicated to the memorialists until late fall. Otherwise, Meyer later recalled, the college might have opened for business in the fall of 1888![48]

An 1888 starting date is hard to credit. A board of trustees had yet to be formed, a provisional charter had yet to be submitted to the New York state legislature for approval, and a name for the college had yet to be determined. The third task either fell to or, more likely, was commandeered by Meyer, but either way shows her at her most Machiavellian.

At the same May 1888 meeting where the Columbia trustees approved the annex proposal, the seventy-nine-year-old President Barnard, now blind as well as deaf, announced his plan to retire in 1889. He remained opposed to the idea of a separate women's college, as did his wife. Eleven months later, at the April 1889 meeting, with Barnard absent and terminally ill (he died three weeks later), the board approved the provisional charter, which for the first time identified the institution as "Barnard College." This had been at Meyer's instigation, hoping thereby to prevent the proposed namesake and his about-to-be widow from objecting from his deathbed to what was transpiring. The stratagem worked. "I cannot very well fight a College which bears his name," Margaret Barnard told Meyer upon hearing of the board's action. So Barnard College it became, just another of the necessary, albeit ironical, steps in the shrewd Meyer getting to yes.[49]

OF NEW YORK'S "VERY EARNEST, PHILANTHROPIC, PUBLIC-SPIRITED CLASS"

Barnard College became the great sustaining cause of Annie Nathan Meyer, but it was not her cause alone at its founding. Nor was it solely the doing of a small group of like-minded women. Barnard was, in its beginnings, a collective effort of a multitribal social class distinctive to turn-of-the-century New York City. For one of its members, Edith Wharton, the class consisted of "the rich, the well born, the best educated." An English visitor to New York in 1888, James Bryce, famously labeled its male members as "the best men . . . eminent in rank, wealth, and ability." Not everyone belonging to this class participated in Barnard's beginnings, but the twenty-two New Yorkers who formed Barnard's original board of trustees all had certifiable claims to membership in a privileged circle that another English visitor, Charles Philip Trevelyan, mischievously called New York's "very earnest, philanthropic, public-spirited class."[50]

In the selection of the original board of trustees, Meyer admitted "knowing nothing whatever of the ramifications of New York society," and relied on the wider social networks of women she had enlisted in her cause. Ella Weed, the headmistress of one of the city's fashionable private girls' schools, and Caroline Dutcher Choate, the founder of the even more exclusive Brearley School for Girls, whom Meyer met during canvassing for petition signatories among the earlier Union League petitioners, proved crucial. But even in this instance, Meyer had very definite views about the board's composition. One was to reject the urging of one of Weed's nominees, Frances Fisher Wood, then the president of the Vassar Alumnae Association, that the board be made up exclusively of women. Meyer insisted instead the board be evenly divided between men and women by inviting "certain well-known, more or less impecunious, literary women as well." Here, as with the earlier selection of signatories to the Columbia trustee petition, Meyer later recalled, she was determined to "steer her way safely between the Charybdis of ultra-conservatism on the one hand, and on the other, the even more dangerous Scylla of radicalism or queerness, or whatever term was used in those days to express advanced vision and a spirit too independent to be harnessed."[51]

Meyer was also committed to having a Barnard board broadly representative of the religious composition of the upper reaches of contemporary New York society. This would be in pointed contrast with Columbia's board, which was dominated by Episcopalian, Dutch Reformed, and Presbyterian Protestants. On Barnard's original board there was to be, in addition to herself, a daughter of the city's Sephardic community, a second Jew, Jacob H. Schiff, head of the merchant banking firm of Kuhn, Loeb & Co., and leader of the city's German-Jewish community. The city's Catholics were represented in the person of the attorney Frederic Rene Coudert; its Baptists in Laura Spelman Rockefeller, the wife of John D. Rockefeller; and the Unitarians by Caroline Dutcher Choate and the publisher George Hoadley. Few New York governing boards of the day could match the original Barnard trustees in their ecumenism.[52]

Perhaps because her own were skimpy, Meyer sought out board members with impressive educational credentials. In an era when few women had attended college, four of the original eleven women trustees were Vassar graduates: Ella Weed (class of 1873), Virginia Brownell (1873), Frances Fisher Wood (1874), and Helen Dawes Brown (1878). A fifth, Alice Williams, was an alumna of the University of Michigan (1876). Three others, Meyer, Laura Rockefeller, and Clara Stranahan, had some college experience. Two of the other three women trustees were married to college men. Of the eleven male trustees, only Schiff, who migrated from Germany to America at age seventeen, was not a college or law school graduate. The others included two Harvard and two Williams graduates, plus one each from Amherst, Western Reserve, Union, Princeton, and Columbia, plus two graduates each from the Harvard Law School and the Columbia Law School.[53]

Six of the eleven original male trustees were lawyers; two were ministers; and one each a publisher, banker, and journalist. Three of the women were teachers or school administrators, two others had founded girls' schools, and three were professional writers. Only three might be called, as by Meyer acidly later, "important as being the wives of influential men."[54]

LIFT OFF!

With a name and board now in place, next came securing a state charter. Here again, Melvil Dewey, recently relocated to Albany, provided useful assistance. A provisional charter was issued by the New York State Board of Regents to the twenty-two members of the board on August 8, 1889. Final details again fell mainly to Meyer and Weed. The former, with her husband as cosigner, leased a brownstone at 343 Madison Avenue, the second building on the east side of Madison Avenue between Forty-Fourth and Forty-Fifth streets, as the first site for the college. One of hundreds of brownstones throughout the city, the building had four floors and was 25 feet wide by 52 feet deep, with buildings abutting both sides. The back looked out on the backsides of yet another row of eastward-facing attached brownstones. The lease was for four years, the rent $3,250 for the first two years (with the owners allowed for the first year to reside on the top floor) and $3,500 for the next two years.[55]

Hiring an instructional staff fell principally to Weed. Here the brownstone's location, five blocks south of the Columbia College campus, simplified the task. By 1889, Columbia College, if not yet in name a university, consisted of five schools, three of which, the college proper, the School of Political Science, and the School of Mines, were located on Madison Avenue between Forty-Ninth and Fiftieth streets. The law school was downtown in the court district, and the loosely affiliated but soon-to-be integrated College of Physicians and Surgeons was across town at Fifty-Ninth Street.

FIGURE 1.3 Rented brownstone at 343 Madison Avenue, East Side of Manhattan, first site of Barnard College. Barnard Archives.

The three schools on the Madison Avenue campus employed about fifty professors, a junior teaching staff of twice that number, and another one hundred graduate students pursuing PhDs in the arts and sciences. All but the professors could be hired for stipends that ranged from $600 to $800 for a four-course teaching program. The fact that Barnard's curriculum would be identical with that of Columbia College meant that those already teaching required courses at Columbia could simply repeat them four blocks away to a classroom of young women. The services of seven instructors for the opening year were quickly secured.[56]

All that was needed now were students. Public notices went out in the early summer that entrance exams, identical with those used by Columbia College, were to be administered to interested women on September 30 and October 5. Of the women taking them, fourteen were enrolled in the class of 1893, along with twenty-two so-called specials (nondegree students who enrolled for one or two courses), all of whom appeared at the scruffy brownstone at 343 Madison Avenue on Monday morning, October 7, 1889, for the start of classes. Lift off!

DONE IN HASTE?

Much about the founding of Barnard College has a provisional, patched-together, on-the-fly quality. Its gestation period of thirty months—from February 1887 when Meyer and Dewey hatched the idea of a women's college in New York City to Barnard's opening in October 1889—surely ranks among the shortest in the history of college founding. It happened fast because many aspects of the normal process were simply skipped or left for later. Vassar opened with rooms for four hundred students; Wellesley could house three hundred students and thirty full-time faculty. Barnard began without either a proper campus or a faculty: in place of the former was a rented brownstone with a four-year lease; in place of the latter was a handful of moonlighting young men hired on a course-by-course basis.

More fundamentally, unlike most private colleges established in the late nineteenth century, Barnard had no single driving personality—no Matthew Vassar, Ezra Cornell, Sophia Smith, Leland Stanford, or Henry and Pauline Durant—behind its creation. Clearly its namesake did not qualify: Frederick A. P. Barnard favored a very different solution to the problem of providing college-level instruction to the young women of New York City. Nor did Annie Nathan Meyer, who deserved credit for the idea and for rounding up support for an affiliated women's college but lacked many of the attributes generally ascribed to a founder.[57]

Chief among Meyer's absent attributes was disposable wealth sufficient to endow a college and provide land for its site. Vassar, Cornell, Smith, Wellesley, Bryn Mawr, Stanford, and the University of Chicago all had wealthy backers who in every case, except that of John D. Rockefeller and the University of Chicago, made these institutions the principal beneficiary of their estates.[58]

When Meyer and her husband signed the lease for 343 Madison Avenue, it was more an act of faith than evidence of deep pockets. To be sure, several of the original trustees were men and women of substantial wealth, with Laura Spelman Rockefeller married to America's richest man at the time, but none of the board's wealthy members were committed to being or later became underwriters of first resort, as Matthew Vassar ($768,000), the Durants ($500,000), Joseph Taylor ($1,500,000), and the Stanfords ($20,000,000) did. Nor did Meyer or any of Barnard's other prime movers have strong denominational connections that could produce both tuition-paying students and financial assistance, unlike the Baptist Matthew Vassar, the Presbyterian Durants, the Quaker Joseph Taylor, or the Baptist William Rainey Harper at the University of Chicago. Barnard's independence from any religious affiliation, however liberating, came at a cost.[59]

The result was that Barnard was, from its start, seriously undercapitalized, a fact that Meyer seems not to have fully grasped, despite Arthur Gilman's warning that no college could survive without a steady infusion of gifts. (She later acknowledged that arithmetic was not her strong suit.) Fifty years after its opening, a Barnard memorialist proudly stated that the college "started with nothing except that most irresistible and indestructible thing, an idea." True enough. But at its founding and for two more decades, the idea that brought Barnard into being was not sure to take permanent root.[60]

2

EAST SIDE, WEST SIDE

A Tale of Two Cities

For whom was [Barnard] intended and from what class of women is it to draw its students?

—REV. ARTHUR BROOKS, 1894[1]

The haste with which Barnard College came into being made its early going tenuous. A rented brownstone on a crowded urban thoroughfare suggested impermanence. So did a nonexistent endowment and the absence of a principal benefactor. Nor could the sufferance of the Columbia College authorities be counted on to secure safe passage should difficulties be encountered in the early stages. At best, Barnard was in for a shaky start; at worst, a failure to launch.

WHO'S IN CHARGE HERE?

Barnard opened its doors in the fall of 1889 without a full-time administrative head. Instead of a president or dean, one of the younger women trustees, Ella Weed, was designated "chairman of the Academic Committee" and handed the day-to-day operations of the college. None of the original male trustees showed interest in the job, while among the women trustees, Weed, thirty-four years old, single, and headmistress of the fashionable Miss Annie Brown's School, at Fifth Avenue and Fifty-Fifth Street, was a plausible choice. A Vassar graduate and professional educator, she made a respectable local spokesperson for the cause of women's higher education. The plan was for her to split her workday shuttling the ten blocks between the two schools, mornings at Miss Brown's and afternoons at Barnard. She received a salary of $1,200 and, beginning in 1890, had the assistance of a full-time staffer, N. W. Liggett, another Vassar graduate, as college registrar. Liggett became the face of the College when Weed was

FIGURE 2.1 Photo of Ella Weed (1851–1894), first administrative head of Barnard College (1889–1894). Barnard Archives.

away at her morning job or, as increasingly became the case, when she was absent due to illness.[2]

However devoted to Barnard, Weed was neither charismatic nor forceful as an academic leader in the mold of Wellesley's Alice Freeman Palmer or Bryn Mawr's M. Carey Thomas. Before illness sidelined her in the fall of 1893, she quietly saw to the admission of four classes and to the college's first graduation earlier that spring. She had one notable success as a fundraiser, an early gift of $5,000 from J. P. Morgan, but otherwise her tenure left the viability of Barnard still in doubt. She died on January 10, 1894, at forty-one.[3]

Weed's job included hiring staff to teach the curriculum prescribed by Columbia College. Her first year's hires consisted of seven officers of instruction, all young men (average age twenty-eight) affiliated with Columbia College, a couple of whom already impressively credentialed. Of the seven, the classicists Mortimer Earle and Nelson McCrae continued moonlighting at Barnard through the 1890s, while Thomas S. Fiske in mathematics and William H. Carpenter in Germanic languages soon acquired permanent places at Columbia. The English assistant, Henry Wasson, later entered the ministry and the French assistant, Guiliarme Scribner, dropped from sight. But the botanist Nathaniel Britton, the most senior of the first group of instructors, who taught for only one year before returning to Columbia and later to the directorship of the New York Botanical Garden, had the most important impact on the college. He did so by securing as his replacement in 1890 Barnard's first female instructor, Emily L. Gregory.[4]

An 1878 graduate of Cornell University, the forty-nine-year-old Gregory earned her PhD in botany at the University of Zurich (1886), the first woman to do so. Prior to Barnard, she taught at Smith (1881–1883), the Harvard Annex (1884–1886), and jointly at the University of Pennsylvania and Bryn Mawr College (1886–1888), where she was a colleague of Professor E. B. Wilson, who subsequently moved to Columbia; there, he achieved international notoriety for his pioneering work in genetics. Gregory was well known to New York City's botany community through her publications in the *Journal of the Torrey Botanical Society*. Her initial appointment at Barnard was that of lecturer and director of the Barnard Botany Laboratory, then located on the third floor of 343 Madison. Independently wealthy, she taught without

FIGURE 2.2 Emily L. Gregory (1851–1897), Cornell AB 1881, Zurich PhD (1881), botanist and first woman to teach at Barnard College. Barnard Archives.

a salary, alternating her summers in Europe purchasing equipment and conducting research at the Marine Biological Laboratory in Woods Hole, Massachusetts. Although an elective, botany under Gregory became one of the college's most heavily subscribed courses among degree candidates and non-degree seeking "specials" alike. She died in 1897, at the age of fifty-six, the author of fifty-five papers and Barnard's first "scholar-teacher."[5]

FIGURE 2.3 Botany lab at 343 Madison Ave. Barnard Archives.

Weed's subsequent hiring forays yielded no other women and only one other officer of instruction who stuck. Charles Knapp came in 1891 as a twenty-three-year-old instructor of Latin and stayed on until retirement in 1937. Several of Weed's subsequent hires later made careers at Columbia, among them Benjamin Woodward in German literature, George Rice Carpenter in American literature, and William T. Hallock in physics. Woodward was twenty-three and Hallock twenty-four when they first taught at Barnard.[6]

Weed seems not to have consulted with Columbia authorities in making her instructional appointments. The turnstile nature of the process and its resultant instability sufficiently disturbed Columbia president Seth Low that, following Weed's death he interjected himself into Barnard's faculty hiring process. In doing so, he gave the as-yet-to-be-so-designated Barnard faculty its first semblance of continuity.

DEAN EMILY JAMES SMITH

Four months passed between Ella Weed's death in January 1894 and the installation of her successor, Emily James Smith. A member of Bryn Mawr's first graduating class of 1889, Smith went on to Girton College, Cambridge, where she was one of the first women to do graduate work in Ancient Greek. From there she proceeded to the Packer Collegiate Institute in Brooklyn, where she taught Greek for two years. In 1892, she was awarded a graduate fellowship at the newly opened University of Chicago. A Barnard trustee familiar with her success at Packer, longtime Brooklyn resident, Ann Wroe Scollay Low, likely suggested her as Weed's successor. On May 11, 1894, Smith became Barnard's second administrative leader and the first to be designated dean of Barnard College. She was twenty-nine.[7]

Eight months later, in January 1895, President Low presented the Barnard trustees a proposal for making three outside appointments of senior scholars who would divide their teaching between Barnard and one of Columbia's three newly created graduate faculties. Their salaries for the first three years were to be paid from a $36,000 anonymous gift from Low on the condition that the Barnard trustees assume responsibility for their salaries thereafter. While we "fully appreciate the necessity of permanence," board chair Arthur Brooks could tell the president only that Barnard "will make every effort" to do so. Undeterred by the lack of assurance, Low and the newly installed Dean Smith announced three appointments, each selected in consultation with the respective Columbia graduate school dean and department: in history, from Amherst, the American colonial historian Herbert Levi Osgood; in economics, from Johns Hopkins and the current president of the American Economic Association, John Bates Clark; in mathematics, from Michigan, Frank N. Cole. On the occasion of these professorial appointments, Low wrote to Dean Smith that "in regard to Dr. Gregory's position, it seems to me only just to make her under the circumstances that she should enjoy the title of 'Professor of Botany at Barnard College.' "[8]

The way these professorships worked in practice was as inventive as the idea of creating them. For every course Osgood, Clark, and Cole taught at Columbia, Barnard was provided a substitute of comparable rank. This meant that Barnard students were regularly taught by several of Osgood's,

FIGURE 2.4 Emily James Smith (later Putnam) (1865–1944), first dean of Barnard College (1894–1900). Barnard Archives.

Clark's, and Cole's equally distinguished departmental colleagues, among them the historian James Harvey Robinson, a future president of the American Historical Association; the economist E. R. A. Seligman, a future president of the American Economic Association; and the mathematician Edward Kasner, a future member of the National Academy of

Science. No turn-of-the-twentieth century American college offered a more celebrated lineup of professors. These joint appointments also established a precedent for faculty sharing between Columbia and Barnard that has continued with differing intensity ever since.[9]

While Dean Smith's role in the creation of the three Barnard professorships at the outset of her deanship is unclear, her subsequent cooperative dealings with Columbia president Seth Low set a standard for all future Barnard administrators. In 1898, she took the lead in persuading Low of the wisdom of setting aside a place on the Barnard board for an alumnae-elected member, a practice the Columbia board took another decade to adopt. In January 1900, she and President Low presented the Barnard board with the intercorporate agreement formalizing the relationship between Columbia and Barnard that remains in force today. Its key provision was the establishment of a separate and freestanding Barnard faculty, discussed in chapter 3.[10]

The 1900 intercorporate agreement was the climactic act of Smith's deanship. Having married the New York publisher, Civil War veteran, and widower George Haven Putnam in early 1899, and some months later becoming pregnant, she chose the signing of the agreement in January 1900 to announce her departure. "The adoption of the agreement with Columbia puts my conscience at rest as regards any inconvenience to the college from my resignation." Her departure was especially felt by Barnard students, who related to a dean only a decade older than they, a dean who brought Greek alive by bringing Homer to freshmen and Plato to sophomores. The now Mrs. Putnam remained a New Yorker and returned to Barnard in 1914 as a part-time and unremunerated instructor of Greek, continuing in that role until she retired in 1930 upon the death of her husband. If too briefly in place to be viewed as one of the great Barnard administrations, her deanship of active leadership and effective collaboration with Columbia stood in stark contrast to that of her successor.[11]

FOOLS AND ANGELS

When Jacob Schiff accepted the invitation of Annie Nathan Meyer to join the Barnard board of trustees in the spring of 1889, he also reluctantly agreed to become college treasurer. He did the first out of a sense of duty as a leader the city's German-Jewish community, and the second because of his reputation for financial probity as head of Kuhn, Loeb, one of the nation's two largest merchant banking firms. But one look at what served as the college's business plan at the first meeting of the board's finance committee in the summer of 1889 gave him second thoughts. It assumed that once four classes were enrolled, the college could subsist on the continuing income from tuition and fees, plus the occasional outright gift. With tuition for degree candidates set at $150, and "specials" charged $50 per course, tuition income was expected to grow from around $3,000 the first year to $12,000 in 1893 and thereafter. During the four-year ramp-up phase, annual pledges of $100 annually from thirty-five or forty or fifty-four "Associates" (their number varies with the teller) were figured to yield an additional $4,000, with one-time gifts projected to produce another $6,000.[12]

Upon seeing these numbers, Schiff urged the committee to hold off opening the college for a year until more capital could be raised. But a majority of the committee voted to proceed with the fall 1889 opening. "Those who were less versed in finance were braver," was the way that Meyer blithely recalled the decision forty-six years later. "It was a good deal the case of the old adage concerning fools and angels."[13]

Schiff stayed on as treasurer for four years, during which time he made donations of $4,500 and two additional loans of $6,000. He often absented himself from board meetings and increasingly left the day-to-day financial affairs of the college to a younger member of the finance committee, the textbook publisher George A. Plimpton. When in attendance, Schiff regularly objected to the practice of annual deficits being made up by dunning individual trustees and having them go hat-in-hand to Barnard's early subscribers. At the board meeting of May 12, 1893, which Schiff made a point of attending, his dissatisfaction became all too apparent.[14]

Four converging considerations made this moment in the college's history critical. With Barnard's first class set to graduate, the annual subscription fund that had provided a quarter of the college's budgeted revenue for four years was at an end. Recent efforts to meet operating deficits with individual solicitations had met increasing instances of what latter-day fundraisers would call donor fatigue. Furthermore, Columbia had just announced plans to move its campus to the city's Upper West Side, on Morningside Heights, which meant physically severing ties with Barnard unless its trustees could come up with the resources to accompany Columbia across town. Finally, and perhaps most pressing, in response to Columbia's announced move, an anonymous donor (later acknowledged to be Mary E. Brinckerhoff, the widow of the merchant Van Wyck Brinckerhoff) had offered Barnard $100,000 in 1892 for the construction of a building if Barnard could raise an estimated $140,000 for a site adjacent to the planned Columbia campus. A year after the offer had been made and the Barnard board had yet to respond, Mrs. Brinckerhoff's lawyer (and later Barnard trustee), Frederick S. Wait, remarked to Plimpton: "I trust the College is not in deep water."[15]

Treasurer Schiff's response to this cascading bad news was to resign. Upon doing so, he offered to forgive his loans, thus allowing the college to close. Other trustees were less despairing, but even the most upbeat could not dismiss the financial judgment of one of the city's leading bankers. Only a gift of $5,000 from J. P. Morgan the following month (solicited by Ella Weed) allowed the college to eliminate its projected annual deficit and end the 1892–1893 budget year free from debt. "What should we have done if it had not been for that five thousand from Mr. Morgan?" Plimpton wrote to Miss Weed upon its receipt. "I certainly don't know. You deserve no end of credit." Even with this gift, Barnard remained, five years into its history, as Plimpton later acknowledged, "an institution on the verge of bankruptcy."[16]

Upon Schiff's resignation as treasurer, trustee George A. Plimpton became the Barnard board's acting treasurer. At thirty-nine, with a young family; already heavily involved in the affairs of his own alma mater, Amherst; and regularly on the road as Ginn & Company's principal textbook salesperson, he at first declined to become treasurer. Effective persuasion came from President Low, who told him that "no one can do as much as you can for Barnard College." Once committed, Plimpton became not only treasurer but, for more than four decades, Barnard's principal fundraiser. Of all the men who have contributed to Barnard's financial well-being, George A. Plimpton stands second to none.[17]

Plimpton's first act as treasurer was to publish a four-year financial statement that, while demonstrating Barnard's continuing needs, acknowledged by name and amount the support of the dozens of New York families that had contributed to Barnard since 1889. It specifically mentioned four benefactors who had matched J. P. Morgan's lead gift of $5,000 by designating Morgan and all future givers at that level the honorific title of founder. He then launched a "site fund" to raise the $140,000 needed to acquire property on Morningside and thus secure the Brinckerhoff gift. When Plimpton began making calls on potential donors, he found he enjoyed asking for money, particularly in amounts greater than his prospects were prepared to give, and soon acquired a reputation as one of the city's great fundraisers. "When your drag-net is thrown out," one $5,000 donor told him, "the fish give up: no use trying to fight."[18]

The socially prominent trustee Caroline Dutcher Choate introduced Plimpton to the first of Barnard's major donors. Elizabeth Milbank Anderson was joint heir with her brother Joseph to the estate of their father Jeremiah Milbank, a successful merchant and founder of the Borden Evaporated Milk Company. At her father's death, Elizabeth, who was married to the artist and rancher Abraham Archibald Anderson, received half of his estate estimated at $32,000,000. Choate knew Anderson socially and through their respective involvements in the founding of two East Side private schools for girls, the Brearley School, which Choate help found in 1880, and the Spence School, which Anderson helped finance in 1892. The occasion in early 1894 for bringing Anderson and Plimpton together followed the decision of the trustees of Roosevelt Hospital to decline a proposed gift from Anderson of $100,000 for a maternity ward. The meeting produced a gift of $10,000 from her to the Barnard site fund. An announcement followed shortly, and on May 11, 1894, Anderson joined the Barnard board.[19]

In the spring of 1896, with the site fund fully subscribed, the Barnard trustees acquired the vacant city block between 119th and 120th Streets directly across Broadway from the planned Columbia campus. This met the terms of the Brinckerhoff building gift and allowed plans for construction to begin. Anderson then announced a second gift, initially for $100,000 and later raised to $170,000, to pay for the construction of a second building on the site. This was followed a year later by a gift of $140,000 for a third building from Mrs. Josiah M. Fiske, a friend and parishioner of the recently deceased board chair Arthur Brooks. Plans were drawn at Anderson's direction by her architect Charles Rich of the

FIGURE 2.5 Elizabeth Milbank Anderson (1850–1921), legatee of the Jeremiah Milbank fortune, philanthropist, generous donor and trustee of Barnard College (1894–1922). Barnard Archives.

firm Lamb & Rich, wherein Milbank Hall was to face south, with Brinckerhoff Hall attached at the 120th Street end on the east and Fiske Hall on the west. A courtyard enclosed on three sides opened to the south.[20]

Even as the Milbank and Brinckerhoff parts of the impressive brick and limestone complex opened in the fall of 1897 (Fiske opened in 1898),

Plimpton secured the offer of a gift of $10,000 for the college from John D. Rockefeller Sr. to establish an endowment conditioned on Barnard raising $90,000 from other sources. Although it took Barnard longer to make the match than the two years stipulated, Rockefeller was sufficiently impressed by the number of contributors that Plimpton had secured that when the match was made in 1901 he increased his gift to $25,000. Although still financially shaky, Barnard entered the twentieth century with a treasurer of the bullish view that he shared with Fiske's estate lawyer: "There is no question in my mind that ultimately Barnard College will have a great deal of money; it cannot be otherwise."[21]

Meanwhile, the board's first chair, Rev. Arthur Brooks, a transplanted New Englander and rector of the Episcopal Church of the Incarnation, died on shipboard returning to New York from a European vacation in the summer of 1894. By agreeing to head the board, he had given the college an added measure of respectability among the city's other church leaders and Episcopal laity, and his untimely death came as a blow. Fortunately, an even more widely acknowledged member of the city's cultural leadership, and certified Knickerbocker to boot, the seventy-six-year-old Abram Hewitt, agreed in 1897 to join the board as its second chair. A Columbia graduate and active alumnus, as well as a generous backer of Cooper Union, Hewitt served for seven years until turning over the position of chair to Silas Brown Brownell, one of the original trustees and a leading member of the New York bar. Whatever Barnard's early problems, attracting members of the city's professional and cultural elite to its board was not one of them.[22]

SMALL WORLD

Three members of the original board of trustees, Laura Spelman Rockefeller; Francis Lynde Stetson, J. P. Morgan's personal attorney; and the Rev. Henry Van Dyke, rector of Brick Presbyterian Church, resigned after only one year of service. But they were the exception. The average tenure of the twenty-two original board members and the thirty-one subsequently elected trustees between 1890 and 1914 was eighteen years. Three original trustees—Annie Nathan Meyer (1889–1951), George A.

Plimpton (1889–1936), and Caroline Spurgeon Choate (1889–1929)—
served sixty-two, forty-eight, and forty-one years, respectively.[23]

Throughout the board's first quarter century, the original gender balance was scrupulously maintained, even after the change in membership
rules that reserved for an alumna a four-year term on the board. Similarly,
the original religious ecumenism persisted, except in the instance of
Schiff's resignation in 1896, which left the board without a member of
the city's German-Jewish community until Sarah Straus Hess (Barnard
class of 1900) was elected an alumnae trustee in 1919. Meanwhile, the
board's original contingent of Knickerbockers and transplanted New
Englanders increased, ensuring a continued predominance of Episcopalians and Presbyterians. Coudert's resignation in 1902 to accept a position
on the Columbia board was followed in 1906 by the election of another
Catholic, the retailer Charles Stuart Smith. Collegiate origins remained
predominantly Ivy League and leading women's colleges, with Columbia
and Barnard graduates, beginning with the election of Florence Colgate
Speranza (Barnard class of 1893) in 1898, as the first designated alumna
member of the board. Among the male trustees, lawyers increased their
already substantial representation.[24]

Most of the New Yorkers Annie Nathan Meyer approached to serve on
the original Barnard board were persons of wealth, but not all. Three of
the women elected to the board—Ella Weed, Helen Dawes Brown, and
Alice Williams—were single and educators with college credentials but
no known independent incomes. Nor did Meyer herself, her husband's
medical practice notwithstanding, have access to substantial wealth. The
rest of the early trustees, including three of the first four alumnae-elected
trustees, had either inherited wealth or had accumulated fortunes on their
own by the time they joined the board. Included were several of the city's
richest families, including the Rockefellers, the Choates, the Harrimans,
the Milbanks, and the Schiffs.[25]

If not themselves persons of wealth on this monumental scale, other
board members enjoyed privileged access to other people's money, among
them the estate attorneys Frederick Wait and George W. Smith, plus the
early board's four ministers, Arthur Brooks, Henry Van Dyke, Roderick
Terry, and William Grosvenor, along with the husband of Mrs. Henry
Sanders, each the spiritual adviser to one of the five richest congregations

in the United States. Even before he became wealthy himself, Plimpton socialized with people of wealth and felt comfortable asking the likes of Andrew Carnegie and Joseph Pulitzer to send some money Barnard's way.[26]

One rough quantitative measure of the wealth of Barnard's early trustees was the number of live-in household servants they employed. Of the fifty-three early trustees, thirty-nine have been located in state and federal census records, which show they enjoyed the services of an average of four live-in servants. The Schiffs had ten; the Choates and the Andersons had eight.[27] Of the city's turn-of-the-century monied and culturally favored groups, five had places on the early Barnard board. They are listed here in order of their arrival to the city:

1. Knickerbockers—a mix of seventeenth-century Dutch, Huguenot, and pre-Revolutionary English families, they were originally Dutch Reformed and Anglican and, following the Revolution, increasingly Episcopalian. They took a proprietary interest in Columbia College and Trinity Church and, of course, the Holland Society and the Knickerbocker Club. Of this group, the early Barnard board could boast Henry Van Dyke, Abram Hewitt, William M. Grosvenor, and George Rives.

2. Grandees—a small number of Jewish families who first arrived in New Amsterdam in the 1650s from Spain and Portugal by way of the West Indies. They included the Cardozos, the Nathans, the Lazuruses. They were Sephardic Jews who were proud of their American pre-Revolutionary origins kept a social distance from both the more recently arrived and often wealthier German-speaking Jews and even more from the Eastern European and Russian Jews arriving in the 1880s. Board Grandees included Annie Nathan Meyer.

3. Transplanted Yankees—New Englanders who came to New York in the nineteenth century but laid claim to American lineages dating back to the seventeenth century. They possessed multigenerational ties to New England colleges such as Harvard, Yale, Williams, and Amherst. Transplanted Yankees enjoyed a clear plurality on the early Barnard board and came in three denominational types: Unitarians— Augusta Foote Arnold, Caroline Choate and George Hoadley; Episcopalians—Arthur Brooks, Anne Scollay Low, Mary Harriman Rumsey, and Lucretia Osborn; Presbyterians—Silas Brown Brownell, George A. Plimpton, and Roderick Terry. Both Brownell and Terry, as well as

Lucretia Perry Osborn, claimed Mayflower descendants, while George Plimpton and Mary Harriman Rumsey traced their family lineage to the Puritan migrations of the 1630s.[28]

4. Our Crowd—German Jews who came to New York after the Civil War, having left Germany and Austria for America from the 1840s onward. They acquired prominence in finance, retailing, and publishing; worshipped at the reform synagogue Temple Emanu-El on Fifth Avenue; and sent their children to Dr. Sacks School or to Ethical Culture. These families included the Altschuls, Goldmans, Goodharts, Guggenheims, Lehmans, Seligmans, Speyers, and Warburgs. Their representative on the early Barnard board was Jacob H. Schiff and, later, Sarah Straus Hess.

5. Outsiders-with-New-Money—recently arrived families headed by fabulously rich self-made men whose early business successes were achieved elsewhere but who were drawn to New York as the nation's corporate capital and for its cultural attractions. Often evangelical Protestants, they included the Baptists Laura Spelman Rockefeller and Elizabeth Milbank Anderson.

Another indicator of the Barnard board's class homogeneity was residential propinquity. At the time of the consolidation in 1897, New York City was even more physically segregated by class, ethnicity, national origin, race, and religion than it is today. The outer boroughs of Queens and the Bronx were fast becoming home to new arrivals from Eastern Europe. Brooklyn was a mix of old families and newcomers. Parts of Manhattan had become ethnic and religious enclaves—the Lower East Side being home to recently arrived Italians and East European Jews; the West Side around Five Points was largely an Irish neighborhood; the far East Side, Germantown. Harlem was Jewish on the way to becoming Black. Staten Island and the upper reaches of Manhattan awaited future development, which, in the case of the latter, came with the opening of the Interborough Rapid Transit (IRT) subway in 1904.[29]

All but one of the fifty-three early Barnard trustees lived in Manhattan. The exception, Clara C. Stranahan, lived in Brooklyn, a condition dictated by the fact that her husband James S. T. Stranahan had represented that city for two terms in Congress, helped with the development of Prospect Park, and was called Brooklyn's First Citizen. Of the Manhattanites, all but five lived on the East Side, home to both the city's old money and to the socially ambitious new arrivals, including the families of German Jews. This so-called silk stocking district encompassed a two-mile-long and one-mile-wide quadrant of the thirty-three-square-mile island, between Twenty-Fourth and Seventy-Fifth Streets, which defined the south-north boundaries of the homes of the city's "arrived." Below Fifty-Ninth Street, the favored east-west boundary extended two blocks west of Fifth Avenue to Sixth Avenue, while above Fifty-Ninth Street, it extended east from Fifth Avenue along the lower Central Park over to Lexington Avenue. Thus, in a city of five boroughs covering 300 square miles, and in the single borough of Manhattan, encompassing twenty-three square miles, all but a half dozen of the fifty-three early Barnard trustees lived within walking distance of each other.[30]

They had their reasons. Manhattan's East Side included the city's wealthiest religious institutions, from the Madison Avenue Baptist Church at Thirty-Fifth Street, where the Rockefellers worshipped; the Presbyterian Brick Church on Park Avenue, favored by the Plimptons; the Episcopal Church of the Incarnation, where Barnard chair Arthur Brooks served as rector and the birthright Baptist Elizabeth Anderson Milbank attended. Temple Emanu-el was located at Fifth Avenue and Forty-Third Street, where the Schiff family attended Reform services. Here, too, on Fifth Avenue and Forty-Eighth Street, was St. Patrick's Cathedral, where the Couderts and the Charles Stewart Smiths worshipped. And here as well were the city's most socially exclusive private day schools, including Columbia Grammar School, on Fifty-First Street near Madison Avenue, and its two newest and most fashionable private girls' schools, Brearley, at 6 East Forty-Fifth Street, and in 1892, Spence, at 6 West Forty-Eighth Street.[31]

The minutes of the Board of Trustees in 1897, following the college's move from the East Side to Morningside, inadvertently confirm the members' residential propinquity. The first board meetings had been held at 343 Madison Avenue and Forty-Fourth Street, within easy walking distance from most of the trustees' homes, but the move to Morningside Heights now entailed a considerable trek north and west across town. When attendance fell off and trustee Brownell complained to his East Side neighbor President Low, "As you know. It is a long way up to Morningside Heights," it was agreed that future board meetings would be held at the home of board chair Abram Hewitt, on Madison and Thirty-Fourth Street and, following Hewitt's death, at the homes or offices of various East Side trustees. Board meetings on the Morningside campus did not resume until the 1920s.[32]

Two other markers of social standing confirm the early Barnard board's high social standing. Of the forty-seven Barnard trustees residing in New York City in 1901, forty (85 percent) were in that year's *New York Social Register*. The seven trustees who were not listed included three who were not then living in New York City; three women trustees unmarried at the time; and Jacob H. Schiff, who, because the *Register* included clubs that excluded Jews, refused to be listed and insisted his extended family and partners do likewise. A publication that competed with the *Social Register* but listed only men, *King's Notable New Yorkers*, included well over half (twenty-five of forty-six) of the trustees or their male spouses, including Schiff.[33]

Male trustees and husbands of female trustees belonged to all manner of socially exclusive clubs and societies, some related to their occupations, such as the Downtown Club, favored by Morgan-affiliated bankers; some to genealogical organizations like the Holland Society, the Knickerbocker Club, the Order of Cincinnati, or Sons of the Colonial Wars; and some recreational, such as the New York Yacht Club and the Automobile Association. Others belonged to the Grolier Club, home of dedicated bibliophiles. Women trustees joined the Colony Club upon its opening in 1903 and four years later the Junior League, founded by Barnard trustee Mary Harriman Rumsey. All these club memberships were by invitation.[34]

Of the clubs, the Century Association, founded in 1847 for "Artists, Literary Men, Scientists, Physicians, Officers of the Army and Navy, members of the Bench and Bar, Engineers, Clergymen, Representatives of the Press, Merchants and Men of Leisure," located at 7 West Forty-Third Street, had the widest appeal for New York's cultural elite. Of Barnard's twenty-six early male trustees, twenty-two were Centurions, as were ten trustee spouses. The club's informal proscription of Jews precluded Schiff and Dr. Meyer from membership, while its liberal beverage policy kept away Henrietta Talcott's husband, James Talcott, the founder of the New York Christian Home for Intemperate Men. But for others, especially relative newcomers to the city such as the New England transplant George Plimpton, election in 1894 to the Century Association, on a par with taking up residence on Park Avenue, confirmed his transition from "aspiring" outlander to socially "arrived" Gothamite.[35]

TALE OF TWO CITIES

Given their own social homogeneity, did the early trustees envision Barnard serving New Yorkers other than their privileged selves? Put differently, was Barnard intended primarily as an instrument of class certification and consolidation or as an engine of interclass assimilation? This is not to insist that Barnard had to be one or the other, either in the service of Edith Wharton's "Old New York" or Jacob Riis's "The Other Half," or that it could not be both. Barnard's early trustees participated in several efforts of social uplift, among them the Charity Organization Society and the settlement house movement. However, Barnard was not founded as a charitable outreach to the city's poor and recently arrived *by* the city's "very earnest, philanthropic, public-spirited class" but *for* them as an instrument of class consolidation.

Support for this argument begins with Annie Nathan Meyer's 1888 letter to *The Nation*, where she identified four groups of New York women from which a day college for women would draw its students. Two of them, those attending college elsewhere for want of a New York women's college and those "bemoaning their fate because their parents will not allow them to leave their homes," she assumed came from families of economic means and social standing. As for the third group she identified, the 1,600 New York women attending the Normal College, Meyer specifically excluded those "whose parents could not afford to pay tuition fees" while laying claim to those with "parents who could easily afford it, and would gladly send their daughters to a private college where a degree could be procured." The fourth included those girls, like herself, again for family reasons rather than financial constraints, were bound to the city.[36]

Neither in *Barnard Beginnings* nor in her autobiography, *It's Been Fun*, did Meyer retrospectively suggest an institutional purpose for Barnard other than providing New York young women of the comfortable class local access to higher education equal to young men of the same class. During her sixty-two years as a trustee, she occasionally described Barnard as a meeting place where New York girls from Christian and Jewish families interacted to their mutual benefit, but she never went beyond commending such intraclass mingling of wealthy

Christians and Jews to suggest that the college function as a class-dissolving melting pot.[37]

In a statement published in 1894 in the *Barnard Annual* entitled "The Constituency of Barnard College," board chair Rev. Arthur Brooks directly posed the question, "[F]or whom was [Barnard] intended and from what class of women is it to draw its students?" He then proceeded to identify two classes. The first was "the large number of New York women who are not likely to be compelled to earn their own living and whose sphere of life, in all probability, is to lie in the family or in New York society." The second were "women dependent upon their own efforts for their support." Further on he argued that "the education which the college offers" was intended for "no one class of lives, but for every possible position in life." Still, one can easily imagine this well-born, Harvard-educated Episcopal priest thinking the college's primary mission was providing a collegiate education for the wealthy and socially connected daughters of the families who made up his East Side congregation.[38]

Another attempt to define Barnard's anticipated clientele, this by trustee Helen Dawes Brown in an 1891 report to the board from the Students Committee, identified "two classes of girls in New York for whom my sympathies are enlisted: the girls who are too rich to go to college, and the girls who are too poor." Brown went on to call for the establishment of a scholarship fund to assist those "hungering for just what this college gives, but without the means to come here," to no immediate effect. It would be seven more years before Barnard's first scholarship was established, the funding coming not from the board but a gift from the Daughters of the American Revolution, hardly a champion of social inclusion. No Barnard trustee publicly stated the board's institutional aspirations for Barnard as plainly as founder Joseph W. Taylor did for Bryn Mawr—"The advanced education and care of Young Women or girls of the higher and more refined classes of Society"—but this does not imply a more expansive social mandate. In the absence of contrary evidence, it is at least arguable that Barnard's founders and early backers expected the college to serve primarily the families of New Yorkers that Columbia trustees referred to as "our own kind": not New York girls in general and even less the poorest or most recent arrivals among them, but their own daughters and nieces, those of their professional colleagues; those with whom they played golf on Saturdays and worshipped on Sundays; and those they hoped to see their sons, grandsons, and nephews marry.[39]

How then to account for the fact that so few of the families of New York's turn-of-the-twentieth-century social elite, including those of trustees, sent their daughters to Barnard? Trustee and later board chair Silas Brown Brownell had five daughters. His two older ones (Louise and Matilda) were attending Bryn Mawr when Barnard opened in 1889 and stayed on there; his three younger daughters (Sylvia, Eleanor, and Grace) all subsequently attended Bryn Mawr. Henry Van Dyke had three daughters, Frederic Coudert (1889–1902) and Hamilton Wright Mabie (1889–1905) each had two college-age daughters, and Roderick Terry had one, but none attended Barnard. Jacob Schiff had a daughter, Frieda, who attended the Brearley School but did not go to college. Henrietta Talcott had two college-age daughters, one of whom, Edith, attended Barnard briefly before transferring to Oberlin, where her younger sister Grace followed her. Elizabeth Milbank Anderson's only daughter, Eleanor, graduated from the Spence School in 1896 and proceeded to Bryn Mawr. Of the forty-five families represented among Barnard's first generation of trustees, only one, Annie Nathan Meyer's, had a daughter graduate from Barnard.[40]

Additional evidence attesting to the infrequency with which not only Barnard trustees but the city's moneyed elite generally sent their daughters to Barnard in those years can be inferred from the college placement patterns of Manhattan's most socially exclusive private girls' schools. The Brearley School opened in 1884 with an explicit purpose to prepare its girls for admission to the newly opened Harvard Annex. Barnard trustee Caroline Dutcher Choate was one of its founders, and Barnard trustee Alice Williams taught there. The Spence School opened in 1892 on West Forty-Fifth Street to serve much the same social clientele. Its founder, Clara Spence, and major financial backer, Elizabeth Milbank Anderson, were both Barnard trustees, as was Charlotte Baker, the Spence School headmistress. Despite these links, neither Brearley nor Spence became a significant feeder to Barnard. Both sent most of their college-going graduates to Bryn Mawr or Vassar. One early Brearley graduate, who, for family reasons, transferred to Barnard from Bryn Mawr later recalled Brearley's college selection process: "Nobody ever mentioned Barnard."[41]

"WE WERE NOT IN 'SOCIETY' EXACTLY; WE WERE PROFESSIONAL PEOPLE"

The evolving social makeup of the families from which the early Barnard student body came was not what Barnard's founders had expected nor was it likely what at least some of them wanted. The evidence here is admittedly more qualitative than quantitative, less statistically verifiable than anecdotally inferable. Yet a comparison of two early graduating classes, separated by a dozen years, suggests a widening gap between the social world of the college's New York founders and trustees and the social world of its students. The first such class, that of 1899, the seventh class to graduate and the one that split its four years between the original East Side campus and Barnard's second home on Morningside Heights, was profiled by its most notable member, Virginia Crocheron Gildersleeve. Gildersleeve's portrait serves two narrative purposes: an early introduction to the single most important person in Barnard's history, and an early indication of my abiding ambivalence about Gildersleeve's reliability and her legacy.[42]

In 1954, seven years after her retirement, Virginia Gildersleeve published her autobiography, *Many a Good Crusade*, to favorable reviews. Undertaken in part—as with most instances of the genre—to preempt posthumous scrutiny by telling her story first as she wanted it told, her account of her early life offers a portrait of a privileged family in the New York society of her youth. It also includes an extended account of her four years as a Barnard student, including descriptions of her classmates. However compelling her affectionate rendering of "Old New York," that of her classmates should be read with a skeptical eye.[43]

Virginia Crocheron Gildersleeve was born on October 3, 1877, in New York City. Her childhood passed as part of a family on both sides socially and economically secure, safely "arrived." "We were not in 'society' exactly," her mother explained, "we were professional people." They resided at 28 West Forty-eighth Street, just off Fifth Avenue, "a very quiet and respectable street in those days."

> Our house was brick with brownstone trim, but practically all the other houses on both sides of the street were the orthodox brownstone complete, four stories and basement, high stoop in front. They were inhabited

by solid American families. I recall the names of the Griswolds, the Whit-
fields, the Rhinelanders, the Frelinghuysens. A few of them were more
wealthy and more socially prominent than we were.

Andrew Carnegie's future wife, Gildersleeve recalled, "lived just across the
street."[44]

The autobiography describes the domestic servants the Gildersleeves
employed, along with a passing assessment of the New Yorkers then in
service:

> They [the Gildersleeves] had two maids,—a cook and a chambermaid-
> waitress—and they had someone come in to do the washing. The ser-
> vants were almost invariably Irish. From my third-story rear bedroom I
> could often hear fiddles playing Irish jigs as maids in neighboring kitchens
> danced at night. I grew up with the vague and utterly preposterous idea
> that domestic servants were the only variety of persons produced by that
> brilliant race.[45]

Both sides of Virginia's family claimed old American lineages. The
Gildersleeves went back eight generations to a New England landfall in
1635; the Crocherons were part of the French Huguenot diaspora that
came to Staten Island in the 1690s. Such geneaological credentials mattered enough to Gildersleeve to devote fourteen pages of her autobiography to them, including a nonjudgmental account of the Crocherons'
stake in an Alabama cotton plantation, with 200 slaves held as disposable property.[46]

While Virginia's mother and namesake was depicted as a powerful force
domestically and "loved very dearly," the family's men garnered most of
her attention. Her father, Henry Alger Gildersleeve, was a Civil War veteran; organizer of the American Rifle Association; prominent lawyer; and
an elected municipal judge, who later served as a justice on the Supreme
Court of the State of New York. He is described as "spectacularly handsome," with a picture of him at seventy to prove it. Of her older brothers,
Alger and Harry (two sisters died before Virginia was born), the younger
Harry, seven years her senior, is depicted as "this radiant figure of my
childhood" and "the brilliant member of the family." Her early childhood,

as she wrote, was one where "no sorrow had ever touched me," until tragedy intervened when Harry, in 1891, just after completing Columbia law school, contracted typhoid fever and died. "At that moment," she wrote, "a black curtain cut my life in two."[47]

To help with their daughter's grieving, the Gildersleeves enrolled fourteen-year-old Virginia at the city's most exclusive girls' school, Brearley. They did so on the recommendation of Frederic Coudert, a colleague of Judge Gildersleeve and a fellow member of the Century Club. In the fall of her senior year at Brearley, Virginia decided that, if she were to go on to college, it would be to Bryn Mawr, where most of her college-bound classmates were headed. Her mother ruled otherwise. "There is a perfectly good college here in New York," by which she meant Barnard, she informed her distraught daughter. It had been recommended by Mrs. Choate, Counsellor Coudert, and likely others of the Gildersleeve social acquaintanceship who served on the college's board.[48]

The decision did not sit well with Virginia. Barnard's admission requirements, identical with Columbia College, still required knowledge of Greek, which Brearley did not teach at the time. This necessitated a cram course on top of her regular program and produced much anxiety about the entrance exam to be administered in the spring. She passed the exam and was accepted to Barnard, the only Brearley girl to have applied. On October 3, 1895, her eighteenth birthday, Virginia appeared along with the other entering twenty-one members of the class of 1899 on the steps of the scruffy brownstone at 343 Madison Avenue, by her own alliterative account, "shy, snobbish, solemn."[49]

"ALL MORE OR LESS ON THE SAME SOCIAL LEVEL"

A year later, Virginia had become a class leader and was elected as sophomore class vice president. What explains this turnabout? Her academic success made her an early favorite of her teachers, but her social success among her peers is less easily accounted for. She likely benefitted from her home's proximity to Barnard, a ten-minute walk, during Barnard's last two years at the Madison Avenue site and by her mother's hosting student gatherings; she was made an honorary member of the class of 1899 in Virginia's first year.[50]

Of the twenty-five young women who were members of the class of 1899 at some point, five are specifically mentioned in Gildersleeve's account. Grace Goodale is cited briefly for the novelty of her not coming from New York City but from upstate. Two other classmates were also residentially demarcated: Edith Striker was "gay and laughing and loyal, whose home was in East Orange, New Jersey"; Alte Stilwell was "nimble-witted and warmhearted, who lived in a pleasant, dignified Harlem street."[51]

Considerably more attention is given to East Sider Alice Duer, who entered the class as a junior. She was the granddaughter of William A. Duer, president of Columbia College (1829–1842) and great granddaughter of Rufus King, a signer of the U.S. Constitution and chair of the Columbia board of trustees. Her father, James Gore King Duer, was a well-known speculator who went bankrupt the year his daughter was to be presented in society, leaving the family financially adrift. Alice delayed college until she was able to pay her own way through journalism and writing fiction for magazines. Three years older than her Barnard classmates and financially on her own, Alice Duer was the class exotic. Five months after graduating, she married a wealthy New York broker, William Miller. Her husband's success on Wall Street allowed her to devote herself to writing fiction and poetry and later screenwriting for Hollywood. She remained a lifelong friend of Virginia Gildersleeve, who, more than a half century after making her acquaintance, recalled Alice as a schoolgirl: "She was beautiful and she was brilliant and she was charming. She brought into our classrooms a glamour from the outer world and her friendship gave me the romance of my youth."[52]

Another East Sider, Marjorie Jacobi, also joined the class of 1899 as a junior and merited extended mention from Gildersleeve. She was the daughter of Dr. Mary Putnam Jacobi, one of the first women physicians in the United States, and Dr. Abraham Jacobi, professor of pediatrics at the College of Physicians and Surgeons (which had been integrated into Columbia University in 1892) and "the father of American pediatrics." Shortly after graduation, Marjorie married George McAneny, a wealthy, socially connected New Yorker, who later served as chair of the New

York City Board of Aldermen. Left unmentioned by Gildersleeve were classmates Rosalie Bloomingdale, Ella Seligsberg, and Sarah Straus, all from prominent German-Jewish families residing on the East Side; Eliza Kupfer, whose parents were Jews from Russia and lived on the West Side; and Martha Ornstein, whose mother was from Hungary and lived in Brooklyn.[53]

For Gildersleeve and her Barnard crowd, those the New York Times called the "socially, intellectually and athletically prominent" (Virginia played golf and was familiar with guns), membership in a Greek sorority (then called a fraternity) provided a desired measure of exclusivity that Barnard's otherwise more egalitarian environment lacked. The college's first fraternity, Kappa Kappa Gamma (KKG), was established in 1891 and initially included all regularly enrolled students. By the spring of 1896, when Gildersleeve was inducted, its membership had become more exclusive and included less than a quarter of the student body. Virginia was the only member of her freshman class to be inducted. During her sophomore and junior year, she saw to the induction of her friends, Duer, Jacobi, Striker, and Stilwell. Never included was a majority of her class, among them its five identified Jewish members—one of whom, Sarah Straus, was the daughter of Isidor and Ida Straus, the owners of Macy's Department Store, who would in 1919 be elected as alumnae member of the Barnard board of trustees. Virginia's sorority sisters were the narrow sample from which she derived two conclusions about her class contained in her 1954 autobiography: that it was "far less varied in make-up than a college class of today" and that its members were "all more or less on the same social level." The first was probably true, but the second is questionable and ignores the social tensions at the anything but inclusive Barnard of her day.[54]

Also unmentioned in her autobiography was an incident that occurred in Virginia's sophomore year. That spring, Stella Stern, a popular junior from New Orleans, was denied admission to Kappa Kappa Gamma because she was Jewish. Stern and three of her Christian classmates, Jessie Hughan, Helen St. Clair (Mullan), and Elizabeth Wyman, all of the class of 1898, protested the decision and set out to end the KKG monopoly by forming their own sorority, Alpha Omicron Pi (AOPi), with a chapter charter that explicitly prohibited religious discrimination. Over the next decade, six more chapters of national sororities were established at Barnard, all closed to the college's growing number of Jewish students.[55]

It was not that Virginia was indifferent to changes occurring around her. In the spring of her senior year, she published an undergraduate essay, "The Changing College Population," lamenting the declining focus on academics and the increasing attention to the social side of attending college. Whatever the validity of these observations, the essay ignored more sweeping changes occurring in the economic circumstances of Barnard students and certainly gave no indication that these reportedly more fun-loving newcomers were any less well off or less socially credentialed than "the studious middle-class daughters" of her later imagining.[56]

GUESS WHO'S COMING TO BARNARD?

By the time of their graduation, Virginia Gildersleeve and her privileged KKG sorority sisters were already a declining presence at Barnard. For every incoming student whose socially prominent New York parents sent her to Barnard, several equally credentialed New York parents entrusted their daughters to Bryn Mawr, Smith, Wellesley, and Vassar. This was particularly true for the daughters of Protestant East Side families who prepared at private day schools such as Brearley and Spence, where both institutional influence and social pressure directed them to one or another of the out-of-town "country colleges." This was not true of the daughters of the city's East Side, German-Jewish elite who attended Dr. Sacks' School or Ethical Culture and who, either because of suspected anti-Semitism on some women's college campuses or tighter familial bonds, were more likely either to forego college altogether (the fate of the Schiffs' daughter Freida) or attend nearby Barnard.[57]

By the early 1900s, Barnard served a portion of the city's German-Jewish community as one of its colleges of choice for their academically inclined but homebound daughters. If their presence distressed some Barnard trustees, no evidence of such has been found.

Whatever her private reservations about Jews more recently arrived to the United States, Annie Nathan Meyer applauded this development in her dealings with the Guggenheims, whom she assured in the course of seeking financial help for the college that Barnard welcomed Jews. But what even Meyer had not anticipated, and almost certainly disapproved of, was the appearance of increasing numbers of applicants from the daughters of Yiddish-speaking Jewish families now residing in the city's outer boroughs and only a generation removed from the shetls of Eastern Europe and Russia. In complaining to President Butler in 1905 about her daughter's rejection by Miss Keller's School, a private school with Columbia faculty on its board that discriminated against Jews, Annie Nathan Meyer agreed that "no school need accept more than a certain proportion [of Hebrews]."

> No Hebrew objects to that. The loud or coarse or those that are too German or Russian to affiliate with the students may with justice be rejected. A common, unrefined brewer may send his boys or girls to these schools but a cultured Hebrew with American traditions, and even if belonging to the oldest families of the country is not permitted the same liberty.

For added effect, Meyer copied the Guggenheims. To all of which Butler coolly responded on behalf of Columbia: "We are much more often charged with favoring Jews than with discriminating against them." Clearly the "Hebrew problem" was not Virginia Gildersleeve's classmates Rosalie Bloomingdale, Ella Seligsberg or Sarah Straus, but the other unremarked upon classmates, Elise Kupner and Martha Ornstein.[58]

Or if not Ornstein or Kupner (the latter going on from Barnard to a distinguished career as chair of the botany department of Wadleigh High School), then what about the "most unsavory girl" who appeared unannounced on campus in the summer of 1901, as Bursar N. W. Liggett reported to the newly arrived Dean Laura Drake Gill:

> Not a creature has been here . . . save a most unsavory girl, named Fox, who took the examinations for Barnard at Fall River, and who has never received any word as to the results. We have been taken in by this girl.

Her home and locality where she lives persuaded me that she was of saintly Puritan stock, but not quite orthodox, since she turned her back upon the colleges of New England for those of New York. She turns out to be an unwashed (I crave pardon for the word, but it required a strong one) Jew! She has friends living on the lower east side of Third Avenue, with whom she proposes to live! I gave her almost an hour of my time, and wish heartily she would partake herself to Radcliffe.

What Bursar Liggett, a Vassar graduate, had yet to understand and Gill, a graduate of Smith, would never grasp, was that the nature of going to college for New York girls had fundamentally changed in the dozen years since Barnard's founding. Once limited to the East Side daughters of the wealthy, well born, and privately prepared, college was becoming a possibility for a wider segment of New Yorkers, not least for the academically ambitious daughters of immigrant families "living on the lower east side of Third Avenue" and in the city's outer boroughs.[59]

To be sure, a few of the city's wealthiest white, Anglo-Saxon, Protestant families did send their daughters to Barnard. Subsequent trustees Florence Colgate (class of 1895) and Mary Harriman (class of 1905), the daughter of the railroad magnate Edward Harriman, granddaughter of an Episcopal bishop and the founder of the Junior League, are cases in point. More common, but still a minority, were the daughters of wealthy German-Jewish families, as with future trustees Sarah Straus Hess (class of 1900) and Helen Lehman Goodhart Altschul (class of 1907). Florence Samet Rothschild, the daughter of an Alsatian Jewish real estate developer, who attended religious services at Temple Emmanu-El on the Upper East Side of Manhattan, entered Barnard in 1904 and later described her background: "I came from a very wealthy family. . . . We were fancy people."[60]

The fact remains that fewer of the city's "fancy people" availed themselves of Barnard than Meyer and others active in the college's founding anticipated. Having described itself in *King's Handbook of New York* in 1893 as mainly for "New York girls, whose parents prefer that their daughters should live at home during their collegiate educations," the college soon found that whatever parental preferences might have been operative in the Meyer and Gildersleeve household, turn-of-the-twentieth-century college-bound girls from New York families of means preferred to go to one of the country colleges than live at home and commute to Barnard. By Barnard's second decade of operations, following its move from Madison Avenue to Morningside, it was attracting fewer socially credentialed East Side residents than it had in its opening decade.[61]

It was more than just the loosening of parental ties among the city's elite families and a greater willingness to grant daughters the same away-to-college experience provided sons that confounded the expectations of Barnard's founders. Equally disruptive was the demographic transformation of turn-of-the-century New York. The earlier influx of German immigrants slowed and that of Irish immigrants continued apace, but the city also witnessed a new wave of immigrants from Italy and Eastern Europe, the latter mostly impoverished and often illiterate Jews who spoke Yiddish, a "mongrel" language that bespoke centuries of dislocations. For some settled New Yorkers, including quickly acculturating German Jews who arrived a generation earlier, these newcomers posed a threat to the standing social order greater than did the Irish, who, after all, spoke English and were Christians of a sort. By 1910, Eastern European Jews made up 25 percent of the population of the consolidated city. A year earlier, a survey indicated that three out of four New York residents had a foreign-born parent.[62]

Another unanticipated development was the remarkable upgrading of the city's public schools begun in the 1870s and accelerated in 1896 with legislation providing for the opening of public high schools throughout the five boroughs, several of which now offered instruction in the subjects required for admission to college. These included coeducational high schools like Jamaica High School in Queens and Morris High School in the Bronx, both opened in 1897, and Curtis High School opened on Staten Island in 1904. And then there were the new high schools for girls, including the Girls' High School in Brooklyn (1886) and Wadleigh High School for Girls, which opened in 1902 on Manhattan's West 114th Street in the largely Jewish neighborhood of Harlem, only four blocks from Barnard. A similar boom in high school building was underway in the towns in Westchester County and northern New Jersey.[63]

In 1906, some 9,000 eighth-graders entered one of the city's eighteen public high schools. A majority of them left at age sixteen to enter the workforce. Of those from Irish families, who constituted 19 percent of the city's population, only 6 percent stayed to graduate. Those from Italian families, who made up 6 percent of the city' population, only 3 percent stayed to graduate. Meanwhile, students whose parents immigrated from Russia, and made up 7 percent of the city's population, comprised 12 percent of all graduates. A 1911 report on *Causes of Elimination of Students in Public Secondary Schools in New York City*, using 1906 and 1908 data, concluded: "The Hebrews far exceed all others, including native-born Americans, in their appreciation and use of New York City high schools."[64]

The report also concluded that girls enrolled in high school were more likely to stay on through graduation than boys, describing the operative family dynamic: "When resources are meagre the older boys are sent to work; the older girls on the other hand are frequently sent to high school." This applied with more force within Irish families, where ten girls went to high school for every six boys, whereas Jewish families sent five boys to high school for every four girls. For both immigrant groups, the report speculated that "older boys are sent to work and only the youngest boys are sent to high school. The older girls, on the other hand, are frequently sent to high school, it appears, possibly in the hope of making teachers of them."[65]

In 1908, a majority of the 24,000 students enrolled in New York City public schools were girls. Of these, only an estimated 7,000 were from native-born families, some living in "two, rarely three rooms in a crowded tenement house section in the least attractive neighborhood." Many of the 3,600 Jewish and 1,000 Irish girls came from even worse residential circumstances. But if only a quarter of these girls stayed on to graduate from high school and then sought further education to enable them to teach in the public schools from which they graduated, they constituted a vast local student pool, one that Barnard's founders had not anticipated twenty years earlier. The question became: Would Barnard embrace this new demographic reality—young women in numbers "from the least attractive neighborhoods" in search of higher education—or remain favoring those trustee chair Arthur Brooks called "New York women who are not likely to be compelled to earn their living"?[66]

Three other turn-of-the-twentieth-century developments, which were unanticipated by Barnard's founders, were technical in nature but together further democratized New Yorkers' access to higher education. The elimination of Greek as a prerequisite for college admission, led by Harvard in 1886, was soon followed by others; Columbia and Barnard did so in 1897. Public high schools offering Latin to their most ambitious students now found themselves legitimate pathways to college.[67]

Another development can be directly credited to Columbia's Nicholas Murray Butler. Before ascending to the Columbia presidency, he worked for a decade to persuade twelve colleges, including Columbia and Barnard, to forego their entrance exams in favor of a uniform admissions examination to be administered by a consortium of college administrators called the College Entrance Examination Board. Once Harvard signed on in 1904, other colleges followed and the so-called College Boards became the national mechanism by which colleges determined the eligibility of an applicant. Entrance exams administered by single colleges soon became a thing of the past.[68]

A third development specific to New York State was the 1904 decision by the Board of Regents to offer state-administered, subject-specific examinations to graduating high school seniors. Passing scores on these Regents exams quickly became an acceptable basis for admission to colleges throughout New York State and beyond. Columbia and Barnard announced in 1906 that they would automatically accept any applicant who scored above 60 percent on four of the Regents exams.

FIGURE 2.6 Milbank Hall (including Brinkerhoff Hall attached on right, Fiske Hall, on left), circa 1900.

The combined effect of these developments would almost certainly make Barnard more diverse and inclusive than any of the college's founders envisioned. Accepting the idea of an inclusive Barnard would take time, and even more time would be required if those favoring a more exclusive Barnard sought to evade the social imperative that came with the college's New York location.

3

BECOMING BARNARD

A Place in the City

A student body of 600, heterogeneous in the extreme.
—PROFESSOR OF LATIN CHARLES KNAPP, (1910)[1]

I n May 1893, Barnard College graduated its first class of eight seniors with appropriate fanfare. Joseph H. Choate wrote of the occasion to his wife, the trustee Carline Dutcher Choate, who was away from the city: "Last night's *Post* has such an excellent account of the first Commencement of the Barnard girls that I have cut it out and enclose it. Mr. Brownell tells me that they made a great sensation as they appeared upon the stage and were received with overwhelming applause." That fall, 106 students returned to the rented Madison Avenue campus to continue the work begun by the college's first graduates, not least of which was the fashioning of an extracurriculum.[2]

INVENTING A COLLEGE LIFE

The first students consisted of fourteen young women, enrolled as "regulars" on the basis of examination as degree-seekers, plus twenty-two "specials," nondegree candidates who registered for one or two courses.

Of that class, eight regulars stayed on to graduate in the spring of 1893. That same fall, Barnard began its fifth academic year with nearly half of its 106 enrollments nondegree specials. Of the regulars, seven stayed on to graduate in 1894, another eight in 1895.[3]

The small size of these first graduating classes and the absence of a discernible upward trend were troubling. Equally concerning was the heavy reliance upon specials, who were expected to be eliminated once four regular classes were in place. Their persistence in numbers, a matter of financial exigency, gave the impression that Barnard's academic standards were lower than other women's colleges who admitted only degree students. Yet their continued presence after the move to Morningside, when they again briefly became a majority of all enrollments, reflects Barnard's continued problem attracting full-time students in sustainable numbers. Not until 1900 did regular enrollments again exceed specials and not until 1905, by which time Barnard had graduated thirteen classes, did specials make up less than one-third of all enrollments. One special in 1910, Iphigene Ochs, described her status as "students who were not very bright or who were inadequately prepared for regular college courses." In Ochs's case, she passed the entrance exams at the start of her third year and became a member of the class of 1914. Specials would not be eliminated until 1927, not coincidentally the same year Barnard became a founding member of the prestigious Seven Sisters College Conference.[4]

Given that all the 200 or so students enrolled at Barnard during the first eight years on the East Side commuted to school, the creation of even a semblance of college life outside the classroom is impressive. During the second year of operations, an Undergraduate Association was introduced that provided the college with a rudimentary student government. A year later, the first chapter of a Greek national fraternity, Kappa Kappa Gamma (KKG) was established. In 1894, the first yearbook, *Barnard Annual*, was published, succeeded three years later by *Barnard Mortarboard*. The first issue of the college's campus newspaper, *Barnard Bulletin*, appeared in 1901. By 1904, students had formed teams in basketball, tennis, and ping-pong; clubs included La Société Française, Deutscher Kreis, the Greek Club, the Botany Club, the Barnard College Young Women's Christian Association, and a chapter of the Church Students' Missionary Association. For those interested in music, there was the Barnard Chorus and the Mandolin Club; for those interested in social service, a chapter of the College Settlement Association. Literary undertakings included the *Barnard Bear*. The invention of an early student life at Barnard reached its imaginative highpoint in 1903 when the sophomores (class of 1905) challenged the incoming freshmen (class of 1906) to a series of athletic contests in what came to be known as the Greek Games. These were thereafter faithfully repeated every spring for seven decades.[5]

Despite the many extracurricular activities, the absence of a residential dimension made the early Barnard experience fundamentally different from that of the other women's colleges and that of "country" colleges in general. This shortcoming was made all the more glaring by the fact that a year after the move to Morningside, with the opening of Fiske Hall in 1898, some twenty-five Barnard students from outside New York City took up temporary residence in the as-yet-unoccupied top floor. The experiment lasted only two years before the space was reassigned

FIGURE 3.1 Annual enactment of Greek Games, 1914.

as a planned laboratory. Despite the brevity of the residency, it was long enough to provoke two different reactions. Trustee Henrietta Talcott, on the basis of a single visit, declared the dormitory "a godless place," and trustee Augusta Arnold agreed, complaining that there were "no limits to the hours that the girls could dance." But trustee Annie Nathan Meyer, while declaring herself to Treasurer Plimpton no fan of country colleges, with their extensive residential quarters conveying "a sense of self-importance, or of mental isolation, or eccentricity," lamented the closing of the temporary dormitory, it having "succeeded in attracting the finest women from all over the country." She closed her letter with a plea: "Do get us a gift of a dormitory. I am sure you will, you have never failed us as yet in any of our great needs."[6]

The ever-resourceful Plimpton already had set his sights on Elizabeth Milbank Anderson for such a gift. Although she had never attended college, Anderson had taken to heart the calls of others on the importance of a dormitory if Barnard was to compete with the country colleges for the daughters of New York's well-to-do families. Indeed, her own daughter, Eleanor, a Brearley graduate, had opted for Bryn Mawr. Anderson's purchase in 1902 of the three acres of land between 116th and 119th Streets, contiguous with the original site, was intended for Barnard's first dormitory, which she likely expected other trustees to underwrite. When none did and Meyer took it upon herself in 1904 to try to interest the Guggenheim family in making a naming gift of a dormitory, Anderson shortly thereafter announced her third major gift to the college, in the amount of $150,000, for a dormitory to be named after the Reverend Arthur Brooks, first chair of the trustees and Anderson's spiritual counselor at the Episcopal Church of the Incarnation.[7]

The building that became Brooks Hall faced inward on the southern edge of the Milbank Quadrangle, with its back facing 116th Street. It was not just another utilitarian college dormitory. Historian Helen Lefkowitz Horowitz, in her illuminating *Alma Mater*, described it this way:

> Designed as an urban residence by Lamb & Rich. The architects of Barnard's first buildings, Brooks Hall rose nine stories in brick and limestone to match the Milbank group some distance away. Built on a steel skeleton, it was a vertical rectangle. A handsome portico fitted with

FIGURE 3.2 Brooks Hall, opened in 1907 to attract residential students from beyond New York City. Barnard Archives.

white limestone columns, an ornamental cornice, and bay windows kept
Brooks from looking severe.

Severe it was not. Brooks consisted of eight floors of outward-facing
rooms and suites designed to accommodate just ninety-seven students,
with interior public rooms on each of the upper floors as well as on the
first floor off the elegant entry. Anderson selected the in-demand Elsie de
Wolfe, who had decorated the Andersons' Fifth Avenue apartment and
countless other East Side homes, to decorate the public spaces. They were
to have, DeWolfe assured her client, referring to New York's most fashionable women's club, "gilt applique like [the] parlor and tea room at [the]
Colony Club."[8]

Annual room rents in Brooks varied significantly, with the smallest
double rooms going for $160 a year, while the suites, which consisted of

FIGURE 3.3 Interior of Brooks Hall room. Barnard Archives.

two rooms, a private bath, and fireplace, a princessly $1,000. Board was fixed at $500, making the total cost of residence several times the tuition of $150 and substantially higher than the other women's colleges. Horowitz convincingly argues that the opening of Brooks Hall "began Barnard's partial transformation into a women's college along the lines of Vassar or Bryn Mawr."[9]

The opening of Brooks Hall in the fall of 1907 was clearly intended to attract wealthy applicants, both New York City residents with resources to live away from home and those from beyond the city. Yet four years after Brooks opened, it had still not attracted enough undergraduates to be fully occupied. In their absence, Barnard rented suites to Columbia female graduate students and offered them to unmarried Barnard women instructors as part of their compensation. When full occupancy by undergraduates was finally achieved in 1913, it was only after the introduction of resident scholarships explicitly designed to attract out-of-state applicants. If early Barnard wanted more out-of-town girls, it seemed it would have to buy them.[10]

SCHLEPPING TO BARNARD

When Barnard was located on Madison Avenue on the East Side, it became one of many cultural institutions within walking distance of the homes of the city's wealthiest families. Situated midway up the island, the college was accessible by trolley car from other parts of Manhattan. Students coming from the boroughs of Brooklyn and Queens required the additional services of a ferry across the East River; those coming from the Bronx and lower Westchester County used a bridge across the Harlem River; and those from northern New Jersey rode a ferry across the Hudson. The longest trek was from eastern Queens and involved a combination of ferry; trolley car; and, from western Long Island, the Long Island Railroad. But whether a leisurely five-minute walk or an arduous two-hour slog, the fact that each school day began and ended with a commute is what most distinguished the Barnard student experience from their country sisters.[11]

The move to Morningside in 1897 only reinforced this distinction. Now East Siders confronted a daily trek by trolley car over the top of Central Park to the thinly populated and considerably more down-market Upper West Side. The commute from northern New Jersey, with its river-crossing terminus at the 135th Street Ferry pier, was shortened by the college's relocation, but the commute was made longer for students from Queens. A more determinative development in confirming Barnard as a commuting school was the 1904 opening of the IRT (Interborough Rapid Transit) subway between City Hall in lower Manhattan to 145th Street. This was soon followed by rapid transit links between the Upper West Side and the Bronx, Queens, and Brooklyn, extending Barnard's commuting zone from ground zero, the Broadway and 116th Street IRT station, outward to a radius of thirty miles. This tristate region included New York's suburbs, plus the densely populated southwest Connecticut and northern New Jersey: a total area of 3,800 square miles, and, by 1900, home to 15,000,000 people, or roughly one-fifth of all Americans.[12]

While hardly cloistered in its original East Side location, the Upper West Side where Barnard now found itself permanently located put the college at the geographical center and cultural heart of the American urban condition, with its fast-paced tempo, rough-edged diversity, and social heterogeneity. Whatever second thoughts these facts of life prompted among its founders and early backers, Barnard's distinct urban essence had to be acknowledged; accepted; and then, if possible, embraced. This last condition would be decades in coming, but as early as 1901, a graduating senior, Florence L. Sanville, gave voice to the "thoroughly cosmopolitan nature of the student body which Barnard's situation in New York makes possible."

> Our situation in a great city with its counter attractions, the home ties and demands which bind a large proportion of the students, the hurrying comings and goings in crowded trolley cars, trains, or ferry boats. . . . In no other college, probably, do the students represent as many different classes as they do at Barnard College. Barnard satisfies the demand of every type—from the girl who cannot afford the expense of an out-of-town college, to the girl who seeks to combine higher studies with a continuance of social life and pleasures. The result of this intermingling of classes is a broad democratic spirit which makes itself felt throughout our ranks.

Not everyone shared Sanville's urban ethic.[13]

"SHE IS NOT A NEW YORKER": THE MISBEGOTTEN GILL DEANSHIP

Dean Emily James Smith Putnam, newly married and in anticipation of motherhood, resigned as dean in February 1900. Her abbreviated tenure, surprise resignation, and the reason prompting it led President Low to urge that her successor be a man. To this end, he appointed the thirty-seven-year-old historian James Harvey Robinson, a popular instructor of history at Barnard and Columbia, as acting dean. Although Elizabeth Milbank Anderson had favored Putnam resigning, she opposed the idea of a male dean for Barnard and urged fellow trustee Silas Brown Brownell to convey her sentiments to Low, his personal friend and fellow Centurion. Brownell did, arguing that "I cannot avoid feeling that the financial support of Barnard is quite as essential as her new administration, and that that support depends upon women, whom Barnard, therefore, cannot afford to alienate." Although Low ceded the point in this instance, he refused Brownell's request to alter the intercorporate agreement to require the Barnard dean be a woman. A new search was then undertaken, in which Anderson played a leading role, and in January 1901, the forty-one-year old Laura Drake Gill was named Barnard's second dean. She proved to be a bad choice. During her seven-year deanship, the progress that Putnam had made in collaboration with Low in securing Barnard's stability was undone.[14]

Effective service as a hospital administrator in Cuba following the American assault in the summer of 1898 had brought Laura Drake Gill to the attention of the Barnard search committee. Born and raised in rural Maine, a Smith graduate, she taught mathematics at Smith's preparatory school in Northampton before joining the Red Cross. That she was single and available counted in her favor; the fact that she was a stranger to New York and, as it turned out, hostile to urban life seems not to have been thought disqualifying. In her very first dean's report to her trustees, she declared "that most unlovely form of provincialism [was] the provincialism of a great city."[15]

Within nine months of Gill's appointment, a newspaper account reached Treasurer Plimpton that Gill had resigned following an early encounter with Columbia's newly installed president Nicholas Murray Butler. Unlike Low, who treated Dean Smith like a partner in the larger university enterprise who reported to her own board of trustees, Butler expected all deans of Columbia schools to report directly to him. In Gill's case, Butler wanted her to limit her dealings with the Barnard board, on which he sat *ex officio*, by funneling all communications through him. It took Gill several years to grasp Butler's notion of their relationship and too late to salvage any semblance of mutual trust. Butler also blamed Gill for rendering Barnard's biggest benefactor and her defender, Elizabeth Milbank Anderson, unwilling to direct some of her largesse Columbia's way.[16]

In ways large and small, Gill offended would-be allies. While the 1900 intercorporate agreement gave Barnard full responsibility for the undergraduate instruction of women within the university, it did not take into account that Teachers College (TC), a party to the agreement, had among its women students some who did not possess ABs. Rather than propose an amicable resolution to a sister institution with overlapping missions, Gill insisted that TC cede all responsibility for instructing undergraduates

FIGURE 3.4 Laura Drake Gill (1860–1932), second dean of Barnard College (1901–1907). Barnard Archives.

to Barnard. For good measure, she publicly made disparaging remarks about the "heterogeneous" students attending TC. Although she prevailed in this dispute, it earned her and Barnard the enmity of TC Dean James Earl Russell and ended space-sharing arrangements in which Barnard students had used the TC gymnasium.[17]

Gill was equally maladroit in lesser ways, for example, in offending trustee Meyer by neglecting to keep the college's Steinway piano in tune. The dean also alienated a leading young alumna, Alice Duer Miller, class of 1899, by declining her application in 1905 for an unpaid part-time teaching appointment because Miller was married. Three months after that happened, Miller, a future chronicler of Barnard history, organized a group of fourteen alumnae from different classes who wrote to President Butler asking him "to consider the removal of Miss Gill." Among their complaints was her "imposing on Barnard the attitude of isolated colleges." But their most damning indictment: "She is not a New Yorker."[18]

The following spring, Gill declined to renew the appointment of a popular English instructor, alumna, and Miller classmate, Virginia Gildersleeve. Here again she demonstrated a flair for offending those who could retaliate. When Gildersleeve later explained her reasoning for accepting the Barnard deanship in 1911, she said that she wished to avoid having "another stranger come in as Miss Gill had done and mess up my College again."[19]

Even in posterity Gill has attracted critics. In her estimable *Women Scientists in America: Struggles and Strategies to 1940* (1984), the historian

FIGURE 3.5 Class Day marchers in 1908. Barnard Archives.

Margaret W. Rossiter cites Dean Gill as responsible for cutting short the promising scientific career of Harriet Brooks. A Canadian by birth and one of Sir Ernest Rutherford's most promising graduate students at McGill University, Brooks was hired as a physics instructor by Barnard in 1903. Four years later, she informed Dean Gill of her engagement to marry, while stating her intentions to continue teaching and conducting research. Gill, over the objections of Margaret Maltby, Barnard's senior physicist, promptly terminated Brooks, who, as it turned out, did not marry the man to whom she was engaged but did abandon her research. Thus, Barnard lost the woman who, at her death in 1933, the *New York Times* called "one of the leading women in the field of nuclear physics, second only to Marie Curie."[20]

A final instance of Gill's innocence of New York City's folkways was her attempt, prior to the Steinway kerfuffle, to help Annie Nathan Meyer find an appropriate school for her daughter, Margaret. This happened after several of the city's fashionable day schools, all with Columbia officials on their boards, had declined to consider Margaret because she was Jewish. Dean Gill then suggested Margaret apply to the Sacks Collegiate Institute, only to receive from Meyer this pointed lesson in New York tribal distinctions:

> I do not like the atmosphere of the Sachs School simply because the girls there come almost exclusively from a wealthy class—one which has not had the stability of *generations* of wealth—and which is unfortunately an intensely materialistic class. Margaret comes from a family in America since the 17th century and I do not care—another reason—to have her in such an exclusively German atmosphere.[21]

It may well have been Gill's cluelessness about New York ethnic and social mores that kept her out of the discussions occupying the boards of both Columbia and Barnard during her deanship on the subject that went by the anodyne label "the Hebrew Problem."

COLUMBIA'S—AND BARNARD'S—"HEBREW PROBLEM"

Columbia College, from its founding as King's College in 1754, had been open to the sons of New York City's pre-Revolutionary Sephardic Jewish community. A similar receptivity characterized the college's dealings with the sons of the more newly arrived German-Jewish community when they began applying in the 1860s. This remained the case into the 1890s. Nicholas Murray Butler's graduating class of 1882 of fifty included a half-dozen Jews. It was only in the early 1900s that the presence of Jews became the so-called Hebrew Problem, which was in fact three related problems.[22]

Beginning in the early 1890s, leading members of the German-Jewish community, some of whom were alumni and donors, called upon Columbia to acknowledge their relationship with the university by naming a Jew to the Board of Trustees. That no Jew had served on the board since the death of Gershon Seixas in 1816 was a source of consternation among would-be and certified Columbia benefactors, including Jacob H. Schiff, who was not an alumnus but had endowed a Columbia professorship in Hebrew studies in 1892. Schiff had the support of President Low for such an appointment, who in a 1901 letter to Columbia trustee Bayard Cutting proposed Isaac N. Seligman (Columbia College class of 1886) for membership. An informal polling of trustees by Cutting revealed resistance to the idea. "I admit that on this subject I am strongly prejudiced," Columbia trustee and future board chair William Barclay Parsons wrote to George L. Rives, a fellow Columbia trustee and later a member of the Barnard board, "and it is possible that my prejudice leads me to give undue weight to my point of view."[23]

With Butler's installation, Schiff abandoned his lobbying for a Jewish appointee and turned to urging Columbia's Jewish alumni to withhold their support until an appointment was made. In 1910, Barnard treasurer Plimpton wrote to Columbia alumnus and Barnard trustee Horace W. Carpentier:

> I had a long talk with Mr. Schiff about Columbia. He says he will not give a dollar more to Columbia University until they have a Jew trustee. He thinks that with a million Jews in this city, and the large number of students they have there, that they ought to be represented on their board. He says that the Jews are represented on every institution board in this city.

Schiff's ongoing generosity to Harvard and subsequent gifts to Cornell and Barnard were intended to remind Columbia of the cost of its prejudice. In 1911, trustee Seth Low withdrew from further participation in the

Columbia board after the trustees, with Butler's acquiescence, refused to grant to Jewish organizations the same access to the Columbia chapel that it granted Christian groups.[24]

A second part of Columbia's Hebrew Problem was the increasing presence of sons of the city's most recently arrived Eastern European Jewish families attending Columbia College, some as a means of securing early admission to one of the university's professional schools. Admission to Columbia's law school and the College of Physicians and Surgeons was limited to college graduates, except for those students attending Columbia College, who could transfer into either school after their second or third year, which attracted professionally ambitious but financially pressed but young men who otherwise would have attended City College of New York (CCNY) or New York University (NYU) for four years. Even more economical planning had a student enroll at tuition-free City College for three semesters, then transfer to Columbia, and after three semesters in the college gain admission to the Columbia professional school of choice. With the college admitting all applicants with passing scores on the Regents exams or College Boards, exams that students could prepare for at one of the city's public high schools, Columbia College, once limited to prosperous New Yorkers, was now within reach of all but the most financially straitened sons of New York City's newest arrivals.[25]

The prospect of Columbia College becoming overwhelmed with the sons of Eastern European immigrants, mostly Jews and products of the city's public high schools, produced for Columbia trustees the most worrisome part of Columbia's "Hebrew Problem": the flight of white Anglo-Saxon Protestants. The sons of New York's leading families with multigenerational ties to Columbia and who attended one of the city's private boys' schools such as Trinity and Collegiate or who studied away at boarding school found the prospect of four years at a Columbia with socially disadvantaged classmates, wholly given over to academic success, increasingly unattractive. Nor did it help matters when Columbia in 1905 temporarily dropped intercollegiate football from its athletic program. Better to follow one's school chums to Harvard, Yale, or Princeton, where "our own kind" remained in a comfortable majority.[26]

This concern was sufficiently salient among old Columbians and would-be applicants that, in 1914, the college's dean Frederick P. Keppel addressed the question directly in his otherwise promotional *Columbia*

College, a contribution to a series of institutional biographies published by Oxford University Press. "Isn't Columbia overrun with European Jews," he preemptively asked, "who are the most unpleasant persons personally?" His answer, meant to be reassuring, came in four parts. The first was that "the proportion of Jewish students is decreasing rather than increasing." The second was that "by far the majority of the Jewish students who do come to Columbia are desirable students in every way." Keppel then went on to make two further distinctions, which however well-intentioned at the time, a century later make for difficult reading. The first of these:

> What most people regard as a racial problem is really a social problem. The Jews who have had the advantages of decent social surroundings for a generation or two are entirely satisfactory companions. Their intellectual ability, and particularly their intellectual curiosity, are above the average, and the teachers are unanimous in saying that their presence in the classroom is distinctly desirable.

The second:

> There are, indeed, Jewish students of another type who have not had the social advantage of their more fortunate fellows. Often they come from an environment which in any stock less fired with ambition would have put the idea of higher education wholly out of the question. Some of these are not particularly pleasant companions, but the total number is not large, and every reputable institution aspiring to public service must stand ready to give those of probity and good moral character the benefits which they are making great sacrifices to obtain.[27]

Keppel privately conceded that Columbia's battle to retain the loyalty of Old New Yorkers was already lost. In 1913, Columbia trustee Francis S. Bangs, whose sons Henry and Francis, classes of 1906 and 1910 respectively, had attended Columbia and bemoaned the experience, floated the idea of limiting admission to Columbia College to residential students, but Keppel dismissed it as financially suicidal and demographically ineffective: "To put it frankly, I do not think such a plan, or any other, will bring us the sons of men like Mr. Rives, Mr. Cutting and Mr. Parsons."[28]

FIRE BELL IN THE NIGHT

We know less of the internal discussions of the Hebrew Problem among Barnard trustees than among their more voluble and more document-retentive Columbia counterparts. To be sure, the institutional circumstances were different, with the Barnard board from its opening being relatively more open to Jewish representation. But might we not assume that these otherwise equally well-placed New Yorkers, with their many social interactions, shared some of the same concerns and prejudices regarding the prospect of the institutions with which they identified being inundated by the city's newest and rawest arrivals? In one instance, the specter of Barnard's inundation may have been seen as even more imminent. In the case of Columbia College, the local presence of CCNY and NYU meant that its admissions officials could redirect academically qualified but socially objectionable local male applicants elsewhere. Barnard, still the city's only four-year liberal arts college for women (the Normal College did not achieve full college status as Hunter College until 1915), remained the principal recourse for New York City girls who, for economic reasons, were limited to colleges within commuting distance.[29]

The first Barnard official to give voice to these concerns was N. W. Liggett, the college bursar. "Personally I am discouraged," she began her letter on June 20, 1906, to Treasurer George Plimpton, "considerably discouraged."

> During the summer I want you to look carefully over the names and addresses of the enclosed candidates. You will observe, I think, that we are drawing a very large percentage of Hebrews, and others of foreign extraction; that our students are coming from neighborhoods unknown to most residenters. This contingent might not be open to criticism if we had plenty of the children of well-to-do New York families also, for the affiliation would do much to neutralize race limitations.[30]

Liggett then provided Plimpton with the list of names, addresses, and collegiate preparation of the 102 applicants. Those she thought Jewish she marked with a check. "Only thirteen private schools in New York, Brooklyn, and Staten Island (the city proper) send us pupils," she reported. "Of these, five send us only Hebrew students. Of 62 taking preliminary

examinations, twenty-nine are Hebrews; of 102 taking complete examinations, 40 are Hebrews." "It seems to me," she warned Plimpton and
his fellow trustees, "that this condition cannot be longer ignored. We are
certainly losing ground."[31]

As Liggett saw it, the problem was also not susceptible to simple reme-
dies such as increased publicity.

> We are not able to do any successful missionary work in the schools, for
> things have reached the pass where this sort of zeal but brings us more
> Hebrews, and all history proves that any cause which attracts the support
> of large numbers of Hebrews is a losing cause in the end.[32]

Liggett then pivoted to questioning the utility of a new dormitory that
trustee Meyer had been soliciting with the Guggenheim family. Acknowledging that it was "our only opportunity of winning a new constituency,"
she warned,

> a dormitory which will receive any number of Hebrews from all parts of
> the country as resident students, will do us incalculable harm. Already
> Hebrews are coming to us from other sections of the country. They are
> not from good Jewish families. . . . A gift of a dormitory building from a
> Hebrew would be the most embarrassing gift that could come to us.

She then concluded her letter with a bearish assessment of Barnard's current "material":

> Every year we are drawing less and less from the private school element,
> and from the well-to-do classes. Much of the material which we graduate
> we cannot place advantageously, where we can ever expect any return,
> for while their minds are trained, the social limitation and environment
> is such that only the public school is available, and we already have too
> much of this sort of material coming to us.[33]

What to make of this extraordinary letter, its unvarnished anti-Semitism aside? It contains several assertions that hold up to subsequent scrutiny. Barnard's entering classes in the opening decade of the twentieth
century did contain a growing proportion of Jewish students, although

perhaps not as many as Liggett suggests. Her identifications square pretty well with other indicators, including census information about parents' birthplaces and language spoken at home, as well as subsequent self-identifications. They also comport with the almost complete absence of the incoming students Liggett identified as Jews later becoming members of Barnard's sororities.[34]

Mapping the homes of the incoming class of 1910 similarly confirms the veracity of Liggett's snide comment about their coming "from neighborhoods unknown to most residenters." Of its ninety-four graduates four years later, only seven of the fifty-eight Manhattanites (12 percent) came from the affluent East Side, while thirteen came from the upper reaches of Manhattan and fourteen from the newly residential Upper West Side. A majority of the others came from the outer boroughs, Westchester, and northern New Jersey. Three came from outside the New York region.[35]

Liggett was also correct in saying that the city's leading private schools, with the exception of the Sachs School and Ethical Culture School, were not sending their college-bound graduates to Barnard, preferring one or another of the women's country colleges. This held for Brearley and Spence but also the coeducational Horace Mann School on Broadway and 120th Street, administered by Columbia University and where many children of faculty went. When asked by a Columbia official in 1908 why so few of his graduates went to Columbia, Horace Mann headmaster Virgil Prettyman responded bluntly that the perception of Columbia among his students was that it had become filled with graduates of the city's public high schools, making it unappealing. Horace Mann's female seniors almost certainly felt the same about Barnard. When accounting for Columbia's failure "to command the support of many of the better New York families," Prettyman explicitly included Barnard students when he wrote of "the belief that the University's undergraduate body contains a preponderating element of students who have had few social advantages and that in consequence, there is little opportunity of making friendships of permanent value among them." His advice to both Barnard and Columbia: "Careful consideration of new channels which bring desirable candidates and the careful turning in other directions such streams as have been proved deleterious."[36]

Barnard's leading feeder schools in 1906, accounting for one-third of the entering class, were Wadleigh High School for Girls on West 114th

Street, with twelve admissions; Morris High School in the Bronx, with nine admissions; Jamaica High School in Queens, with four admissions; and Girls' High School in Brooklyn, with three admissions. Four other city high schools provided at least one member each, while public high schools in northern New Jersey and Westchester provided another one-third of the class. In all, 72 percent of the entering class of 1910 were prepared at public schools. (Of the students attending Bryn Mawr between 1885 and 1908, 70 percent studied at private schools or were taught by private tutors.) What was said of the girls attending Brooklyn's Girls' High School in 1895 by the *New York Times* applied more generally for the city's public schoolers: that it was "the ambition of every Brooklyn girl [is] to enter the Girls' High School where she may enjoy the advantages of an advanced education and be prepared for college."[37]

Liggett also proved prescient about the occupational outcomes of the incoming "material." Of the forty-three students entering in 1906 and identified as gainfully employed in 1925, twenty-four (56 percent) were employed as teachers, fifteen by a public high school in New York City, Westchester, or northern New Jersey. (Teaching was the occupational outcome of only 16 percent of all Wellesley students between 1889 and 1918.) Liggett's disparagement of Barnard graduates aspiring to careers in secondary education notwithstanding, for many it was precisely their hard-come-by Barnard AB that enabled them to secure the most gainful and respectable employment that their economic circumstances required and that was open to women. Whatever happened to the Reverend Brooks's "New York women who are not likely to be compelled to earn their own living and whose sphere of life, in all probability, is to lie in the family or in New York society"?[38]

We do not have Plimpton's response to Liggett's screed, although his continued insistence in approaching potential Barnard donors, Christian and Jewish alike, with the message that "there isn't a race or nationality that is not represented there," suggests he did not share her prejudices, as does his retention of her letter among his carefully archived papers.[39]

Another recipient of Liggett's letter was Dean Gill, who by 1906 was on the outs with both her registrar and the college's Jewish constituency. The latter alienation followed on Gill's insistence that Barnard classes continue to be scheduled on Saturday mornings, despite Columbia making them optional for observant Jewish students. Rather than acknowledge the conflict, Gill charged those complaining with trying to avoid a sixth day of commuting to campus. She similarly dismissed her registrar's warnings about Barnard's declining appeal among "the privates" and its increasing reliance on the city's public schoolers coming to Barnard "looking to self-support." "We may have no fear," Gill informed her trustees in 1906, "that the college is losing its hold upon those who regard higher education as chiefly ministering to general intellectual ends." Such a cheery view confirms Gill's disconnect with both the college and New York City during her last months as dean.[40]

Some trustees almost certainly shared Liggett's concerns—if not her anti-Semitism. Those with teenage daughters or familiar with the private school scene must have been aware of the reputation Barnard had acquired among wealthier private schoolers. One Brearley graduate from Richmond Hill, a wealthy neighborhood in Queens, who, against her wishes ended up at Barnard in 1913, later described the contrast: "I had never seen a Jew. I didn't know about Jews. Barnard, of course, was full of them. Such interesting delightful people. Many of their mothers were scrubbing floors so they could go through college."[41]

Not all Jews attending Barnard had mothers scrubbing floors or worked their way through college. But one who did work her way through college was Augusta Salik, class of 1902, born of Jewish parents from South Russia, who paid her way through Barnard doing social work in Harlem. More typical was Hannah Falk, who entered Barnard in 1905. Born to Jewish parents in 1889 in a railroad flat on Fourteenth Street, she moved with her family at least four times in her early years, the last to an apartment on East Ninety-Third Street, between Park and Madison, several blocks north of the then upper limits of the wealthy Upper East Side. "It was on the south side of the street," she recalled eight decades later. "On the north side it was farm land and squatters lived there in their little houses. It was the end of the city." But it was also within trolley car range of the newly opened Wadleigh High School for Girls on West 114th Street, where she and three Jewish classmates went before going to Barnard. While Hannah's parents could afford Barnard's $150 tuition, they were of the view that "to go out of town [for college] would have been ridiculous in my day." Once enrolled at Barnard, the college's lack of social amenities for its commuting students led Hannah, who regularly went home after lunch, to conclude, "It wasn't much of a college experience."[42]

4

WHO'S AFRAID OF VIRGINIA GILDERSLEEVE?

A flower from Barnard's own garden.

—NICHOLAS MURRAY BUTLER (1911)[1]

"FAR FROM ADEQUATE FINANCIAL PROVISION"

In 1894, while seeking a successor to Ella Weed as dean, Barnard's new treasurer George A. Plimpton wrote to his friend, Johns Hopkins President Daniel Coit Gilman, "I have no doubt in my mind but that within a few years Barnard College will be the richest women's college in the country." Two years later, Plimpton doubled down. "There is no question in my mind," he wrote to the attorney of Mrs. Josiah Fiske, "that ultimately Barnard College will have a great deal of money; it cannot be otherwise." This statement came in the immediate wake of his successful $140,000 "site fund" campaign that also secured the conditioned $100,000 Brinckerhoff gift for a building and the announcement of a $170,000 gift of a second building from Elizabeth Milbank Anderson, which in turn produced a gift of $130,000 from Mrs. Josiah Fiske for a third building. Yet eleven years later, the same Treasurer Plimpton. in an appeal to the Rockefeller-funded General Education Board, described Barnard as "far from having adequate financial provision for its necessary work." These conflicting assessments, one boasting and the other poor-mouthing, reflected the ongoing volatility and shifting fortunes of the young college's finances.[2]

On the plus side of the ledger, Barnard in 1907 owned four buildings, the original Brinckerhoff, Milbank, and Fiske buildings, plus the just opened Brooks dormitory, with a combined book value of $750,000. These were located on a four-and-a half-acre site assessed at $1,250,000. Barnard also owned securities and mortgages with a market value of $700,000. This last amount, in effect the college's endowment, was largely the result of Plimpton's tireless solicitations of gifts from many of New York's biggest benefactors, among them J. P. Morgan, Andrew Carnegie, the Harriman family, and Joseph Pulitzer.[3]

In one instance, that of John D. Rockefeller Sr. and later the Rockefeller-funded General Educational Board chaired by John D. Rockefeller Jr., Plimpton proved to be a more successful fundraiser on Barnard's behalf than his counterparts at Columbia, where the Rockefellers' recent arrival in New York made them socially suspect in the minds of some Columbia trustees. Plimpton, by contrast, was an equal opportunity mendicant. He was also lavish with praise for those who responded. "I doubt there ever would have been a Barnard College," he told John D. Rockefeller Jr. in 1910, "such as we have today had it not been for your generosity." But even escapees, as with one who reneged on a pledge of $1,000, were handled with care:

> I note what you say about not liking my way of raising money. I can assure you that this whole money-making business is most disagreeable to me. . . . The position of treasurer I did not seek. It was thrust upon me. . . . Now my good woman, do not give yourself any anxiety or uneasiness about the matter.[4]

One problem Plimpton faced with fundraising was that several of his prospects had more compelling calls on their largesse. This was certainly the case with Abram Hewitt, one of the city's wealthiest men and the Barnard board's second chair, the bulk of whose estate went to Cooper Union. So, too, with the original trustee Henrietta Talcott and her merchant husband, James Talcott, whose $4 million estate went to the Young Women's Christian Association (YWCA), the Northfield Seminary, and the New York Bible Society. Even in the case of Elizabeth Milbank Anderson, early

Barnard's greatest benefactor, the bulk of her $32 million estate, and that of her cousin, Albert G. Milbank, who became a Barnard trustee in 1903, was committed after 1907 to the Milbank Memorial Fund Association (later the Milbank Memorial Fund). Another original trustee of substantial wealth, Caroline Dutcher Choate, left most of her estate to the Brearley School and to a fund that endowed her forty-acre estate, Naumkeag, in Stockbridge, Massachusetts. None of the early board's many lawyers or ministers proved to be major donors, with several directing their wealth to their own alma maters. This was even true of Plimpton, whose benefactions were distributed among Amherst, Wellesley, Columbia University, the Presbyterian-sponsored Robert College, and the American College for Girls in Istanbul.[5]

On the expenditure side of the ledger, Barnard in its second decade operated regularly with annual deficits that were covered by end-of-year borrowing from the endowment or commercial loans. All the other leading women's colleges had endowments substantially larger than Barnard. With nearly all the college's operating income coming from student tuition and fees, the only long-term solution to Barnard's financial situation was to increase the size of the entering classes or increase the tuition from its original $150. The latter was deemed inadvisable until Columbia did so and, in any event, would almost certainly have resulted in fewer enrollments.[6]

Increasing enrollments posed other problems, especially after the Gill-advised decision in 1904 to reduce drastically the number of "specials" to get in step with the other women's colleges. In 1905, the year the decision went into effect, enrollments dropped from 500 to 366, with tuition income dropping accordingly. Total enrollments would not return to 1904 levels for five more years. Meanwhile, the college's shaky finances did not escape scrutiny or comment.[7]

BARNARD'S FIRST MERGER CRISIS

Doubts about Barnard's long-term financial viability were voiced by Columbia's new and aggrandizing president, Nicholas Murray Butler. "The fact ought to be faced," Butler informed Annie Nathan Meyer, who had written him on another matter in 1905, "that Barnard is the only branch of the University which is not springing vigorously forward with full and increased prestige. It is not getting the financial or the personal support which it ought to have." Over the next five years, this complaint became a standard part of communications passing westward across Broadway. As a student, Butler opposed President Barnard's efforts to have Columbia College admit women; now, as an administrator, he was open to the idea that undergraduate women should have a place in his university, just not in Columbia College. As dean of the Faculty of Philosophy, he had opened graduate instruction in the humanities to women. One of his first moves as president was to insist that the Faculty of Political Science do likewise. No less than his predecessor, Seth Low, Butler was very much disposed to putting every educational entity within reach under the direction of the Columbia trustees, which is to say, under his direction.[8]

Part of Dean Gill's problems with Butler was her opposition to his hopes of consolidating Barnard within Columbia. In 1904, Butler called for the merger of the registrar offices of Columbia College, the School of Mines, and Barnard College, under the direction of a Columbia administrator. When Gill objected, she was overruled by her own trustees, with Plimpton supporting the move on grounds of efficiency and economy. This followed on a note from Butler to Plimpton in which he called for a talk between them about "enrollment at Barnard . . . which is one part of the University that lags behind in the present advance."[9]

Butler likely urged the resignation of Dean Gill in 1907. And it was Butler who appointed William Tenney Brewster, recently promoted to a professorship in English at Barnard and a seat in the Columbia Faculty of Philosophy, as Barnard's acting dean. What followed was a four-year standoff between the Columbia president and a set of Barnard trustees, led by Anderson, with Plimpton as her behind-the-scenes ally in keeping the permanent position of dean of Barnard from going to Brewster. In 1909, Butler added to Brewster's formal duties by naming him to the new post of provost of Barnard. In so doing, he signaled to the Barnard trustees that they might choose a woman as their titular dean, who would be the public face of the college, as long as the academic and financial side of the college was entrusted to his man Brewster.[10]

Butler also maneuvered to put Barnard under the administrative leadership of the dean of Columbia College. In 1909, he proposed that the admissions process of all three undergraduate schools—Columbia

College, the School of Mines, and Barnard—be consolidated under the University Committee of Undergraduate Admissions, to be headed by a Columbia College appointee, Adam Leroy Jones. Barnard officials, at the urging of its acting dean, went along.[11]

Brewster wanted the job as Barnard's permanent dean and favored the college being merged into Columbia, with its governance transferred to the university's trustees. "I find myself in complete agreement with what you say in your recent letter," Butler wrote to Brewster in 1908, "regarding the feebleness of the Barnard Faculty as a Faculty, that I move to propose that we begin a reform without delay." But at the same time, Brewster was the antithesis of the country college wannabes, seeing Barnard instead as an urban institution in the service of the city's academically ambitious women of limited means. As he wrote in his first report as acting dean in the summer of 1907:

> It is evident that in all probability a city college like Barnard will draw a large part of its membership from nearby, and that it will be made up largely of students who are unable to enjoy the opener life afforded at country colleges. Students other than the class described will be attracted to Barnard College by the soundness of its scholarship.[12]

However enlightened his views on Barnard as an urban institution, Dean "Billy" Brewster was not to be. Elizabeth Milbank Anderson opposed his candidacy and objected to Butler's strong-arm tactics. Plimpton agreed that the Columbia president could be overbearing and that his objections to several women Barnard had proposed as Gill's successor were unreasonable. "I believe if I should find the Angel Gabriel," he wrote to Anderson in June 1910, "Butler would probably turn him down. Possibly he may think he has Brewster, and he may be indifferent as to what woman there is." Knowing that Anderson was set against Brewster and determined to have a woman as dean, Plimpton further endeared himself to Barnard's principal benefactor with a closing call: "I say let us select a Dean after our own hearts."[13]

Two months later, on November 10, 1910, Butler informed Plimpton that he wished to see Alice Duer Miller as Barnard's next dean. "She is a graduate of Barnard, a New Yorker, born and bred, and a lady of distinction of both mind and person." That she was married, Butler assured

Plimpton, was not a problem. He did not add that she was also the daughter of a Columbia graduate; the granddaughter of Columbia's tenth president, William A. Duer (1829–1842); and the great-granddaughter of Rufus King, a longtime chair of the Columbia Board of Trustees, nor that she was the Barnard alumna who led the call for Gill's dismissal five years earlier. Her nomination made clear Butler's intention to divide Barnard's administrative responsibilities between a socially presentable woman, in Miller's case, a journalist and writer without academic credentials, who would oversee the social and external affairs of the college, with the academic and financial affairs of the college entrusted to a man.[14]

When the Barnard board rejected the Miller nomination, citing her lack of academic credentials, Butler proceeded with an offer he likely thought too good for the Barnard trustees to refuse. It was nothing if not clear-cut. "I want to put myself on record now," he wrote to Plimpton on November 18, 1910, "as saying if Barnard College can be turned over bodily to the Trustees of the University, I will make myself responsible for raising the money to pay the outstanding debt of Barnard College."[15]

Butler's offer, if accepted, would have transformed Barnard from a free-standing, financially independent institution with its own trustees into one of the several schools of the university (but separate from the all-male Columbia College) under the control of the Columbia Board of Trustees. Barnard's thirty-person faculty would be disbanded, with some of the male members finding places in the lower ranks of the Columbia faculty. All that Butler implied was needed to effect Barnard's dismemberment was the acquiescence of its treasurer. As an added inducement, Butler told Plimpton, with reference to their mutual friend, fellow Centurion and Barnard's current board chair, "It is also Mr. Brownell's wish."[16]

Indeed it was. Two years earlier Brownell wrote privately to Butler:

> For many years it has been my aim to turn Barnard College over to the Trustees of the University for their management, and I have set my mark at an endowment of $500,000 as the suitable time for proposing to the University to take Barnard's property and good will, very much as it took over the College of Physicians and Surgeons.[17]

What made Barnard, in its twenty-first year of operations, so vulnerable to a takeover? Butler cited three factors: "Barnard's finances shaky;

salaries too low; faculty restless." All true, especially the "faculty restless" assertion, at a time when several of Barnard's senior male professors had recently transferred to Columbia for the higher salaries and professional status, while others were actively angling to do so. Those who stayed on at Barnard could not help but begrudge those who decamped.

But there was more. Butler's call for Barnard's absorption likely had as its precipitating factor the evolving social composition of the university's undergraduates, which Columbia's troubled trustees and their eager-to-please president had recently determined to put right. The earlier consolidation of the admissions process was a step in that direction, but a more direct way to address the perceived problem affecting all three undergraduate schools would be simply to have Columbia take Barnard over. But when the Barnard trustees, at Anderson's insistence and with Plimpton's support, rejected Columbia's buyout offer, Butler quickly reverted to plan B. On December 10, 1910, he offered the Barnard deanship to a junior member of the Columbia English Department, the thirty-three-year-old Virginia C. Gildersleeve. Whether this had been his plan all along we will never know.[18]

"A FLOWER FROM BARNARD'S OWN GARDEN"

Among Virginia Gildersleeve's academic prizes at her graduation from Barnard in 1899 was a Fiske Graduate Fellowship, which provided for a year's graduate study at Columbia. She used it to pursue an MA degree in medieval history under the guidance of James Harvey Robinson, with whom she had studied at Barnard. Degree in hand in the summer of 1900, she was offered an assistantship in English at Barnard with responsibility for a section of freshman English. For the next four years, she held the rank of tutor and taught two sections. But when in the spring of 1905, William Tenney Brewster, in charge of staffing Barnard's English courses, informed Gildersleeve she was to teach all five sections of required sophomore English—which would involve reading and grading 100 essays a week—she resigned.[19]

Travel in Europe that summer was followed by the offer, coming through Annie Nathan Meyer's intervention with President Butler, of a graduate fellowship for doctoral studies in English at Columbia. During her first two years of graduate study, Gildersleeve renewed her teaching ties to Barnard, only to have them severed in the spring of 1907 for budgetary reasons in one of Laura Gill's last acts as dean. Three more years of study, research, and writing resulted in her completing requirements for a PhD in English and the ensuing publication of her dissertation, *Government Regulation of the Elizabethan Theatre*.[20]

In the fall of 1908, with PhD studies over and Gill gone, Gildersleeve returned to Barnard for an $800 lectureship to teach a section of William P. Trent's course on Chaucer. She was then offered $500 to teach Shakespeare on a Columbia salary as part of the Columbia-Barnard faculty exchange. A year later, she was promoted to an assistant professorship in the Columbia English Department, making her the first woman to achieve professorial rank at Columbia. When a senior male colleague accepted a full professorship at the University of Wisconsin and offered to take Gildersleeve along as an associate professor, she declined, explaining, "I could not leave New York." To which her would-be patron rejoined: "Good heavens, you will never make a career for yourself that way." Her decision does lend credence, however, to the self-deprecatory chapter title from her book given to her work before becoming dean: "I drift into a profession."[21]

The noontime meeting Butler called on December 10, 1910, to offer the Barnard deanship to his thirty-four-year-old Columbia assistant professor of English was to be followed by a meeting of the Barnard trustees to proceed with her election. But when Gildersleeve sought assurances that she, as dean—and not any provost—would have authority over Barnard's academics and budget, the board meeting was postponed. Four days later, Butler gave his personal assurances that "the provost is just a lieutenant of the dean," and Gildersleeve agreed to become Barnard's third dean. "There seemed to be no other Barnard candidate. So I told the president I would accept."[22]

Whether Gildersleeve was his real choice all along or not, Butler appreciated her appropriateness for the position. The Gildersleeves were only slightly less established in New York society than the Duers and currently in better standing. Virginia's father, Henry Alger Gildersleeve, like Butler, was a convert to the Episcopal religion after being raised a Presbyterian and graduated from Columbia law school before becoming a judge

FIGURE 4.1 Virginia Gildersleeve, 1912. Barnard Archives.

and a political force among the city's veterans' organizations. "Alger" and "Murray" were members of the Century Club and friends. It was Butler, encountering Gildersleeve on the Fifth Avenue trolley, who told the judge that his daughter had been chosen as dean just minutes earlier at the Barnard board meeting.[23]

Despite assurances that she would be in charge of the academic and budgetary affairs of the college, the first public announcement of her appointment by Columbia implied a more limited mandate. This prompted Anderson's nephew, attorney Albert G. Milbank, himself now a Barnard trustee, to relay to Plimpton his aunt's complaint about "the inaccurate statement which appeared in connection with Miss Gildersleeve's appointment, to the effect that the Provost had charge of the educational administration of the College." As with so much else in Barnard's early history, it fell to Plimpton to secure reassurances from Columbia that Gildersleeve would be Barnard's dean in full and that Columbia would cease all talk of a merger. Although the office of Barnard provost was not eliminated until 1922, Brewster's return to full-time teaching in 1914 confirmed Plimpton's success on both counts.[24]

Still, Butler likely harbored at the outset of Gildersleeve's deanship the happy thought that, should Barnard falter, the new dean's youth, her Columbia ties, and her deferential ways with him would make her amenable to a later merger offer. Barnard's condition under her long deanship never became dire enough to prompt such an offer, but neither at any point during the thirty-five years of their overlapping tenures did she ever publicly challenge her beloved father's friend. Butler in turn was said by other Columbia deans to treat Gildersleeve as a daughter. At Gildersleeve's inauguration on February 11, 1911, Butler called her "a flower from Barnard's own garden."[25]

MAKING HER BONES

An early indication of where the new dean stood on the issue of Barnard's proper constituency appears in her initial correspondence with Plimpton about the wording of his fundraising letter intended to launch a $2 million campaign in celebration of the college's upcoming twenty-fifth anniversary in 1914. "An Appeal for Barnard College" was circulated among the trustees and drew several responses. Two were relayed to Plimpton by Dean Gildersleeve, one from President Butler, who thought its focus was "too New Yorkey." To this the dean appended, "I am inclined to agree with him."[26]

The second came from Mrs. George McAneny (née Marjorie Jacobi), Gildersleeve's college classmate and Kappa Kappa Gamma (KKG) sorority sister, recently elected alumnae representative to the board, and the spouse of a wealthy and politically active clubman. McAneny objected to a sentence in the letter's second paragraph. "[The] enumeration of the various races makes Barnard sound too much like an indiscriminate melting pot," Gildersleeve reported. "She feels it might offend the sensibilities of some persons and discourage them from sending their daughters here." The dean suggested leaving the offending sentence out.[27]

Plimpton responded the next day. "I thoroughly approve of President Butler's revision of your appeal." But as for McAneny's objection and the dean's suggested solution: "Under no conditions would I leave out the enumeration of the different nationalities. I think it a strong appeal and I am sure we will get our $2 million." Indeed, three years earlier, Plimpton had approached Mrs. Russell Sage for support, boasting that "there isn't a race or nationality that is not represented here." That Plimpton located himself on the opposite side of the inclusive/exclusive divide from the new dean may have contributed to their early frosty relationship. It would be several years before they put each other on a first-name basis.[28]

An early controversy not of the new dean's making—the move to dissolve Barnard's fraternities (i.e., sororities)—sheds further light on where Gildersleeve wished to take Barnard. At the outset of her deanship, Barnard had eight fraternities, their members making up less than a third of the student body. Among Jewish students, the percentage of fraternity participation was close to zero. An interviewer in 1989 asked a member of the class of 1909, Hannah Falk Hofheimer, "Did you join a fraternity?" She answered: "No. There was only one I think open to Jewish girls. . . . We knew that Kappa Kappa Gamma was 'the' sorority. And we knew we weren't going to be asked."[29]

Bursar Liggett took Barnard's fraternities discrimination against Jewish students in stride. Not so Treasurer Plimpton, keenly alert to their fundraising implications. "I deplore the social prejudice which causes the discrimination at Barnard College," he wrote in 1912 to Mrs. Adolph S. Ochs, whose daughter Iphigene (class of 1914) had just enrolled as a regular student after two years as a special. "We all know that the Hebrews of this city, by their financial and commercial integrity, by their intellectual culture, by their broad-minded philanthropy, have brought us much nearer to the day when there will be no prejudice against their race." Plimpton then closed with an interrogative and uncharacteristic shilly-shally: "Is it not in this gradual but absolute way that we may expect the barriers to come down at Barnard?"[30]

Only part of the issue with Barnard's fraternities was their discriminatory covenants; membership also entailed substantial expenditures that many of Barnard's commuting students could not afford. Several fraternities rented rooms off campus where members congregated at safe remove from their less clubbable classmates, adding a spatial exclusivity to their doings. Other critics complained that fraternities undercut class spirit and drew students away from all-college events.[31]

In the fall of 1912, an on-campus campaign to abolish fraternities got underway. The precipitating event was the publication of an editorial in the student literary magazine, *Barnard Bear*, entitled "Fraternities vs. Democracy." The author was sophomore Freda Kirchwey, the daughter of Columbia law professor George Kirchwey and sister of Dorothy Kirchwey (class of 1910), who had been a member of KKG. The younger Kirchwey was joined by her classmate Sarah Schuyler Butler, the Columbia president's daughter. The student council responded to their call for an end to fraternities by petitioning Dean Gildersleeve to convene a committee to investigate their place at Barnard.[32]

Gildersleeve appointed a fourteen-person committee of four faculty members, four alumnae, four students, the provost, and herself. The alumnae and students were drawn equally from the ranks of fraternity supporters and critics. Recruiting new members by the fraternities was suspended until the committee completed its investigation. In April 1913, the committee issued two reports. The "majority report" found fraternities to be, on balance, "highly beneficial" to the college but said they should be more transparent in their operations. The "minority report" concluded that fraternities were "distinctly harmful" to the college and should be abolished. Dean Gildersleeve authored the majority report, Provost Brewster the minority report.[33]

Community sentiment aligned with the minority report. The faculty, already on record as critical of the outsized role that fraternities had on campus, joined the opposition, as did the parents of some Jewish students. What followed were two separate polls, one of the students and one of the faculty members, both of which endorsed the committee's minority report. A story in the *New York Times* took the same position, prematurely congratulating Barnard officials for its "ban on secret societies." The faculty voted overwhelmingly to do away with fraternities, citing them as deflecting students from their studies. With the ban on rushing indefinitely extended, most of the fraternities lacked the members to carry on. The editors of the 1914 *Barnard Mortarboard*, which, in prior years, had given fraternities extensive coverage, dropped all mention of them. By 1915, when a student referendum supported the elimination of fraternities by a vote of 255 to 159, they had ceased to exist at Barnard.[34]

While the standard accounts of Barnard's history, including one by her lifelong friend and sorority sister, Alice Duer Miller, have Gildersleeve favoring the elimination of fraternities, her position was less clear-cut. In a 1915 follow-up story in the *New York Times*, she pointed to a negative consequence of the ban that "Barnard women wishing to pledge sororities [now] go over to Columbia, and that the social life of these students becomes less centered around Barnard as their time spent across Broadway lengthens." Later that same year, responding to the dean of Swarthmore College inquiring about life after fraternities, Gildersleeve waxed nostalgic:

> In many ways we miss the fraternities very much in our scattered college life where normally only a third of the student body is in residence. . . . They were very useful in getting hold of certain students and helping to interest them and adjust them to college life. On the other hand these secret societies caused a great deal of bad feeling and suspicion. Life has certainly been more peaceful since they have been given up.[35]

Four decades later in her autobiography, without ever mentioning Barnard's elimination of fraternities early in her deanship, Gildersleeve said of her own student days as a member of KKG: "It did me lots of good."[36]

"DESERVING AND ASPIRING CROWDS"

The point Gildersleeve made to the Swarthmore dean, that at Barnard "normally only a third of the student body is in residence," became a target for corrective action and provided another opportunity to put her personal impress on the college. "It will add greatly to the interest of our resident life," she wrote in her first report in 1911, "if we can draw more extensively than hitherto on other states and countries." The opening of Brooks Hall in the fall of 1907 had not, as its donor and Dean Gill had hoped, given Barnard the feel of one of the country colleges. Part of the problem was that the dorm could accommodate only ninety-seven residents when, at the dorm's opening, the college enrolled 400 full-time students. By the time Gildersleeve became dean in 1911, enrollments stood at 600.[37]

A more revealing problem was that, for Barnard's first five years Brooks, failed to attract enough residential students to achieve full capacity. In this instance, the new dean quickly devised a solution to Barnard's underoccupied and overpriced dormitory that advanced her personal agenda for the college. Five months into her deanship, Gildersleeve learned that Barnard was to receive $100,000 from the estate of the newspaper publisher Joseph Pulitzer. An earlier gift from Pulitzer to Columbia had been for scholarships for Brooklyn high school graduates to attend Columbia College and Barnard. These Brooklyn scholarships had been in keeping with Pulitzer's efforts, paralleling those of his fellow Jew, Jacob Schiff, to encourage both schools to be more welcoming to the bright children of the city's immigrant communities. It is doubtful that Pulitzer would have endorsed on ideological grounds the use to which Gildersleeve put Barnard's share of his last benefaction: the creation of twelve annual residential scholarships, by which applicants *from outside New York City* would receive scholarships covering the cost of room and board in Brooks Hall. In the fall of 1913, Dean Gildersleeve announced that, thanks to these residential scholarships, Brooks Hall was now fully occupied with undergraduates.[38]

Meanwhile, increasing numbers of commuting students sought cheap lodgings close to campus. Ongoing improvements in public transportation had girls coming to Barnard from further away. In 1910, a quarter of the Barnard student body traveled to campus from the outer boroughs of New York City and another quarter from northern New Jersey and New York's Westchester, Nassau, and Rockland counties. Two-hour, three-connection commutes each way were common. Neither Dean Gill, acting dean Brewster, nor Dean Gildersleeve displayed much interest in confronting the "schlepping" problem. Nor did the trustees. It was the Barnard alumnae, the majority of whom had experienced the travails of commuting, who took it up.[39]

By 1915, the Barnard Alumnae Association, founded in 1891, included 1,500 members. Its first action of consequence had been to convince the trustees of the wisdom of having one of the trustees be a Barnard alumna elected by the college's alumnae. Such a provision in the statutes was added in 1899, followed by the election of Ellen Fitzgerald Bryson (class of 1894) to a three-year term. By 1910, the board had two places reserved for alumnae-elected trustees, one of whom, Florence Colgate Speranza, was subsequently elected to life term. Several of these early alumnae trustees took a special interest in the financial circumstances affecting student life. In 1915, that interest involved seeking the college's help on behalf of "students whose circumstances do not permit them to live in Brooks Hall."[40]

The alumnae urged the College to rent rooms in the neighborhood—much as the fraternities had done for social purposes—where students could live more cheaply than in Brooks. Economies would be achieved through cooperative arrangements, with residents contributing time to housekeeping and preparing meals. In 1916, with a personal contribution from the ever-generous trustee Anderson, the alumnae association rented rooms for 15 students in an apartment at 99 Claremont Avenue. The following year they moved to 606 West 116th Street directly across from Brooks. The 44 students in residence paid less than half Brooks's going rates. The lease on "606" was extended for two more years, housing 43 and 44 students, half on them on scholarships.[41]

The plight of the dozens of would-be residents from outside Manhattan was only partially met by these apartments. In 1920, a sophomore transfer from Indiana, Margaret Mead, attracted by the social diversity they fostered, availed herself of these apartments. At the same time, she and her classmates enjoyed little institutional favor in living there, garnering from the Brooks resident director a description of them as "a mental and moral muss." They in turn dubbed themselves the "Ash Can Cats." There is no indication that Dean Gildersleeve showed any interest in promoting these cooperative arrangements. In 1922, Barnard's experiment in cooperative living was terminated by administrative fiat, prompting the *Barnard Alumnae Magazine* to provide the obituary: "Thus was closed the second successful effort of the Alumnae to aid in the development of the residential life of the college."[42]

Another indicator of a new direction Dean Gildersleeve sought to take Barnard involved her in a disagreement with board chair Silas Brown

Brownell and put her at cross purposes to the educational egalitarianism of New York. Here, too, she seemed intent on limiting the numbers of New Yorkers coming to Barnard, specifically public school graduates from the city's ethnic communities, while preserving a place for the daughters of the American heartland. In the 1880s, as municipalities opened high schools, the New York State Board of Regents began administering tests in four fields to give school administrators a means of certifying degree eligibility. For young New Yorkers, completing public high school at the turn of the century, scores on the Regents exams provided a ready means by which they, their parents, and their teachers could gauge readiness for college. The tests were administered on site and without charge, whereas the College Boards were administered offsite and carried a fee. In some cases, it was a daughter's high scores on the Regents exams that convinced parents that the heretofore unthinkable prospect of her going on to college, if the costs could be managed, a lively prospect.[43]

By 1910, more than half of those applying to Barnard did so with results from Regents exams. In and of itself, the widespread adoption of these exams had significantly increased access to college for the city's public high school graduates, who were more than half the state's graduates, a fact not lost upon Bursar Liggett nor on members of the Barnard community who saw the college's proper student body as the privately prepared daughters of the city's socially arrived families. More troubling still was the action of the New York State legislature in 1912 to create New York State Regents scholarships to be awarded to seniors with the highest scores on the Regents exams in each of the state's 150 assembly districts. This meant that, in New York City, some 750 scholarships would be awarded annually to graduating seniors, more than half of them girls and a majority of them Jewish.[44]

The Regents scholarship program provided winning students an annual grant of $100 for four years to offset costs of tuition at a New York State college, public or private. The immediate effect for a prospective Barnard student was to cut the effective annual tuition by two-thirds. College suddenly became much more affordable for many more New York families with daughters doing well in high school and prepared to commute.

Among Regents Scholarship winners that first year was Fanny Rosenman, a sixteen-year-old girl from a Yiddish-speaking Bronx family, one residential move from the Lower East Side. Her father was from Russia and worked as a cutter in a cloak shop. The household included an older brother and four boarders, all cutters. Prior to receipt of the notice of the $100 scholarship in her senior year at Brooklyn Girls High School, Fanny later reminisced, attendance at a college, much less a "pay-college," was out of the question. With scholarship in hand, she entered Barnard in the fall of 1913, graduating four years later. She went on to become head of the science department at Rye High School.[45]

That same fall, nearly one-third of Barnard's 184-member entering class held Regents scholarships, with fifty-four of them graduates of New York City public schools. Dean Gildersleeve chose the occasion to recommend to the board that the college raise its tuition from $150 to $200, citing the need to increase the salaries of the teaching staff and build up the college's modest endowment. Left unmentioned was that doing so would cancel half the financial benefit of a Regents scholarship to attend Barnard, thereby reducing the number of students like Fanny Rosenman in attendance. At its January 27, 1914, meeting, the board unanimously approved the tuition increase, effective that coming fall.[46]

Absent from the January meeting was board chair Silas Brownell, who subsequently submitted a memorandum to the board dissenting from its decision. In doing so, he provided posterity with a rare early statement of the "inclusive Barnard" persuasion and a rejoinder to the Liggett exclusionary view, which in a less virulent form, was also the Gildersleeve view. Barnard, he wrote, should be trying "to make college education accessible as far as possible to those who would otherwise be precluded from its advantages." Warming to the subject, and exploiting his being one of the board's remaining half-dozen original members, he offered his colleagues a bracing (if factually dubious) origins story:

> Barnard was not founded to make money or to get income for the College, nor to make a more comfortable place for its instructors and teachers, but to provide and popularize college education, especially for those who except for it might not have the golden opportunity.

This call for inclusion came from a pillar of the city's dominant white, Anglo-Saxon Protestant legal establishment, communicant of the Church of the Incarnation, resident of Fifth Avenue, father of Bryn Mawr daughters, and active Centurion! Brownell closed by reiterating his position:

"Barnard should not be limited to people of means and position. It should open its doors and leave them open to the deserving and aspiring crowds."[47]

To no effect. At its next meeting, on February 10, 1914, the board confirmed the tuition hike, with no recorded reference to the chair's dissenting memorandum. For some board members their vote had been the simple one of approving a means by which the college could increase needed future income. But for some others, including the dean, the tuition hike provided a partial check against the college being swamped by the city's "deserving and aspiring crowds."[48]

THE PLIMPTON TOUCH

The early Gildersleeve deanship was attended by modestly improving finances, a welcome relief from the chronic budgetary problems of her predecessor and the acting dean. During Gill's administration, the college had experienced a succession of budgets where expenses outpaced income and produced annual deficits as high as $15,000 (on operating budgets of $100,000), which were covered each spring by private subscriptions or by borrowing. Available income from the college's endowment in 1912, which had a book value of $1,000,000 but was tied up in mortgages, was unable to fill the gap. Thus, the trustees, with a new and young dean just installed and an upcoming silver anniversary in 1914, announced a $2,000,000 fundraising campaign, with half to go for capital improvements and half into endowment.[49]

It quickly became clear that fundraising was not one of Gildersleeve's strengths. She disliked asking for money from past donors or cultivating new ones, jokingly acknowledging in her autobiography that the two major campaigns launched during her deanship were both promptly interrupted by world wars. As earlier, the college's fundraising responsibilities fell to the board's treasurer.[50]

Plimpton enjoyed many triumphs over the course of forty-four years raising money for Barnard, securing repeated benefactions in excess of $100,000 from the Rockefellers, John Sr. and John Jr.; from Elizabeth Milbank Anderson; and smaller ones from Andrew Carnegie and the

Harrimans. But it was his two successes in the first years of the Gildersleeve deanship that gave Barnard its margin of financial well-being during the subsequent decade and a half.

The first was Plimpton's protracted cultivation of Jacob H. Schiff. As mentioned earlier, Schiff was recruited by Annie Nathan Meyer to serve as Barnard's first board treasurer in 1889. The experience was wholly unsatisfactory and prompted his resignation in 1893. In 1896, he also gave up his seat on the board, presumably washing his hands of the college. Perhaps the only good to come of his Barnard board years was making the acquaintanceship of Plimpton, who had quietly covered for him during frequent absences and then succeeded him as treasurer. From this chance meeting—there is no reason for their having met before—they developed a friendship marked by a lively correspondence. Much of what they wrote about involved Schiff's many efforts to convince Columbia's trustees to elect a Jewish member, which Plimpton agreed was in Columbia's best interest, even if its trustees and president continued to believe otherwise.[51]

Sympathetic listening was only one form Plimpton's cultivation took. In 1912, he made a gift of a rare early book on mathematics from his personal collection to the Library of the City of Frankfurt, Schiff's birthplace, in his honor. On other occasions, he made himself available for visits to Schiff's summer compound in Long Branch, New Jersey. In 1910, he accompanied Schiff, twenty years his senior, on a four-week trip from Seattle to Alaska aboard a private train. One subject of conversation that came up often was how Schiff might mark the upcoming fiftieth anniversary of his coming to America.[52]

The result was a gift of $500,000 to Barnard in 1915 for the construction of Students Hall (later Barnard Hall), which would contain a gymnasium and pool, along with space for a library and faculty offices. At its announcement, it was the largest single building gift Barnard had received and one that Schiff later increased to $550,000 when building costs exceeded original estimates. It was—and remains—one of the more impressive buildings on Morningside Heights, and at its 1917 opening, it was one of the largest. An argument Plimpton had used in soliciting the gift was that such a building would obviate the need for fraternities.[53]

Even the building's placement, on Broadway (at what would have been 117th Street) directly across from and facing Columbia, was at the donor's direction. So was his insistence that the use of the building be at the direction of an advisory board to include Jewish and Catholic representatives. These conditions negotiated with Plimpton were in keeping with what Barnard board chair Brownell, in accepting them and anticipating Columbia's negative reaction, referred to as Schiff's "well known intent and purpose to promote and exploit the equal opportunities of the Jewish race." Both Plimpton and Brownell understood that, by giving generously to Barnard, Schiff was stiffing Columbia for its board's continuing prejudice against his fellow Jews.[54]

If Schiff, a merchant banker, member of Temple Emanu-El, and person not known for his companionability, and Plimpton, a ninth-generation New Englander, publisher, communicant of Brick Presbyterian Church, and person considered eminently clubbable, made an odd couple, so did the latter's long friendship with Horace W. Carpentier, four decades his senior. Carpentier was one of those young New Yorkers who, upon graduating from Columbia College in 1848, anticipated Horace Greeley's advice by fifteen years, by setting out for California. Once there, he passed on the possibilities of mining to focus on real estate. In 1852, he saw to the incorporation of the city of Oakland and proceeded to become the largest landowner in the East Bay. He briefly served as Oakland's mayor and then was appointed a major general in the California State Militia (hence his occasionally going by the name General). A few questionable real estate transactions involving East Bay waterfront properties and dealings with Spanish land-grant owners led him to diversify his investments, becoming in the process a principal in the Overland Telegraph Company, which proceeded in 1861 to complete the intercontinental telegraphic connection and make him one of California's richest men.[55]

In 1888, at age sixty-four and a confirmed bachelor, Carpentier returned to New York. Taking an interest in alumni affairs, Carpentier made a gift to Columbia in 1901 of $100,000 to endow the Dean Lung Chair in Chinese Studies, in recognition of his longtime servant. When asked by President Low to join the Columbia board, he declined, citing his age (seventy-six). Yet two years later, when approached by Plimpton, who had befriended him back in 1896 when Carpentier had given $10,000 to the Barnard site fund, to join the Barnard board, he accepted. At the time, he admitted to Plimpton that since his return to New York he had made few friends. "Then," Plimpton told him, "I shall be your friend."[56]

Three years later, when asked again by President Butler to join the Columbia board, Carpentier accepted and resigned from the Barnard board. Upon doing so, he gave $200,000 to Barnard, establishing the Henrietta Carpentier Scholarship Fund in honor of his mother. During the next four years, he alternated between making substantial gifts to Columbia and urging Butler to convince his board to elect a Jew to its membership. When his urgings produced no action, he resigned from the Columbia board in 1910 and returned, at age eighty-six, to the Barnard board. Five years later, citing his age, he again announced his intention to leave the board. Upon doing so, he proposed an additional gift of $100,000 to provide Barnard scholarships for "deserving Chinese girls seeking an education there." When apprised of Carpentier's intentions, Plimpton urged him to word the gift to allow that when "not so used to be applied to the general expense of the College." Carpentier readily agreed and further proceeded to honor his mother with yet another gift for scholarships, this time one of $500,000.[57]

At Caprentier's death in 1918, his estate included another $1,000,000 for Barnard. His total gifts of $1,760,000 made him, along with Elizabeth Milbank Anderson and Jacob Schiff, one of the college's three largest benefactors, a status they held for another four decades. (Most of the financial aid Barnard made available during the ensuing interwar period came from Carpentier's benefactions.) Of the approximately $4 million from these three individuals, only Anderson's gift to Barnard of the Milbank Quadrangle site, which came as a total surprise, came without Plimpton's direct involvement. Gildersleeve played no discernible role in any of these solicitations, other than gratefully acknowledging the successful efforts of her treasurer.[58]

Elsewhere on the fundraising front, the results were mixed. The Quarter Century Fund, seeking to raise $2,000,000 by the fall of 1914 on the occasion of Barnard's twenty-fifth anniversary, got off to a promising start when Plimpton secured a conditional pledge of a $250,000 endowment gift from the Rockefeller-funded General Education Board—if Barnard raised the other $750,000. But in August 1914, with Barnard still well short of matching the pledge, Dean Gildersleeve pointed to "the appalling calamity abroad" as the reason for deferring the twenty-fifth birthday for a year and suspended the campaign for the duration of the war. The Rockefeller match would not be met until 1920.[59]

BARNARD IN THE GREAT WAR

The outbreak of war in Europe was received at Barnard with shock and dismay. Few members of the community showed early interest in becoming part of it. One exception was the French instructor, Henri Muller, who returned to his native France upon the mobilization of his army unit. A few other faculty members, including the German-born and Columbia-based but Barnard-teaching Franz Boas, and possibly some students of Irish extraction (and thus anti-British by inheritance), declined to blame Germany for starting the war. Among Barnard faculty members, Professor of English William Peterfield Trent, a native Virginian, publicly aligned himself with the "white Teutonic race" when the French army used black Senegalese troops against the invading Germans.[60]

For most Barnard instructors, trustees and students, while less critical of the British and their allies, the policy advocated by both the president of the United States and the president of Columbia University during the first two years of the fighting in Europe—not our fight; neutral in word and deed—reflected their sentiments as well. But as the war and the killing dragged on into 1916 with no end in sight, some Columbians, including the philosopher John Dewey and some trustees, shifted away from a principled neutrality toward intervention on the side of Britain and France. President Butler, however, remained firmly in the anti-interventionist camp and rejected efforts by ex-president Theodore Roosevelt to have Columbia host a training school for reserve officers.[61]

Similarly disposed was Barnard's dean. She later acknowledged that it was in 1916 that she became a Democrat out of her admiration of President Wilson, who that fall won reelection on the campaign appeal, "He Kept Us Out of War." But with Germany's renewal of submarine warfare in February 1917 and Wilson's shift to a more combative stance with respect to Germany, Butler belatedly aligned himself and the university with the interventionists. Six weeks after the United States entered the war in April 1917, he conveyed to the alumni—but with his real audience antiwar instructors and students—the university's wartime policy: "What had been tolerated before, became intolerable now. What had been wrong-headedness was now sedition. What had been folly was now treason." Dean Gildersleeve's charge to the Barnard convocation in the fall of 1917, if less bellicose and more resignedly phrased, was of a kind: "The cause for which we are called upon as College women to do our share."[62]

Meanwhile, several Columbia trustees seized the moment to settle scores with faculty members whose past public statements they believed had done the university one disservice or another. Their principal target was the psychologist James McKeen Cattell, whose oft-stated opposition to trustee governance had been met with stony silence from his bosses but whose opposition to the military draft and support of the antiwar demonstrations of his son made him fair game. At the trustees' direction and with the acquiescence of a committee of senior Columbia faculty, Cattell was fired in September 1917 for "actions detrimental to the University." Also caught up in the trustee witch hunt was the economist Henry R. Mussey, who had for a decade divided his teaching time between Columbia and Barnard, where he was a member of the faculty. Mussey barely escaped being fired, along with Cattell and Columbia assistant professor of English Henry Wadsworth Longfellow Dana, for protesting the draft.[63]

Such instances of trustee high-handedness gave Butler pause, but not before two of his most prominent and popular faculty members, the American political scientist/historian Charles A. Beard, and the European intellectual historian James Harvey Robinson, resigned in protest. Both men had close ties to Barnard. Robinson had taught at Barnard for twenty years, served as acting dean in 1900, and was a member of its original faculty. Beard, a member of Columbia's Department of Government and Public Law, had been recruited by Dean Gildersleeve in 1912 to introduce a two-semester sequence in American history required for acceptance into the newly opened Columbia School of Journalism. During his four years of teaching at Barnard he developed a following among students and faculty members alike.[64]

Beard's was the more dramatic resignation. It came at the start of the 1917 fall term in a public letter addressed to President Butler in which he excoriated Columbia's trustees as having "no standing in the world of education, who are reactionary and visionless in politics, narrow and medieval in religion." The *New York Times* condemned Beard's actions in an editorial entitled, "Columbia's Deliverance."[65]

Three weeks after Beard submitted his resignation, Mussey submitted his, citing the failure of the Columbia faculty to protest the firing of Cattell. To their collective credit, and in contrast with official Columbia,

Dean Gildersleeve, the Barnard faculty members, and the student editors of the *Barnard Bulletin* all publicly acknowledged Beard's services to the college and lamented the circumstances that brought about his resignation. One of the few public expressions of support for Beard appeared in the *New York Herald-Tribune*, the day after the *Times* denounced him, from the Barnard-based philosopher, William P. Montague. Mussey's departure was similarly regretted in a resolution made by history instructor Maude Hutman to the Barnard faculty in December, although, likely out of deference to official Columbia, it was tabled.[66]

Robinson waited to submit his resignation until the spring semester of 1918, when he joined the economist Alvin Johnson (who had taught briefly at Barnard in 1905–1906) with other New York–based academics and public intellectuals (including Emily James Smith Putnam) to establish the New School for Social Research. Here, too, Barnard proved to be more generous to this departing faculty member than was his principal employer. When Columbia declined Robinson's request that he be paid for an unused sabbatical, Barnard treasurer Plimpton promptly authorized payment of Barnard's share.[67]

However ambivalent the Barnard community may have been about the decision to enter the war, once it was made, many members took an active part in its prosecution. Faculty members Franklin Giddings and James T. Shotwell took up civilian positions in one of the several war agencies that sprung up. On campus, other instructors joined with about sixty Barnard students under the lead of the geologist Ida Ogilvie to supplement wartime agricultural production by planting and growing some of their food on a borrowed family farm in Bedford, New York. Still other students and staff members volunteered their services at the Boathouse Canteen, a recreational center for soldiers and sailors passing through New York City located in Columbia's boathouse jutting out into the Hudson River at 122nd Street.[68]

Barnard's biggest contribution to the war effort came from its alumnae. Three members of the class of 1917 joined the Navy upon graduation and spent the war decoding and translating enemy documents. Sarah Schuyler Butler (class of 1915) organized the Barnard War Service Corps, which in turn recruited five alumnae volunteers for a Barnard Red Cross Unit; it set up a field unit in Bordeaux, France. Another ten Barnard alumnae saw service at a YWCA canteen within hearing of the front lines in France. In all, some thirty-five Barnard alumnae saw wartime and immediate post-war service in Europe.[69]

On the home front, Dean Gildersleeve used the occasion of the war to press for opening Columbia's medical school, the College of Physicians and Surgeons, to qualified Barnard graduates. Her earlier success in gaining access for women to Columbia's School of Journalism in 1912 had occurred without resistance and was in keeping with Joseph Pulitzer's wishes, but cracking either the medical or law school's opposition to admitting women was another matter. Facing a shortage of male applicants and heavy calls on the medical profession to staff field hospitals in Europe, College of Physicians and Surgeons officials reluctantly agreed to a temporary lifting of its ban on women students. Gildersleeve then recommended a graduating senior, Gulli Charlotte Lindh, who was duly admitted. Lindh subsequently graduated at the top of her medical school class, while two other wartime female admissions finished third and fifth. These results prompted the medical school to rescind its ban permanently. Columbia law school would be next.[70]

By war's end in 1918, the now forty-one-year-old Dean Gildersleeve had consolidated her position as Barnard's chief administrative officer and as an effective operative within the university. It was time to look for other crusades.

5

GOOD TIMES

Barnard in the Twenties

I found [at Barnard]—and in some measure created—the kind of student life that matched my dreams.

—MARGARET MEAD, CLASS OF 1923[1]

THE DEAN GETS A LIFE

American entry into World War I, called the Great War at the time, marked Dean Gildersleeve's entry into the world of public affairs. Her appointment by President Butler in the spring of 1917 as chair of the Columbia University Committee on Women's War Work brought her into contact with city officials, including a renewed contact with New York's mayor John Purroy Mitchell, an 1899 Columbia classmate, who appointed her to the Mayor's Committee of Women on National Defense. Soon came calls from Washington, where she was asked to be a member of the Committee on War Service Training for Women College Students. In her autobiography, Gildersleeve recalled some frustration with these committee assignments as "fighting an armchair war," but she also acknowledged their more lasting effect: "It committed me to international affairs as the principal work of my life next to my immediate task as Dean of Barnard College." The Great War also became the occasion for her finding love.[2]

Gildersleeve had toured Europe as a schoolgirl with her parents and again with a Brearley friend after graduation. Both paternal ancestry—the Gildersleeves were from Suffolk—and her dissertation subject—governmental regulation of the Elizabethan theatre—made England a special place of interest. An invitation to visit followed Barnard hosting a delegation of English women academics in the fall of 1918. The invitation came from Caroline Spurgeon, professor of English literature, a Chaucer scholar and academic administrator at Bedford College, University of London. Gildersleeve, who was still living with her parents (an arrangement Bryn Mawr's M. Carey Thomas took exception to on feminist grounds), put up her guests in Brooks Hall. Eight years Gildersleeve's senior, Spurgeon and the dean almost immediately established an intimate relationship that would define their personal lives for the next quarter century.[3]

Before her guests returned to England, Gildersleeve arranged for a visit the following summer and initiated plans to establish an International Federation of University Women (IFUW). The trip included a stay with Spurgeon and her women friends, who shared a summer cottage in the Cotswolds. Such reciprocal visits thereafter became the norm, with Spurgeon spending three months every fall in New York, often as a visiting lecturer at Barnard. In 1925, Gildersleeve took up residence in the Deanery, private quarters at the north end of the newly opened Hewitt Hall, with Spurgeon joining her there, while she spent summers in a thatched cottage in Alciston, Sussex—the Old Postman's Cottage—with Lillian Clapham and Gildersleeve's beloved Cara, her nickname for Spurgeon. From there, they frequently traveled across the English Channel to France or elsewhere in Europe, sometimes on business relating to the IFUW or Reid Hall, a residence for American students and artists in Paris, which, beginning in 1922, was administered by the IFUW, but often simply for the pleasure of traveling together. Upon Clapham's death in 1936, the ailing Spurgeon moved to Arizona, where Gildersleeve became a regular visitor until her companion's death in 1942.[4]

Summers abroad became only part of a more comprehensive pattern of off-campus excursions by Barnard's dean. With the adoption of the Nineteenth Amendment to the U.S. Constitution, American politics lost its male-only character and became an arena for women as well. Several Barnard alumnae were among the first to become active in state and national party politics. Jessie Wallace Hughan (class of 1898) became a leader in the Socialist Party; Sarah Schuyler Butler (class of 1915) was vice chair of the New York Republican State Committee; Juliet Poyntz (class of 1907) was active in the Socialist Party and later joined the Communist Party. But it was Gildersleeve's involvement with successive New York Democratic governors Al Smith and Franklin Roosevelt, and still later with New York City mayor Fiorello La Guardia, that received the most public notice for breaking with the studied apolitical stance of other college leaders of her day.[5]

This enlargement of Gildersleeve's life followed on the almost simultaneous loss of both her parents. In 1912, her mother's increasing problems with vertigo prompted the sale of the family brownstone on Forty-Eighth Street and a move into an apartment on 113th Street and Riverside Drive. Judge Gildersleeve, who had retired from the bench at seventy-two but continued to practice law, died in February 1923. His wife followed six months later.

Gildersleeve needed only to look across Broadway to Columbia's President Butler for the very model of the interwar academic leader as public celebrity, as Michael Rosenthal's spirited biography makes clear. Butler served as a New York delegate to every Republican national convention from 1888 to 1936 and twice came close to being the party's nominee for vice president. He was a force in the Carnegie Endowment for International Peace for four decades and its president from 1925 to 1945. While never as internationally recognized as Nicholas Miraculous, which is what Theodore Roosevelt called his one-time political ally, Nicholas Murray Butler, Gildersleeve became in her middle years as Barnard's dean the most frequently cited woman academic in America. She was regularly called upon by the New York press for her opinions on subjects relating to domestic politics and later on the state of international affairs, especially with regard to the Middle East.[6]

The dean's interest in global issues was another product of her midcareer invention. In her autobiography, she credits the Chicago-based businessperson Charles Crane with sparking her interest in the Middle East, where his philanthropic, religious and commercial interests overlapped. Gildersleeve's other New York acquaintances, including Barnard trustees George A. Plimpton and later Harry Emerson Fosdick, minister of the Rockefeller-founded Riverside Church, were also actively engaged in matters relating to the Middle East, with Plimpton serving on the boards of the Presbyterian-sponsored all-boys Robert College and the American College for Girls in Istanbul. In 1924, Plimpton and Gildersleeve had tried to arrange a joint appointment with the Museum of Natural History to bring to Barnard the Chicago-based Egyptologist James H. Breasted, author of *Ancient Times: A History of the Ancient World.* Trips with Spurgeon to North Africa in 1921, followed by an extended visit to Cairo in 1930, solidified Gildersleeve's connection with things Arabic. This would later complicate her already strained relationship with some of Barnard's Jewish alumnae.[7]

Of Virginia Gildersleeve's four decades as dean of Barnard, the 1920s decade was easily her most enjoyable. By then she had established a good working relationship with the trustees, as more and more of the original trustees were succeeded by replacements that she had a role in selecting. While Annie Nathan Meyer continued to find occasions to criticize her, Gildersleeve seems to have won over the succession of white, Anglo-Saxon Protestant (WASP) lawyers who dominated the board, and her dealings with Treasurer Plimpton became, if not warm, companionable.[8]

President Butler remained paternally disposed toward Gildersleeve, and she was ever loyal to him. Meanwhile her dealings with various university deans produced outcomes favorable to Barnard's students seeking professional careers. The decision of the College of Physicians and Surgeons in 1920 to lift permanently the ban on women allowed admission of a handful of Barnard graduates annually. Negotiations with Columbia Law School deans Harlan Fiske Stone and Huger Jervey led the school to admit women starting in 1927, although an earlier negotiated arrangement that the law school would only accept Barnard women was vetoed at the last moment.[9]

A FACULTY OF ITS OWN

Getting an instructional staff in place in the fall of 1889 had been one of the easier challenges that the founders of Barnard faced. So, too, in 1900, Barnard's physical proximity and the newly negotiated intercorporate agreement with Columbia greatly facilitated the constitution of a freestanding faculty of considerable scholarly distinction. Here, as well, the willingness of Barnard to copy the undergraduate curriculum of Columbia College simplified matters. What subsequently complicated them were two developments. The first was the gradual recognition that Barnard's curricular needs as a women's college differed from those of a men's college, especially one designed as Columbia College was as a feeder to the university's professional schools. But second and more immediate was the unresolved question of what place, if any, were women to have in the Barnard College faculty.

During Barnard's first eleven years, when fifty or so individuals offered instruction, the botanist Emily L. Gregory was the only woman. Upon her death in 1897, she was succeeded by Herbert Maule Richards. When President Low underwrote the outside appointments of three senior scholars at Barnard, all were men. When the college's first faculty was organized in 1900, it consisted of sixteen men of professorial rank, and thirteen "officers of instruction," including two women, the forty-year-old physicist Margaret E. Maltby and the just-graduated Eleanor Keller (class of 1900) as an assistant in chemistry. The fact that the 1900 intercorporate agreement contains the explicit statement that "Members of the Faculty of Barnard College may be either men or women" suggests this had been negotiated.[10]

By Barnard's twenty-fifth anniversary in 1914, the forty-five-person instructional staff included five women of faculty rank:

Margaret E. Maltby (1900–1931), assistant professor of physics
Gertrude M. Hirst (1901–1943), assistant professor of classics
Ida H. Ogilvie (1903–1941), assistant professor of geology
Marie Reimer (1903–1945), associate professor of chemistry
Mabel Foote Weeks (1907–1939), assistant professor of English

Only one woman of faculty rank had come and gone. This was the settlement house leader Mary K. Simkhovitch, who was appointed adjunct professor of sociology in 1907 but resigned in 1910. Men chaired all but three of the college's fifteen departments, the exceptions being Margaret Maltby, chair of physics; Marie Reimer, chair of chemistry; and Ida H. Ogilvie, chair of geology. All three women were accomplished scientists as acknowledged by their inclusion in successive editions of James McKeen Catell's *American Men of Science*.[11]

These three scientists also reflect a discernible pattern of gender differentiation: women who joined the Barnard faculty generally stayed, while half the men who did so eventually moved on, some by transferring to Columbia and others by being hired elsewhere. With no possibility of transferring to the all-male Columbia faculty (its first female appointment occurred in 1938 and the first transfer of a Barnard woman faculty member to Columbia was in 1949) and with few other academic institutions hiring women faculty—even most women's colleges preferred men—Barnard's women faculty members were occupationally stuck.[12]

The effect of these gender-differentiated career trajectories became even more evident in the next decade. By 1925, Barnard's instructional staff had grown to eighty-five, with just over half of them women. Men, however, held three-quarters of the faculty-rank positions and all but one of the twenty-two full professorships. Still, the increased presence of women in the lower faculty ranks and their three-to-one majority among the subfaculty ranks suggested to some observers that, if left to its own devices, the Barnard faculty was on its way to becoming all-female. Unless checked by administrative action, Barnard's faculty seemed equally at risk of inundation as its student body, only here it was not the threat of city ethnics driving away country WASPs but female academics outlasting their male counterparts. And if so, who better to address this "problem" of excess women faculty than a dean already addressing that of excess New Yorkers?[13]

One difference between the two problems was that Dean Gildersleeve was more willing to discuss the second than the first. "How many women teachers should we have at Barnard? That was a puzzling problem," she recalled in her autobiography. She then specified the "problem."

When I was an undergraduate, there were none [women teachers] except one able lecturer in botany with whom I never came in contact. But women gradually drifted into the departments, generally to the position of assistant or instructor, and then as they showed themselves able and useful got promoted. We could, as a rule, secure for an assistantship a better quality of woman than of man. Thus if we filled our higher posts only by promotions from below, we tended to acquire a faculty predominantly feminine.

And then, still very much the interventionist Progressive and social engineer, she continued:

Was this a good thing? I was inclined to think it was *not*, and for this some feminists blamed me, saying that there were so few collegiate posts in the country open to women that a woman should be appointed at Barnard in every possible case. It seemed to me, on the other hand, that it was our first obligation to provide the best professors we could secure for our students irrespective of sex, but that we should also try to preserve a balance between the sexes. We seemed sure to have plenty of women in any event, as the unusually competent ones in the lower grades were promoted to professorial rank.

How then to keep "plenty of women" from becoming "all women"? The dean's solution: "When we were bringing in a new professor or associate professor, we were likely to try to bring in a man. Perhaps this was discrimination against women, but it was, I am sure, for the good of the college as a whole."[14]

The preferential hiring of men at the professorial level was an interwar fact of Barnard faculty life. Of the twenty-one initial faculty appointments between 1915 and 1939, all but one went to men. The only woman hired at professional rank was the French scholar Marguerite Mespoulet, in 1936. The distinguished classical archeologist, Margaret Bieber, who came to Barnard as an externally funded visiting lecturer in 1934 after losing her professorship in Germany because she was Jewish, became an associate professor three years later.[15]

Another gendered fact of the period was that men initially appointed to subfaculty ranks either left shortly thereafter or secured faculty rank twice as quickly as did women. The average time for the eight male instructors to achieve professorial rank was seven years; for the thirty-four women, it was thirteen years. At the other end of the academic life span, women who achieved faculty rank had careers at Barnard lasting twenty-eight years, while the average for men was twenty years. The women did so only after staying in subfaculty ranks on average four times longer (13.8 years) than did their male counterparts (3.3 years).[16]

Could explanations other than gender discrimination account for these differences? Were the women who hired hired less academically credentialed than the men? This would appear not to be the case, neither in terms of the degrees held or the source of graduate training. That a majority of Barnard interwar faculty appointees of both genders received their professional training and advanced degrees from Columbia also implies parity.[17]

What about differences in subsequent scholarly productivity? It may be that male faculty members more often achieved scholarly prominence than did women faculty. But here, too, gender plays a role. One way that male Barnard faculty members got themselves transferred to Columbia or came to the attention of other universities is through regular publication of their research. They wrote their way across Broadway or to universities elsewhere. But because the same opportunities were not available for women, their incentive to publish became less compelling.

This is not to argue that interwar Barnard women faculty members published less frequently than their male counterparts. By recent norms, neither gender published all that much, with the majority having as their principal publication their doctoral dissertation. Interwar science faculty at Barnard of either sex lacked the laboratories and graduate students available to university-based scientists, making it almost impossible to maintain an active research program, except as staff members of projects led by Columbia professors. Among women in the social sciences, however, the anthropologist Gladys Reichard, political scientist Jane Perry-Clark Carey, and sociologist Mirra Komarrovsky all achieved national standing through their publications and professional activities. The fact that none of them was ever offered a faculty appointment at Columbia, although all three were Columbia PhDs, and two of Komarrovsky's male departmental colleagues, Robert M. MacIver and Willard Waller, were speaks to their occupational condition.[18]

Outside faculty hires initiating instruction in a new field went exclusively to men. These included Raymond Moley in government in 1923 and Douglas Moore in music in 1926. Only after two successive males hired to start a program in fine arts, Ernest De Wald in 1923 and Norman

MIRRA KOMARROVSKY
"Secret   joys   and   secret
     smiles."

FIGURE 5.1 Mira Komarovsky, class of 1926, later professor of sociology (1934–1968). Barnard Archives.

W. Haring in 1925, went elsewhere did Barnard secure the long-term services in 1929 of Marion Lawrence, a specialist in early Christian art. Meanwhile, Eleanor Keller in chemistry, Ethel Sturtevant in English, Grace Langford in physics, and Grace Goodale in classics spent between seventeen and nineteen years in subfaculty ranks before being promoted to assistant professor, in Sturtevant's case, only on the eve of her retirement.[19]

Another possible exculpatory explanation for the different treatment of men and women instructors might be that the latter were made less mobile by marital circumstances that included a spouse whose career required New York residence. While this would limit mobility for many after World War II, nearly all interwar Barnard female faculty members were single. But this subjected them to yet another form of discrimination.

Income disparities resulting from the systemic lag in female promotions were exacerbated by salary determinations by marital status. Married faculty members, which included most of the male instructors, were assumed to be principal breadwinners with family responsibilities (and stay-at-home wives) that necessitated higher salaries, while single faculty members were thought to be able to survive on lower salaries. There were instances of single women of independent means, the geologist Ida Ogilvie is a case in point, or married women faculty with husbands earning high incomes, like Mirra Komarrovsky, who acknowledged their financial independence and did not need raises. But there were also instances of single women faculty members with financial responsibility for parents or unemployed domestic partners.[20]

Similar discriminatory compensation policies existed at other interwar institutions, and remained in place at Columbia and other universities into the 1970s. What is unusual, and for an historian helpful, about their functioning at interwar Barnard was that nobody made any bones about them.[21]

A CURRICULUM OF THEIR OWN

Unlike Cornell, whose founders in 1865 promised "instruction in all subjects," or Harvard at the outset of the presidency of Charles W. Eliot in 1869, who set about to reinstall a "free elective system," Barnard began with no plans for disrupting the standing curricular order. Its founders simply sought to make the classics-heavy curriculum of the all-male Columbia College available to women. That meant a curriculum largely of required courses for the first two years, with a few choices in the last two years, but even these were heavily weighted in favor of classical languages and light on science.[22]

An unintended consequence of Barnard acquiring its own faculty in 1900 was that it acquired ownership of its curriculum. Unlike President Barnard, who unsuccessfully sought trustee support to junk its traditional and fixed classical curriculum in favor of an elective system, Seth Low succeeded in implementing his favored curricular reforms. Rather than opt for Harvard's elective system, Low took Columbia College in the opposite direction with an undergraduate curriculum that could be completed in two or three years and consisting mainly of required and broadly conceived courses akin to those that later came to be designated "general education." In the 1920s, these courses coalesced into Columbia's hallmark core curriculum. This decidedly nonspecialized curriculum was taught mostly by faculty permanently assigned to Columbia College or by junior faculty on loan from one of the three graduate faculties, thereby freeing most senior faculty for graduate instruction. Low's successor, Butler, essentially endorsed this arrangement even as he proceeded to remove first Greek and then Latin courses from the required curriculum while further isolating those teaching in the college from the privileged disciplinary specialists in the graduate faculties. Successive deans of the college, Frederick Keppel and Herbert Hawkes, maintained the commitment to nonspecialized learning.[23]

However well this pre-professional, unspecialized curriculum served Columbia College's many profession-bound and its few learning-for-learning's-sake men, it presented several problems for Barnard students. Not least was that many of Columbia's professional schools did not accept women, college graduates or not. The exceptions were the graduate programs in the arts and sciences, where early Barnard graduates beginning in the 1890s could and did pursue advanced degrees in the humanities, social sciences, and sciences at a rate higher than that of any American college. This was also the case with Columbia's Journalism School, which at the direction of its patron, Joseph Pulitzer, admitted women from its opening in 1912. The College of Physicians and Surgeons began admitting a handful of women in 1917, the law school in 1926, engineering in 1943. Meanwhile, there were other medical, law, and engineering schools that earlier accepted women (NYU being a local instance), and professionally aspiring early Barnard graduates availed themselves of them. But for most Barnard students, an undergraduate curriculum that fed into Columbia's professional schools or was otherwise occupationally irrelevant made little sense.[24]

Most of the interwar Barnard students who went on after graduation to take a master's degree in one of Columbia's three graduate faculties did so to enhance their job prospects as high school teachers. For most of the rest, securing a level of competence in an academically recognizable field—mathematics, zoology, history, Spanish as undergraduates made them more likely to find the employment that for all but the few trust-fund-blessed Barnard students necessarily followed on graduation. The fact that proportionally more interwar Barnard graduates pursued advanced and professional degrees than the women of any other colleges (with the possible exception of Hunter College graduates) speaks to both their intellectual ambitions and the quality of the instruction they received as undergraduates and also to the occupational imperative that had prompted their matriculation.[25]

Barnard's faculty members had their own problems with the Columbia College curriculum. The privileging of "general education" and pre-professional subjects meant that teaching these courses would leave them at still further remove from the intellectual issues engaging their disciplinary specialties. This may have been an acceptable trade-off for those few Morningside instructors who, like John Erskine or Irwin Edman, saw themselves primarily as teachers, but self-identified scholars who wished to stay abreast of their fields—and occasionally make contributions to them—needed to teach their subject. And not just at the introductory level. This was especially so for Barnard faculty, with few or no opportunities to work with graduate students.

The cumulative effect of these considerations led Barnard to develop a curriculum that encouraged immediate exposure of students to a variety of disciplines followed by early specialization in a given one. The difference between students "majoring" in a subject pursued in depth through electives—the Barnard way—and having them "concentrate" in a set of prescribed courses—the Columbia way—became even more pronounced in the 1920s, when Columbia College gave over the first two years of its curriculum to an increasing number of required courses of no specific discipline that constituted its fabled core curriculum. As long as the occupational prospects of male and female college graduates favored men, colleges such as Columbia could afford to be disdainful of job readiness considerations and focus instead on what the godfather of Columbia's core curriculum John Erskine called "the obligation to be intelligent." Not so women's colleges, or at least not one serving the "aspiring crowds."[26]

Subjects added to the Barnard interwar curriculum included studio courses in theater and dance and, in 1939, interdisciplinary programs in medieval studies and American studies, the latter arguably the first such undergraduate program in the country. Other subjects taught on both sides of Broadway—anthropology, botany, mathematics, music, and fine arts—generated more faculty and undergraduate interest at Barnard than at Columbia. Overall, however, it was the unique combination of student emphasis on acquiring competence in a specialty, access to advanced courses in these specialties taught by Columbia's three graduate faculties, and the preference Barnard faculty members had for teaching within their disciplinary specialty that produced the extraordinary number of inter-war Barnard graduates who went on to earn PhDs and take up academic careers. When Barnard's discipline-centered curriculum was put in place in 1927, Columbia College's Dean Hawkes patronizingly described it as "certainly not one which I should wish to have in any college of which I was Dean," before going on: "But if the Barnard Faculty wants it, then, on behalf of Columbia College, I have no objection." Left unmentioned by Hawkes was that Barnard women under their new curriculum were more likely to major in one of the sciences than his Columbia men.[27]

INTERWAR ADMISSIONS: NEW YORKERS NEED NOT APPLY

Dean Gildersleeve was a latitudinarian when it came to curricular mat-ters, giving her faculty a free hand to determine what should be taught. In her autobiography, she allowed that "personally I came to believe that it did not matter greatly which subjects a student studied." Not so, when it came to which kinds of students should be admitted to Barnard, an issue she cared deeply about and where her views aligned with those prevailing across Broadway.[28]

Enrollments in Columbia College dropped sharply in the fall of 1917. Administrators initially attributed it to previously enrolled undergrad-uates going off to military service. But when applications from students seeking to transfer to Columbia in the spring of 1918 spiked, they became concerned. The increase came mostly from students at the City College of New York (CCNY) who were seeking admission to Columbia after three tuition-free semesters and willing to pay for two or three semesters in Columbia College to enhance prospects of admission to one of the uni-versity's professional schools. The admission of transfers to the college was still determined wholly by Regents exam results or College Boards and high school grades, which meant that most of these applicants were admit-ted. And when it was estimated that, as a result, Jews made up a third of the class of 1919 (some estimates had it at 40 percent), alarms went off.[29]

Whatever the number, the incoming dean of the college Herbert Hawkes complained to Butler that his inherited class of career-focused sons of immigrants "have no use for college affairs and regard Columbia less as an Alma Mater than as an Efficens Pater." This was an instance of preaching to the choir. Butler had already pronounced on the quality of the class entering in the fall of 1917 as "depressing in the extreme," where "boys of old American stock" were in shorter supply than the "foreign born and children of those who have recently arrived in this country."[30]

Hawkes and Admissions Director Adam Leroy Jones, with the active support of Butler and concerned trustees, now instituted sweeping changes in the admissions process. Among them was an application form that for the first time required the following information: the birthplace of the applicant's parents, the family's religion, the language spoken at home, the father's education, the mother's education, the father's occupation, the family's previous last name if it had been changed. A photograph of the applicant was also required, as was a psychological test, the results of which would inform the decision to admit. Finally, and most bizarre, a physical exam was now required, along with a swimming test, for the ostensible purpose of weeding out those afflicted with diseases thought to be prevalent among newly arrived immigrants.[31]

Because these changes applied equally to Barnard applicants, no longer would Bursar N. W. Liggett be left to guess the religion of applicants by their names or neighborhoods. Henceforth, as President Butler had earlier urged Dean Keppel, admission could turn on "treating the candidate for graduation as one treats a candidate for admission to a club, that is, having his personal qualifications examined." If the club Butler had in mind was his and Keppel's Century Association, both knew Jews and women were systematically excluded.

The effect of these changes was immediate enough for Dean Hawkes to boast to Keppel after admitting his first class for the fall of 1919: "The like of [it] you have never seen in this place. I would like to have you read a list of the Freshmen. You could pronounce every name without tying a double knot in your tongue."[32]

Beginning in 1920, Columbia College placed an upper limit on the size of entering classes of 550 students. This cap allowed the admissions staff to refuse admission to academically eligible applicants because the class was filled, presumably but not necessarily (as in the case of athletes or legacies) with more academically qualified applicants but also with those whose social profile suggested they would make a "better fit."

In 1922, when press criticism of these new policies put Columbia on the defensive, Hawkes defended them in a letter to Massachusetts Institute of Technology (MIT) Professor Edwin B. Wilson. After a prefatory disclaimer that "I have no desire whatever to eliminate the Jew from Columbia College," he got down to numbers.

> Situated as we are in New York we ought to furnish the best education we can to a good many of them and as a matter of fact the cream of the Jews constitutes a very fine body of people in my opinion. I believe we ought to carry at least 15 percent of Jews and I do not think that 20 percent is excessive for Columbia College.[33]

To the allegation Wilson passed along that "our Intelligence Examinations are intended to discriminate against the Jew and are judged with that idea in mind," Hawkes declared it to be "an absolute perversion of the truth." To the anticipated follow-up question, "What, then, is the rationale for the mental examination," Hawkes demonstrated the usefulness of an enrollment cap: "What we have been trying to do is to eliminate the low grade boy. We had 1200 applications for admission last fall and could accommodate only 550. This meant that somebody had to lose out. We have not eliminated boys because they were Jewish."[34]

The concerns of Barnard administrators are less a matter of record than those of Columbia. But we do know that the admissions procedures at Columbia and Barnard were administered by some of the same staffers. We also know that the social composition of the Barnard classes were, in terms of their religious character, strikingly similar, that is with Jews making up between 18 percent and 22 percent of entering interwar classes.[35]

No evidence has been found to indicate that Dean Gildersleeve had any problems with these new admissions procedures. In November 1920, she wrote to Butler of Barnard's intention to adopt the psychological test in place at Columbia, seeing it as giving Barnard more "elasticity" in putting together future classes. Anticipating some resistance from her faculty, the dean was careful to describe the desired effect of these new procedures as aimed at attracting more students of the "conventional middle class" from beyond the New York region rather than a conscious effort to limit the number of Jewish New Yorkers at Barnard. The use of the psychological test was approved as an experiment and helped shape Barnard entering classes into the 1930s.[36]

Barnard also joined Columbia in announcing a cap on the size of entering classes, setting it between 250 and 275 for any given class once overall enrollments reached 1,000. Finally, the new policies allowed Barnard to admit a socially attractive applicant who came up short on her entrance exams by establishing categories such as "admit with conditions" and "admit/irregulars." In 1922, these categories encompassed half the admitted class. Getting away from their earlier and heavier reliance upon New York City public schools as the source of preparation became a cross-Broadway competition, with Columbia declaring itself the early winner in 1926 when 66 percent of the Barnard girls still came from public high schools, but only 57 percent of entering Columbia boys.[37]

Admissions practices further privileged private school applicants by waiving personal interviews for those with a recommendation from the head of a recognizable private school. New York City public schoolers were admitted only after a personal interview. Together these practices placed a double burden on applicants from New York City public schools, where well into the 1930s Jewish boys and girls were six times as likely to stay on and graduate as were the children of the city's two other major immigrant populations, the Irish and the Italians. With New York City in 1930 home to three-quarters of America's Jews, and with Jews making up 30 percent of the city's population, one does not have to accept the notion that "New Yorker" was code for "Jew" to conclude that the cumulative negative impact of such policies on Jewish applicants was not collateral but intended.

And it worked. Although Eli Ginzberg, the son of a university professor and later a Columbia business school professor and distinguished economist, managed in 1926 to secure admission to Columbia College as a Jew from DeWitt Clinton High School, he estimated the cap on admissions for applicants like himself to be twenty-five members of his 500-member class. His equally bright sister, he later recalled, refused to risk almost certain rejection in 1931 by even applying to Barnard.[38]

Columbia's admissions policies in general and its use of a psychological test in particular attracted considerable negative press, including in the *Nation*, where Barnard alumna Freda Kirchwey (class of 1915), who opposed fraternities as an undergraduate, was editor and writer. In

successive issues in June 1922, Kirchwey laid into Columbia for procedures that privileged extracurricular activities that she believed unfairly
discriminated against "the boy from an immigrant family who is excluded
from some of the social life of his fellows by prejudice and the need of
earning his own way."[39]

Kirchwey did not mention Barnard in her June articles. On October 4,
1922, however, the *Nation* published a letter from Rebecca Grecht headed
"Anti-Semitism at Barnard." The letterwriter was identified only by name
in the publication. The New York State Census data described her as eighteen years old and the only daughter of Russian-born parents (her father
Adolph made ladies' hats) residing in a tenement building along with
other Russian immigrant families at 304 East Fifth Street when, in 1918,
she applied to and was rejected by Barnard. In her letter, she described
herself as one of three Jewish girls from her unnamed New York City high
school to apply and be rejected. In her case, having finished fourteenth on
her Assembly District's Regents Scholarship Exam and gone on to Hunter
and graduated from NYU *cum laude*, she subsequently wrote to Barnard
asking why she had been rejected. Her persistency extracted three different explanations:

—Her high school was considered "not high enough."
—Barnard preferred applicants who submitted College Board scores
    over those who submitted Regents Exam scores.
—The class was already filled by the time her application was reviewed.

Rebecca Grecht was clearly dissatisfied with these explanations, proposing
instead that she had been rejected because she was Jewish, a discriminatory practice that she contended had become so widespread that "several
prominent Jewish women who had in previous years assisted Barnard
financially now refused a contribution."[40]

Six issues later, on December 6, 1922, the *Nation* published a response
from Dean Gildersleeve, under the banner "Class and Creed at Barnard."

—To the question why was the applicant in question rejected?
[Virginia Crocheron Gildersleeve] VCG: "She did not seem as prom
    ising a student as the others whom we accepted."

—To the insinuation that the applicant's academic achievements were ignored:

VCG: "The mere ability to pass a certain set of examinations with high marks is not necessarily the most important evidence."

—To Barnard's inferred discrimination against New York City applicants, a partial admission:

VCG: "We are particularly anxious to have Barnard a college where New York girls, of every class and creed, can meet girls from other parts of the country and from other nations."

—To the accusation that Barnard was anti-Semitic, a categorical denial:

VCG: "Personally I am deeply interested in the problem of getting Jew and gentile to live together helpfully as useful fellow-citizens in our country."[41]

Meanwhile, Gildersleeve made certain that any success she had in nationalizing the Barnard student body received public notice. In 1921, she informed the faculty and alumnae that the proportion of residents of New York City in the entering class had dropped from 90 percent a decade earlier to 50 percent. "Clearly the College has been relatively losing in the City," she noted of her decade as dean, "and gaining in the country." This shift, she indicated, was ongoing, and the Barnard student of the future "will become cosmopolitan in type."[42]

I have found only two other statements by Gildersleeve on Barnard's admissions policies, both framed to emphasize the positive end of advancing Barnard as a national institution while sidestepping the negative consequences this had on academically qualified applicants from New York City public schools. The first appeared in 1939 in the *Barnard College Alumnae*:

Of course we always want a generous proportion of New Yorkers; but we want to be a national and not merely a local college. . . . So we are fairly generous in admitting girls from Alaska or Hawaii. [We want] a variety of economic, social, racial and national backgrounds.[43]

The other statement appears in her 1954 autobiography, *Many a Good Crusade*:

From what I have been saying it must sound as if a Barnard class was excessively cosmopolitan and a polyglot mixture, but as a matter of fact the vast majority were just plain Americans, whatever their descent, and though half were from New York City or its neighborhood they generally represented almost every state in the union.

Neither statement counters the anecdotal evidence that this "Old New Yorker" shared the social anti-Semitism that was endemic to her class and time nor does it gainsay the damage it has done to her historical standing.[44]

FLAPPERS AND ASH CAN CATS

Whatever temporary success Gildersleeve had in her social engineering efforts to nationalize the student body in the 1920s, Barnard retained much of its local and decidedly urban character. As enrollments overall increased, with the proportion of Jewish students limited to around 20 percent, the percentage of Catholics grew to comparable levels. Most of these students came from the city's Irish and Italian immigrant communities, along with others from New Jersey and upstate New York. Catholics do not seem to have been the object of discriminatory practices in the application process. Their problem, particularly if they attended a parochial school, was securing permission to apply to a so-called heathen college. Many of those Catholics attending Barnard maintained their religious ties through membership in the Craigie Club and later the Newman Club, and through services provided by Corpus Christi Church on 121st Street, where Father George Barry Ford acted as Catholic chaplain to Columbia University. By the mid-1920s, Barnard, founded primarily by mainline Protestants and employing a faculty and administration dominated by Protestants, had, along with Columbia, become one of the first American colleges to have a student body in which Protestants were in the minority.[45]

Catholics matriculating at Barnard in the 1920s included Anna Anastasi, who entered Barnard in 1924 at fifteen; she was the daughter of Italian immigrants living on Fordham Road, in the Bronx. While completing her doctorate at Columbia, she taught psychology at Barnard from

1930 to 1939 before accepting a professorship at Queens and later at Fordham, where her work on psychological testing led to her election as president of the American Psychological Association in 1972. Another Catholic attending Barnard in the 1920s was Theresa Carbonara, class of 1927, whose parents were Italian immigrants living in Brooklyn and who stayed on at Barnard as an instructor in Italian from 1929 to her death in 1951.[46]

Barnard's Jewish students represented a mix of rich and poor, the former including those whose ancestors were German-speaking and came to the United States in the post–Civil War era. Among them were the occasional legacy, Ruth Strauss, class of 1923, the daughter of Hilda Newborg Strauss, class of 1900; and Josephine Sperry, class of 1925, the daughter of Rosalie Bloomngdale Sperry, class of 1900, and resident of upscale 345 Park Avenue. Other Jewish students came from families recently arrived from Eastern Europe and Russia. Esther Biederman entered Barnard in 1927; she was the daughter of parents born in Ukraine who arrived in New York only months before her birth. Esther grew up in Brooklyn and the Bronx and attended Girls High School. A Girls High School scholarship and a Regents scholarship made it possible for her family to send her to Barnard. For two and a half years, she commuted three hours a day from Brooklyn before winning a residence scholarship that allowed her to live on campus. Six decades later, she recalled that, while "there were also some very wealthy girls," at least three in her class had fathers "who were either firemen or cops."[47]

Included among those from comfortable circumstances was Mirra Komarovsky, class of 1926, whose parents fled Russia in 1917, alighting first in Wichita, Kansas, before establishing themselves in Brooklyn. There, Komarovsky attended public high school before coming to Barnard. Following graduation and despite the warning of her Barnard professor, Robert MacIver, that an academic career was not possible for a woman and a Jew, she took up graduate studies in sociology at Columbia. She commenced her teaching career at Barnard in 1935 and remained twenty years beyond her retirement in 1968. In 1972, she was elected president of the American Sociological Association.[48]

Somewhere in the middle of the family income interwar spectrum was Eleanor Rosenberg, class of 1929, who attended Hunter College High School. Her parents could not afford to send her to an out-of-town college, so Eleanor spent all four years at Barnard as a commuter. She later recalled a rivalry between the "dorm girls" and the "city girls," declaring the latter "more intellectually ambitious."[49]

Two other Barnard students in the 1920s speak to the variety of circumstances from which they came. The Pennsylvania-born Margaret Mead entered Barnard in 1920 as a transfer after one year at DePauw College in rural Indiana. Her parents were both college graduates (her father an academic who taught at Wharton) and Episcopalians. Margaret attended a mix of private and public schools and spent some years educated at home by a grandmother. Why she went to DePauw rather than Wellesley or Bryn Mawr, her autobiography leaves unstated. But it is clear why she left: "It was a college to which students had come for fraternity life, for football games, and for establishing the kind of rapport with other people that would make them good Rotarians in later life and their wives good members of the garden club."[50]

Although finding the DePauw faculty committed and engaged, her literary aspirations and a New York City–based boyfriend sent here back east to New York and Barnard. There, she later wrote in *Blackberry Winter*, "I found—and in some measure created—the kind of student life that matched my dreams."[51]

That life involved three years of cooperative living in apartments on West 116th Street and Claremont Avenue with a group of young women from varied circumstances, "half Jewish and half Gentile." Successively designated by disapproving overseers of the residence halls as a "mental and moral muss" and "Communist morons," or by the label they took up as their own, the "Ash Can Cats," the group included Leonie Adams, class of 1922, poetry editor of *Barnard Bulletin*; Viola Corrigan, a Catholic; and Mary Anne "Bunny" McCall, "the perfect flapper." Their apartment became a refuge for like-minded commuter students. "We belonged to a generation of young women who felt extraordinarily free—free from the demand to marry unless we chose to do so." Mead was a psychology major until her senior year, when courses taught by Franz Boas (with Ruth Benedict his teaching assistant) were opened to Barnard students and redirected Mead to a storied career in anthropology.[52]

Yet another different kind of student appeared among Barnard's incoming class in the fall of 1925 in the person of Zora Neale Hurston. In her early thirties, having earlier attended Howard University, the already published Hurston was the first black student to attend Barnard. Her

admission had been engineered by Annie Nathan Meyer, whose involvement with Harlem theater people had brought them together and who
took responsibility for her tuition and fees. Gildersleeve went along with
the arrangement, once it was confirmed that Hurston would be living off
campus and that no precedent be set by her admission. Hurston stayed
three semesters before graduating with the class of 1927, having accumulated a strong academic record in anthropology. In her *Dust Tracks on a
Road: An Autobiography*, she recalled the experience:

> I have no lurid tales to tell of race discrimination at Barnard. I made a few
> friends in the first few days. The *Social Register* crowd at Barnard soon
> took me up. And I soon became Barnard's sacred black cow. . . . I set out
> to maintain a good average, take part in whatever went on, and just be
> part of the college like everybody else.[53]

The Hurston "experiment" passed without incident but did not produce a more welcoming stance toward Black applicants. In the decade
after 1927, only three Black women graduated from Barnard—Belle Tobias
in 1931, Vera Joseph in 1932, and Jean Blackwell Hutson in 1935—and all
lived off campus. Anecdotal evidence suggests that in the case of Black
applicants, unlike Jewish applicants, a hard quota was firmly in place so
that no class would have more than two Black members. In 1934, when a
Black transfer from the University of Michigan, Jean Blackwell, appeared
on campus to register, she was stopped from doing so on the grounds that
her race had not been disclosed in the admissions process and that her
admission would exceed the two-per-class quota. A compromise was then
effected by which Blackwell was allowed to matriculate if she gave up her
assigned room on campus and instead boarded in Harlem. She graduated
in 1935 and twenty years later, as Jean Blackwell Hutson, was appointed
curator of the Schomburg Center for Research in Black Culture at the
New York Public Library.[54]

For Gildersleeve, the problem in the 1920s was less how Barnard might
provide low-cost cooperative living arrangements for students of limited
means and long commutes than how it might properly provide for the
kinds of students attracted to Vassar, Smith, Wellesley, and Byrn Mawr.
Her solution was a second dormitory, to be built along the same generous
lines as Brooks. It was on the occasion of first proposing such a project to

her trustees in 1920 that the dean indicated her long-term goal to reduce the proportion of Barnard's commuting students from the current 75 percent to 50 percent.[55]

The trustees, in the absence of funds, deferred action on the dean's proposal, but four years later, with steadily increasing enrollments producing budgetary surpluses, they approved the construction of a 250-bed extension to Brooks Hall dormitory. Named for Abram S. Hewitt, Barnard's second board chair, the project was unusual because it went ahead without a capital campaign or a naming gift to help pay the $1,000,000 cost. Clearly much of the impetus behind the second dormitory was to increase out-of-town enrollments.[56]

The cost of living in Hewitt was comparable to Brooks, which made the cost of attending Barnard for those who did so substantially higher than any of the country colleges, but this does not seem to have been a problem. More likely it was viewed in many quarters as a solution. With Hewitt's opening in 1925, its 250 beds added to the 100 in Brooks and the fifty in the John Jay apartment building on adjacent Claremont Avenue. Gildersleeve's goal of ending Barnard's days as a commuter's school for the daughters of New York's "aspiring crowds" now seemed within her grasp. The impact of the second of three tuition increases during the 1920s, this from $250 to $300 in 1925, she assured her trustees, was negligible. "The great majority of our students do not seem to feel any burden in paying the additional sums." As for "the comparatively small number who are burdened," the allowable inference was that they should seek less costly educational opportunities.

Meanwhile, all that was needed to confirm Barnard's transformation was gaining the public acceptance of the nationally recognized elite women's colleges that Barnard belonged in their company.[57]

INVENTING THE SEVEN SISTERS

Barnard stopped admitting specials in 1927, thereby bringing itself into conformity with the prevailing admissions practices among the other northeastern women's colleges. Indeed, that likely prompted the decision. Doing so fit the ambitions of Virginia Gildersleeve to have Barnard considered in the public mind as one with the half dozen northeastern women's colleges that had preceded it. Barnard's relations with these colleges into the 1920s were limited to occasional correspondence between college heads over specific issues, such as the treatment of married women faculty members or the admission of Black students. Barnard athletic teams occasionally scheduled games with nearby Vassar and Bryn Mawr, as did its debating team. But when the leading women's colleges were mentioned collectively in the national press into the 1920s, Barnard was seldom included.

In the early 1920s, the Massachusetts-based Smith, Wellesley, Mount Holyoke, and Radcliffe formed the Four College Conference. Nearby Vassar was thereafter informally included in some of their meetings and, on occasion, Bryn Mawr. The absence of Barnard is readily understandable. Differences in the mix of residential and commuting students, the Protestant-denominational circumstances of their founding and ongoing character, the absence (for all but Radcliffe) of a university affiliation, their larger endowments, their locational circumstances—small town or suburban as opposed to inner city—all set Barnard apart.[58]

When Dean Gildersleeve set out to ensure that Barnard was considered among the top women's colleges, she brought several advantages to the task. First was Barnard's unmatched access to the national press, in the case of the *New York Herald Tribune* through Helen Rogers Reid, class of 1903; the *New York Times*, through Agnes Ernst Meyer (BC 1907); and Iphigene Ochs Sulzberger, class of 1914. Second, with the retirement of President M. Carey Thomas of Bryn Mawr in 1922, and with the presidents of Smith, Mount Holyoke, and Vassar all men, Dean Gildersleeve was already better known than any of the country's women college presidents. A third advantage was Barnard's location in New York City, giving it direct access to the nation's leading foundations, including the Rockefeller-funded General Education Board and the Carnegie Corporation, which by the 1920s had become the two most important underwriters of private higher education.[59]

If it was publicity that women's colleges sought in gaining the attention of foundations, Barnard, Gildersleeve suggested, needed to be in the room. In 1927, the heads of the seven colleges jointly published an article in the *Atlantic Monthly* laying out the case for supporting women's colleges. This was followed by the setup of a committee of alumnae from the seven colleges in New York to publicize their collective cause. The money raised was never great and, after a few years, the collaborative fundraising aspect of the relationship gave way to annual meetings focused on common challenges. By then, Barnard had secured itself a place, by common consent, alongside Bryn Mawr, Mount Holyoke, Radcliffe, Smith, Vassar, and Wellesley, among the Seven Sisters, one of higher education's most elite clubs, second only to the Ivy League, another of the decade's academic inventions.[60]

PROSPERITY DECADE?

If the key to an institution's financial wellbeing is to minimize the negative impact of bad times and take full advantage of good times to increase solvency, Barnard failed in the prosperous 1920s to do the latter and left itself unprepared for the tough times to follow. The decade did represent a relatively easy patch in Barnard's financial history. Enrollments increased from 700 to 1,100, while three tuition hikes, from $250 to $300 in 1922, to $350 in 1925, and to $400 in 1927 produced substantial increases in revenues. Financial aid outlays increased only moderately during the period. Surpluses were used to cover some of the $1,000,000 cost of Hewitt Hall, with borrowing for the balance. Hewitt went to full occupancy much faster than Brooks but with comparable room rates, allowing the dormitories to operate on a break-even basis.[61]

The tuition increases were all accompanied by assurances to the trustees from Gildersleeve that families of current students could accommodate them. In the case of the 1929 increase, she estimated that the 33 percent hike "will apparently be no burden to at least three-quarters of our student body." She then proceeded to describe the kind of students she thought Barnard, as a member of the Seven Sisters, should be using its financial aid funds to attract: "The group we are most concerned about is the daughters of professional men and women with modest incomes—teachers, professors, clergymen, country doctors and similar professional workers. The women's colleges have found that in the long run their best students come from this class." She then added: "In such families there are likely to be brains, some tradition of culture and intellectual interests,

and not enough money to make life too easy for the children." To this
end, Gildersleeve announced the introduction of new "open scholarships,
especially intended for the daughters of professional families." The dean
appended a coda in which she lamented the practice of "working your way
through college," which brought to Barnard "students who are entirely or
almost entirely penniless." Better, she advised, "to borrow." From whom
she did not say.[62]

Even as the dean was securing a coveted place among the wealthier, more rustic, and more WASP Seven Sisters and reserving spaces at
Barnard for the daughters of country doctors while privileging those
from families with "some tradition of culture and intellectual interests,"
another initiative of the 1920s squared more with Barnard's urban locale
and the social makeup of its student body. "The Barnard Summer School
for Women Workers in industry" was established in 1927 to provide six
weeks of instruction to women from all segments of the labor movement.
When Bryn Mawr allowed its own summer outreach program to the labor
movement to lapse the year before, Gildersleeve was given formal credit
for bringing it to Barnard as part of Columbia's regular summer session.
More likely the move came about at the urging of Emilie Hutchinson, class
of 1905, then an assistant professor of economics with a scholarly interest
in the female workforce, who became the school's director. Only four of
the first twenty-six women were American born; the others were immigrants from Russia, Poland, Rumania, Czechoslovakia, and Germany. A
group photograph includes at least one Black woman. They received six
weeks of instruction in economics, English, and general science, much
of it provided by members of Barnard's teaching staff. This early experiment in labor education continued for four summers, accommodating
more than 100 industrial workers drawn from the garment, millinery,
upholstery, and electrical trades, and many of them selected by their local
union, until terminated after 1932 when funding from the Carnegie Corporation ran out and the school was closed.[63]

The prosperity that seemingly attended Barnard in the 1920s was not
only short-lived but also illusory, at least in part. Two aspects of the decade
should have given the trustees cause for concern. One was the absence
of any major gifts after those coming from the Carpentier estate in 1918,
which remained the largest received through the next quarter-century.
(The only exception occurred in 1926, when the estate of Mrs. Adrian

FIGURE 5.2 Group photograph of members of the Barnard Summer School for Women Workers in Industry, which was housed at Barnard from 1928 to 1932. Barnard Archives.

Joline gave Barnard $100,000 to endow a chair in music, Barnard's first and, for the next twenty-five years, its only endowed chair.) Another was Gildersleeve's disinclination to involve herself personally in fundraising, leaving the task to the college treasurer. "Mr. Plimpton was so wonderful at money-raising," she later wrote, "that everybody else tended to sit back and let him do it." Everybody included herself.[64]

A larger problem related to fundraising involved the college's failure to follow the lead of other colleges in hiring one of the professional fundraising firms that had sprung up during the war. Here the reluctance is traceable to Columbia and President Butler's hesitancy in doing so. Unlike Gildersleeve, Butler was personally comfortable asking for money, especially among his trustees, friends, and social acquaintances. But deep into the 1920s, he remained resistant to approaching members of the German-Jewish community, including Columbia alumni, lest their support confer a measure of control over university affairs. In 1928, he only reluctantly agreed to engage the services of the fundraising firm John Price-Jones, which by then had managed fourteen college and university campaigns and raised nearly $68 million for endowments and buildings. He also dutifully arranged for the requisite election of a Jew to the Columbia board, in the person of the jurist Benjamin Cardozo, a cousin of Barnard's Annie Nathan Meyer, but it was too little, too late. Ten months after Cardozo's election to the Columbia board, the stock market collapsed, and all plans for a massive fundraising campaign were shelved.[65]

Meanwhile, Dean Gildersleeve and her board eschewed the services of Price-Jones that Smith, Wellesley, and Bryn Mawr employed to mount campaigns that yielded $4 million, $2.7 million, and $2.2 million, respectively. Mount Holyoke engaged the firm of Tamblyn and Brown to conduct a 1923 campaign that added $2.6 million to its endowment. The 1920s marked the decade that Columbia, once the richest of American universities, fell behind three of its Ivy competitors; for Barnard, always the poorest of the sister colleges and now even more so, the decade was a missed opportunity to make provisions against lean times ahead.[66]

6

TOUGH TIMES

Depression, War, and Other Distractions

I want to thank this place for not pretending to be our parents, for not inviting us to remember bright college days when we had no cares, and for insisting instead on the value of the life of the mind. It was tough at times, and I think almost every alumna has a little bit of resentment tucked away somewhere for the fact that Barnard was not, is not, and never has been a nest of singing birds in a golden age of nostalgia. Instead, what we learned—I think—was how to live in the world as it was becoming then and as it is now. . . . Back when we went to school, they gave us the straight stuff.

—ELIZABETH HALL JANEWAY, CLASS OF 1935[1]

At two points in her memoir, *Many a Good Crusade*, Virginia Gildersleeve interrupted her narrative to mark a crucial turning point in her life. The first occurred in 1891, when she was fourteen, with the death of her older and beloved brother Harry "At that moment a black curtain cut my life in two." The second, when she was fifty-one, involved both personal and global loss. "For me," she wrote, "the last days of health unbroken—the last year of man's assurance that his civilization moves 'ever upward and onward' . . . was 1928." That year very much marked an inflection point in the case of her beloved Barnard, which had enjoyed, in the 1920s, eight years of increasing enrollments and accumulating surpluses, allowing her to advance her agenda of increasing the college's national recognition by attracting residential students from outside New York City. But then all her calculated distancing of the college from its urban setting was undercut by the stock market collapse in 1929, the ensuing Great Depression, and World War II, all of which dramatically affected Barnard's financial and demographic situation. And with all of that also came personal tragedy.[2]

HOW BAD DID IT GET?

The effects on Barnard of the stock market crash in October 1929 were first thought to be manageable. That year's entering class of 247 members pushed total enrollments to an all-time high of 1,076, with all safely enrolled and their fall tuitions in the bank. However disastrous the crash may have been for speculators, the college's small endowment of under $4 million ($59 million in 2019 dollars), mostly in railroad and utility bonds, was spared the immediate paper losses suffered by investors in equities. In the spring of 1930, the editors of the *Barnard Bulletin* assured graduating seniors that, temporary dislocations in financial markets notwithstanding, they would have their pick of jobs.[3]

The first hint of serious trouble came in the fall of 1930, with a smaller-than-expected entering class, down by forty students. This was accompanied by a comparable drop in returning students and an increased call from those who did return for financial assistance. These developments, acting dean George Mullins told the trustees, "may be attributed to business depression." No one at the time could have known—or likely even imagined—that this was to be the first of five straight years of declining entering enrollments and shrinking graduating classes.[4]

The class entering in 1931 was smaller than the previous one by forty-eight students; that entering in 1932 by another fifty students. In the fall of 1932, sixty-five rooms in the two dorms went unoccupied. A growing majority of the first-year and transfer students were commuters, which by the spring of 1933 resulted in a 20 percent vacancy rate in the college's two dormitories and a corresponding drop in revenues. Nor did a cut in room rents that fall alter the fact that residence hall rooms were again going to junior female faculty members as part of their compensation.[5]

Unlike the 1920s, many of the transfers now applying to Barnard were New Yorkers who had gone away to college in more prosperous times, only now to find the room and board expenses of doing so beyond their parents' reduced means. Much of the progress Gildersleeve had made in nationalizing the student body in the 1920s was undone by the pressing need to keep enrollments from falling to levels that would force the college to close. In 1925, Gildersleeve's social engineering had produced a graduating class in which only half (51 percent) were from New York City; in 1934, the percentage of New Yorkers had climbed back to pre–World War I levels (61 percent). She despondently reported to alumnae in 1933 sixty-five vacant rooms in the dorms and the "reduction in the numbers of our students coming from a distance."[6]

STARTING OUT IN THE THIRTIES

Sixteen-year-old Helen Phelps entered Barnard as a freshman in the fall of 1929. Her mother was a first-generation Irish immigrant and her father a self-educated newspaper pressman. Helen was born in the Bronx and attended public high school in Palisades, New Jersey. An excellent student, having shown an early talent for languages, she wanted to attend Vassar but family finances did not allow it. She learned from a high school friend that Barnard students became eligible for competitive tuition scholarships after their first year. She applied and was accepted as a tuition-paying freshman. This one year "on family," she later recalled, came "at considerable sacrifice."[7]

Helen's commute from Palisades involved a ferry across the Hudson to 125th Street and a short walk to campus. She did well enough academically in her first year to earn a tuition scholarship as a sophomore and to keep it thereafter. She majored in French and, while lacking the funds for a semester abroad, managed to spend the summer between her junior and senior years at McGill University. Upon graduating, she hoped to find a job teaching French in a public school. None were open as the Great Depression took hold.[8]

By the fall of 1932, calls on Barnard's student loan fund managed by the Alumnae Association for students in temporary need outran the fund's capacity to help. Requests for financial aid that year were up 300 percent from the prior year. In 1935, New Deal legislation extended relief support in the form of campus jobs administered by the National Youth Administration, and 140 of Barnard's 1,000 students were eligible. Nor did students who managed to make it through to graduate fare much better. Six months after graduation, half the class of 1934 had yet to find employment.[9]

Little wonder that many Barnard students of the 1930s took up leftist politics, permanently souring on the capitalist system and the liberal

FIGURE 6.1 Student in physical education class, Students Hall, 1922. Barnard Archives.

political institutions that, their critics insisted, allowed capitalists to run roughshod over underpaid workers and unemployed students. Others aligned themselves in the presidential campaigns of 1932 and 1936 with Norman Thomas and the Socialist Party; still others, among them Florence Dubroff, class of 1940, became active in the American Student Union. Some Barnard students took the Oxford Oath against participating in future wars, and still others became Communists. Among the latter, Judith Coplon, class of 1943, a member of the Young Communist League while at Barnard, was later convicted of spying on behalf of the Soviet Union. Some of these student activists were "red diaper babies," their radicalism acquired from their immigrant parents whose politics were either Marxist or Zionist or both. In the case of Helen Simon, class of 1934, however, she belied her privileged circumstances on Fifth Avenue to become a member of the National Student League.[10]

Barnard students joined in the political protests that roiled the Columbia campus in the 1930s. These included demonstrations critical of President Butler's response to a strike by cafeteria workers in April 1932, which resulted in the suspension of Reed Harris, editor of the *Columbia Spectator*, and protests after Butler's welcoming to campus German Ambassador Hans Luther in November 1933, following the election of Adolf Hitler as chancellor. When the *Barnard Bulletin* joined in condemning both actions, Dean Gildersleeve pointedly reminded its editor-in-chief, Mary Dublin Keyserling, class of 1933, that "many of the trustees will be very annoyed." More typical were the Depression-era Barnard graduates who took up employment and then pursued careers in government agencies identified with the New Deal, where gender-based discrimination was less pronounced than in private industry and where a college degree had currency.[11]

Given Barnard's Depression-era reversion to a mostly commuting student body, the percentage of Jewish students almost certainly increased. In a singular nod to transparency, the *Barnard Alumnae Magazine* in its fall 1935 issue provided data on the incoming class that included reported religious affiliation. It was likely prompted by the regular publication of such data by other Ivy and Sister colleges. Princeton, for example, annually published the religious affiliation of its incoming classes. The dependably less than 10 percent of Jewish students, in any class, was likely intended to be reassuring. Barnard Jewish students seem to have been fully aware of

TABLE 6.1   Barnard Class Entering in Fall 1935 (and Transfers) by Reported Religious Affiliation

Religious Affiliation	Number	Percentage of Total Number of Students	Percentage with Affiliation
Episcopalians	77	21%	24
Presbyterians	48	13	15
Methodists	24	7	7
Congregationalists	15	4	4
Lutherans	11	3	3
Baptists	10	3	3
Other Protestants	29	8	
All Protestants	214	59	66
Moslems	1	0	0
Catholics	61	17	19
Jews	46	13	14
None reported	42	12	
All	364	100	
All with affiliation	322		

the existence of limits on their admission. "We knew there was a quota," Shirley Adelson Siegel, class of 1937, stated in a recent interview. "We just didn't really care."[12]

The inclusion of 150 transfers likely inflated the proportion of Protestant students at Barnard, on the assumption that most transfers in the middle of the Depression consisted of non-Jewish New Yorkers who had originally enrolled elsewhere but returned home as a cost-cutting measure. Second, the substantial number of applicants either not providing their religious affiliation or claiming none likely included a disproportionate number of applicants with Jewish backgrounds who were wary of acknowledging it. Anecdotal evidence puts the percentage of both Jews and Catholics higher than these data, with Jews making up 20 percent of any given class and Catholics as much as one-quarter. Comparable percentages were reported by Columbia College.

Still, I found no explicit evidence that Barnard officials in the 1930s sought to help solve Columbia's putative interwar Hebrew Problem by discriminating against Jewish applicants simply because they were Jewish. The closest approximation to a smoking gun is to be found at Columbia but almost certainly applied to Barnard. In 1934, Adam LeRoy Jones retired after twenty-five years as chair of the University Undergraduate Committee, to be succeeded by Frank Bowles. Bowles's report to President Butler on his first incoming class of Columbia College specified the role of his committee in determining its religious makeup. Whereas half of all non-Jewish applicants to the class of 1938 were admitted, he reported, the admission ratio for Jewish applicants was one in six. Bowles did not suggest that these results represented a break from those produced by his predecessor or that comparable ones did not obtain for Barnard. He simply sought the president's endorsement for the committee's ongoing efforts to secure "desirable students of upper middle class American stock." Butler responded in kind: "Continue to build up the Freshman Class along the lines that have recently been followed." Are we to assume that Gildersleeve would have responded differently?[13]

THE GRAYING OF THE BARNARD FACULTY

Of the many areas of college administration during most of the long Gildersleeve deanship, when Barnard made do without full-time staffing, that of faculty affairs stands out. Despite having secured Butler's assurances that her authority encompassed matters relating to the faculty and that the newly created position of provost of Barnard College was merely "a lieutenant to her," Gildersleeve eliminated the provost position altogether in 1922. It was not until 1932 that Gildersleeve finally established the position of associate dean of the college, to which she appointed the zoologist Louise Gregory. Gregory's duties were more secretarial than operational and focused on students. While they also extended to administrative matters with faculty, department chairs continued to report directly to Dean Gildersleeve. Even in her last decade as dean, with her health deteriorating and her absences from campus longer and more frequent, Gildersleeve retained full authority over her faculty, subject only to the consent of her relatively unengaged trustees and, of course, the approval of President Butler. Younger faculty members found her manner intimidating and imperious.[14]

The effect of this arrangement was that responsibility for the day-to-day operation of the faculty fell upon a half dozen senior faculty members on the dean-appointed Committee of Instruction, to which Associate Dean Gregory was not invited. Faculty meetings were largely informational sessions and limited to officers of instruction of the rank of assistant professor or higher, and maybe this was just as well. During the Depression and into the war years, with no money to appoint new faculty or promote continuing faculty, with instructional salaries frozen and curricular renewal similarly limited by financial exigencies, there was not all that much faculty business to transact. Keeping to their posts, while fending off the specter of salary cuts and the massive layoffs occurring on other campuses, pretty much constituted the faculty response to those downbeat times. With each passing year, not just individually but collectively, the Barnard faculty got older. In 1931, the median age of the Barnard instructional staff was forty-three; eight years later, it was forty-nine.[15]

By 1934, when the Depression sunk to the first of its two lows, the fifty-eight women teaching at Barnard made up a majority (54 percent) of its 107-member instructional staff. They remained, however, a minority (40 percent) among those of faculty rank and held only one of the college's twenty-one full professorships (5 percent). This last had been filled since 1927 by the chemist Marie Reimer (1903–1945). By 1939, two years after the Depression hit its second low, women had increased their majority among Barnard's instructional staff to 59 percent and their percentage of faculty positions to 44 percent, and they occupied four of the seventeen full professorships. In addition to Reimer, they now included the classicist Gertrude Hirst (1903–1941), the geologist Ida Ogilvie (1903–1941), and the philosopher Helen Parkhurst (1917–1952).[16]

Perhaps more telling of the state of the Barnard faculty than the numerical advances made by its long-serving women members was its ongoing retrenchment. Between 1934 and 1939, while the size of the instructional staff declined by only one member, faculty ranks had declined by eight (from 54 percent of all ranks to 50 percent) and the number of professors from twenty-one to seventeen. Not a single promotion from below into the professorial ranks occurred between 1930 and 1940. This freeze allowed Barnard to stave off the massive faculty cutbacks occurring on other campuses during the Depression, with both Butler and Gildersleeve rejecting the strategy of Harvard's President Conant to use the economic crisis to impose an "up or out" system that allowed for new faculty appointments in an era of no growth.[17]

A major contributing factor to the changes in the gender composition of the Barnard faculty had to do with male departures. With Columbia committed to avoiding the kinds of faculty cuts occurring elsewhere, transfers of midcareer Barnard male faculty to Columbia slowed. Still, Hoxie Fairchild, who joined the Barnard English Department in 1927, and the mathematician Paul Smith, who came the same year, both transferred to Columbia, Fairchild in 1939, Smith a year later. The botanist Edmund Sinnott, who had come to Barnard in 1927 as chair of the Botany Department, also transferred to Columbia in 1939 before making a more permanent move to Yale.[18]

More numerically significant were the resignations of five male professors to take up better-paying positions elsewhere, including the historian Edward Mead Earle, who left for Princeton in 1935, and the economist Harry Gideonse, who departed after a single year at Barnard for the presidency of Brooklyn College. In 1939, the newly opened Queens College hired away both the economist Arthur Gayer and the psychologist Anna Anastasi, the only woman I have found on the Barnard faculty in the 1930s to leave for an academic position elsewhere. Although they maintained ties to Barnard, both the political scientist Raymond Moley and the musicologist Douglas Moore shifted most of their teaching and administrative duties to Columbia during the 1930s.[19]

Yet even in these straitened circumstances, Dean Gildersleeve's dealings with prospective faculty allowed some observers to detect bigotry. As the Columbia Business School economist Eli Ginzberg told the story a half century later, sometime in the late 1930s (likely upon Gideonse's departure), Dean Gildersleeve asked the chair of the Columbia economics department to recommend a possible appointee to the Barnard teaching staff. He suggested Moses Abramovitz, one of the department's most promising recent PhD students and a friend of Ginzberg. Abramovitz came away from his interview with Gildersleeve, "who did not even ask him to sit down," convinced that she had dismissed his candidacy out-of-hand because he was Jewish. He later became a founding member of the Stanford University Economics Department. To her credit, Gildersleeve did take in the art historians and intellectual émigrés Margarite Beiber and Julius Held, whose initial hiring in the mid-1930s was made possible

by outside funding. Beiber, one of Europe's leading classical archaeol-
ogists, was appointed an associate professor upon arrival, but in Held's
case, his appointment only became permanent after Gildersleeve's retirement twelve years later.[20]

STARTING OUT IN THE THIRTIES: A FACULTY VERSION

While serving as a student teacher at the Lincoln School of Teacher's College in the spring of her senior year, Helen Phelps, class of 1933, was offered
by Dean Gildersleeve an assistantship in French for the following year,
with a salary of $1,400 and a room in Hewitt. She married in 1934 and the
following year began studies at Columbia for an MA in French. Her intention, she later recalled, "was not to be a professor—but a teacher." The
now Helen Phelps Bailey earned her MA in 1938 and divorced two years
later, all the while teaching at Barnard, first as a tutor and then instructor.
During the war, she taught French to naval officers attending the Military
Government School housed on the Columbia campus and started work
on a dissertation. Upon completion of "Hamlet in France" in 1950, for
which she was awarded her PhD, she was promoted in her seventeenth
year of teaching to the rank of assistant professor. Further promotion
was blocked by the fact that her dissertation research had been done in
the United States rather than in France and that it went unpublished for
fourteen years. Her teaching program involved twelve hours of classroom
instruction per week.[21]

Bailey's subsequent career speaks to both the possibilities and the limits
for members of her interwar generation of Barnard graduates—and of the
era's women college graduates more generally—who entered academe. In
1955, President McIntosh appointed Bailey the Dean of Studies, the administrative post in which she served until her retirement in 1977. Asked by a
junior faculty member in 1979 whether she ever regretted giving up her
scholarly pursuits by going into administration, she initially acknowledged
that she sometimes "felt exploited" before saying that she did as she was
asked because "I felt I owed Barnard an awful lot." Subsequent generations
of less occupationally limited faculty might wonder why.[22]

By the fall of 1931, it was apparent that the stock market's collapse would have long-term consequences for the college, and Dean Gildersleeve announced that the trustees had ordered a freeze on all faculty salaries and a moratorium on faculty hiring and promotions, and warned of likely pay cuts. The moratorium on hires and promotions was vigorously enforced and included involuntary thinning throughout the subfaculty ranks. This decade-long stoppage of hiring, combined with few resignations and even fewer retirements, resulted in a significant graying of the Barnard faculty. In 1929, the median number of years of service of a Barnard faculty member was twenty; by 1939, it had increased to twenty-nine.[23]

Other budgetary economies included the closing in 1932 of the Barnard Summer School for Women Workers in Industry. But such measures could not prevent annual budget deficits beginning in 1931 and continuing for all but one of the next eight years. The reported deficit for 1938–1939 was $68,000, which treasurer Francis P. T. Plimpton called "staggering." Some of these annual deficits were covered by the trustees borrowing from the college's modest endowment, but as the Depression deepened, the market value of the railroad bonds making up most of the endowment had depreciated so much that they could be sold only at a fraction of their book value. The only other alternative was adding to the college's long-term debt through successive and increasingly hard-to-come-by bank loans.[24]

The only significant gift received by Barnard during the 1930s came from the Rockefeller-directed General Education Board, which in 1936 gave the college $250,000, half the amount needed to acquire one of the last vacant properties on Morningside Heights, the block immediately west of Milbank and south of Riverside Church, running from Claremont Avenue to Riverside Drive and from 119th Street to 120th Street. However generous the gift, it did nothing to ease the college's cash flow or chronic budgetary squeeze. Nothing was built on the property for another seventeen years before being bought back in 1953 to be the site of the Rockefeller-sponsored Interchurch Center.[25]

In 1936, Barnard lost to death its most effective fundraiser and, next to Annie Nathan Meyer, its most senior trustee, George A. Plimpton, shortly after a celebration of his forty-seven years as a trustee and forty-three years as treasurer. Plimpton was succeeded as treasurer by his son Francis T. P. Plimpton, but fundraising was effectively stalled by the Depression and would not resume until after the war and the installation of a new dean. Meanwhile, Gildersleeve informed the alumnae in 1935, "In the past two years, our problem was to keep the college alive—keep our students in college, maintain salaries without cutting."[26] What made the Great Depression so emotionally draining for the dean was its duration. After five years of only dismal numbers to present, Gildersleeve managed in her 1935–1936 report to the trustees to express some optimism that "conditions were improving." This followed on a modest uptick that year in student enrollments, although the increase was almost entirely in the so-called unclassifieds: students who seldom stayed on for more than a semester. "We did not lack students," Gildersleeve told her trustees, "but a great number of them could not pay the fees."[27]

The perceived upturn in the college's fortunes in 1935 coincided with a temporary one in national economic indicators attributable to the deficit spending underwriting governmental relief efforts. This "recovery" promptly sputtered when budget deficit–minded Congress cut back on such spending and induced a second slump. In 1937, Barnard enrollments were down again. Two years later, in 1939, the ninth year of the economic crisis, Gildersleeve was back to declaring "the financial situation very grave."[28]

BATTLE OF THE BOOKS

The economic strains of the Depression years were exacerbated by quarrels within the Barnard family. Unlike Gildersleeve's relationship with Plimpton, which warmed over the years, the dean's dealings with the last original trustee, Annie Nathan Meyer, remained frosty. Early efforts to find common ground in their standing as Daughters of the American Revolution or in their shared discomfort in the company of what Meyer called "new people," never quite worked. The death of Meyer's only daughter, Margaret, class of 1915, in 1925, likely by suicide, proved another missed opportunity for the two women to bond in their common loss of a young family member. One clash occurred when Gildersleeve casually referred to Jews as a race (she applied the same term to the Irish), to which Meyer objected, insisting that they constituted a religion with no distinctive racial aspect. Gildersleeve dutifully apologized; she also remembered to include the incident in her autobiography and the comment that "as the years went on, Meyer's dynamic energy became a bit crabbed."[29]

As the only Jewish member of the board from 1896 upon Jacob Schiff's resignation to the election of Sarah Straus Hess (class of 1900) as alumnae trustee in 1919, Meyer resented her quarter century as the board's "token" Jew. Nor did the coming of Hess provide much company; Hess was a member of the city's wealthy German-Jewish clan who had attended Bryn Mawr before returning to New York and transferring to Barnard after an injury. She got on so well with the board's White, Anglo-Saxon Protestant leadership that at the end of her alumnae term she was elected to life membership. What Meyer especially resented were the recurrent celebratory retellings of the college's early history in which she figured as merely one among many "founders." Such refusals to acknowledge her singular role by college and university officials, she concluded, reflected their determination to minimize the role played by Jews in Barnard's beginnings. The board's decision in 1926 to rename Students Hall in honor of the college's namesake, F. A. P. Barnard, and not after its donor, Jacob Schiff, upon Columbia designating one of its new buildings Students Hall, confirmed her suspicions and brought these resentments into public view.[30]

When a contributor to the *Bulletin of the Associate Alumnae of Barnard College* reasonably asked, "Why not call it Schiff Hall?," the official explanation seems to have been that would have been contrary to the "gentleman's agreement" reached in 1904 between the Columbia trustees and the German-Jewish mining entrepreneur Adolf Lewisohn when he offered to make a gift of $200,000 for a building to house the School of Mines. The board accepted the gift, but not before specifying that the building not bear his name. This stipulation, which Lewisohn accepted, was said to comport with a tradition that no university building should be named for someone still living; its real purpose, others said, was to keep the university from attaching a Jewish name to any of its buildings. But with Schiff having died five years earlier, Meyer argued that the building's donor should be appropriately acknowledged, but to no avail. Students' Hall became Barnard Hall.[31]

Sometime in the early 1930s, Meyer decided that the story of Barnard's beginnings could be told only by telling it herself. An accomplished writer and journalist and assiduous keeper of documents, including a journal of her early years, she was singularly equipped for the role of Barnard's first in-house historian. With Plimpton the only other participant during the college's early years still alive, she might well have been commissioned by her fellow trustees to write such a history. It bears noting that she was not.

Barnard Beginnings appeared in the spring of 1935 from Houghton Mifflin, the publisher of two of Meyer's earlier books. It drew almost entirely on the author's own memory of events and on relevant documents in her possession. There is no indication that she interviewed anyone else about events leading up to or following immediately upon the college's founding. Nor does it appear that she shared drafts of her history with those who had an interest in the college. The result was decidedly one person's account, with almost everything that transpired in the making of Barnard either beginning with or ending with the author. Self-referential and opinionated to be sure, aggrandizing on occasion, and possibly slighting of the role of others also present at the creation, but as institutional histories go (a modest threshold), *Barnard Beginnings* is eminently readable and factually reliable.[32]

Early reviews of *Barnard Beginnings* in the general press were respectful and generally positive. The chief exception was the three-paragraph review that appeared in the November 1936 issue of *Barnard College Alumnae Monthly*. Unsigned, it was likely written by the *Monthly*'s editors, Helen Chamberlain and Helen Erskine, both devoted admirers of Gildersleeve and in the employ of the college. To add insult to injury, the review appeared side-by-side with a glowing review of Caroline Spurgeon's "remarkable" and just published *Shakespeare's Imagery*, written and signed by Dean Virginia Gildersleeve. After complimenting Meyer for pulling together materials relating to Barnard's founding, the review took exception to the publisher's dust jacket comment that it is the story of a "one woman fight for an idea." "It is one woman's story of the fight," the review allowed, "but certainly not 'a one woman fight' as Mrs. Meyer should be the first to insist."[33] Warming to the task, the reviewer(s) turned the second paragraph into an all-out assault:

> The chronological sequence of events is confused by the author's many digressions, digressions which make of the book a complete autobiography, an intensely personal picture of the author, her activities and her opinions in the 1880's and 90's. For this reason the book is in no sense a complete or altogether accurate history of the early days of Barnard.[34]

The review concluded with a call upon the *Alumnae Monthly*'s readers to produce "a complete and accurate history," one that would make more room for the roles of Ella Weed, Dean Smith, and Treasurer Plimpton, but also for "our present dean [NB: twelve at the college's founding!], whose influence on the lives and thoughts of Barnard students for the past twenty-five years has been incalculable. It is a great story crying to be written."[35]

To this revisionist task was assigned Gildersleeve's college classmate and friend, the poet, author, and screenwriter Alice Durer Miller (class of 1899), and another college friend and the dean's longtime personal secretary, Susan Myers (class of 1898). Their brief *Barnard College: The First Fifty Years* duly appeared three years later in 1939. The two subsequent official histories published in 1954 and 1962 adhered closely to the Miller-Meyers handling of Barnard's founding, wherein Annie Meyer's role is as one of many. None of these histories directly challenged anything claimed in *Barnard Beginnings*. Along with a retelling in *It's Been Fun*, her autobiography published posthumously with no mention of what she called in her journal "the sly, hateful review," Meyer's remains the fullest and most human telling of Barnard's origins.[36]

CALLS AWAY

Second only to the perennially gallivanting President Butler, Dean Gildersleeve may have been the most traveled American academic of the interwar period. In addition to annual summer visits to England, she regularly managed trips to Europe and parts farther south and east. In the early 1930s, Italy became a favorite repeat destination. There, again second only to Butler, whose position as head of the Carnegie Endowment for Peace assured him visits with Pope Pius XI and Mussolini, Gildersleeve, as a representative of the International Federation of University Women, was shown every consideration by leading university administrators and government officials. Reports on these visits regularly appeared in *Barnard Alumnae*, and they occasionally touched on Italy's political situation without criticism of Mussolini's Fascist regime, which Butler had on several occasions in the late 1920s and early 1930s extravagantly praised. In 1930, Gildersleeve did report approvingly to alumnae that "the strong arm of the fascist government has finally made inland Sicily safe for foreign travelers." When an editorial in April 1934 in the *Barnard Bulletin* criticized President Butler for his failure to criticize Hitler, Gildersleeve defended him in a letter to the editor as "a brave, sincere, and tireless worker for peace."[37]

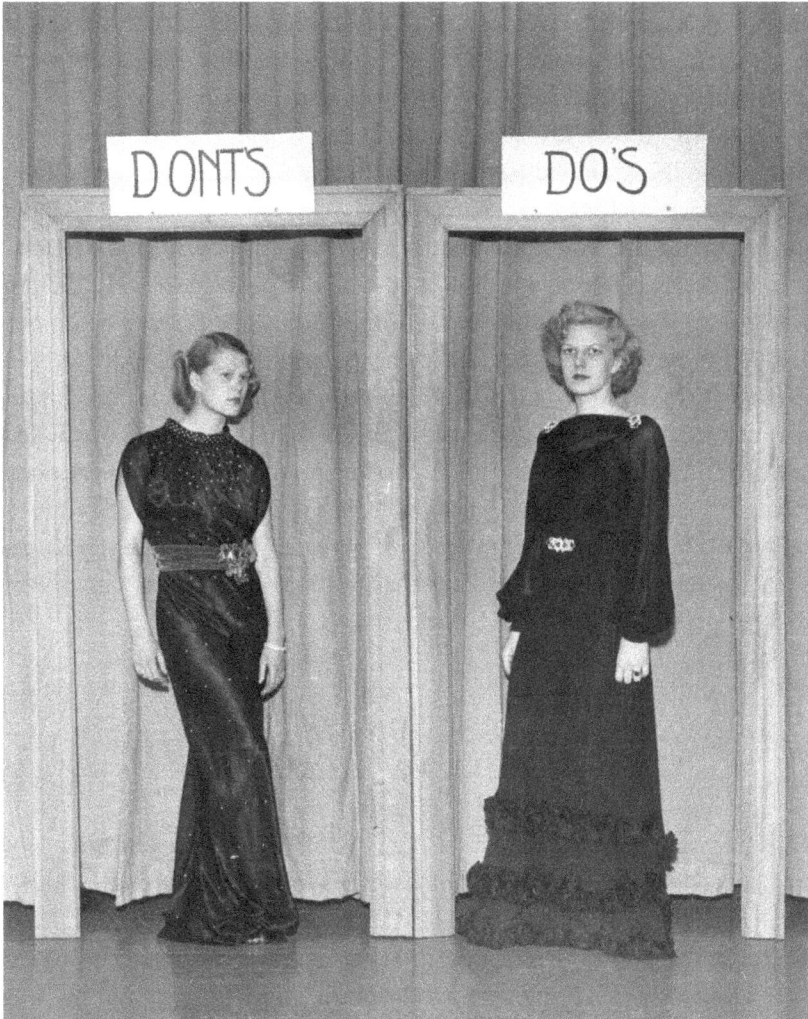

FIGURE 6.2 Posture do's and don'ts, 1930s, Barnard Archives.

A Gildersleeve visit to Germany in the summer of 1934, officially on International Federation of University Women (IFUW) business and within months of Hitler's coming to power, garnered more attention. The *New York Times* had a reporter at dockside when the dean disembarked in September to seek her reactions to the new order in Germany. Her remarks allowed the impression that she sympathized with Germany's need for "natural expansion" and that German restrictions on Jewish admissions to universities were economically justifiable because "professions were apparently overcrowded." A follow-up interview by a *Barnard Alumnae Magazine* staffer came away with a somewhat different account but not sufficiently different to satisfy subsequent critics.[38]

Closer to home, calls came regularly all through the 1930s from city hall, where the dean had become a particular favorite of Mayor Fiorello LaGuardia, as well as from Albany from governors Roosevelt and Lehman for her to head up one committee or another, or to sit on one commission or another. She seldom declined her services, considering them a way to keep Barnard in the news. A supporter of the League of Nations and a loyal New Deal Democrat, having campaigned for Franklin Delano Roosevelt (FDR) in 1932 and again in 1936, she was also on call for all manner of national service. Some of these assignments could be carried out from her Barnard office, but others required her to spend time away from campus for days or weeks at a time. She was also committed to periodic visits to Arizona, where Caroline Spurgeon had moved upon retirement in hopes of finding the dry climate restorative. New York City seems to have lost its hold on Dean Gildersleeve.[39]

BARNARD AND THE GOOD WAR

Gildersleeve's desire for public service only increased after war broke out in Europe in September 1939. She soon made her interventionist views public by joining the Committee to Aid the Allies along with Alice Duer Miller. In sharp contrast to her position before American entry into World War I, but very much in line with President Butler's turnabout, she was especially anxious in 1940 to have the United States come to the immediate aid of Britain, which, since 1920, was her second home. The sentiments of the concluding stanza of Alice Duer Miller's poem, "The White Cliffs of Dover," were also the dean's:

> I am American bred,
> I have seen much to hate here—much to forgive,
> But in a world where England is finished and dead,
> I do not wish to live.[40]

When American entry into the war came with the Japanese attack on Pearl Harbor in December 1941, the now sixty-four-year-old dean placed herself at her nation's call for the duration. As adviser to the Navy's efforts to recruit women to serve in noncombat roles, she recommended Elizabeth Reynard, a member of the Barnard English Department and soon to be her companion, for a commission in the newly organized Navy-affiliated Women Accepted for Volunteer Emergency Service (WAVES). She also encouraged Barnard alumnae to sign up for government service as cryptographers, translators, and intelligence operatives. With victory in sight in the spring of 1945 and only days before his death, President Roosevelt asked Gildersleeve to be a delegate to a conference planned for August in San Francisco to found the United Nations. She was to be the only woman asked to serve and she agreed to do so, despite the extensive preparation required leading up to the conference. Once in San Francisco, she took an active role in shaping the Charter of the United Nations. After that, she served on a commission to advise the Japanese and the American occupation authorities on educational reforms.

Meanwhile, at least a dozen members of the Barnard faculty joined the military or served the war effort in some civilian capacity. And unlike World War I and all America's wars to follow, campus sentiment throughout World War II was united as to the righteousness of the cause.[41]

DO NOT GO GENTLE

Dean Gildersleeve had long planned to retire when she reached age sixty-five in 1942. In recurrent ill health since 1931, she subsequently experienced two heart attacks, and she was emotionally drained by the lingering illness and death in 1941 of Caroline Spurgeon, her compan-ion of twenty-four years. When she informed Butler of her intentions, the then eighty-three-year-old president, himself deaf and partially blind, insisted she remain in place until he left office. Ever dutiful to him, she agreed. In staying on for what turned out to be another five years (Butler was forced into retirement in 1945), her last years in office saw her entan-gled in four different controversies, none of which added to her legacy.[42]

The first was in regard to race. Between 1925, when at the urging and with the funding of Annie Nathan Meyer, Zora Neale Hurston enrolled as a junior transfer, and 1942, Barnard admitted only twelve Black students. Of these, eight stayed on to graduate, two of whom, Belle Tobias, class of 1931, and Vera Joseph, class of 1932, were elected to Phi Beta Kappa. This was substantially fewer Black women then attending either Wellesley or Smith. At no time during these eighteen years were there more than two Black women in any Barnard class. None were allowed to live on campus. Given Barnard's location abutting Harlem, the largest Black community in the United States, and the fact that dozens of Black girls graduated every year from Harlem high schools and went on to Hunter College, the record is at least suggestive of intentional discrimination.[43]

In 1943, Rev. James Robinson, pastor of a Harlem congregation, at an interfaith conference held at Teachers College, publicly charged Barnard with maintaining a quota for Black women, a maximum of four every two years. Gildersleeve immediately denied the accusation. "This is quite untrue," she wrote in a letter reprinted in the *Barnard Bulletin*. "We have no Negro quota. We never receive many applications for admission from Negroes. If we are going to have a quota, we certainly would not have such a foolish one as that reported in the strange rumor which seems to have reached you." She then went beyond the historical record in assuring Rev. Robinson and *Barnard Bulletin* readers that "[w]e always have some Negro students in Barnard."[44]

Privately, however, Gildersleeve informed Robinson that Barnard was prepared to offer a full tuition scholarship to a deserving Black student of his choosing, which Robinson then proceeded to produce in the person of Charlotte Hanley, a graduate of Yonkers High School who was prepar-ing to attend Hunter College. Hanley entered Barnard in the fall of 1943, graduating with her class in 1947. An economics major, she later became the first African American hired at the Federal Reserve Bank of Chicago as an economist, becoming assistant vice president. (She later served on the Barnard Board of Trustees from 1977 to 1984.) Yet the historical judgment on Gildersleeve's treatment of African Americans, if equivocal, has not been exculpatory. "The primary reason Barnard had so few Black students," historian Linda Perkins has written, "was that Black women believed the school did not welcome them."[45]

The second controversy in which the about-to-retire Gildersleeve became embroiled involved the future place of the world's displaced and persecuted Jews. Since the 1880s, Zionists argued that Palestine should be that place. But it was only with the revelations about Nazi atrocities against Jews during World War II that some leading American political leaders aligned themselves with the Zionist cause. All through the 1930s, the *New York Times*, owned by the husband of Barnard trustee Iphigene Ochs Sulzberger, had opposed the creation of a Jewish state. Other Americans known for their support of various philanthropies in the Middle East, including Barnard trustees George A. Plimpton and Rev. Harry Emerson Fosdick, also actively opposed the creation of Israel. But many of these opponents, in light of the compelling evidence that Hitler had killed millions of Jews and concerned that continued opposition would be interpreted as anti-Semitism, either muffled their criticisms of the plan or now subscribed to it. Not so Gildersleeve. A letter she wrote to the *New York Times* in October 9, 1945, as Congress was taking up the issue of Israel, both made clear the reasoning behind her anti-Zionism—that it came at the cost of the Arabs residing in the land being claimed—and undercut whatever latter-day progress she might have made convincing Barnard's Jewish constituency (and some scholars) that she was not an anti-Semite.[46]

The third controversy at the end of Gildersleeve's deanship combined elements of the first two: charges of discrimination and insinuations of anti-Semitism. While directed more at and played out on the Columbia side of Broadway, legislative efforts led by Jewish organizations in 1946 to have Columbia's state charter revoked because of past discrimination against Jewish applicants applied to Barnard as well. Both Butler in retirement and Gildersleeve in her last months as dean denied that their institutions had practiced discrimination. (Butler simultaneously directed a selective purge of relevant university records.) Legislative censure of Columbia and Barnard was avoided by a deal brokered by the Catholic

Archdiocese of New York between the private universities and Governor Thomas Dewey whereby the state would not press its discrimination case if the universities agreed to drop their opposition to the governor's proposed expansion of the State University of New York. Meanwhile, by common accord, whatever discriminatory practices might have been used by private universities and colleges in the past against Jews were to end.[47]

The last controversy was arguably the most personally demeaning. It involved the selection of her successor. In 1942, a delegation of Barnard trustees, in anticipation of the dean's retirement, had identified a possible successor in the headmistress of the Brearley School, Millicent Carey McIntosh, the wife of Dr. Rustin McIntosh, dean of the Columbia Babies Hospital. As the seasoned head of an East Side private girls school favored by the city's wealthy families, she impressed the trustees with her administrative experience and fundraising potential. At the time, McIntosh showed little interest in the job and, when Gildersleeve decided to stay on, the search was suspended. Four years later, with Gildersleeve set to leave, and McIntosh still uncertain that she wanted to leave Brearley, her candidacy was reactivated.[48]

Upon hearing who her successor might be, and ignoring the academic convention that outgoing administrators recuse themselves in the selection of their successor, Gildersleeve proposed an alternative candidate, Elizabeth Reynard (class of 1922) a member of the Barnard English Department since 1922, a founder of Barnard's American Civilization program in 1939, and during World War II (at Gildersleeve's nomination) assistant director of the WAVES. She had also been, since shortly after Caroline Spurgeon's death in 1942, Gildersleeve's live-in companion, although she was twenty-three years Gildersleeve's junior.[49]

Both the search committee and McIntosh regarded Gildersleeve's intrusion into the selection process as inappropriate. They thought Reynard unqualified as an administrator, as evidenced by her poor performance as program director and naval officer. She also had demonstrated no talent for or interest in fundraising. Her appointment would also undercut the search committee's determination to come up with a wife and mother who would counter Gildersleeve's public image as a critic of marriage and champion of the single life. Shortly after McIntosh accepted the deanship, Reynard resigned from Barnard and spent the rest of her life with Gildersleeve, first in Bedford, New York, and then on Reynard's native Cape Cod. She died in 1962, three years before Gildersleeve's death. Only once in retirement did Gildersleeve ever return to Barnard. She did allow, however, upon the selection of the then single and scholarly Rosemary Park to succeed Millicent McIntosh in 1962, that Park was in keeping "with Barnard tradition." McIntosh did not miss the dig.[50]

Might Gildersleeve's deanship have ended more serenely if it had happened earlier? What if, in 1931, instead of staying on for another fifteen years, she had resigned when she first became seriously ill? Butler, still fit himself, would likely have let her leave. Her departure would have been received by the Barnard community as regrettable but understandable, and her accomplishments, especially in securing Barnard a greater measure of national recognition, would have been duly acknowledged. She might even have received credit for Barnard's stable—at that point— finances. Her standing as the most recognizable woman in higher education would have been universally acknowledged. After two decades as dean, but only fifty-four, she could have permanently settled with Cara on one side or the other of the Atlantic, instead of them continually shuttling back and forth. Had her health permitted, and depending on where they took up residence, she could have kept her hand in Democratic politics and Middle East affairs when in the United States, or, when abroad, in the business of the IFUW. And best of all, she would not have had to oversee Barnard during the Great Depression, when so much of what she seemed to have accomplished in her first two decades as dean unraveled.

She might as well have been spared the critical assessments of her personality that attended her later deanship. Emma Stecher, class of 1925, who returned to Barnard in 1946 as a member of the Chemistry Department in 1946, later recalled how Gildersleeve "held aloof from most students and most faculty." An entering freshman in 1939, Barbara Valentine Hertz, class of 1943, agreed. "She welcomed you all to Barnard and I think that was the last time I ever saw her. She was very busy." John Kouwenhoven, who joined the English Department in 1946 following four years of wartime service, later described Gildersleeve as "a quite terrifying person, really. . . . A rather dark and ominous figure." He recalled her handshake technique to discourage guests from holding up the procession, that it had "turned me through two quadrants of a circle and quite unsettled the grace of my exit from her office." Kouwenhoven's department colleague Eleanor Rosenberg remembered her as "respected, admired, somewhat

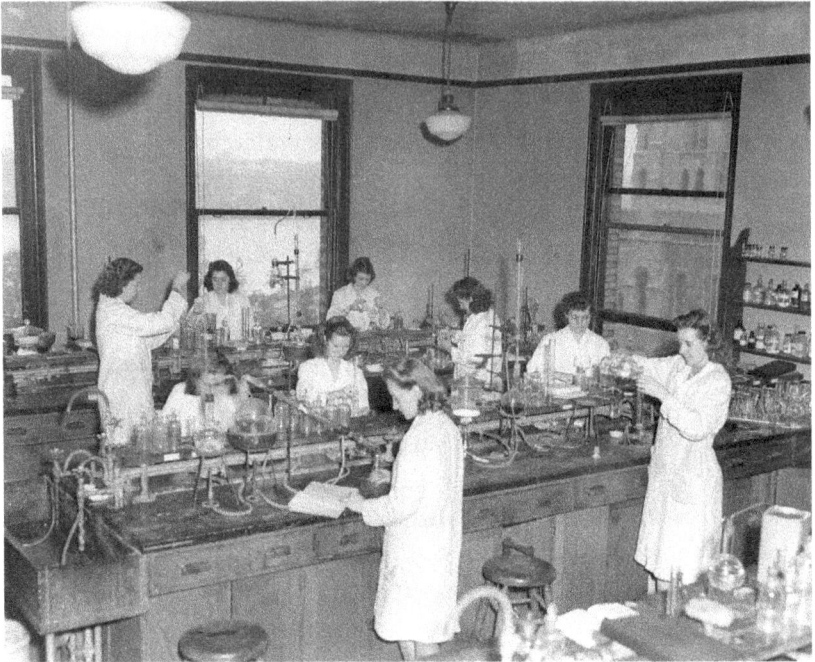

FIGURE 6.3 Organic chemistry lab, Milbank Hall, 1940s. Barnard Archives.

feared, and seemed almost completely detached." The art historian Julius Held, a refugee from Hitler's Europe who taught under five different Barnard administrative heads, allowed that "none . . . were ever as much a ruling figure as was Dean Gildersleeve."[51]

So why didn't Gildersleeve pull the plug? It bears noting that she seriously considered doing so. As the full impact of the Depression first revealed itself, Gildersleeve in 1931 seems to have experienced something of a personal crisis of confidence. Akin to Butler's pronouncement that same year on the collapse of the American financial system, that maybe Mussolini's was the better way, Gildersleeve worried aloud about the fallout from "the hectic flush of the twenties" and "whether there has not been some dire deficiency in the education provided the last 20 or 30 years in our secondary schools." At other times, in her later years as dean, she appeared to take less interest in the day-to-day management of the college, gradually turning over functions to a still small (by subsequent standards) but growing cadre of administrative assistants.[52]

Keeping herself at the wheel was in keeping with the example set by the three most important men in her life. Her father, Henry Alger Gildersleeve, worked well into his seventies; her academic mentor, Nicholas Murray Butler, did so into his eighties and then had to be told to retire; her treasurer and friend, George A. Plimpton, died at seventy-eight still in the service of Ginn & Company, Barnard, Amherst College, and a string of philanthropies. And then there was the negative example of her beloved brother Harry, whose life ended at twenty-one before his life's work began.

What likely kept Gildersleeve in the Barnard deanship is what she said prompted her to take it on in the first place: "my reluctance to have another stranger come in as Miss Gill had done and mess up my College again." However later generations may judge her personal shortcomings and ideological blind spots, her commitment to Barnard College was lifelong and unconditional. Her college pal and lifetime friend, Alice Duer Miller, on the occasion of the college's fiftieth anniversary in 1939, admonished Barnard alumnae: "Don't ever dare to take your college as a matter of course—because, like freedom and democracy, many people you'll never know anything about have broken their hearts to get it for you." None who labored for the college did so as assiduously and none for so as long as Virginia Gildersleeve, "this flower from Barnard's own garden."

7

AGAINST NOSTALGIA

The McIntosh Era

Never be on the subway without a book in your hand.

—MILLICENT McINTOSH[1]

T he two decades after World War II seem in retrospect for Barnard a period of unusual rapport among faculty members, students, trustees, and administrators. Alumnae of the period regularly recall it as such. This singularly placid interlude in an otherwise tumultuous saga can be credited in part to the consensual national mood of the postwar period, the blight of McCarthyism notwithstanding. During these years, Columbia allowed Barnard to set its own course, which contributed to the general sense of wellbeing. But so, too, did the attentive and sensitive leadership of Dean (and later President) Millicent C. McIntosh. And while all three favorable conditions persisted into the early 1960s, and have since cast a nostalgic glow over the period, each took time lining up.

MRS. MAC

Upon President Butler's retirement at age eighty-three in 1945, the sixty-eight-year-old Dean Gildersleeve secured her own release. One local possibility to succeed her remained Millicent Carey McIntosh, the forty-nine-year-old headmistress of the Brearley School. McIntosh had been approached by trustee Helen Rogers Reid in 1942 when Gildersleeve broached the subject of retiring, but she had expressed no interest in the job. When asked again in 1946, and again by Reid in the company of Agnes Ernst Meyer, class of 1909, McIntosh again demurred. Only after talking with her husband, who told her, "You might regret not having taken this job for the rest of your life," did she reconsider.[2]

A native of Baltimore, Maryland, Millicent Carey McIntosh came from that city's civic-minded Quaker gentry. Her father was a manufacturer and her mother a member of Bryn Mawr College's first graduating class (1889), the mother of six children who pursued a lifelong interest in prison reform and civic activism. McIntosh attended the Bryn Mawr School in Baltimore, where she learned Greek from the noted classicist Edith Hamilton, before proceeding to Bryn Mawr College, where her mother's sister, M. Carey Thomas, was president. Upon graduation in 1920, disappointing her aunt by ranking only third in her class, and following a stint of social work in England, she returned to Baltimore to Johns Hopkins University, where she earned a PhD in English in 1926.[3]

McIntosh then returned to Bryn Mawr as an assistant professor of English. In addition to teaching, she took on administrative responsibilities and found them to her liking. "I'm not, by nature, a scholar," she later acknowledged. "I have a good scholarly background, but that's quite different." Three years into her appointment and with no top administrative post at Bryn Mawr in sight, she agreed to talk with the trustees of the Brearley School, New York City's most academically demanding and socially exclusive independent girls' school, about their vacant headmistress position. They hired her. Two years into the job, McIntosh announced her pending marriage.[4]

Her husband-to-be, Dr. Rustin McIntosh, was an up-and-coming pediatrician and administrator at the Columbia-affiliated New York Babies Hospital. Once married, they proceeded in rapid order to produce four boys, two of them twins, and a girl. The youngest, their only daughter, Alice, was seven when the Barnard search committee, represented by the trustees Reid and Meyer, along with Professor of German Hugh Wiley Puckett, came calling. McIntosh's academic credentials; administrative experience; familiarity with New York's wealthy; and, not least, her domestic situation as a wife and mother, all commended her to the two trustees on the search committee. The board was especially keen on the prospect of a married woman, having grown weary of complaints from parents about Miss Gildersleeve's jaundiced view of the marital state, and of someone for family reasons likely to stay in town.[5]

Some faculty members, including Puckett, were less impressed, holding her years as head of an elementary and secondary school, even the academically demanding Brearley, as disqualifying. Meanwhile, Gildersleeve continued to press for her companion Elizabeth Reynard. In the end, the committee chose McIntosh, the board concurred. and disappointed faculty members took to their tents to await developments.

WOLF AT THE DOOR

Calling on Gildersleeve after her election but before her installation, Dean-elect McIntosh heard for the first time the true state of Barnard's financial affairs. The college needed an immediate infusion of $10 million. A labor contract with the newly unionized facilities staff, repairs to buildings whose maintenance had been deferred by the Depression and the war, the need for a third dormitory, and the imperative to raise faculty salaries or risk losing the college's best young teachers: all these issues required immediate attention.

None of the trustees during the search process indicated anything near as dire a situation as Gildersleeve described. McIntosh later concluded that they likely did not know because Gildersleeve and her chief financial officer, John J. Swan, a retired naval officer well into his seventies, had systematically spared them the bad news. The $1,400,000 operating budget Dean McIntosh inherited in the fall of 1947 included an anticipated deficit of $135,000. "Had I known the true state of affairs at Barnard when offered the position as its dean," she later reminisced, "I might well have stayed at Brearley."[6]

Part of the financial problem turned on the college's aging physical plant. In 1947, then in its fiftieth year on Morningside, the plant consisted of a four-and-a-half-acre campus bisected north and south by 119th Street, about a quarter of it occupied by four substantial buildings:

—Milbank Hall (1897), four stories, housing administrative offices, faculty offices, and classrooms
—Brooks Hall (1907), eleven stories, serving as a dormitory for 100 residents
—Barnard Hall, (1917), four stories, serving as a student center as well as an academic space for athletics, faculty offices, classrooms, and the Ella Weed Library
—Hewitt Hall (1925), eight stories, serving as Barnard's second dormitory for 250 students; its northern end consisted of the Deanery where Gildersleeve had resided

All four buildings needed repair, with the fifty-year-old Milbank Hall requiring a major renovation. The most recent addition to Barnard's building stock, Hewitt, dated back more than two decades.

The land not taken up by buildings consisted of four tennis courts, open space, and an overgrown section referred to as the jungle. The college also owned the vacant corner lot across Claremont from Milbank Hall on the southwest corner of 120th Street and Riverside Drive, a gift of the Rockefeller-funded General Education Board in 1936, for which funds to build upon remained wanting.[7]

Meanwhile, the wider Morningside neighborhood was showing its age, with many of the once handsome pre–World War I apartment buildings along Riverside Drive, Broadway, and Morningside Drive and on the cross streets between Ninety-Sixth and 125th Streets now cut up into ever smaller units until some had fallen into such disrepair as to be rentable only as single-room occupancies (SROs). Other buildings were abandoned by landlords unable to pay the taxes on them. Some became occupied by squatters and put to various illegal uses, including prostitution and the sale of drugs. Efforts to stem the neighborhood's decline became a prime consideration for all its institutional landlords, not least Columbia University and the Rockefeller-funded Riverside Church. Both made extensive defensive investments in residential and commercial real estate.[8]

Trustee Agnes Ernst Meyer, class of 1909, journalist, civil rights activist, art patron, and wife of the publisher of the *Washington Post*, was a member of the dean search committee. Yet she remained uninformed about the state of Barnard's finances in 1946, which speaks to the board's minimal involvement in the college's management during the later years of Gildersleeve's deanship. In the 1920s and 1930s, the board had been chaired successively by three distinguished attorneys, all senior partners in leading New York law firms—John George Milburn (1918–1930), James Rockwell Sheffield (1931–1937), and Lucius Hart Beers (1938–1947). All deferred to the dean on most matters, as did other male members of the board. Board treasurer Francis T. P. Plimpton told a prospective biographer of Gildersleeve in 1952 that "she babied the trustees too much, and they had little knowledge of what was going on inside the college." Among the women trustees, Helen Rogers Reid and Agnes Ernst Meyer were the most knowledgeable about the state of the college but not up to questioning Gildersleeve. "My only lasting contribution," Meyer wrote in her autobiography in reference to Barnard, "was made when Helen Rogers Reid and I sat on Millicent McIntosh's doorstep until she consented to be the successor of our distinguished retiring dean Virginia Gildersleeve."[9]

Once apprised of the situation, the trustees and their new dean promptly launched the aptly named Operation Bootstraps, a development campaign to raise $2,000,000. This was the first Barnard campaign in which trustee members (other than Plimpton back in the day) took active roles in the solicitation process. They were led by Reid, who became Barnard's first female trustee chair in 1947, and Helen Goodhart Altschul, class of 1907, a recently reengaged alumna who was elected to the board in 1949. Both became major contributors to the campaign and encouraged other trustees, not heretofore distinguished by their benefactions, to do likewise. A development officer was hired; a fundraising pamphlet was produced; and McIntosh, Reid, and Altschul enthusiastically took to the mendicant trail. The development officer, Jean T. Palmer, a Bryn Mawr graduate and no-nonsense administrator who had been an officer in the Women Accepted for Volunteer Emergency Service (WAVES) and initially hired as admissions director, stayed on at Barnard as general secretary of the college into the early 1970s. By 1950, the campaign had secured $1,700,000 in gifts from 1,400 donors. The contrast with the half hearted fundraising efforts of the Gildersleeve years and the willingness of previously resistant Jewish alumnae to support the college did not go unnoted.[10]

A $50,000 gift in 1949 from Mr. and Mrs. Eugene Meyer to build an annex to Barnard Hall started a wave of gift giving by serving trustees, which culminated in the early 1960s. The fact that the Meyers, his parents Alsatian Jews, along with Helen Goodhart Altschul, the daughter of German Jews, led the way signaled to Barnard's Jewish alumnae and the wider New York City Jewish community that Dean Gildersleeve had left the building. It is also noteworthy that the Meyers' gift was for a building not designed to attract residential students from outside the region but to improve the lives of Barnard's long-neglected commuting students by providing them with an on-campus social space of their own. Meanwhile, to contain the cost of boarding, Brooks and Hewitt residents became responsible for their own linen. What Anderson or Elsie de Wolfe or Dean Gildersleeve might have thought of this déclassé cut in services went unmentioned.[11]

The largest single gift of the Operation Bootstraps campaign came from John D. Rockefeller Jr. Asking was assigned to McIntosh and involved several detailed discussions with Rockefeller Foundation officials before a personal visit was scheduled. When that day came in the spring of 1950, the dean brought along her then nine-year-old daughter Alice, home from the Putney School in Vermont. When the seventy-five-year-old Rockefeller spotted her in the waiting room and was introduced, he and Alice immediately fell into a detailed discussion of machinery used to milk cows. "He's very much like a farmer," Alice said after the visit, without knowing that in the course of their chat, "the farmer" had doubled his intended gift of $500,000 to a million.[12]

The Rockefeller gift came in Standard Oil Company bonds, which provided an annual yield of 9 percent, or $90,000, enough to cover the anticipated shortfall in the 1949–1950 budget. With no matching requirement, it was singularly responsive to the college's immediate needs. McIntosh later called it for Barnard "one of the most strategic gifts that was ever made." Three years later, the same John D. Rockefeller Jr. pressed Barnard to sell back the still-unbuilt-upon Riverside and 120th Street site for $510,000 so that the Rockefeller-financed Interchurch Center building could be constructed on it. Barnard acceded. "Some people felt very bitterly about it," McIntosh recalled in 1966. "But I didn't feel bitterly, because I knew he had really saved us."[13]

In 1951, two developments occurred that marked Barnard's belated entry into the era of twentieth-century fundraising. The first was a gift of $300,000 (later raised to $500,000) from trustee Helen Goodhart Altschul to underwrite the college's first internally endowed chair, the Millicent McIntosh Professorship in English. The inaugural chair holder was professor of English Cabell Greet, an expert on pronunciation of English, followed upon his retirement by David A. Robertson Jr., a scholar of nine-teenth-century English travel literature. The gift allowed Barnard to pay its holder what was then the college's highest faculty salary of $10,000 ($129,000 in 2019). The second development was to establish the Barnard Fund, an annual appeal to alumnae that, by 1956, had raised $2,370,000.[14]

It was the imperative of fundraising—as McIntosh discovered in early 1953, when seeking funding from the Ford Foundation—that led the Bar-nard trustees to secure agreement from the Columbia trustees to change the title of head of the college from dean to president. The former title, Ford officials told her, normally applied to the head of a school within a university and put into question Barnard's institutional autonomy and thus its claims to funding considerations distinct from those of Colum-bia. *President* bespoke the head of a freestanding college. The Columbia trustees and their newly inaugurated President Grayson Kirk promptly acceded to the request. Dean emerita Gildersleeve opposed the title change as minimizing Barnard's ties to Columbia but to no avail. On June 30, 1953, Millicent McIntosh became the last dean to be head of Bar-nard College, and a day later its first president. Two years later, when the Ford Foundation distributed $500,000,000 in faculty-support funding to 200 freestanding private colleges, Barnard received $900,000. The same year, upon the retirement of John J. Swan as comptroller, Forest "Duke" Abbott, already on the staff, became the college's chief financial officer.[15]

"A STUDENT BODY AS VARIED AND INTERESTING AS NEW YORK ITSELF"

For all Gildersleeve's tireless efforts to nationalize the Barnard student body, the college she left to her successor in 1947 retained a distinctly local and nonprivileged character. It consisted of just under 1,200 women, half of them New York City residents. Two out of three Barnard students commuted to campus, half of them from one of the five boroughs, with others trekking in from surrounding towns within a thirty-mile radius of Morningside Heights. Less than 10 percent of the graduating class of 1947 hailed from outside the Northeast.[16]

Some commuters did so by choice, but for many the 1947 tuition of $700 already strained family resources. Even with a Regents scholarship and after the first-year, merit-based financial assistance from the college, an additional $500 for room and board would have made attendance prohibitive for a large number of commuters. Financial assistance with room and board remained limited to students coming from outside New York City, a policy dating back to the start of the Gildersleeve era. Many commuters had jobs in their neighborhoods, while some residents worked part-time on campus or downtown. As for latter-day equivalents of the Social Register girls that Zora Neale Hurston recalled meeting at Barnard in the mid-1920s, they were noticeable mostly in their absence.[17]

Somewhere between a quarter and a third of the Barnard students in 1947 were either Jewish or Catholic, with a likely majority of them first in their families to attend college. A plurality were the children of immigrants. The college enrolled fewer legacies—the daughters of Barnard graduates—than did any of the other Seven Sister colleges. Fewer still were graduated from private schools, either the private girls' day schools clustered on the city's East Side—Brearley, Spence, Nightingale—or nationally known boarding schools. Approximately 70 percent of Barnard students in the early 1950s had attended public schools, half of them in New York City public high schools. Of those with Manhattan addresses, only a few were from the wealthy East Side, with most from the less affluent reaches of Upper Manhattan and the West Side. Students from lower-middle-class neighborhoods in the Bronx and Queens outnumbered those from the more comfortable Westchester suburbs.[18]

This socioeconomic profile of Barnard students was markedly different from those McIntosh had known at Bryn Mawr or Brearley. Yet her response was not, as Gildersleeve's had been in 1911, to try to make Barnard more like Bryn Mawr or Brearley. Instead, she chose to applaud the college's acquired distinctiveness. "We are blessed," she declared in her inauguration, "with a student body as varied and as interesting as New York itself."[19]

McIntosh's decision at the outset of her deanship may have been an acceptance of the situation as she found it. But almost immediately she demonstrated an easy acceptance of—even pride in—what distinguished Barnard from wealthier and more socially comfortable schools. "Because of the nature of our student body," she told the trustees in 1949 as part of a larger discussion on setting the tuition rate, "it is probably better for us to be a little under some of our more plutocratic women's colleges." "We have always drawn from the lower economic groups," she proudly told her interviewer in 1966: "Barnard has never been a fashionable college."[20]

A confidential report commissioned by the Educational Testing Service at the request of the Seven Sister colleges in 1952 confirms Barnard's unique position within the sisterhood. Postwar Barnard attracted fewer applicants than any of the other sister colleges except for Bryn Mawr, which was substantially smaller and whose applicants were the least likely to limit themselves, as nearly two out of every three Barnard applicants did, to a single application. Most women who applied to Barnard in the 1950s did not do so because it was part of an elite collegiate sisterhood but rather because of its academic standing, propinquity, and economy.[21]

Other findings support the notion that postwar Barnard applicants came from less affluent and less distant circumstances than those applying to the other sister colleges. Nearly a third (32 percent) of Barnard applicants requested financial assistance, a substantially higher percentage than any but Radcliffe's applicants. Only 15 percent of Smith's applicants and only 20 percent of Wellesley's sought financial assistance. With four of the sister colleges located in New England and three in the Mid-Atlantic region, all attracted substantially more applicants outside their respective region than did Barnard, with an outside-the-Northeast applicant pool of only 12 percent, half that for all the other sister colleges. Finally, a breakdown of applicants by the type of secondary schools they attended had nearly three-quarters of Barnard applicants coming from public high schools, whereas only about half of the applicants of the other sister colleges did so. When the Middles States Accreditation Committee visited Barnard in 1960, its chair, Jeremiah Finch, from Princeton, to his apparent surprise, discovered that "Barnard is, in fact, predominantly a commuting college."[22]

While the composition of the student body remained consistent, McIntosh's years at Bryn Mawr and Brearley did inspire a new approach in student services. Gildersleeve was very much of the sink-or-swim school and showed little interest in her students' lives beyond the classroom. Academic advising had remained ad hoc and makeshift well into the late 1930s, when it first acquired institutional recognition and formal staffing, with the appointment of Lorna McGuire, a junior member of the English Department, as associate dean for students. Similarly, the provision of health services and psychiatric counseling under Gildersleeve fell outside the realm of college-provided services. All this changed under McIntosh. A college physician was appointed in 1948, and in 1953 a member of the French Department and Barnard alumna, Helen Phelps Bailey (class of

1933), became the college's first dean of studies, with responsibilities that extended beyond academic matters.[23]

A more significant administrative adjustment occurred in the wake of the 1946 state investigation into possible instances of religious discrimination in admissions: the elimination of the University Undergraduate Admissions Committee. The job of recruiting Barnard students, a university-wide function for the last thirty-eight years, was now put back wholly in Barnard's hands. The newly created position of admissions director first fell to Jean Palmer, who held it for three years before being put in charge of development (fundraising). Then the position went briefly to Marion Smith, who soon gave way to her assistant, Helen M. McCann, class of 1940, who became director in 1953. McCann shared her boss's non-elitist perspective on admissions, as suggested by her statement to alumnae in 1955 concerning Barnard's few legacies: "I am not so interested in whether her mother went here or not. I am interested in the daughter."[24]

Barnard's student recruitment effort in the 1950s faced two new challenges. The first was temporary and common to all colleges: the drop in the college-age population attributable to the decline in births during the Great Depression and the war. This resulted in a drop-off in college enrollments throughout the 1950s, particularly among women's colleges, which did not get the offsetting bump from returning veterans that men's and coeducational colleges did. Thus, Barnard annual enrollments declined in the immediate postwar years, from 1,267 in 1946–1947 to 1,046 in 1951–1952. Even with a growing reliance on transfers, graduating classes in the same years stayed around 300. Any modest increases in the mid-1950s came in the face of stark demographic realities.[25]

The second challenge was unique to private women's colleges located in New York City, who relied on the city's high schools for a plurality of their applicants: increasing competition from the state's newly upgraded and publicly supported coeducational colleges. Whereas Hunter College earlier represented Barnard's only tuition-free local competition, the opening of Brooklyn College in 1930 and Queens College in 1937, both coeducational, and the opening of City College to women in 1951, meant that Barnard now had to compete with three taxpayer-supported and academically ambitious institutions situated in the very boroughs from which it drew half its commuting students.[26]

A decade later, beginning in the early 1960s, several once noncompet-
itive state teachers' colleges in the State University of New York (SUNY)
system were upgraded, while others, such as Stony Brook University on
Long Island, were created from scratch. All were soon competing for the
same students from upstate and eastern Long Island, which by the 1950s
provided a quarter of Barnard's enrollments. The proliferation of upstate
campuses (Binghamton, Albany, Buffalo) further threatened to undercut
what had become for Barnard, thanks to the Regents scholarships, an
increasingly fertile recruitment pool. And unlike the nationwide drop in
college-age students, this increased statewide competition came with no
expiration date.[27]

Barnard's response was to mount an aggressive recruitment program
among the city's most academically demanding public schools as well as
parochial and Jewish day schools throughout the New York metropolitan
region. It was at Admissions Director McCann's urging in 1955 that the
faculty begrudgingly accepted Hebrew as a foreign language for purposes
of admission, thus accommodating yeshiva students, after first rejecting
the change on the risible grounds that Hebrew lacked a literature.[28]

A network of Barnard graduates teaching in high schools throughout
the region joined in this recruitment effort. The result was that between
1951 and 1955, Barnard increased its applications from 569 to 991 (74 percent), its admissions from 456 to 585 (28 percent) and its accepted students
from 212 to 309 (46 percent). No apologies were made for the fact that its
admissions rate hovered around 60 percent and that the proportion of
the entering class prepared by public high schools climbed to 75 percent.
Rather than complain, faculty members later recalled these years with
nostalgia. "I remember happily," professor of philosophy Joseph Brennan
recalled in 1977, "all the bright Jewish students of the 1950s who came to
Barnard from the upper 10 percent of the graduating classes of their New
York City high schools. What philosophers they made!"[29]

Despite McIntosh's initial resistance (acting on the advice of the university's rabbi) early in her administration to a student-formulated proposal
for a kosher kitchen, which she later called "my worst political mistake,"
McIntosh's relations with Barnard's Jewish students were marked by
mutual appreciation. One, a transfer from the University of Rochester and
a member of the class of 1962, shared with the author this postcard she
received from Mrs. Mac at the birth of her first daughter:

Dear Hazel,

I was delighted to get the notice of your little daughter's arrival, and to read your note.

I can well understand your joy, and send you my congratulations and best wishes.

You will not want to work until your family are well started.

Yours very sincerely,

Millicent McIntosh.[30]

BARBARA WATSON
Government

FIGURE 7.1 Yearbook photograph of Barbara Mae Watson, Barnard class of 1939, the first black woman to serve as assistant secretary of state, Barnard Archives.

Less commendable in retrospect is Barnard's postwar record enrolling Black women. During McIntosh's fifteen years at the helm, Barnard never had more than a half dozen Black women enrolled at one time. During that period, Barnard averaged one Black graduate per year. None of the other Sister colleges did much better, but given Barnard's urban location abutting Harlem, in a city where in 1960 more than 1,000,000 African Americans resided, it might have done more. The appointment of a Black scholar as a visiting lecturer for one semester in 1949 would not be followed up by a full-time appointment for a decade.[31]

Barnard did better enrolling students from abroad. McIntosh built upon Gildersleeve's initiatives, and several young women from diplomatic families attached to the United Nations attended Barnard in the 1950s, among them Bhinda Malla, class of 1956, the first woman from Nepal to graduate from an American college. That same year, the *Barnard Alumnae*

FIGURE 7.2 Students from Barnard's international exchange program, Barnard Archives.

Magazine reported that Barnard enrolled "more foreign students than any college in the country."[32]

The second half of the McIntosh era was marked by a steady upswing in enrollments, several successes on the fundraising front, a surge in construction on campus, and a period of singularly cordial relations with Columbia. All followed on initiatives undertaken in the first half of the McIntosh era. Between 1952 and 1962, Barnard enrollments increased every year, climbing from 1,046 to 1,549. Admittance rates remained in the 60 percent range, high by subsequent standards, but acceptances from outside the Northeast region modestly increased so that, by the early 1960s, they accounted for a quarter of entering classes. Meanwhile those from within the New York region, reflective of larger demographic trends, were now coming from the surrounding suburbs more so than from Manhattan.[33]

However, the college's distinctly urban ethos remained intact, with the daughters of first- and second-generation American families outnumbering those with longer lineages. Firsts-in-family to attend college were commonplace and public school students the rule, even as a few more daughters of trustees were in attendance than earlier.

A SILENT GENERATION?

Possibly because the sixties generation was so outspoken and critically disposed, college students of the 1950s have been characterized then and since as a silent generation. Philosophy professor Joe Brennan, who taught during this period, viewed the 1950s generation at Barnard as "pretty tame in its desires and aspirations, timid in its respect for the law laid down by the social group." The period seems in retrospect to have been remarkably free of student discord. What little campus attention was given to presidential politics found a majority of polled students in 1952 and again in 1956 favoring Republican Dwight Eisenhower over Democrat Adlai Stevenson. Widespread participation in the civil rights movement was a decade away and opposition to nuclear testing was little evident.[34]

For many students of the 1950s, their energy was focused on extracurricular activities, specifically using their college years to secure a suitable

FIGURE 7.3 Barnard dean Millicent McIntosh (1947–1962) and Columbia president Dwight Eisenhower (1948–1953), 1949, Eisenhower. Barnard Archives.

marriage partner. Many succeeded. Whereas only 4 percent of the class of 1940 were engaged or married at graduation, this was the case with 20 percent of the class of 1960. Substantial numbers of students left before graduation to marry, while others stayed enrolled but moved out of the dorms to be with new husbands, and a substantial portion of transfer students came already married. It may be an exaggeration to say, as some pundits did, that college women of the postwar era were focused on the "Mrs." degree, or as John Updike allowed, "the 50s . . . when everybody was pregnant"—at Barnard many were. Otherwise, it was graduate school and securing a PhD, which Barnard graduates also did all out of proportion to their numbers.[35]

Keeping recently married women in college for four years became both an advising challenge for faculty and an economic imperative for the college. McIntosh encouraged Barnard students to marry and raise families, but she also urged them—and implicitly offering herself as an example—to complete college and acquire the means for economic self-sufficiency first. She also advocated giving the single life, a near requirement for professional careers at the time, serious consideration. In any event, we have the contemporary testimony of Anne Bernays, class of 1957, who became Anne Bernays Kaplan in 1958 by marrying Justin Kaplan, Columbia College class of 1957, that "[t]he girls at Barnard, first of all, are not conformists. They are a bristling crowd of individualists: irritated, cynical, yes; apathetic, perhaps, conformists, no."[36]

A FACULTY IN PLAY

A young member of the all-male pre–World War I Amherst College faculty, John Erskine, described his colleagues as falling into three camps: "old giants," "middle lazies," and "young, soon-to-be-gones." The post–World War II Barnard faculty might be similarly categorized, but with Erskine's tripartite division further complicated by gender.[37]

As discussed earlier, one consequence of the economic distress of the 1930s and the massive dislocations attending World War II was to delay faculty members' departure beyond the normal retirement age. Eight of those staying on into the war years had initial appointments antedating Gildersleeve's deanship. These pre-Gildersleeve "giants" were followed into deferred retirement shortly after the war's end by five others and, soon thereafter, by three more whose appointments came before World War I.[38]

Another factor complicating the faculty situation at the end of the war was the uncertain return of several younger male faculty members who had served in the armed forces. These included mathematician Edgar Lorch, physicist Henry Boorse, geologist Henry Sharp, economist Raymond Saulnier, psychologist Richard Youtz, American historian Basil Rauch, and a member of the English Department, David A. Robertson. Saulnier, Boorse, Youtz, Rauch, and Robertson all returned to Barnard and stayed on for their careers, but their return could not have been assumed.[39]

And then there was uncertainty about the extent to which Columbia would fill its depleted ranks by hiring away Barnard faculty. Lorch and Sharp returned to Barnard in 1946 but shortly thereafter transferred full-time to Columbia, as did three interwar faculty straddlers: musicologist Douglas Moore, Italian scholar Peter Riccio, and English literary biographer James Clifford. Meanwhile, historian James Oliver (1936–1946) did not return to Barnard from wartime service but took up an appointment at the University of California, Los Angeles (UCLA).[40] In all, retirements, transfers, and resignations occurring during the war and immediately thereafter resulted in more than a quarter of the 107 full-time faculty departing from Barnard classrooms from 1940 to the immediate postwar years. Some of these—Shotwell, Montague, Moley, Haller, Moore—had divided their teaching and administrative service between Barnard and Columbia, and were better known through their Columbia affiliation, but had retained professorial standing at Barnard. But others had passed their entire careers at Barnard, with some of the women among them—Maude Hutmann, Jane Perry-Clark Carey, Elizabeth Baker, Gladys Reichard—acquiring outside professional recognition for their scholarship. All labored long and loyally in the college's classrooms. As much as the college's longest-serving trustees and its most committed alumnae, these teachers provided the sinews that bound early Barnard into a vibrant teaching and learning community and helped sustain it through the lean Depression and war years. Like the passing of the deanship from Virginia Gildersleeve to Millicent McIntosh marks an inflection point in the history of the college's leadership, the concentrated departure of the better part of two generations of faculty members and the arrival of a third in the immediate postwar era marks a crucial divide between the Barnard faculty that was and the Barnard faculty that was to be and is.[41]

The situation called for the launching of a faculty replenishment of the sort undertaken by other colleges faced with similar challenges. Instead, McIntosh later ruefully recalled that she spent her first years as dean "cutting down faculty because we were so broke." In 1948, Barnard instruction in astronomy and Portuguese was ceded to Columbia. Responsibility for Italian and mathematics followed shortly after, each subject retaining only a token instructional presence at Barnard. Similarly, all instruction in music, the classics, and physics beyond the introductory level became the responsibility of the cognate Columbia departments.[42]

The imperative of faculty retrenchment became the occasion for a more sweeping overhaul of Barnard's long-standing hiring practices, perhaps the most sweeping in the college's history. In 1948, overriding resistance from her department chairs and six years before Columbia did so, McIntosh put in place at Barnard the Harvard-pioneered up-or-out policy with regard to junior faculty. It required department chairs either to recommend long-serving junior members for tenure, which required attesting to their scholarly accomplishments, or to terminate them. Newly hired assistant professors would now serve a probationary period of six years, after which they would be promoted to a tenured associate professorship or be required to leave. The term of an instructorship, formerly open-ended, was now limited to four years. With the imposition of this policy, the earlier distinction between "faculty," everyone of professorial rank, and "other officers of instruction" gave way to the operative division between "on ladder" and "off ladder" faculty. Once occupationally secure, assistant professors now became probationers, while those serving in the nonprofessorial ranks of lecturer, instructor, and tutor, which earlier included about half Barnard's instructional staff members, were now subject to termination as economic circumstances warranted.[43]

One immediate effect of this new policy was to reduce sharply the number of full-time women instructors, many of whom had been kept on for years because, as McIntosh later put it, "they liked their jobs, and they worked along with starvation wages." Among the faculty members McIntosh inherited in 1947 were a dozen women instructors who had taught at Barnard for nearly a quarter century before being promoted to professorial rank, some only on the eve of their retirement.

While prompted primarily by cost-cutting considerations, adoption of the up-or-out policy—which later mutated to that of publish or perish—turned also on the issue of gender equity. "One of the things I saw," McIntosh recalled of her early days as dean, "was that young women were being kept on as department assistants, without any hope of promotion . . . simply because the heads of departments [almost all male] didn't want to tell them they had to leave." Whatever the immediate costs, in the long run the new policy advanced gender parity within the ranks of the faculty. That McIntosh began to transform the character of the Barnard faculty during a period of serious financial belt tightening and under a trustee mandate not to increase its size presents one of the best early examples in Barnard's history of administrative adherence to the Winston Churchill dictum: "Never let a good crisis go to waste."[44]

Yet it bears noting that many of the older instructors and department heads McIntosh inherited never warmed to her and her ways. Some begrudged her limiting their authority in the matter of staff retention, others for ceding instructional responsibility for "our" subjects to Columbia. Still others suspected McIntosh of favoring Columbia's core curriculum and even a merger with Columbia. Others complained about her expansion of student services, with funds they thought could be better spent on faculty salaries. Behind much of this criticism remained the more fundamental unease of their being led by a school mistress who made no pretense to being a scholar and who downplayed her own PhD by asking to be called Mrs. Mac, noting that her family already had a Dr. McIntosh.[45]

The feeling was mutual, as evidenced by McIntosh's dismissive assessment of the faculty member on the dean search committee and later her chief antagonist, the senior Germanist, Hugh Wiley Puckett. "He had never been anywhere except Columbia," she later recalled. "He had graduated from Columbia, he was a Columbia PhD, he had all his teaching

FIGURE 7.4 Barnard students as Columbia cheerleaders, 1940s. Barnard Archives.

career at Barnard." Similarly, veteran faculty member, Columbia-trained professor of government, Thomas Peardon, she believed "regarded anything new with a jaundiced eye." In Peardon's case, however, McIntosh shrewdly made him her first dean of the faculty precisely because of his conservative bona fides. She later acknowledged that his counsel had saved her from pressing too hard for reforms that the faculty could not possibly abide. Referring to her years at Brearley, McIntosh went on: "The experience I'd had running a rather obstinate and contrary faculty of conservative schoolteachers [was] a great help to me," she later said of Puckett and company, "partly because I didn't pay much attention to their complaints."[46]

McIntosh found her allies among the younger faculty members she inherited, many just back from military service. These included economist Raymond ("Steve") Saulnier; philosopher Joseph Brennan; chemist Edward King; botanist Donald Ritchie; and classicist Helen Bacon, a Bryn Mawr AB and PhD who came to Barnard after wartime service

FIGURE 7.5 Columbia College visitors to Barnard campus, 1940s. Barnard Archives.

in the WAVES and resigning a tenured position at Smith when a male colleague was fired for being a homosexual. Others hired in the 1930s but promoted under McIntosh included sociologist Mirra Komarovsky, class of 1926, and art historian Julius Held (1937–1980), both aligned with the new dean. So did appointees from her first years, among them the American studies scholars John Kouwenhoven (1946–1972) and Annette K. Baxter (1952–1983). Many of the newcomers took an interest in curricular reform, something that had received little attention at Barnard after the mid-1920s. Another hire, the sociologist Gladys Meyer (1948–1975), later said that McIntosh "took [Barnard] out of this kind of elitism so that the whole atmosphere breathed better." Julius Held remembered her with affection as "the mother type."[47]

An emblematic McIntosh-led curricular initiative was the introduction of an Education Program intended to prepare Barnard students for careers as primary and secondary school teachers. Some faculty members objected to the program's vocational character, and specifically its student-teaching component, seeing it as a departure from the college's steadfast commitment to the liberal arts. Others thought such instruction should be left to the normal colleges and that Barnard graduates ought to be directed to careers of a more prestigious character than school teaching. Support from the Carnegie Corporation and Joe Brennan's enthusiastic endorsement helped McIntosh overcome faculty opposition for the program that, since its founding in 1951, has provided a vital link between Barnard and the city's schools, public and private.[48]

Other curricular undertakings included the creation of a religion department in 1949 thanks to a $500,000 gift from the estate of Thomas Lamont, to which Ursula Niebuhr, the wife of Union Theological Seminary theologian Reinhold Niebuhr, was named chair. In 1952, the American Civilization Program, begun in 1939 under Elizabeth Reynard, was relaunched with a $75,000 Carnegie Foundation grant, with historian Basil Rauch its director. That same year, a drama program was added to the English Department, led by Howard Teichmann (1946–1970), playwright and biographer of George S. Kaufman. Following the transfer of Douglas Moore to Columbia, Barnard's Music Department continued first under electronic music pioneer Otto Leunig and then Hubert Doris.[49]

McIntosh advanced meritocratic principles in the Barnard faculty hiring process by making appointments on a more universalist basis than

Eleanor Rosenberg

FIGURE 7.6 Eleanor Rosenberg, class of 1929, later professor of English (1953–1978), 1950s. Barnard Archives.

earlier. Examples of this included the retention of philosophy professor Joseph Brennan, whose Catholicism had made him suspect in Gilder-sleeve's eyes. She also approved the appointments of several faculty members of Jewish background, including the sociologists Herbert Hyman and Bernard Barber, and in English, the cultural critic Barry Ulanov and the Renaissance scholar Eleanor Rosenberg, class of 1929. One of Rosenberg's students, Anne Bernays, described her as "a soft-spoken middle-aged woman with no particularly striking trait other than her mind."[50]

Despite an extended freeze on the size of the faculty, ending only in 1955, and falling further behind Columbia in faculty salaries, Barnard managed under McIntosh to appoint, promote, and retain a new generation of faculty members that would serve the college into the 1980s. This postwar generation differed from their interwar counterpart in two ways:

newer members were now subject to a specified probationary period before consideration for tenure, and they accepted the reality that effective teaching and departmental service would no longer suffice for permanent retention. These conditions in turn produced a growing commitment to scholarship—to research and publication—which set a portion of the postwar generation apart from not only their Barnard predecessors but their peers at other liberal arts colleges. The notion, if not yet the full reality, of the Barnard faculty as a community of scholar-teachers, as distinct from teacher-scholars, has its origins in the McIntosh era.

This raising of the scholarly profile of the Barnard faculty, a product of changes in college policy and the ambitions of those entering the academic profession after the war, had its problematic side. It left the college open to faculty raiding by rapidly expanding second-tier universities intent on building or upgrading their faculties. Due to an absence of endowed professorships and a salary policy of across-the-board raises, the college's bargaining power was limited in trying to retain faculty members who had outside offers. Meanwhile, Columbia continued to lure promising Barnard male faculty members over to its side of Broadway with higher salaries, lab space, and graduate instruction. Defectors to Columbia included sociologist Conrad Arensberg, medieval historian John Mundy, and geologist John Imbrie, while zoologist Aubrey Gorbman left Morningside altogether for the University of Washington. And poaching was no longer limited to male faculty: in 1952 French literary scholar Jeanne Varney Pleasants transferred to Columbia and botanist Ingrith Deyrup, class of 1940, decamped with Gorbman for Washington. In 1955, sociologist Renee Fox left Barnard for a full professorship at the University of Pennsylvania. Faculty raiding would become an even more serious problem for McIntosh's successor.[51]

In addition to the increasing mobility and turnover in the Barnard faculty, other long-term changes in the McIntosh administration included the gradual reduction in the reliance upon Columbia PhD programs as the major supplier of starting Barnard faculty. Into the early 1950s, about 60 percent of male faculty appointees, and an even higher percentage of female appointees, had been trained at Columbia. The practice of Columbia department chairs sending over to their Barnard counterpart one of their promising graduate students, particularly one of their otherwise hard-to-place women graduate students, became less common under

McIntosh. But it still happened. When Gladys Meyer was finishing her PhD in sociology in the spring of 1948 under Columbia's Robert MacIver, he discharged his placement responsibilities by telling Meyer, "Go over [to Barnard] and see Professor Arensberg."[52]

Not yet as transparent as the federally mandated open-search procedures introduced in the late 1960s, the faculty appointment process in the later McIntosh era had widened the college's recruitment range to include more PhDs from other Ivy League schools, the University of California, and Stanford, and especially in the sciences, from the large state universities of the Midwest. By the mid-1960s, the percentage of Barnard faculty with Columbia PhDs had dropped below 50 percent and would continue to decline to the point today (2020) where the Columbia-trained contingent makes up only 10 percent of today's Barnard faculty.[53]

Even as the two administrations worked more effectively together, the two faculties became more distinct entities. On balance, this was a positive development, allowing the smaller Barnard to be more innovative in terms of its undergraduate curriculum and less constrained by Columbia's privileging of its graduate programs. But it also had a downside, particularly when the instructors of larger and less integrated Columbia departments lost contact with their Barnard counterparts, contacts that had been maintained earlier by joint membership and coordinated hiring/tenure policies. English and psychology are cases in point: by the early 1960s, the mutual estrangement had reached a point where the senior members of both departments ceased all but the most pro forma consultations on personnel and curriculum matters. Tenure appointments were sometimes made at Barnard in instances where the cognate Columbia department chose to keep its reservations about the candidate's scholarship to itself while appointments were made at Columbia in specialties already covered by Barnard faculty. When such consultation became required in the 1970s, one veteran member of the Barnard English Department referred to his Columbia departmental counterparts as being for him and his Barnard Hall mates "a great distraction." But another member, the prolific John Kouwenhoven, described the department's tenure criteria in the McIntosh era: "The person who hadn't published a damned thing [but] was a first-rate teacher and a very valuable member of the college community, the [advisory] committee would almost uniformly recommend promotion all the way up to full professor." The old had yet to give way to the new.[54]

MRS. MAC AND MCCARTHYISM

Postwar Barnard gets high marks on another of the era's tests of presidential fair-mindedness: how to respond to the McCarthy-led congressional probes into leftist leanings and the political pasts of faculty members. In 1950, in anticipation of being the target of such an investigation, McIntosh proposed the following response, taking her cue from Harvard:

FIGURE 7.7 No hands, just knees. Barnard Archives.

1. If a faculty member is called for questioning, he or she should be encouraged to answer questions freely.

2. If the faculty member acknowledges prior membership in the Communist party but is no longer a member, and that is confirmed, no action should be taken by the college.

3. If a faculty member invokes the Fifth Amendment, he or she is to be suspended with pay while a committee of faculty and trustees investigate the situation.

FIGURE 7.8 Helen Bacon, professor of classics (1961–1989) and students. Barnard Archives.

Her guidelines provided three institutional options for dealing with a faculty member with a Communist past: reinstatement of the faculty member with no penalty, reinstatement with probation for a specified time, and dismissal.[55]

When McIntosh presented these guidelines to the Barnard trustees, they staked out even higher ground by rejecting the option of dismissing an instructor for invoking the Fifth Amendment. Trustee Samuel Milbank pointed out that, by invoking the Fifth Amendment, a faculty member was invoking a right protected by the Constitution. Among other Barnard trustees to take the same principled public stand on the fraught issue of ex-Communists in the classroom were Agnes Ernst Meyer and Iphigene Ochs Sulzberger.[56]

In the proposed hiring in 1956 of an admitted former Communist, the philosopher Stanley Moore, who had been fired from the Reed College faculty following his refusal to testify before the House Un-American

FIGURE 7.9 Barnard student teacher with neighborhood kids, late 1950s. Barnard Archives.

Activities Committee (HUAC) in 1954, Barnard held the high ground. Both McIntosh and the board accepted the philosophy department's recommendation in 1956 to appoint the then-unemployed Moore as an assistant professor. (Moore left in 1964 for the University of California, San Diego, when McIntosh's successor declined to recommend his promotion to associate professor with tenure.) Meanwhile, despite an otherwise good record in responding to McCarthyism, the Columbia administration terminated the anthropologist, Gene Weltfish, class of 1925, an avowed radical, from her position as a research associate after she charged the United States with using germ warfare in Korea.[57]

Moore's appointment came late in the McIntosh administration, when the economic constraints of the late 1940s and early 1950s were loosened and the college could afford a cautious optimism about its future prospects. Indeed, looking back six decades later, Barnard in the mid-1950s appears to have entered a period of quiet prosperity that provided those who partook of it a decade-long respite from the difficult earlier years and the tumultuous ones to follow.

BRINGING IN THE SHEAVES

By 1956, the modern fundraising structure that had been installed earlier began to produce major results. That year, the trustees announced the creation of a Library Development Campaign that would underwrite construction of a freestanding library (150,000 volumes) to replace the Ella Weed Library that had occupied a portion of the second floor of Barnard Hall since 1917. Trustee Iphigene Sulzberger (class of 1914) was campaign chair and the needed $1,700,000 was quickly raised from four principal sources:

$750,000 from the Wollman Foundation, where Sulzberger served on the board

$750,000 from the Lehman family in honor of Adele Lewisohn Lehman, class of 1903

$125,000 from Helen Goodhart Altschul, class of 1907

$75,000 from campaign chair Iphigene Sulzberger

The Wollman Library/Lehman Hall groundbreaking took place in April 1958, and the building opened in 1960. The four-story structure was north of the Barnard Annex, with its glass front facing Broadway across a swath of lawn and its back on Claremont. It became home to the departments of economics, history, and political science. In 2016, it was demolished to make way for the more architecturally striking Milstein Teaching and Learning Center, which opened in the fall of 2018.[58]

Another major fundraising/building project of the McIntosh era was the construction of Barnard's third dormitory, Reid Hall, with principal funding from the family of Mary Louise Stewart Reid, class of 1946, in honor of her mother-in-law and longtime trustee Helen Rogers Reid. The funding announcement took place in December 1957 and groundbreaking two years later. The eight-story Reid Hall was next to Brooks Hall and along Broadway, but it faced inward to form the third and southeastern side of the Milbank Quadrangle. Upon opening in 1961 with accommodations for 150 residential students, along with an additional 150 with the purchase of the first of three apartment buildings (616 West 116th Street) across from Brooks/Reid, Barnard now provided housing to half its incoming students.[59]

The last major fundraising/building project initiated in the McIntosh era and completed later was for a student center. Groundbreaking for what became the Millicent McIntosh Student Center occurred in May 1962, four weeks before its namesake retired after fifteen years of service. It was a fitting climax to her presidency. Having inherited a balance sheet with chronic deficits, an endowment of $10 million, and a moribund fundraising apparatus, she bequeathed to her successor a string of budgetary surpluses, an endowment of $20 million ($168 million in 2019 dollars), and a fundraising apparatus that had underwritten construction of four buildings and the purchase of a fifth. McIntosh also inherited a four-and-a-half-acre, four-block campus distinguished by two sets of buildings clustered at the north and south ends, with only Barnard Hall in between, and the rest occupied by tennis courts, some bushes, and semirustic pathways, but she bequeathed to her successor a campus with eight buildings taking up most of the campus and unoccupied space at a premium. After sixty-seven years on Morningside Heights, Barnard had become as densely urban as its surroundings.[60]

FIGURE 7.10 President McIntosh on a bulldozer during excavation for Reid Hall, 1960. Barnard Archives.

COLUMBIA'S BENIGN NEGLECT

Critical to any Barnard leader's standing has been her relations with Columbia. The two deemed least successful in this regard were Laura Drake Gill (1901–1907) and Jacquelyn Mattfeld (1975–1980), who had many disputes with their Columbia counterparts. Here, McIntosh enjoyed singular success. Her administration coincided with the Columbia presidencies of Dwight D. Eisenhower (1948–1953) and Grayson Kirk (1953–1968). She worked well with and liked both, if differently. On

Ike: "He was exceedingly kind to me, very pleasant and nice and under-standing. But his academic work was nil. He once told me that he very much resented just being a public relations person." On Kirk: "I'm one of Mr. Kirk's greatest admirers. I think he made [this in 1966] an excellent president for the University. He's a professor's president." The feelings were mutual.[61]

McIntosh's relations with Columbia's provosts and professional school deans, with whom she met weekly, also went smoothly. At these meetings, all faculty promotions under consideration at Barnard were discussed, as were proposals to share resources. Here, too, some Barnard faculty members thought her too eager to find ways by which Barnard departments might cooperate with their Columbia counterparts on appointments. A few even suspected she was open to a merger with Columbia, a charge she addressed in her 1966 oral history:

MCM [Millicent Carey McIntosh]: "Mr. Kirk thinks we should give up our separate identity and be merged with Columbia College."
Interviewer: "How would you feel about that?"
MCM: "Very strongly against it."[62]

In 1962, McIntosh and Kirk agreed to eliminate the past practice of Barnard making annual payments to Columbia for any imbalance in the student exchange, even though Barnard students typically took more courses at Columbia than Columbia students took at Barnard. While subsequent financial exigencies at Columbia (more about this in the next chapter) led to the reinstating of payments in 1970, its temporary abey-ance marks a singularly placid period in an institutional relationship of thirteen decades and counting. When later asked about that Barnard College/Columbia University relationship, Mrs. Mac described it as "some-thing that is impossible to explain to anyone," before characteristically adding: "It's one of the most interesting things about the job."[63]

Barnard students in this period had only limited access to Columbia courses, and vice versa, but some of the fondest memories of Barnard alumnae of their undergraduate years involve venturing across Broad-way in search of academic enlightenment. That such trips initiated or cemented relationships of a social nature that led to marriage may also have distinguished the postwar years on Morningside. But undoubtedly they also reinforced in other instances a commitment to graduate studies and scholarly or professional careers.

In 1960, when her husband reached the mandatory retirement age of sixty-five and prepared to leave his deanship at Columbia's Babies Hospital, Millicent McIntosh informed her trustees that she wished to accompany him into retirement. Reid persuaded her to remain until a replacement could be found, a process in which she was asked to participate. In 1962, she commenced her retirement on the family farm in Tyringham, Massachusetts. She thereafter kept in regular contact with succeeding presidents and returned several times to campus, twice to events at the Millicent McIntosh Student Center. The first was its delayed opening in November 1969, when she was sixty-nine; the second in 1999, during the presidency of Judith Shapiro, when Barnard and Brearley celebrated her 100th birthday. She died two years later, in January 2001. Based on where the college was when she became its head compared to its situation at the time of her retirement, Millicent McIntosh ranks as one of Barnard's two most successful leaders to date.[64]

THE ROSEMARY PARK INTERREGNUM

During McIntosh's last year in office, a presidential search committee chose Rosemary Park as her successor. Park was president of Connecticut College and a scholar of German literature. A Radcliffe graduate with a PhD from the University of Cologne, she hailed from a family of academic administrators. Her father, Edgar Park, had been president of Wheaton College and her brother, William, president of Simmons College. Her fifteen years at Connecticut College had been marked by great success in fundraising and additions to the New London campus's physical plant. By all accounts, she was loved by students and alumnae and admired by her faculty. Her motives for coming to Barnard are not known, other than looking for a change and seeing the Barnard presidency as a new and exciting challenge in the nation's cultural capital. McIntosh had championed her candidacy and Dean emerita Gildersleeve approved, calling the appointment of a scholarly, unmarried woman "a return to the Barnard tradition." Mrs. Mac let both swipes pass.[65]

Once installed in November 1962, Park demonstrated strengths in two crucial areas of presidential responsibility. First, she quickly made good on her reputation as a formidable fundraiser, both among the trustees and with the major foundations. In 1965, she secured from the Ford Foundation $2,500,000 by raising from other sources a match of three times that amount. The major funding for the Altschul Science Tower, $750,000, came from the Milbank Memorial Fund. Two more apartment buildings, at 600 and 620 West 116th Street, were purchased to be used as student dormitories, as was the Bryn Mawr Hotel on 121st Street and Amsterdam as the future site for Plimpton Hall. Even as these capital projects proceeded, Barnard's endowment edged upward to $25 million ($198 million in 2019).[66]

Park also got on famously with Columbia's President Kirk and with the intellectually formidable University Provost Jacques Barzun, who shared Park's love of classical music and her habit of sneaking off on Wednesday afternoons to attend performances by the New York Symphony. As she had with Barzun, Park won the instant respect of her faculty, many seeing her as the scholar and public intellectual that Mrs. Mac never pretended to be. Several veteran Barnard faculty members and administrators mentioned Park as their favorite president when they were interviewed.[67]

But all this goodwill did not stop several of Barnard's most promising faculty members from accepting academic positions elsewhere. McIntosh had presided over the beginning of what Barzun called "the era of the packed suitcase," and it was Park's fate to experience it at floodtide. In 1962, the economist Robert Lekachman left Barnard for SUNY Stonybrook, where he doubled his salary; two years later, English professor Marcus Klein left for the University of Buffalo, for what McIntosh called "a big, fat state university salary." Such raids became less common after the cooling of the academic job market in the late 1960s, first in the humanities and then spreading across all disciplines, but it constituted a significant challenge for a college with many faculty publishing at rates expected of university appointees. Nor did Park escape all responsibility for these departures. "Some of these losses I think she could have avoided," McIntosh suggested tartly in her 1966 oral history, "if she had spent more time getting to know her faculty."[68]

Park's biggest challenge came in adjusting to the contrast between the students she encountered at Connecticut College and those at Barnard.

Some of the differences were in part generational (consensual 1950s versus confrontational 1960s), others demographic (White, Anglo-Saxon Protestants versus first-generation ethnics), and still others locational (New England suburbs versus inner city), but together they were differences Park had trouble bridging. At some point, she may have stopped trying. Again, her predecessor proved less than forgiving, seeing her as "cool and aloof" in her dealings with students. According to McIntosh Park was also unsettled by Barnard's more aggressive students, reporting them "dirty, beatnik, unpleasant." As for Barnard's best and brightest students: "They're just alien to her." One faculty member, the sociologist Gladys Meyer, who was close to some of Barnard's more outspoken students, later said of Park: "Students didn't like her and she didn't have much interest in dealing with students except in a formal way."[69]

Four years into her presidency, the fifty-nine-year-old Park married Milton Anastos, an internationally known scholar of Byzantine history at UCLA. Shortly thereafter she informed the Barnard trustees of her intention to resign effective June 30, 1967, to take an administrative post at UCLA. Her departing words on "relinquishing one of the most rewarding responsibilities in all higher education" were characteristically gracious. She remained an active participant in and commentator on higher education and women's issues for another three decades. She died in 2004, at age ninety-seven.[70]

Park's presidency of four and a half years was too brief to be considered successful. And her unexpected departure left any successor in a tight spot. That campus tensions were higher at her leaving than at her arrival were likely attributable to changing times more than to any specific actions she took during her presidency. Still, it seems she lacked a visceral connection to New York City, perhaps not an absolute requirement for the job, but without it, success has historically proved elusive.

The Park presidency did benefit from good timing, ending as it did before the escalation of student protests that began in May 1965 and would make the Barnard campus a hostile environment for confrontation-averse administrators, faculty members, and students. These protests reached their crescendo in 1968, months after her departure for California.

8

INTO THE STORM

Weeks of demonstrations, committing myself to the student uprising with my body, and the non-stop talking, flirting, and tuna fish sandwich-making, remain an ecstatic blur of happiness and adrenalin.

—SUSAN SLYOMOVICS, CLASS OF 1971[1]

LOOKING AFIELD

By the spring of 1967, Rosemary Park had resigned and decamped with her new husband to California. A search committee for her successor completed its work that fall with its recommendation for Barnard's third president. At the time of her selection, Martha Peterson, then the Dean of Women at the University of Wisconsin, Madison, seemed an unlikely choice. First was the matter of origins. Peterson was born outside Jamestown, Kansas, population 1,900, her father a wheat farmer and mother a newspaper reporter. She attended local public schools and then the University of Kansas, from which she graduated in 1937. She then taught mathematics in a Kansas high school for several years before returning to the University of Kansas, where she combined jobs in student affairs and graduate work in educational psychology. In 1957, she left Lawrence for Madison, Wisconsin, where she became dean of women and a close confidant of President Fred Harrington.

Even more than the ill-fated Dean Laura Drake Gill, it could be said of Martha Peterson that "she was not a New Yorker."[2]

There was also the matter of academic credentials. Unlike most of Barnard's previous chief administrators, Peterson's degrees were from large coed public universities, and in a field that many in the humanities and hard sciences found suspect. The fact that she came from an administrative position focused on students rather than faculty and her classroom experiences were as a high school teacher did not endear her to faculty members hoping for a repeat of the scholarly Park. What Peterson's early skeptics failed to appreciate was that the search committee and board of trustees had settled on a no-nonsense Midwesterner who might just be what the unsettled times ahead called for should Barnard be in for a period of student protest and faculty disquiet,. She arrived on campus in November 1967, just before the roof fell in.[3]

LIFE WITH A WOUNDED LION

Of all the major interwar American universities, Columbia had the toughest time sustaining its standing in the postwar years. It ceased being the richest American university in the 1920s, falling behind Harvard, Yale and Princeton. By the 1930s, it was no longer the largest producer of PhDs, and by the 1950s, its continued placement among the four best American universities was increasingly seen as a classic instance of lagging indicators.[4]

Recruiting and retaining instructors became a significant Columbia problem in the 1950s. New York City was increasingly perceived by recruitment targets as expensive and a tough place to work or raise a family. For scientists, Columbia's already overbuilt campus offered little room for needed laboratory space. Internally, Columbia was slow to see the need to compete not only with its traditional Ivy rivals, Chicago, and the University of California, but also with new challengers such as the Massachusetts Institute of Technology (MIT), Stanford, and Michigan. Many of these institutions had presidents who seized on immediate postwar developments as opportunities to push their universities to the front of the pack. In contrast, Columbia experienced an eight-year gap in

effective leadership, encompassing the last five years of the Butler presidency and the three-year interregnum between Butler's retirement in
1945 and Dwight Eisenhower's arrival on campus in 1948. Nor did Eisenhower, once at Columbia, ever really take up the full responsibilities of the
presidential office. He left fundraising and faculty development to others,
while he remained on call for various military assignments and then presidential campaigning. He was away from campus more than in residence
during his five-year college presidency.[5]

During Eisenhower's absentee presidency, Columbia operated under
the day-to-day direction of Provost Grayson Kirk, who succeeded Eisenhower when he relocated to the White House in January 1953. A competent
and hardworking academic administrator, Kirk was not forceful or imaginative enough to reset Columbia's course, but he saw his responsibilities
less as transformative than custodial. He used federal research contracts
and available foundation support to swell the university's operating budget, but in doing so, he made Columbia increasingly reliant upon annually
appropriated "soft" money. In 1964, federal research funds accounted for
45 percent of the university's income. Meanwhile, the university's endowment remained concentrated in Manhattan real estate, with returns substantially below those of universities with more of their endowments in
equities. In 1965, when the Columbia trustees belatedly recognized their
exposure, they directed a reluctant President Kirk to mount a capital campaign to raise $2 billion, then the largest campaign goal in the history of
academic fundraising.[6]

Two department-by-department rankings of American universities
in the 1950s, one conducted internally in 1957 by the Columbia political
scientist Arthur MacMahon and the other in 1959 by Kenneth Keniston
of the University of Pennsylvania, placed Columbia among the nation's
top four research universities, along with Harvard, Yale, and Chicago. But
rankings published in 1966, by the economist Allan Cartter for the American Council of Education using data for 1964, showed declines in the
standing of nearly every ranked Columbia department. Overall, the university placed seventh. Three years later, when the rankings were recalibrated and now included faculty assessments collected in 1967, Columbia
had dropped to twelfth.[7]

Columbia College had its own problems. Since the early 1900s, it had
enjoyed a virtual lock on the best graduates of New York City public

schools and admitted only a small percentage of those academically qualified Jewish applicants. In the immediate post–World War II years, with
discriminatory practices eliminated, the college enjoyed its geographically privileged access to the top Jewish graduates as well. But by the early
1960s, Harvard, Yale, MIT, Princeton, Amherst, and other elite colleges
were actively recruiting these students. Columbia historian Fritz Stern,
himself a postwar graduate by way of a Jewish family and a New York
City high school, called the 1950s the "golden age" of Columbia College.
A decade later, it had become the safety school of the Ivy League. Add
to the mix a scruffy and questionably safe campus, a core curriculum of
limited national appeal, plus few coed classrooms, and you had, from a
student-recruitment perspective, a tough sell.[8]

Student antiwar protests on the Columbia campus commenced in the
spring of 1965, with a whimsical counterdemonstration during the commissioning ceremony for Naval Reserve Officers Training Corps (NROTC)
seniors. By 1967, with the increasing involvement of members of the campus
chapter of Students for a Democratic Society (SDS), the demonstrations
took on a more disruptive character. Barnard students numbered among
these campus protesters, although most of their fire was directed at the
Columbia administration. A demonstration in Dodge Hall on March 24,
1967, to protest the presence of a Central Intelligence Agency (CIA) recruiter
on campus, and a second on April 21, when marine recruiters were on campus, both protests including Barnard students, represented an escalation of
conflict between irate students and hard-pressed administrators.[9]

PUSH COMES TO SHOVE

The first serious matter to confront incoming President Peterson was stu-
dent-related. In March 1968, a Barnard student, identified initially only
as "from New Hampshire," became the object of a *New York Times* story
about cohabitation with her boyfriend off campus. Because this arrangement violated college housing rules (they permitted off-campus living for
noncommuting students only as live-in caregivers) and because Barnard
had so few students from New Hampshire, the student was easily identified as Linda LeClair, a junior. When summoned to the dean's office to

explain herself, LeClair, instead of apologizing for misrepresenting her housing arrangements, challenged the right of the college to oversee them. She and her boyfriend, Peter Behr, were members of the Columbia chapter of SDS, and both insisted on her right to live as she pleased. Behr was also refusing induction into the army. LeClair's case was referred to the college judicial council, made up of students and faculty members, that conducted a well-attended open hearing and sanctioned her behavior but imposed no penalty other than banning her from the school cafeteria. Student opinion supported LeClair's call for doing away with the parietal rules, seeing them as more restrictive than those that applied to Columbia men. Meanwhile, President Peterson, under pressure from the press and some of her trustees, considered rejecting the council's ruling and expelling LeClair. Before she decided, other more pressing matters intervened.[10]

Developments in the spring of 1968 led to escalated protest activities on the Columbia campus and a series of violent confrontations that collectively became known as Columbia '68. Growing opposition across the United States to the war in Vietnam was intensified by reports of the January Tet Offensive launched by North Vietnam against South Vietnamese and U.S. military installations across South Vietnam. Antiwar demonstrations in New York City's Central Park were regular events attended by Barnard and Columbia students and instructors. On campus, a change in SDS leadership brought Columbia College junior Mark Rudd and a set of like-minded undergraduate confrontationists to the fore, ensuring a disruptive spring semester. On February 23, 200 students marched into Low Library to protest the presence of Dow Chemical recruiters on campus; on March 20, the New York City director of the Selective Service, on campus to discuss changes in the draft law, had a lemon meringue pie thrown in his face by a student many thought to be Mark Rudd. On March 27, SDS mounted a demonstration in Low Library, which prompted staffers to demand that disciplinary action be taken against the demonstrators. Six students, all SDS leaders, were identified and put on probation.[11]

By then protesting students had settled on three non-negotiable demands:

1. Columbia [must] end its membership in the Institute for Defense Analyses (IDA), a quasi-governmental entity where Defense Department officials and university administrators discussed the allocation

of military research funds among research universities. In 1968, Grayson Kirk was the chair of IDA and trustee William Burden was a long-time member.

2. Columbia [must] cancel plans to build a gym in Morningside Park because the provisions for community-access approved a decade earlier by city hall and Harlem officials were now seen as racially insensitive.

3. Columbia [must] rescind disciplinary policies that put SDS student leaders engaged in earlier protests subject to expulsion. Their exposure prompted a demand for amnesty for all protesters, past and future.[12]

One might ask, What do these demands have to do with Barnard? Barnard was not a member of IDA, its faculty conducted no military research, the proposed gym was a Columbia College project and would not be open to Barnard students or faculty, Barnard's disciplinary policies differed from those of Columbia and no Barnard student was at risk of expulsion. Beginning on the night of April 23, when the first of five academic buildings at Columbia were occupied and held until a forced removal by New York City police in the early morning of April 30, none of the buildings belonged to Barnard and Barnard authorities had not called for the police action. But if Barnard had no dog in this fight, why were an estimated 300 Barnard students among the building occupiers? And why did 115 stay on in the buildings to be arrested when the police arrived?[13]

Some Barnard students may have joined boyfriends or for the excitement. However, many others did so to protest one or another university policy in keeping with their ideological principles, and in some cases with those of their parents. They included the Black students who "liberated" Hamilton Hall Tuesday, the "Gene McCarthy liberal types" who occupied Fayerweather Hall on Wednesday, and those who exchanged the laidback Fayerweather for the more militant and star-studded Mathematics Hall on Thursday. The scene in Avery Hall, which was more accurately a sit-in led by architecture graduate students, also had its Barnard participants. The Low Library occupation included Nancy Bieberman, class of 1969, and Barbara Bernstein, class of 1971, among others. Meanwhile, Barnard students such as Mary Gordon, class of 1971, unwilling to risk arrest or jeopardize their scholarships, staffed the SDS communications center in Ferris Booth Hall and helped with the contested resupplying of Hamilton Hall and Low Library.[14]

One demand added at the start of the building occupations did apply to Barnard: to rectify the widely perceived failure of both institutions to follow up their decision in 1964 to recruit Black students, hire more Black instructors, and include in the curriculum Black-focused courses. This demand was linked to the opposition to the construction of a gym in Morningside Park as part of a larger list of issues that Black students had with Columbia and their relationship to neighboring Harlem. The occupation of Hamilton Hall was not an SDS-staged event or even a protest against the Vietnam War: it followed directly on a protest against the Morningside gym project and focused on the demands of Columbia and Barnard Black students. Many of the Black women in Hamilton were Barnard students, and there as an expression of racial solidarity.[15]

On Monday morning, April 29, 1968, with five Columbia buildings occupied and the police preparing for a forced removal after midnight, Martha Peterson was inaugurated as Barnard's third president in the Cathedral of St. John the Divine. The event, attended by Columbia president Grayson Kirk, passed peacefully with a few picketers on hand.[16]

The clearing of the buildings by the New York City police in the early morning of April 30 was accompanied by scattered violence, most occurring during the emptying of the last building, Mathematics Hall, where militant student and nonstudent protesters resisted removal. A subsequent charge by police into a crowd of observers gathered on the South Lawn resulted in several injuries and much recrimination, and was later deemed by a police investigation to have been gratuitous.[17]

None of the 115 Barnard students arrested in clearing the buildings required medical attention. They were taken from campus, booked at precinct courts throughout the city, and later charged with unlawfully occupying private property and resisting arrest. Their release was facilitated in several instances by Barnard trustee Iola Haverstick, who posted bond as needed.[18]

While cooperating with their more exercised Columbia counterparts, Barnard administrators declined to add to the criminal charges against their students disciplinary charges of their own devising. Instead, college counsel moved to have the criminal charges dropped. President Peterson convened an open meeting of students, instructors, and administrators later in the day of the police bust at which she sought advice on how to proceed. Barnard faculty members, while divided over the issues, were uniformly disposed to be forgiving of, if not secretly pleased with, their students' actions, many having strong feelings about the war and perhaps some with their own grievances with Columbia. The Barnard trustees concurred in this conciliatory response. In this case, the center held.[19]

Not so across Broadway, where events struck Columbia in the fifteenth year of the presidency of Grayson Kirk and at the outset of the university's capital campaign. Two months after calling the police on campus and with the capital campaign in tatters, Kirk resigned. Responsibility for salvaging the situation had been seized by a faculty executive committee, brought into being the morning after the police action and headed by Columbia law professor Michael I. Sovern. Upon Kirk's departure, administrative authority passed to acting president Andrew W. Cordier, and then to

FIGURE 8.1 Barnard President Martha Peterson (1967–1975). Barnard Archives.

William J. McGill, who became Columbia's sixteenth president in February 1970. McGill had taught psychology at Columba in the 1950s before becoming one of the faculty hired away, in his case by newly opened University of California, San Diego, where in 1967 he became its chancellor. His handling of controversial scholars and activists Herbert Marcuse and Angela Davis earned him the reputation of "one tough Mick" and was part of his appeal to the Columbia presidential search committee. Once on campus, he received two charges from his board, one immediate and one longer-term: the first, get Columbia off the front page of the *New York Times* by restoring campus order; the second, for which he was given five years (it would take ten), bring the university's budget back into balance by whatever means at his disposal.[20]

"GOOD MARTHA PETERSON"

Barnard's new president was immediately confronted with the challenge of keeping student protests from disrupting the normal business of the college. Her longer-term objective was responding to protest-riddled Columbia, only belatedly reckoning with its dire financial situation. As for the first problem, Peterson quickly established a reasonable level of student-administrative comity, demonstrating a coolness under fire. The Linda LeClair matter was resolved in the summer of 1968 with her suspension, not for violating the parietal rules forbidding cohabitation with a man but for lying to the student-run College Honor Board. This was followed by a significant relaxation of those rules, which were still more restrictive than those applying to Columbia men. (They were also more restrictive than those Peterson monitored back in Madison.) By 1971, most restrictions on male visitors to the Barnard dorms were lifted; two years later, Barnard and Columbia were experimenting with coed dorms. A floor of Plimpton Hall, Barnard's fourth dorm, which opened on Amsterdam and 121st Street in 1968, was one of the first test sites.[21]

Other presidential actions helped lower the temperature on campus. In early 1969, Peterson joined with Columbia College Dean Carl Hovde to form a committee on Barnard-Columbia curricular cooperation. Its recommendations led directly to a mutual loosening of cross-registration requirements and an immediate increase in curricular traffic across Broadway in both directions. A second committee convened by Peterson in the wake of the 1968 disturbances was the inelegantly named Committee on Committees, which successfully pressed for reconstituting standing Barnard committees to include student members. Heretofore, these committees, among them the Committee on Instruction, were made up of instructors and administrators. The trustees introduced a similar reform in 1970, when they approved the inclusion of a nonvoting student representative to the Board of Trustees.[22]

Meanwhile, issues of concern to Barnard's Black students required attending. By 1970, there were now 100 Black students, who were represented by the Barnard Organization of Soul Sisters (BOSS). One of the more pressing concerns was the hiring of more Black instructors. The only course regularly taught on the Black experience was Literary Negritude, first taught by Professor of French Serge Gavronsky and in 1964 by a Black instructor, Louise Jefferson. In 1970, the college made its first full-time faculty appointment of an African American, Quandra Prettyman, whose course on African American literature would soon become a fixture in the curriculum. In 1971, a second African American, Inez Reid, was appointed to an associate professorship in political science.[23]

Another issue for Barnard's Black students related to housing. Many, but not all, wished to live together and separately from White residents. This soon took the form of a demand for a Black corridor in Hewitt Hall. Despite objections that she was countenancing racial segregation, Peterson took this request seriously and had it considered by one of the tripartite (students, instructors, administrators) committees she introduced upon her arrival. On the committee's recommendation, Peterson announced in 1972 that current and incoming Black students could request to be housed on the eighth floor in Hewitt or assigned housing without regard to race. This arrangement, which later was terminated when found to be at odds with New York State laws against racial segregation, spoke to the lengths Peterson was prepared to go to keep the most agitated elements of the fractious Barnard community in the fold. She may also have shared an aspect of their alienation and saw their separatist demand as a legitimate political act.[24]

Another example of administrative flexibility to student demands was Barnard's short-lived Experimental College. One of the upshots of the

FIGURE 8.2 Quandra Prettyman, lecturer on African American literature in English Department (1970–1998), 1977. Barnard Archives.

1968–1970 campus protests was the notion that peer instruction should replace the hierarchical ways of the traditional classroom. At Columbia, in the days after the police bust, this notion took the form of courses designed by students for students, with faculty participation optional and then only in the role of facilitator. It was also thought that such an educational experience should be not only coeducational but also communally residential. As with much of the restructuring talk transpiring at Columbia in those heady days, little came of it once McGill and his budgeteers were in place. However, the Barnard administration and faculty were more receptive to these suggestions. Successively under the leadership of the feminist theorist and critic Kate Millet and the sociologist Hester Eisenstein, and housed in the Hotel Paris on West End Avenue, a mile from campus, the Barnard-Columbia Experimental College tested the patience of Barnard administrators and trustees before quietly passing out of existence in 1975.[25]

Peterson also displayed tactical adeptness when, in 1972, some faculty members became interested in the prospect of securing recognition of the local chapter of the American Association of University Professors (AAUP) as a union with full bargaining authority. Rather than openly opposing the idea of faculty unionization, Peterson encouraged faculty members who were skeptical of doing so to propose an alternative mechanism by which instructors' economic interests could be advocated for without resorting to collective bargaining and foregoing faculty claims to being more than employees. This led to a counterproposal for a faculty finance committee to be made up of a tenured, a nontenured, and an off-ladder member of the faculty, each elected by the respective group, and charged to represent faculty interests in the budgetary process, including annually meeting with the chair of the trustee finance committee. When Peterson supported its adoption before the faculty and helped secure for it trustee approval, and when successive chairs of the finance committee took seriously the presentations of the Faculty Finance Committee (since renamed the Faculty Finance and Resource Committee), unionization dropped from the faculty's agenda, not to appear again until 2014 and then among contingent faculty.[26]

A direct outcome of Columbia '68 with repercussions for Barnard was the recognition among women who had participated in the demonstrations that their own gender-specific interests required attention. This took organizational form in an ad hoc committee of women faculty members pressuring university administrators to look into salary discrimination, which, while directed at Columbia, benefitted from the active participation of several Barnard instructors, including Catharine Stimpson, then an assistant professor of English, later editor of the feminist journal *Signs*, and still later dean of the Graduate School of Arts and Sciences at New York University (NYU) and president of the Modern Language Association, and Patricia Graham, then director of the Barnard Education

Program and later dean of the Harvard Graduate School of Education and president of the Spencer Foundation. Similar gender-specific concerns led to the founding in 1971 of the Barnard Center for Research on Women as one of the nation's first feminist research institutes and home to the nationally recognized Scholar and Feminist Conference. Launched with a founding gift from trustee Eleanor Thomas Elliott, class of 1949, the center had as its founding director the feminist and writer Jane Gould. While some of the center's early activities were edgier than less committed Barnard feminists thought appropriate, Peterson here as well demonstrated a singular capacity to "keep calm and carry on."[27]

BARNARD TRUSTEES TO THE FORE

President McGill's strategy for seizing the financial reins of the university was to wrest control over all tuition and grants going to the eighteen schools nominally reporting to him. While the deans of the engineering school, the law school, and journalism grumbled but complied, those of the wealthier schools and divisions, most notably the medical school, the business school, and Lamont-Doherty Earth Observatory, resisted. As McGill described the always contentious and sometimes brutal process of settling budgetary questions with his school deans, "I decided them and then forced them down the throats of the parties."[28]

Although Barnard was not one of the university's schools in terms of its finances, neither was it exempt from being seen as a potential source of needed income and savings for the university. Among the first changes announced by McGill was that Barnard would now be expected to pay its way. This included an annual payment for the continued use of the university's libraries and athletic facilities. It also ended the Kirk administration's policy of waiving charges for any imbalance in cross-registrations; henceforth, Barnard would make an annual payment to Columbia for the net balance in cross-registration flows. This was to occur at the same time both Barnard and Columbia were expected to open up more courses to undergraduates enrolled elsewhere in the university.[29]

Part of the logic behind Columbia encouraging more cross-registration, aside from the added revenue that would flow eastward across Broadway, was that it would reduce redundancy in course offerings and future faculty hires. If Barnard, General Studies, and Columbia College, for example, all offered courses in Chaucer and each had a Chaucer specialist on the faculty, might there not be substantial savings all round by consolidating these resources? But by this logic, why not simply merge the faculties? This was the conclusion Columbia's Dean of Graduate Faculties George Fraenkel came to and vigorously campaigned for. In anticipation of such an outcome, Fraenkel set about to assure himself that Barnard would not rush to grant tenure to faculty members who could then not be easily dispensed with come the merger. For a merger to save money, junior faculty on both sides of Broadway had to be dispensable. And lest the merger of faculties be considered Fraenkel's hobby horse alone, McGill in his first weeks back on Morningside told the *Columbia Spectator*, "I have always favored the merger of the Barnard and Columbia faculties."[30]

However supportive of faculty merger, McGill was more focused on securing immediate financial help from Barnard. He made his expectations known to the Barnard members of the Joint Trustee Committee on Barnard-Columbia Relations, consisting of board chair Wallace Jones, Treasurer Plimpton and trustees Katherine Woodbridge and Katherine Auchincloss. They in turn directed Peterson to negotiate a comprehensive deal with McGill that would pay Columbia enough to maintain the affiliation but not so much as to bankrupt Barnard. They also directed her to allow Columbia to play a more prominent role in deciding tenure for Barnard faculty while a full merger of faculties remained on the table.[31]

Peterson played her weak hand with considerable skill, at one point prompting a key Columbia negotiator, Vice President Paul Carter, to complain in November 1972 to President McGill:

> In honesty and candor, I feel that the failure of these attempts is a result of Martha's refusal to acknowledge the importance of Barnard's relations with Columbia and her consequent refusal to negotiate in good faith. Where there are tentative agreements, I have made concessions; where there is no agreement, Martha has refused to budge. So long as this dilemma prevails, I see no hope for an agreement.[32]

By the spring of 1973, the outlines of a deal were made known to the two boards. The financial arrangements called for Barnard to make an annual payment (backdated to 1970) for the continued use of the university's libraries and gym facilities. The libraries payment would be determined by a comparison of Barnard's annual expenditures for its own 100,000-volume library with the average library expenditures of the other sister colleges, all with much larger libraries, with the difference payable to Columbia. The negotiated first payment, due July 1, 1973, was for $200,000, a number that could be expected to rise every year. A similar calculation was made in the case of Barnard's use of Columbia's gym facilities. The back-payment agreement covering 1971 to 1973 totaled $600,000, that for 1973–74 another $700,000.[33]

A different formula was used to settle on the annual payment Barnard would make to Columbia for the net balance in cross-registrations; it required Barnard to pay 10 percent of a student's tuition for every net course a Barnard student took at Columbia. First guesses made in 1971 as to the expected range of the annual cross-registration payment: another $300,000 to $400,000.[34]

The third agreed-upon payment by Barnard to Columbia covered general services overhead costs of operating Columbia, much like the indirect costs Columbia charged federal agencies to cover overhead. Annual price tag: $100,000. The total projected costs added to Barnard's operating budget as a direct outcome of the college's 1970–1972 negotiations with the cash-strapped Columbia was between $600,000 to $700,000. Coming on top of the projected 1974–1975 budget deficit of $500,000, the chair of the finance and budget committee Robert Houget reasonably called the situation "unacceptable."[35]

However much a strain these payments placed on Barnard, they did not measurably improve Columbia's balance sheet, which in 1972 still showed a deficit of $17 million. But that may not have been Columbia's purpose. A Columbia finance staffer explained the operative strategy to the incoming University Provost Peter Kenen: "The object of the negotiation is not optimum pricing of [cross]-registration, but maximum pressure for academic merger."[36]

The deal struck about Barnard's tenure procedures was qualitatively more sweeping. It effectively transformed a process in place since the late 1940s by which Barnard departments nominated junior members for tenure to an elective committee of Barnard full professors called the Appointments and Tenure Committee (ATP) for college-wide consideration.

The ATP then passed positive recommendations to the president for her approval. If the president approved, the candidate's name then went to the Barnard trustees for pro forma approval. The view of the cognate Columbia department as to the candidate's qualifications could be and often was sought at some stage of this internal process, as were letters from outside scholars in the candidate's field, but the opinions received were advisory, not dispositive. The Columbia University provost played no role in the process.[37]

Under the new dispensation, favorable recommendation of the ATP and the president's concurrence would now be "subject to review by a University ad hoc committee subsequent to Barnard's internal tenure procedures." The ad hoc committee would consist of five full professors, three drawn from the Columbia faculty and two from the Barnard faculty, all chosen by the university provost. A favorable recommendation from the ad hoc committee and acceptable to the provost then—and only then— went back across Broadway to secure pro forma approval by the Barnard trustees. A negative vote of the ad hoc committee or a rejection of a favorable vote by the university provost effectively ended the process with the candidacy being rejected. Because this arrangement closely matched that for Columbia's professional schools (with the notable exception of the law school), those supporting its adoption argued that it more effectively assured Barnard tenured faculty equal standing in the university, whereas the earlier arrangements did not. It also came under criticism by those opposed to it as a classic instance of "double jeopardy."[38]

Both the financial and tenure arrangements determined by the Joint Trustees Committee were adopted at the June 4, 1973, meeting of the Barnard trustees. This came after Treasurer Plimpton assured board members concerned about faculty reaction that he had polled a number of department chairs—likely all tenured males—and found them amenable to the new arrangements. Although the board's leadership and members of the Joint Trustees Committee pressed for and received a unanimous vote on its handiwork, doing so led directly to an insurrection within the board and a new set of board officers a year later.[39]

The prime mover in this insurrection was Eleanor (Elly) Lansing Thomas Elliott, class of 1949, a board member since 1960 and one of the college's principal fundraisers. As early as McGill's first appearance as an *ex officio* member of the Barnard board in October 1970, Elly Elliott

had challenged his assurances that he intended no harm, citing his statement favoring merger of the Barnard and Columbia faculties. Two years
later, when Plimpton again sought endorsements of the tenure plan from
some senior members of the faculty, Elliott did her own polling of women
faculty members with different results. Behind-the-scenes references to
the trustees who had negotiated the deal with Columbia as "the Gang
of Four"—Jones, Hoguet, Auchincloss, and Woodbridge—suggested that
the comity characterizing earlier board dealings had left the room.[40]

Custom dictated that, at the end of a board chair's term, she or he would
stay on for a second term or call for the election of the vice chair, who in
the fall of 1974 was Robert Hoguet. But custom was not followed and upon
Jones's departure, Eleanor Elliott was elected to become the ninth chair
of the board, only the second woman to do so. This was followed in short
order by the departure of two of the reputed Gang of Four, Katherine
Auchincloss and Catherine Woodbridge, and thereafter by Robert Hoguet.
Meanwhile elected in rapid succession to the board were William T.
Golden at the October meeting prior to Elliott's election; Helene Kaplan,
class of 1953, at the December meeting; plus Arthur Altschul in 1975 and
Gedale Horowitz shortly thereafter. All became dependable allies of the
new chair, who also had the support of ongoing board members Blanche
Graubard, class of 1936, and Ellen Futter, class of 1971.[41]

Although dispositive evidence is lacking, it was widely thought that the
new chair of the board made it her first order of business to urge President
Peterson to seek employment elsewhere. Elliott had served as social secretary to John Foster Dulles in the Eisenhower administration, was married
to the advertising executive John (Jock) Elliott, and had been Barnard's
principal fundraiser since 1959. She was very much the sophisticated
New Yorker but also a committed feminist. Some have suggested that she
viewed the matronly Midwesterner Peterson unsuited to the task of fundraising among New York's wealthy, still others that she disapproved of the
president's domestic circumstances, which by 1974 involved a possibly
lesbian relationship with a frequent visitor from Wisconsin. Still others
pointed to Peterson's absenting herself from Barnard for three weeks in
the fall of 1974 to tour China with an American Council of Education
mission as the event that turned the board chair against her.[42]

Finally, there was Peterson's string of five annual deficit budgets, an
accumulated debt of $913,000 and a shrinking endowment that, while in

part attributable to the inflationary times, had occurred on her watch. The meeting minutes for the board meeting immediately prior to her resignation state: "Mr. Jones spoke of the larger issue of survival and the maintenance of independence." Yet the unstated charge against Peterson was that she had been insufficiently attentive to Barnard's needs in her dealings with Columbia and had become too close to the Gang of Four and its accommodationist strategy. As one board member later put it, she had been a party to very nearly "giving away the store."[43]

For her part, after seven years Peterson had tired of the Barnard job and by her admission "pretty weary of living in New York." In 1974, she was sixty-eight years old and not in the best of health. She was said to be uncomfortable among sophisticated New Yorkers, not excluding Barnard board members. Her newly elected position as president of the American Council of Education and her professional and personal ties with Midwest academics produced several job offers, among them the presidency at Beloit College in Wisconsin, located within a few miles of her ailing mother. In May 1975, President Peterson announced that she was resigning from Barnard to accept the Beloit presidency. There she served effectively as its first female president for six years before retiring in 1981. She died in 2006.[44]

Peterson's quiet departure did not placate her faculty admirers (the author among them) or prevent some from characterizing her decision as coerced and the result of an unrepresentative contingent of faculty members urging the trustees to force her out. "She was fired," one faculty member with friends on the board at the time later declared. Another, professor of classics Helen Bacon, protested to Wallace Jones that trustees "in touch with a small and unrepresentative group of faculty [were] mistaken [about] what they heard from them for faculty opinion."[45]

How to assess Peterson's presidency? She was an effective day-to-day manager for seven of the most tempestuous years in American higher education; no academic visionary and no public intellectual, she was personally inclusive, listened to students, supported junior faculty members, and earned Columbia's respect. She experienced budgetary and student-recruitment problems that she was not able to solve. When caught in a trustee crossfire, she extricated herself by going back home. She was the right person at the Barnard helm during the most intense period of student protest, when neither the faculty nor the trustees could have kept the ship from being swamped. And then she left quietly. Her dear friend and philosophy professor Joe Brennan offered this epitaph a year after her departure: "Good Martha Peterson! She gave Barnard seven years of her generous life, but unlike Dorothy, her fellow Kansan, she did not find her Emerald City. Not in New York, anyway."[46]

STUDENTS OF THE FALL

Perhaps no four-year cohort of Barnard undergraduates ever experienced so complete a transformation of the prevailing student culture than those entering in the second half of the 1960s. Part of what made the changes so dramatic, and for many disorienting, was that the prevailing parietal rules governing student conduct were antiquated. Curfews for residential students, strict limits on male visits to the dorms (4:00 to 10:00 p.m. on weekdays, noon to midnight on weekends), and the persistence of dress codes all seemed carryovers from an earlier era. Living off campus with a boyfriend was strictly forbidden. This in a city all too familiar with the "liberating" impact of sex, drugs, and rock 'n' roll, as well as home for the largest gay and lesbian communities in the country. In the fall of 1969, Barnard set about dismantling its parietal rules. A year later, the college allowed students to live where they wished and permitted men in the dorms at all hours. To find a male visitor in a roommate's bed became for some a source of irritation and, if reported, the basis for room reassignment.[47]

The presence of drugs on campus first became an issue of institutional concern in the late 1960s, although by then parts of the Morningside Heights neighborhood, especially along the upper reaches of Amsterdam Avenue, had long been known as drug distribution points. Most of the reported student use involved marijuana, although heroin was not unknown and was available. In the fall of 1970, an incoming Barnard student died of a drug overdose at a Bronx party. Drug dealers were thought to be operating out of Ferris Booth Hall, Columbia College's student center, and were thought to make periodic passes through the dorms. One Barnard student of the class of 1971 recalled four decades later: "Drugs—a big part of Barnard life—pot the first night on campus/mescaline/acid my junior year . . . was tripping all the time." Increased surveillance by dorm advisers and stricter enforcement by the New York City Police Department, along with a growing recognition among students that drugs can and did kill, kept the casualties of this pharmacological infestation limited and allowed the campus within a short period to return to alcohol as the drug of choice.[48]

Barnard students of the late 1960s and early 1970s were the first to deal with racial issues on campus. By 1970, approximately 10 percent of the student body was Black. They included wealthy debutantes from Detroit like Michelle (Micky) Patrick, class of 1971, and others who had studied at private boarding schools, but they also included students coming from inner-city neighborhoods. Those speaking for Black students, including those among the founders of BOSS and later among those pressing the administration for separate living arrangements, did not have interracial harmony as their first priority.[49]

FIGURE 8.3 Dance celebration organized by Black Order of Soul Sisters (BOSS), 1972. Barnard Archives.

The presence of lesbian and bisexual students on campus also became more widely acknowledged. The same could be said about abortion: legally prohibited and grounds for expulsion as recently as 1968, three years later, abortion procedures were covered by the college's medical insurance.[50]

Much of the retrospective attention since paid to Barnard student life in the late 1960s focuses on its radical nature and links to larger social movements (protests against war, feminism, civil rights, environmentalism) and, given its contemporary prominence, rightly so. It is just one of

Arlene Rubenstein

FIGURE 8.4 Students on picket line during employee strike, 1971. Barnard Archives

FIGURE 8.5 Student picket line blocking access to Altschul Hall during the campus protest of the U.S. bombing of Cambodia in the spring of 1970. Barnard Archives.

FIGURE 8.6 Women's peace march. Barnard Archives.

FIGURE 8.7 Protests at the 1970 commencement ceremony. Barnard Archives.

the many strengths of the Barnard Alumnae Class of 1971 Oral History Project that its interviews encompass a representative collection of voices, including Barnard alums of the period who either sat out the revolution or lived through it with earlier beliefs and practices intact. This was more the case with commuting students (in 1970, still 40 percent of the student body) than with residents, and it was more likely the case among those who came to Barnard from religiously observant families than politically radical ones.[51]

Barnard students continued to come from a wide range of family circumstances. Ruth Stuart Bell, class of 1971, described her own as "a Brahmin family, an old Boston family. Both branches of it. . . ." And then there was Josephine Drexel Biddle Duke, whose middle names mark her bloodlines to three of America's richest and socially well-placed families (she left Barnard after a year). Another first-year student in 1967–1968, Katherine Brewster, traced her ancestry back to William Brewster, a founder of Plymouth Colony in the 1620s. At the other end of the class spectrum was Carol Santanello Spencer, class of 1971, whose parents were working-class Italian Americans, while Fay Chew Matsuda was born "in the back of a laundry in Ossining, New York" to Chinese immigrants. The father of Karla Spurlock-Evans, class of 1971, was a factory worker in the mill town of Willimantic, Connecticut.[52]

If somewhat less likely to hail from New York City, Barnard students in the late 1960s and early 1970s were more self-selecting than those attending the other remaining sister colleges (Vassar went coed in 1969 and Radcliffe effectively merged with Harvard in the early 1970s). Factors of propinquity, overall cost, and academic reputation appear to have been more crucial than family ties, social exclusivity, or the desire for an all-women's collegiate experience. In an era when single-sex colleges had become a harder sell, Barnard's link with Columbia and its location in New York City (even for outlanders) remained positive features. Still, most of the young women who applied to Barnard during this period were admitted, although under half of them then came to Barnard. Many who went elsewhere, especially if opting for a public institution, did so in part for economic reasons.[53]

Another view of Barnard students in the late 1960s that belies the retrospective focus on their rebelliousness is the number of alumnae from that period who subsequently went on to play major roles at Barnard. These one-time students include administrators President Ellen V. Futter, class of 1971; Dean of the College Dorothy Denburg, class of 1970; political scientist and Associate Dean of the Faculty Flora Davidson, class of 1971; English Department lecturer and college registrar Constance Brown, class of 1971. Faculty members who were once students include Millicent C. McIntosh Professor of English and Writing Mary Gordon, class of 1971, and trustees include Frances Sadler, class of 1972, one of the founders of BOSS.[54]

For all their political activism and social experimentation, most students of the late 1960s and early 1970s remained focused on academic performance, seeking courses on both sides of Broadway that served their intellectual interests and professional aspirations. They contributed to the first *Barnard/Columbia Course Guide*, with candid assessments of hundreds of courses open to undergraduates by undergraduates. Woe to faculty members who dismissed the immediate impact of a scathing evaluation on their enrollments or assistant professors who dismissed the impacts on enrollments or their tenure prospects, and administrators and historians who dismissed this important step in the rise of student agency.[55]

Proportionally fewer graduates of this period went to graduate school and into academic life than a decade earlier due to the decreasing number of college teaching jobs; however, many more now enrolled in law school or MBA programs and took up careers in law, business, and finance. Barnard continued to send greater proportions of graduates to medical school and into the health professions. Others turned their collegiate interests into careers of social activism. Many of these profession-bound graduates were the academically ambitious daughters of the city's newest residents, now as likely to be from Latin America, Asia, and the Middle East as from Ireland or Eastern Europe. While so much else changed during these years, Barnard remained, if reluctantly early on and proudly since the late 1940s, at the service of New York City's and now the nation's "deserving and aspiring crowds."[56]

9

SAYING NO TO ZEUS

Interviewer: Aside from your understanding both perspectives, did you think that Barnard should merge into Columbia as a whole?

Interviewee: I'll tell you what I thought. I felt like the Greek maiden Leda as the swan approaches her. How do you say no to Zeus? You know. What I felt was overwhelmed. Columbia is big. It's like living—as somebody pointed out at the time at our meeting over this—we had a 10-ton gorilla in the room, and how can we preserve our independence if the 10-ton gorilla wants to take over?

—PROFESSOR OF ENGLISH ANNE PRESCOTT, CLASS OF 1959[1]

REBEL AND MAVERICK

The job of finding Barnard's fourth president fell principally to newly elected trustee and attorney Helene L. Kaplan. Her search committee included another trustee newcomer as co-chair, investment banker William T. Golden, whose mother was a Barnard graduate. Faculty members included professor of sociology Bernard Barber and professor of Spanish Mirella Servodidio, class of 1955. The Columbia representative was professor of history Henry Graff, whose two daughters were Barnard graduates.[2]

Committed to selecting a woman, a scholar, and an experienced academic administrator, and assuming a shallow pool of candidates meeting these conditions, the committee anticipated a long search. The facts that Peterson's departure had been widely seen as a board firing and the testy Barnard-Columbia discussions were regularly reported upon by the *New York Times* did not make their task seem easier. It would take a particular kind of academic to be attracted to the prospect of entering this lion's den.

To the committee's surprise and relief, a candidate with all the stated qualifications turned up early in the canvassing. Jacquelyn A. Mattfeld, a musicologist with scholarly standing, had been at Brown University for five years as dean of faculty and academic affairs, which made her the highest ranked woman administrator among Ivy universities. Three months into the search, the committee unanimously recommended her appointment to the Barnard trustees and the president of the university. At its November 12, 1975, meeting, the trustees unanimously elected Mattfeld as Barnard's fourth president, to take office July 1, 1976.[3]

When Brown terminated Mattfeld's deanship on the announcement of her new post, Barnard board chair Eleanor Elliott asked her to spend the five months before assuming the office of presidency familiarizing herself with the issues and introducing herself to key figures at Barnard and Columbia. Elliott used the announcement of this interim arrangement to assure Barnard alumnae that there was not to be a merger and that the board and the president-elect were now embarked on an aggressive program of "innovative retrenchment."[4]

Jacquelyn Anderson Mattfeld was born in 1925 in Baltimore, Maryland, into a family that would soon be adversely affected by the Great Depression. Her father, a chemist, limited Jacquelyn's college selection to local schools. An accomplished pianist as a teenager, she first attended Peabody Conservatory and then Goucher College, where she graduated magna cum laude in 1948. From there she went to Yale for graduate studies in musicology and music history. While in New Haven, she met and married a fellow musicologist, Victor Mattfeld. Despite her PhD in music history, she could not secure even a teaching assistant (TA) position at Yale, those being reserved for men, and was forced to earn an unsteady income for the next decade giving private piano lessons. With two daughters and a husband intermittently employed editing music, she was often the family's primary wage earner.[5]

Mattfeld's career prospects brightened in 1960 when, at thirty-five, she came within the supportive orbit of Mary Bunting, then president of Radcliffe College. Bunting brought her to Cambridge as Radcliffe's associate director of financial aid. She moved to the Massachusetts Institute of Technology (MIT) in 1963 as its first female dean of student affairs, and then to Sarah Lawrence College as provost and dean of the faculty. There her marriage ended. In 1971, she became associate provost and dean of academic affairs of Brown University. Three years later, in 1974, she became Brown's dean of the faculty. At about this same time, she was offered the presidency of Swarthmore College, only to turn it down because she thought it would be "too comfortable." In 1973, reflecting on her career as a woman in a man's academic world, she characterized herself to a reporter as less "militant" than younger women colleagues:

> Don't forget, I'm 47. I've been tempered in a far different fire than women who have come in the last few years riding the crest of the wave of HEW rulings . . .
>
> I've done all the dirty work. I've been the butt of all the things that used to happen to women. That doesn't mean I'm a martyr. I'm not. I'm here because I'm good. But I'm also here because people have been good to me and I don't forget it.[6]

President-elect Mattfeld became a Morningside presence during the five months between her selection in November and the scheduled start of her presidency in May. She was introduced to the trustees at their December 10, 1975, meeting. At that same trustees meeting, she learned from board treasurer Samuel Milbank that the 1975–1976 budget was $400,000 in the red due to the shortfall from the entering and returning classes of 100 students. Newly elected trustee William Golden, citing the projected drop in endowment from $24 million to $21 million, urged adoption of a budget with a mandated cut of $650,000 over the next two years. While agreeing that "[w]e are operating at a very large deficit," ex-chair Wallace Jones opposed doing so. Matters were not helped when admissions director Helen McCann reported that the enrollment picture for the coming year was not any brighter. The national swing away from single-sex colleges and the uncertain fortunes of New York City were taking a toll.[7]

FIGURE 9.1 Jacquelyn A. Mattfeld (1926–), third president of Barnard College (1975–1980), tangled with Columbia officials and ousted by Barnard trustees. Barnard Archives.

In February 1976, president-elect Mattfeld met Columbia officials, first President William McGill and then Vice President James Young, who headed the Columbia team charged with overseeing Barnard-Columbia relations. These early talks, both sides subsequently agreed, went badly. Mattfeld later said in an open letter to the Barnard community that McGill had tried to get her to go beyond the charge she had from her trustees and commit to a merger of the Barnard faculty. When Mattfeld proposed bringing in consultants under a Ford Foundation planning grant, McGill disagreed about her recommended consultants, who included her mentor Mary Bunting. For his part, McGill suspected Mattfeld was trying to provoke him into a public fight.[8]

Some of the animosity that Mattfeld generated at Columbia might be explained as coming from male academics unused to dealing with women as professional equals and wary of being out-negotiated. Mattfeld and her defenders believed that was the source of her difficulties with McGill and Young. But then there is the case of university provost William T. deBary, whose wife and three daughters were Barnard graduates and who disagreed with the evolving Columbia view that Barnard should merge with Columbia or Columbia College should admit women. His take on Mattfeld:

> She didn't trust Columbia. Period. That's it. She had been brought in by trustees that didn't trust Columbia, once McGill had begun to talk about taking over Barnard. They got her in the search for somebody that would fight McGill, and they sure got somebody who fought him.[9]

A week before formally taking up the presidency in May, Mattfeld obtained from her trustees the following charge: "To maintain Barnard's autonomy and integrity while furthering the Barnard-Columbia relationship through institutional planning and cooperation." On August 30, in her nine-page open letter to the Barnard community, she acknowledged her already strained relations with both McGill and Young, charging them with setting conditions not contemplated in the 1973 agreement.[10]

Nor did she ingratiate herself with Columbia by negotiating in the press. On May 14, 1976, in a *New York Times* interview, under the headline, "Barnard, Columbia in a Merger Struggle," she cast herself in the role of underdog. "If push comes to shove," she told education editor Edward Fiske, "Columbia has the trump card. They can simply say that there will be no cross-registration." This followed on Mattfeld's description of her antagonists' expressed attitude toward Barnard: "Authorities at Columbia can think of no valid reason for the continuance of Barnard's independence." She also quoted Columbia's complaint with Barnard's faculty, specifically "the mediocrity in the female contingent of the faculty." Meanwhile, board chair Elliott installed a new trustee negotiating team to carry on discussions with Columbia, consisting of Helene Kaplan, William Golden, and Richard Furland, all new board members and wary of Columbia's intentions.[11]

Amid the controversies and disputes regarding merging the two schools, Mattfeld was inaugurated as Barnard's fourth president on

November 7, 1976, in a music-filled ceremony attended by 4,000 in Riverside Church. Accompanying events were widely reported as "lavish," with Barnard trustee chair Elliott personally picking up the $35,000 tab.[12]

Five months into her presidency, Mattfeld delivered an autobiographical talk to seventy-five women at the Barnard Women's Center that she entitled "The Life Story of a Maverick and a Rebel." In it, both her father and her ex-husband, and her male Yale colleagues all come up short, whereas it was the "Sisterhood" that saw her through to better times. The *Spectator* reporter covering the talk noted that her remarks left many in the audience in tears.[13]

But already something was amiss. Later reports have some trustees (and their spouses) and members of the presidential search team having second thoughts about their new president. Among those with an early case of "buyer's remorse" was Mattfeld's most enthusiastic sponsor on the board, Eleanor Elliott. During the search, she had personally checked with Mattfeld's former employers, all of whom touted her administrative skills, only later to conclude that the positive assessments from Providence were an instance of "white collar welfare" whereby Brown "just passed her along." In December 1976, Elliott resigned the position of chair after less than three years, ostensibly because of her health. A friend later described her condition as a near nervous breakdown brought on by the prospect of firing a second Barnard president.[14]

The incoming chair Arthur Altschul, financier and son of Helen Goodhart Altschul, class of 1907, was another early doubter who soon found himself unwilling to meet with Mattfeld without having trustee Helene Kaplan present. Altschul's unease with Mattfeld began after he concluded that she had tricked him into publicly aligning the board behind her call for Barnard faculty salary parity with Columbia. He had agreed with the need to reduce the longstanding gap "in principle," but Mattfeld had him committing to parity within three years. He later explicitly repudiated any such agreement.[15]

Meanwhile, the new president began installing her own set of senior administrators. For the retiring Forrest "Duke" Abbott, she appointed Harry Albers as vice president of finance; for vice president for public affairs, Doris Critz; for vice president for academic affairs and dean of the faculty, Charles S. Olton. This last appointment was a departure on two scores: Olton, a thirty-five-year-old American historian, came from outside the Barnard faculty (he had been a recently tenured member of the Buffalo State faculty and an administrative fellow at Swarthmore), and his appointment did not include a tenured position in the faculty. For a new director of admissions, Mattfeld turned to a member of the faculty, Christine Royer, a lecturer in the English Department and beloved academic adviser.[16]

Some president-watchers later suggested Mattfeld had a problem working with colleagues, including some of those she hired. Development officer Doris Critz lasted only two years before she was publicly chastised by Mattfeld and demoted, and she subsequently quit. The president alternately berated her dean of the faculty and increased his salary. The problem may have been particularly acute when it came to men. Two male spouses of trustees were said to have reacted negatively upon first meeting her. One Barnard administrator said of Mattfeld, referring to her reluctance to confront her Columbia counterparts personally: "She could not cross Broadway without feeling faint."[17]

Despite Mattfeld's run-ins with her Columbia counterparts and some of her own trustees, her championing the cause of salary parity won support among faculty members. Many appreciated her standing as a scholar and her administrative experience, while others saw her as an embattled feminist going toe-to-toe with Columbia's male chauvinists. And there was at least one (the author) who admired her calling faculty meetings to order by letting loose a whistle that could break crystal. Of all the constituencies making up the Barnard community, faculty members remained her most consistent allies throughout her star-crossed presidency.[18]

The reasons for such faculty support were not entirely self-interested. Mattfeld was more sophisticated and better attuned to the ways of eastern private institutions than her predecessor. Whereas Peterson's forte was dealing with students, Mattfeld seemed more sure-footed in taking on the financial problems she inherited. Indeed, shortly after taking office, she came up with what her staffers believed might be the answer to them.

THE MATTFELD SURGE AND ITS DISCONTENTS

Barnard's expenditures in the late 1950s and early 1960s consistently matched its income, despite the college's heavy reliance upon tuition

(tuition contributed about 70 percent to its coffers). Foundation support had helped, as well as the sale of the Claremont Avenue property back to the Rockefeller family to make way for the Interchurch Center (locally referred to as the God Box). Rosemary Park's four budgets all produced modest surpluses. Between 1962 and 1971, the endowment doubled from $12 million to $25 million ($162 million in 2019 dollars). Meanwhile, three buildings—McIntosh Student Center, Plimpton Dormitory, and Altschul Science Tower—had been added to the operating plant. Thus, trustee Eleanor Elliott explained in 1970 why Columbia, operating with annual deficits larger than Barnard's annual budgets, began to look to Barnard to relieve its financial difficulties: "Because they were broke and we were in the black."[19]

But not for long. Of Peterson's seven budgets, only the first was balanced, to be followed by six with ever-increasing deficits. These were covered by annual drawdowns on the quasi-endowment (that part not encumbered by explicit provisions), which in turn reduced the amount available for investment. Between 1971 and 1975, Barnard's endowment shrank from $25 million to $21 million. Meanwhile, faculty salaries fell further behind those of Columbia and many of Barnard's collegiate peers located in places where the cost of living was substantially less than it was in New York City.[20]

Upon assuming the position of board chair in 1977, Arthur Altschul asked Gedale Horowitz, a Citigroup financial executive, the husband of a Barnard graduate, and himself a graduate of Columbia College and Columbia Law School, to join the board as its fifth treasurer, succeeding Samuel Milbank. Horowitz found the college to be operating with two balance sheets, one that obscured the amount of debt and "the real one" that showed "[w]e were absolutely broke. . . . The school was in desperate shape." He later recalled the situation as "so close to the edge of being gone [that] Columbia would have taken the place over."[21]

Part of the financial difficulty the Peterson administration faced after 1970 was making the new negotiated annual payments to Columbia, which their negotiators pegged at $4 million and which now fell to her successor to cover. Mattfeld moved quickly to increase tuition income by enlarging the size of entering classes. Her new admissions director, Christine Royer, installed in early 1977 upon McCann's retirement, introduced new promotional literature and more active recruiting efforts that increased applications from 1,546 in 1977 to 2,278 in 1980, an increase of 47 percent. With more applicants came more admissions, reaching with Royer's first class in 1977 an astronomical admission rate of 71 percent before dropping back to 51 percent in 1980. Total enrollments grew proportionally, from 2,006 in 1975 to 2,524 in 1980, an increase of 26 percent.[22]

As early as the fall of 1977, the new chief financial officer Harry Albers credited increased enrollments with eliminating the projected budget deficit for 1977–1978, noting that Barnard "is in a much healthier position than it has been for years." Two months later, Albers acknowledged omitting from his October calculation additional expenditures of $240,000 on financial aid for the additional enrollments, which again put balancing that year's budget in doubt. "He was loved," a member of the board's finance committee recalled of Albers. "Not a good sign. He ran Barnard like a mom-and-pop store." Albers left after eighteen months in the job, assuring his staff, "The budget and my leaving are two separate matters."[23]

The surge in enrollments unaccompanied by a corresponding increase in college housing meant that Barnard applicants from the New York region could not be assured of living on campus. Being so informed, many went elsewhere. Among already enrolled students, it meant that some first-year commuters who been promised housing in their sophomore year were now told to wait until their junior or even senior year to live on campus.[24]

Turning some singles into doubles in Plimpton and in 600 and 620 West 116th Street in 1978 marginally supplemented the capacity of Barnard's dorms, but also made them less livable. Efforts to lease off-campus housing for upper-class students did not alleviate the problem and created new ones. The lease of fifty apartments in the Embassy Hotel on Broadway and Seventieth Street, for example, had to be terminated when the building's owners were arrested for loan sharking. The lease of one floor in an apartment building on 110th Street was plagued by inadequate security that allowed several break-ins and an attempted rape of a Barnard resident.[25]

What turned out to be the final blow to any chance of an administrative-student rapprochement over housing occurred in April 1980, when it was announced that the admissions office had promised too many incoming students on-campus housing, some of whom had to be given rooms slated for commuters who had waited three years for a room on campus and were now out of luck. This prompted a noontime sit-in in McIntosh led by student government leaders; it ended with administrators promising to find more off-campus housing for the incoming class.[26]

Little wonder that when two student leaders from the late 1970s were four decades later asked their views on the much-discussed prospect of merger, each recalled that student priorities of their day were less about merger than housing. When pushed to choose between Mattfeld and the trustees, even students who admired her stance toward Columbia and honored her hard-won feminism could not be counted on to come to her defense.[27]

Mattfeld's problems with providing housing for the increased number of students were complicated by the trustees' insistence that the costs of the college's auxiliary services—the provision of room and board—be income neutral. Accordingly, substantial increases in room and board prompted by inflation (the consumer price index [CPI] increase in 1979 was 12 percent) were imposed. An attempt in November 1979 to supplement the increase with a $150 "energy surcharge" on students living on campus and $60 for those commuting for the spring term prompted parents to express outrage at what they saw as a classic instance of bait and switch. It did not help matters that Columbia imposed no such surcharge and thus Barnard residents in coed Plimpton would have to pay several hundred dollars more than their Columbia hallmates. The Barnard board later rescinded these charges but not before the Student Rep Council charged the administration with "fiscal mismanagement."[28]

Concerns were expressed by a few faculty members and likely by some trustees about two other matters related to the enrollment surge. One was whether more students really increased total revenues via tuition income or whether increased financial aid outlays rendered the surge income-neutral or worse. How many of these additional students were coming simply because of generous financial aid packages that the college could ill afford? And then there was the concern that bigger enrollments unaccompanied by a parallel increase in courses offered by Barnard faculty meant larger classes.[29]

Both questions were referred by Mattfeld to her third Vice President for Finance Jack McBride. He assured the faculty at the April 2, 1980, meeting that the tuition derived from the additional students, after the added financial aid was subtracted, still netted $2 million in additional income. According to McBride, the enrollment increase was a "clear financial benefit." Whatever their nonfinancial costs, the balanced budgets of the Mattfeld presidency were real.[30]

Mattfeld and McBride were equally categorical on the matter of class size. Both cited internal studies that showed the student/faculty ratio had held steady at around 14.4 students per Barnard classroom instructor throughout the surge and even may have declined a bit. How could this be when enrollments had increased almost 20 percent and the number of full-time faculty had declined? The answer was that more and more Barnard students were taking classes at Columbia, thereby keeping Barnard classes from growing. In 1974, Barnard registrations in Columbia-taught courses numbered 5,386 while Columbia registrations in Barnard-taught course was 4,180, for a net balance favoring Columbia of 1,206 registrations; in 1979, Barnard registrations in Columbia-taught courses had increased to 5,999, and the net balance favoring Columbia had increased to 1,764. This explanation, while putting to rest the charge of overcrowded Barnard classrooms, only increased doubts about Barnard's long-term viability. It opened the administration to new charges that the enrollment surge was mostly enriching Columbia and put into play the life-or-death question of the need for a Barnard faculty. Why not just send all the students enrolled at Barnard over to Columbia for all their classes? For Barnard's beleaguered president, it seemed it was damned if she did and damned if she didn't.[31]

Meanwhile, Mattfeld kept pressure on the trustees to make good on her goal to bring Barnard faculty salaries into parity with those at Columbia within three years. She included funds in each of her budgets to help accomplish this and, despite the runaway inflation of the late 1970s, made real progress. The 1978–1979 salary program brought Barnard assistant professors into parity with those at Columbia; the 1979–1980 salary program was expected to do the same for Barnard's associate professors. A sizable gap remained at the full-professor level, but even the most critically disposed faculty members acknowledged their president's commitment to closing it.[32]

Other policy actions relating to senior faculty were less appreciated. At one point in 1978, when the trustees had effectively removed Mattfeld from the ongoing discussions with Columbia, she informed faculty members that they should likewise cease all communications with their Columbia counterparts. For the thirty or so Barnard instructors who regularly taught graduate courses and were voting members of their cognate Columbia departments, that directive went ignored.[33]

EXIT MATTFELD

Two staffers working closely with President Mattfeld in the spring of 1980 agreed in separate interviews that her firing came as a shock to their boss. The decision was delivered by four members of the executive committee of the trustees in the president's apartment on Claremont Avenue immediately after the regular June meeting of the entire board, which had transpired uneventfully. One staffer recalled her being stunned, not least by the trustees' insistence that she "get out today." Another recalled her confusion when "no reasons were provided" for her dismissal. Both faculty representatives to the trustees, Peter Juvilier and Marcia Welles, class of 1965, were also caught unaware. Nor were reasons subsequently forthcoming, either in the minutes of trustees' meeting that followed the firing or in the several interviews of trustees in the room conducted by my colleague Rosalind Rosenberg and me. What follows therefore is necessarily conjecture.[34]

There is no shortage of possible explanations for her termination. Four different ones from as many sources bear consideration. The first turns on Mattfeld's efforts to secure faculty salary parity. To increase the money available for annual salary increases for continuing faculty members, it has been said that she supplemented the trustee-approved budgetary amount going for salary increases for a given year with Columbia's annual payment for graduate instruction by Barnard faculty members to be paid in the next year. Doing so represented a departure from normal accounting rules. When both the dean of the faculty, Charles S. Olton, and the budget officer, Helen Vanides, pointed this out to the president, they were directed to proceed anyway, without informing the trustees.[35]

The trustees, so this explanation goes, inadvertently learned of this practice in early May 1980 when a Finance Committee member did a back-of-the-envelope calculation of what faculty members were being told by the administration they would be receiving against the amount allotted by the trustees. The salary increases exceeded the budgeted amount. When questioned by members of the board, Dean Olton confirmed the board member's calculation and stated that commingling the budgeted amount for salaries with the Columbia payment had been the practice in prior budgets as well, as directed by the president. Olton later recalled that he and a knowledgeable senior member of the faculty jokingly referred to it as "the loaves and fishes strategy."[36]

Once the trustees learned of this practice, and concluding that it was intended to mislead them by understating the magnitude of the salary increases, Mattfeld was fired. Olton narrowly escaped a similar fate by producing the memo he wrote to Mattfeld questioning her instructions as being at variance with standard accounting practices. To the extent that this was the smoking gun, it comports with a view expressed later by some trustees of their president as "unstable" and "manipulative."[37]

A second explanation, this from the Mattfeld camp, has her being fired because she had succeeded all too well in protecting Barnard's autonomy, frustrating board members who wanted to merge with Columbia. By increasing enrollments, balancing the budget, rallying alumnae, and securing the support of her faculty, Mattfeld had eliminated the need for merger. One of her staffers claimed that, in the immediate aftermath of the firing, board members still favoring a merger sought to undercut recent successes in recruiting students by slashing the financial aid budget by 45 percent. This was blocked only by the staffer's impassioned objections and the threat of a story to this effect appearing in the *New York Times*. The financial aid funding was restored, the *Times* story never appeared, and the staffer was fired.[38]

A third explanation was that trustees objected to Mattfeld's open lesbian relationship with a colleague from Providence who was living in the president's apartment on Claremont Avenue. That some students and faculty members were aware of this relationship attests to its visibility if not its role in prompting Mattfeld's firing.[39]

The last proffered explanation implicates Columbia in the firing. In the spring of 1979, President McGill, exhausted after his protracted financial rescue of the university, told his trustees of his intention to retire the following year. With their approval, he then offered the job of university provost to the dean of the law school, Michael I. Sovern, personally assuring him that as provost he had the inside track to become Columbia's next president a year hence.[40]

The new provost and president-in-waiting made it an early order of business to reach out to Barnard's president by inviting her to Columbia for an introductory meeting. Sovern and Mattfeld had previously never met, in itself unusual because of the weekly meeting of all the Columbia deans convened by the university provost, which Barnard presidents and deans had faithfully attended going back to the Gildersleeve deanship.

Mattfeld chose not to attend, however, sending instead a succession of staffers in her stead, one of whom noted that Sovern, unlike some of the other deans, was unfailingly kind to her.[41]

The meeting between the Barnard president and the Columbia president-to-be went badly. Rather than accept the invitation to meet alone and without an agenda, Mattfeld surprised Sovern by showing up with her dean of the faculty in tow. Early in the meeting, she objected to something Sovern said, declaring the remark "an opinion a man would have." It went downhill from there. As for Sovern, he might well have asked, "What's her story?" and relayed his misgivings about working with her to some of Barnard's trustees, several of whom were personal friends and professional acquaintances. It is likely that the message (that the prospects for resolving the Barnard-Columbia impasse would be facilitated by Barnard having a new president) made it across Broadway.[42]

Whatever the explanation, and it may have been a combination of the above and still others, Mattfeld was out after four years as Barnard's fourth president. Hers was the shortest tenure of any administrative head of the college. Her departure elicited objections from her faculty supporters but little in the way of student dismay. She remains the only one of Barnard's six past presidents not to have her portrait in Sulzberger Parlor.

From New York, Mattfeld proceeded to administrative posts in the South, Southwest, and West, later earning an MA in gerontology and consulting about the theories and experiences of late-life development. She retired in 2014 as executive director and director of public programs of the C. G. Jung Center in Evanston, Illinois, at age eighty-nine.[43]

FACULTY IN FLUX

Since 1900, Barnard has had its own faculty consisting of both men and women, with the latter becoming the majority of the instructional staff in the mid-1920s. Equal gender representation in two of the three faculty ranks—assistant and associate professors—had been achieved in the 1950s, although in the rank of full professor, men remained in the majority until 1970. This, of course, placed it in sharp contrast with the Columbia faculty, which tenured its first women in the late 1930s, although up to the 1960s, it had only a handful of tenured women among the 600 members of its three arts and sciences faculties. In other ways, however, the two post–World War II faculties were much alike. Both institutions favored hiring those whose graduate training was acquired at Columbia or, failing that, one of the other Ivy League schools. Also, and even more with Barnard than Columbia, a substantial portion of their faculties had been undergraduates on Morningside Heights. Both faculties looked first to their own junior ranks when filling tenured positions, although Columbia made a higher proportion of outside senior appointments than did Barnard. Until the 1950s, a senior appointee at Columbia usually stayed on to retirement. At Barnard, however, midcareer male senior faculty members regularly transferred to Columbia. Nine did so between 1945 and 1970, whereas only one senior Columbia faculty member during those same years transferred to Barnard.[44]

Several practical considerations helped account for the one-way direction of this interaction. Columbia's salaries were higher than Barnard's, in some years and ranks by as much as 20 percent. Columbia's teaching programs were lighter than Barnard's, by a course or two each year. Columbia faculty members had some choice in their teaching programs: they taught graduate students exclusively (the cases of Richard Hofstadter and Robert K. Merton), mostly undergraduates (Lionel Trilling, Jacques Barzun), or a mixture of both. A Barnard faculty member taught undergraduates, with the occasional graduate course available only at the invitation of Columbia as its needs dictated. Beyond these considerations, a tenured position on the Columbia faculty simply conveyed higher professional status than did one on the Barnard faculty. The first meant identification with a world-class research university, the second with a first-rate undergraduate women's college.[45]

These contrasting institutional circumstances produced equally distinctive internal secondary effects. Standing within the Columbia faculty was primarily a function of one's scholarly eminence in one's field. Teaching effectiveness, especially at the undergraduate level, was a lesser consideration and, where the scholarly eminence was of star quality, dispensable. (Nobel laureates often turned out to be poor or indifferent teachers.) Ditto institutional service, with some of Columbia's faculty luminaries successfully eluding turns serving as department chairs. What made one Columbia faculty member more valuable than another in the eyes of his (the gender attribution still valid) colleagues was the perceived quality of his scholarly output as measured by citations and the prominence his graduate students acquired in a given field. Contributions to institutional well-being were welcome but optional. Trilling's comment in the midst of the 1968 protests is suggestive: "You see, I still can't understand why [students] give a good god damn about how the University runs. I didn't. Why should they?"[46]

Barnard's heavier teaching programs and higher expectations of service cut into time available for scholarship. But other limiting factors included the absence of graduate students and, especially in the case of Barnard's science faculty, the lack of research laboratory space. Scholarly productivity did not go unrewarded at post–World War II Barnard, but it also carried with it in some quarters the suspicion that it had been achieved by shirking one's responsibilities in the classroom or departmental and college service. A Barnard professor's internal standing derived as much from her reputation as a brilliant classroom teacher, a beloved adviser, a devoted department chair, or long-serving committee member as it did from her publications. Promotion to full professor sometimes was accelerated for the most scholarly active associate professors but more often came as a function of years in rank. Similarly, with the exception of the holder of the college's single endowed professorship, faculty salaries were keyed to years in rank, with increases in fixed amounts rather than by individual considerations, such as the publication of a well-received book, the receipt of a research grant, or even an outside offer.[47]

Another post–World War II development that widened the gap between the scholarly profiles of the Barnard and Columbia faculties was a declining involvement in the Barnard tenure process by the equivalent Columbia department. In the absence of this oversight, some Barnard tenure appointments were made to junior faculty whose teaching effectiveness and departmental service were more demonstrable than their scholarly productivity. The subsequent involvement of these faculty with modest scholarly records in determining who among their junior colleagues should be nominated for tenure could only have the effect of keeping scholarly expectations modest.[48]

The shift during the McIntosh administration of the college-wide Appointments and Tenure Committee (ATP), which advised the president on all departmental nominations of junior faculty members to tenure, from appointive by the president to elective by the faculty likely further attenuated the committee's—and the college's—commitment to the expectation that ongoing scholarship was expected, if not required, of Barnard senior faculty. To be sure, many Barnard senior faculty in the post–World War II era continued to pursue publishing agendas beyond tenure, with several of the men who did so transferring to Columbia or taking up university appointments elsewhere. But as long as Barnard's women faculty had few prospects for doing either, the incentive to keep up their publishing was personal and went institutionally unrewarded.[49]

Thus, when Columbia department members in the early 1970s, at the urging of economy-minded administrators, turned their serious attention to their Barnard counterparts as future colleagues, they saw professional profiles markedly different from their own. In the first instance, they, mostly men, saw mostly women. And second, they saw men and women whose careers had been largely shaped by the needs and rewards of an undergraduate college. While the prospect of an infusion of young women faculty had its attraction for departments such as art history and anthropology, conspicuously male-dominated even where their graduate students were mostly women, that of acquiring tenured faculty of either gender who lacked sufficient professional visibility to advance the reputation of their Columbia department was dispiriting. It was this concern, even as no decision had yet been made to merge departments, that prompted Columbia in 1972 to insist upon having a much more active role in the future hiring of Barnard faculty and a determinative role in the tenure of Barnard faculty should a merger happen. While not set to become operative until academic year 1974–1975, two Columbia departments weighed in to attempt to derail the last ad hoc committee nominations going forward at Barnard.[50]

The Barnard constituency most affected by the new ad hoc procedures was the faculty. Some senior faculty welcomed the change, with their place as tenured members of the university confirmed, if only by being grandfathered in. Others saw their opportunities for graduate teaching enhanced and normalized. But some senior faculty members, particularly women, saw a university with a history of discriminatory practices toward women now determining the composition of Barnard's faculty. And, should merger occur, Columbia faculty would be dictating their teaching programs. They had cause for concern.[51]

A few junior faculty members of both genders welcomed the change, for the same reasons as those senior faculty members who saw the new provisions validating their standing in the university and who looked forward to the higher salaries, more varied teaching program, and higher professional standing. Other junior faculty members, especially those nearing the end of their probationary seven years and about to be evaluated under arrangements that privileged scholarly productivity, looked at the prospect as career threatening.[52]

The first four nominations forwarded by Barnard to the Columbia provost's office for consideration by an ad hoc faculty committee in the spring of 1974 resulted in three tenure approvals and one initial rejection, that of Catharine Stimpson, a popular assistant professor of English and already a nationally known feminist theorist. When President Peterson invoked the formal appeal mechanism included in the agreement on Stimpson's behalf, President McGill overrode the negative decision of his provost but said he would not do so again. From that point on, the internal reviews conducted by Barnard's ATP became much more focused on a nominee's scholarship. Cases that earlier would have sailed through faced increased scrutiny. Rejections of Barnard nominees at the university ad hoc committee level or by the provost became annual springtime events and cause for consternation throughout the entire Barnard community, not least among the college's students and recent alumnae, who saw some of their most admired teachers obliged to leave.[53]

Responses to a faculty survey I conducted in June 1974 suggest the several fault lines that characterized the Barnard faculty at the implementation of the ad hoc tenure procedures. The survey consisted of twenty-three questions designed to determine how faculty members identified themselves, either primarily as an undergraduate teacher or as a publishing scholar. A secondary purpose was to collect the range of faculty views on the prospect of closer cooperation and possible merger with Columbia.[54] The survey revealed that:

—Barnard faculty members were pretty evenly divided between those identifying primarily with their scholarly role (48 percent) and their teaching role (52 percent).
—Barnard male faculty members more often self-identified as "scholars," "primarily scholars," or "scholars-teachers" "(56 percent) than did female faculty (43 percent).

—Social science faculty members more often self-identified as "scholars" and "primarily scholars" (53 percent) than did those in the sciences (35 percent), the humanities (28 percent), or modern languages (10 percent).

—Tenured faculty members self-identified as "scholars" and "primarily scholars" (41 percent) more than did untenured faculty members (27 percent).

—Members of small departments (e.g., physics, anthropology, religion) closely linked with their Columbia cognate department more often self-identified as "scholars" and "primarily scholars" than did members of large departments operating in isolation (English, Spanish; psychology).[55]

More than four decades later, the most striking overall picture to be drawn from this novice polling exercise, which in its intrusiveness and transparency could likely not be replicated today, was of a faculty in the midst of an identity crisis that would take years to resolve.

We know in retrospect that the seemingly imminent merger of the faculties in the 1970s did not take place. But the imposition of the ad hoc procedures in anticipation of that non-event nonetheless has had a significant effect on the subsequent composition of the Barnard faculty. Before the 1970s, Barnard faculty members consisted mostly of long-serving and devoted teacher-scholars, along with the occasional scholar-teacher, who, if male, often moved on, and if female, likely stayed. Since the 1970s, the faculty has come increasingly to consist of scholar-teachers regardless of gender, field, or rank. While faculty commitment to classroom teaching and service remains essential to the workings of the college, it is ultimately published scholarship that wins them a permanent place in the faculty and secures for them additional recognition. Almost every new faculty policy adopted since the early 1980s has confirmed and reinforced this shift in professional identity. A similar shift has since occurred at other leading liberal arts colleges, but later and arguably less completely than at Barnard.[56]

10

BARNARD RISING

*We aimed to save the College, and I saw the crisis as an opportunity to
highlight Barnard's story as a high-quality undergraduate college.*

—ELLEN V. FUTTER[1]

TOUCHING BOTTOM—BARNARD IN THE
SUMMER OF 1980

The abrupt termination of the Mattfeld presidency in June 1980 left Barnard
without administrative leadership even as the decade-long negotiations
with Columbia passed into the hands of its new president. During his year
as university provost and president-designate, Michael I. Sovern had made
it clear that he wanted to settle the question of the Barnard-Columbia relationship quickly. As he later wrote, he hoped to avoid being cast as "the
Butcher of Barnard" and was less committed to a merger of the Barnard
faculty than Dean of Graduate Faculties George K. Fraenkel, but he was
alert to calls from college administrators and alumni that any further delay
in admitting women could do permanent damage to Columbia College.[2]

Meanwhile, the Barnard faculty, substantial portions of which had seen
Mattfeld as a champion of the cause of faculty parity and a critic of the ad
hoc system, were further unsettled by the trustees firing her. The absence

of an explanation only added to the disquiet. So did the feeling among some faculty members that the increasing imbalance in the flow of students across Broadway put their jobs at risk.

For their part, students and their parents had other reasons for concern. Not least was the continuing shortage of on-campus housing, along with the likelihood of inflation-fueled steep hikes in tuition and fees. Nor did it help that New York City, just past its brush with bankruptcy, continued to be perceived as dangerous and uninviting to all but the most intrepid out-of-towners.[3]

To be sure, Mattfeld had avoided the annual deficits of her predecessor, but only by increasing enrollments to levels now seen as unsustainable without additional on-campus housing. Whatever prospect of acquiring additional property seemed dashed when a request to the Department of Housing and Urban Development (HUD) for a $4.6 million dormitory loan in 1979 was rejected.[4]

The Barnard endowment in 1980 stood at $20 million ($62 million in 2020 dollars), $3 million less than a decade earlier. Fundraising was hampered by the turnover in presidents and development officers as well as the unwillingness of alumnae or foundations to give to Barnard because a merger with Columbia seemed more likely. As a modestly endowed women's college currently accepting 60 percent of its applicants in an era when women's colleges were closing at a faster rate than at any time since they came on the scene in the 1830s, Barnard was seen as a risky investment.[5]

CHILDREN'S CRUSADE

After their experience with two seasoned academic administrators but strangers to New York, the Barnard trustees turned to one of their own to serve as acting president. Doing so departed from past precedent, when gaps between chief administrators in 1894, 1900, 1967, and 1975 were filled by faculty members. The only exception was in 1946, upon Gildersleeve's retirement, when trustee-chair-elect Helen Rogers Reid filled in as acting dean (chairing faculty meetings in her trademark hat). On July 10, 1980, the trustees announced the results of their internal search.[6]

The appointment of Ellen V. Futter as acting president, two months shy of her thirty-first birthday, surprised everyone outside the Barnard board and likely some within. Faculty representatives to the board learned of her selection in the *New York Times*. Futter's youth was only part of what made the appointment unusual. Futter was a Barnard graduate after transferring from the University of Wisconsin at the end of her sophomore year. (Her home in Port Washington in Nassau County had rendered her ineligible for first-year housing at Barnard.) Her professional training was in law and her occupational experience was as an associate at Milbank, Tweed, Hadley, and McCloy, one of New York's major Wall Street law firms, where she was a corporate attorney. Whereas Barnard's four previous heads had all been academics with extensive administrative and/or teaching experience, she brought neither to the job. (The only previous nonacademic was Laura Drake Gill, not a reassuring precedent.) The post was defined as "acting," with the explicit understanding that Futter would

FIGURE 10.1 Ellen Futter, class of 1970, fifth president of Barnard College (1980–1993), 1972 photograph. Barnard Archives.

return to Milbank, Tweed within a year or earlier upon Barnard's finding a permanent president. This assurance did little to allay the immediate concern among some faculty members and alumnae that the trustees had again acted too quickly, if not in panic. The appointee later recalled her selection being likened in some quarters to the desperate launching of "a children's crusade."[7]

In hindsight, the appointment is easier to understand. The leadership vacuum created by Mattfeld's sudden departure could not wait on a national search; it had to be filled quickly. But who would take the job on the fly was another concern. This called for someone on the scene, someone who was readily available and conversant with the issues. Mattfeld's dean of the faculty, Charles S. Olton, was still relatively new to the Barnard community, was not tenured, and had barely escaped being fired along with his boss. Someone might conceivably have been drawn from the senior faculty, but no one was sufficiently informed on the issues or had the confidence of the board. And because faculty members were divided over both the firing of Mattfeld—seventy members had signed a petition decrying it—and the proper approach to Columbia, the appointment of one of them might further exacerbate the faculty divisions.[8]

Thus, from the perspective of the trustees, turning to one of their own as acting president seemed a more attractive alternative. In Futter's case, a leave of absence from Milbank, Tweed, a firm with many links to the Barnard board, could be arranged without jeopardizing her prospects for a partnership. At the same time, Futter's youth was not the liability that some outsiders assumed it to be. It might make her relations with students easier, not an insignificant factor considering the frayed relations between Mattfeld and student leaders during her last months. That students might see her as an older sister rather than someone at a generation or two remove had its potential advantages. So did the newsworthiness of an elite Seven Sisters college entrusting its presidency to one of its graduates two years short of her tenth reunion. Faculty members who had taught her a decade earlier were prepared to certify both her abilities and her character as being one of the grown-ups.[9]

Futter's youth was also misleading if it implied an absence of relevant experience. Of all her predecessors, only Virginia Gildesleeve, who became dean at age thirty-four, brought as much local and institutional knowledge to the job. Like Gildersleeve, Futter was a New Yorker, born in the city (September 21, 1949) and raised in Port Washington, a close suburb on the North Shore of Long Island. Her father Victor was a graduate of Columbia College (1939) and Columbia Law School (1942), and was counsel for Allied Chemical. He was also an active alumnus and had served as president of the Columbia College Alumni Association. Futter's mother was a middle-school librarian and her grandmother had been a graduate of Teachers College and a friend of Sarah Butler (class of 1915), the only daughter of Nicholas Murray Butler. Like Gildersleeve, Futter was a magna cum laude graduate and student leader. She was also a graduate of Columbia's law school, where Michael I. Sovern, who became Columbia's seventeenth president two weeks before her appointment as Barnard's acting president, had been her dean.[10]

Where Futter's prior experience exceeded that of Gildersleeve was her eight years as a member of the Barnard board of trustees. Appointed in 1972 at age twenty-two to fill the vacated seat of ex–Supreme Court Justice Arthur Goldberg, having just served two years as the board's second nonvoting student representative, she soon became a junior member of the inner circle of trustees, which consisted of trustee veteran Eleanor Elliott, the newly appointed William Golden, Arthur Altschul, and Helene Kaplan, plus the ex-president of the University of Rhode Island Frank Newman and the banker Dale Horowitz, who joined the board in 1977. Together, they shaped board policy with respect to Columbia in the late 1970s and without Futter's involvement forced Mattfeld's resignation. To the extent that the board saw Barnard's future as an autonomous college affiliated with Columbia University, giving the ball to its youngest member made sense.[11]

COLUMBIA RULES

For his part, the newly installed Columbia president Michael I. Sovern had made known his intention to settle the coeducation issue quickly and proceed with his own agenda. Still not ready to risk the public relations fallout from implementing the plan favored by Columbia College deans, that Columbia immediately admit women and good luck to Barnard, he proposed to Futter a less radical alternative: that Barnard and Columbia take steps to ensure that Columbia classes had the same proportion of women students as the other Ivy League schools, with those women being provided by Barnard. Predictably, a plan devised by two lawyers and set to be monitored by a third came with its own label: de facto coeducation. It was to go into effect for the 1981–1982 fall term.[12]

The acting president's charge from her board was straightforward: come to an agreement with Columbia that secured Barnard's autonomy without losing its affiliation with the university. Both the Barnard board and the acting president knew that Columbia could, at any point, with a year's notice, terminate the 1900 intercorporate agreement and begin admitting women to the college. This was precisely what the Columbia College dean Arnold Collery (as had his three predecessors) argued for, as had Columbia faculty identified with the college. As Dean of Studies Roger Lehecka put it, Columbia was being "held hostage" because it was unable to compete with its Ivy peers as a result of Barnard's exclusive right to admit women undergraduates.[13]

For his part, Sovern was alert to the possible costs of moving unilaterally. And as with many pre-1983 Columbia professors with daughters, one of his was a loyal Barnard alumna. There was also concern that Barnard alumnae and donors would not take kindly to Columbia acting in its own self-interest by hanging Barnard out to dry. The Columbia community had its own Barnard loyalists: ex-provost William Theodore deBary, whose wife and three daughters were Barnard alumnae; Joan Ferrante, a professor in the Columbia English Department and a daughter-in-law of Millicent McIntosh; and professor of religion Gillian Lindt were among them. The wider feminist community would see the move as another instance of male chauvinism. In October, at a forum sponsored by Lesbians at Barnard (LAB), eighty Barnard students signed a petition titled "Women Against Merger."[14]

What de facto coeducation required of Barnard was a restructuring of its requirements so that Barnard students would be required to take more classes at Columbia, including those in the college's core curriculum, thereby assuring a level of coeducation at Columbia comparable to that of its Ivy peers. Negotiations with Co-Provost Fritz Stern during the first months of the Futter acting presidency seemed close to achieving such an arrangement, one where Barnard's compliance was to be overseen by a third party, Columbia law school professor Albert Rosenthal, who was acceptable to both Sovern and Futter. Other parts of the proposed package involved Barnard faculty teaching in the Columbia core curriculum, Barnard students becoming eligible to play on Columbia's National Collegiate Athletic Association (NCAA) Title I athletic teams, and students of both Barnard and Columbia having the option of meeting the major requirements of either school. It seemed that spring that a deal could be reached allowing Barnard to retain both its autonomy and its Columbia affiliation, without Columbia College admitting women. In the spring of 1981, some Barnard faculty members (the author among them) began brushing up on the Western classics that were required for Columbia College's core curriculum in the expectation that they might be called upon to help staff it.[15]

In April 1981, the Barnard trustees announced that they had concluded their nine-month national search for a president and offered the job to acting president Futter. She accepted, conditioned upon the search committee securing the endorsement of Barnard's senior faculty. When this was immediately forthcoming, Futter became Barnard's ninth academic leader and fifth president, and at thirty-two, its youngest. President Sovern applauded the appointment. Surely some of the confidence the search committee, board, senior faculty, and the incumbent had in the appointment flowed from what appeared to be the propitious state of the interinstitutional negotiations and the prospect of a successful outcome.[16]

Not so fast. In 1980, the new dean of Columbia College, Arnold Collery, commissioned a committee of college faculty to assess the situation of Columbia as the last of the all-male Ivy League schools. Ronald Breslow, professor of chemistry, was named chair, and in April 1981, issued the Breslow Report. His was not the first declaration from Hamilton Hall that made the case for the college admitting women. Others dated back to the deanship of Carl Hovde, while a subsequent unauthorized endorsement of admitting women had cost Peter Pouncey his deanship in 1976. Reports issued in 1978 and 1980 by committees chaired by professor of history Eugene Rice and professor of physics Gerald Feinberg made much the same case. The view from Hamilton Hall summarized in the Feinberg Report reported that 82 percent of Columbia College respondents found their single-sex situation depressing. "It's not Barnard's existence that anyone attacks; it's the fact that the existence prevents a decent social life."[17]

What distinguished the Breslow Report from its predecessors and helps account for its game-changing impact was the categorical answers it gave to two crucial questions:

1. Q: Could Columbia College restore its place as a highly selective Ivy without moving immediately to admit women?
    A: No.
2. Q: Could Barnard survive were Columbia College to admit women?
    A: Yes.

In defending the first conclusion, Breslow and his committee went beyond earlier descriptions of the college's slippage in student recruitment to portray it as on the cusp of an irreversible decline. All prospects of increasing applications and enrollments turned on Columbia College doubling the size of its recruitment pool by opening its doors to women. Perhaps more revealing was the report's call to replace the bottom quarter of its recent all-male acceptances with more qualified women by moving as quickly as possible to a student body of half women.[18]

Unstated but generally assumed was that the bottom quarter of the college student body, the smallest in the Ivy League, contained a disproportionately high percentage of recruited athletes needed to field the twenty-five teams mandated by Columbia's status as an NCAA Title I school. A third or more of Columbia admissions in 1980 were athletes. Football alone required the recruitment of fifty potential players a year. If the college did not become bigger, the Breslow Report concluded that the college could not get better, and both depended on recruiting their own women. Without women, and given the projected 17 percent shrinkage in the applicant pool in the 1980s, the college would be forced to become even less selective to maintain current enrollment levels.[19]

The Breslow committee reached its second finding by taking Barnard's own upbeat public projections at face value. Thus, when President Mattfeld assured the Barnard community in the spring of 1979 that Barnard "was without peer," this was cited as proof of Barnard's long-term viability. The Breslow Report's bottom line: Columbia College needed to act in its own institutional interest, which was to admit women, leaving to Barnard to sort out its own future.[20]

THE DIME DROPS

Negotiations between Barnard and Columbia on how to implement de facto coeducation for the college continued into the late summer of 1981 but were briefly suspended in August when President Futter experienced complications with her first pregnancy. Both President Sovern and Co-Provost Stern had pressed for a quick agreement that could be communicated at the first meeting of the university senate in September, but that deadline went unmet. Futter took another break from the discussions in late October to give birth to her daughter Victoria. The clock kept ticking. At one point in the late fall of 1981, a Columbia staffer told Barnard Dean of Studies Barbara Schmitter that Barnard had two weeks to commit to the de facto coeducation plan or see Columbia College given the green light by its trustees to admit women.[21]

Meanwhile, Barnard staffers, along with consultants from Peat, Marwick, and Mitchell, developed various models for what achieving coeducational levels of 40 percent in Columbia classrooms meant for Barnard. They concluded it would require a substantially larger number of Barnard students taking classes at Columbia, with a correspondingly larger share of Barnard tuition income being transferred to Columbia, than earlier thought. But how many more students crossing Broadway and how much more tuition income going with them? One scenario, taking into account that Barnard enrolled 400 fewer students than the college: to achieve 40 percent coeducation at Columbia would require 79 percent of all Barnard registrations being in Columbia-taught classes.[22]

Here the historical record is unclear, and my interviews are inconclusive. But in a seven-page letter to President Sovern on November 16, 1981, in which she cited the 40 percent versus 79 percent numbers, President Futter signaled that adoption of the de facto coeducation plan was unacceptable to Barnard. She called for more discussion.[23]

Time was up. At a meeting of the Columbia board of trustees in early December, President Sovern was given authority, upon informing Barnard, to make plans to admit women to Columbia College in the fall of 1983. Co-Provost Stern was delegated to inform Futter, which he did in late December. "The winds have changed," he told her. The other Columbia negotiator, Co-Provost Peter Likins, slated to leave to become president of Lehigh University, later succinctly stated in impressively neutral language why Barnard could not accept the de facto plan: "Because they would end up with most of their students taking courses on this side of the street most of the time." Without disagreeing, Futter later put the outcome differently. "Columbia changed its mind," she stated in an interview. "They walked away from a deal-well-along-in-the-making." As for the need to send so much of Barnard's tuition income to Columbia: "We were prepared to figure how to do that."[24]

Another possibility is that the Barnard negotiators realized early that Columbia could do what it wanted with respect to opening the college to women simply by giving Barnard one year's notice and ending the 1900 agreement. It was only a matter of time before it would do so. They accordingly sought to protract the negotiating period as long as possible to better prepare for the inevitable by sharpening the institution's self-identity, hoping that "when the dime dropped," Barnard would be ready to deal with the consequences. Or as a Barnard staffer recalled working at the time with Peat, Marwick developing scenarios: "What do we do if they do it? And then they did it."[25]

Discussions between the trustees of the two institutions that followed on Columbia's announcement were remembered by one of the Barnard participants as "very difficult." The Barnard team, sensing they were the target of a "hostile takeover," augmented their ranks by the inclusion of Joseph Flom, the famed mergers-and-acquisitions attorney and subsequent trustee. The upshot of these discussions was a two-part agreement:

—Barnard would accept a change in the intercorporate agreement and thus allow Columbia College to admit women in the fall of 1983.
—Columbia would accept an alteration in the standing ad hoc faculty procedures as applied to Barnard tenure cases by replacing one of the three Columbia faculty members of the five-member committee with an academic drawn from outside the university.[26]

While Columbia's concession on the composition of ad hoc tenure committees allowed Barnard to come away with something of importance, particularly to its faculty, few observers missed the asymmetry of the outcomes or its unilateral initiation. President Futter certainly had no illusions about the latter, telling her faculty on January 25, 1982, the day after the agreement was made public: "Barnard did not decide to terminate these discussions. The decision was not for Barnard to make."[27]

WHISTLING PAST THE GRAVEYARD

At that same faculty meeting in January 1982, President Futter concluded her remarks with the message that Barnard was "now, more than ever, in charge of its own destiny." As for Barnard's ties to Columbia: "We are more certain than ever before of a long-term stable relationship." For some in the audience, the author among them, these statements, however brave, fell short of reassuring Barnard's very survival as an autonomous institution.[28]

The challenge facing the Barnard community was threefold:

1. No longer the only source of undergraduate education for college-age women on Morningside Heights, Barnard would now be vying for qualified students with its better-known neighbor in addition to its traditional competitors. Would Barnard be able to continue to attract bright women in sustainable numbers in this new competitive environment? And could it do so while entering the possibility of another multiyear decline in the size of the college-age cohort, especially in the Northeast, with New York City's standing as an attractive college town questionable?

2. With the merger of the Barnard faculty with Columbia's now off the table (Fraenkel had stepped down as dean of the graduate faculties in 1982), maintaining access for the thirty-plus Barnard faculty (out of 150) who were teaching graduate courses as part of their programs became an open question. More broadly, would Barnard be able to maintain a faculty of scholar-teachers under this new dispensation, or would it have to abandon its recently acquired research ethos and revert to its earlier identity as primarily classroom teachers?

3. The outcome of the merger-that-wasn't did nothing to strengthen Barnard's fragile financial situation, except possibly to engage the active financial support of some heretofore inactive alumnae now alerted to

their college's tenuous condition. Would Barnard have the financial aid funds necessary to secure strong incoming classes and support them for four years at Barnard? And what of the salaries and research equipment necessary to attract and retain a quality faculty?[29]

There were also the two issues tentatively agreed upon during the 1980–1981 discussions between Co-Provost Stern and Futter—access for Barnard athletes to Columbia teams and Columbia dorms for Barnard students. Because those discussions were preempted, they needed to be renegotiated.

No one at Barnard could be sure that the college was up to meeting these challenges, while some at Columbia expected Barnard to be in such terminal shape by 1987, when the 1982 intercorporate agreement would be up for renegotiation, that it would then be quietly folded into Columbia and cease to be. To such prognosticators, President Futter responded: "We're here to stay." But also: "This was not a divorce."[30]

Before taking up the long-term challenge of Barnard's survival, Futter had to contend in the spring of 1982 with a dispute within the feminist community between those who saw pornography as demeaning and insulting to women and those who believed opposition to pornography infringed upon women's right to enjoy sex in its many forms. This dispute threatened to turn the annual Scholar and Feminist Conference into a battleground over the issue of pornography. The theme and the organization of the 1982 conference, the ninth in what had become a widely recognized event within the feminist community and the growing number of women's studies scholars, had been assigned to Carole Vance, a Columbia anthropologist. Funding was to be provided by the Helena Rubinstein Foundation. When it appeared from the speakers selected and from early versions of what the organizers called a "diary" to be distributed at the conference (the diary promised "artwork and reproductions of contemporary and historical visual material on sexuality") that the topic choice would permit a full hearing of the sex-positive position, anti-pornography feminists complained to Barnard officials and the Rubinstein Foundation. President Futter, concerned about adverse publicity, insisted that Barnard's name be scrubbed from the program. This led to a countercampaign of letter writing and calls from Vance and her supporters, including some Barnard alumnae, to have Barnard stand by the conference organizers and the program in the name of academic freedom. Meanwhile, the Rubinstein funding was withdrawn, the diary went undistributed the day of the conference, and the controversy around Barnard's so-called sex conference drew national attention. Locally, Futter's stand had the support of most of the Barnard community, even among faculty identified with the Women's Center, while her critics acknowledged that she had acted decisively in what she saw as the best interests of the college. Subsequent Scholar and Feminist conferences have since reverted to less charged subjects.[31]

Futter's first move after the announcement of the new intercorporate agreement was to initiate a sweeping curriculum review, with an unstated goal of revamping Barnard's academic offerings to distinguish them from those of Columbia College and to develop new courses that would attract Columbia students under the ongoing cross-registration arrangements. It was the right place to start. As then Dean of the Faculty Charles S. Olton later characterized the Barnard curriculum of the time, which had not been reviewed in twenty years: "Nothing to write home about." Lawrence A. Cremin, a distinguished historian of American education and President of Teachers College, chaired the curriculum review committee.[32]

In short order (as curricular changes go), the committee produced several recommendations that went directly to the faculty for consideration. The first to come to a full faculty vote, in May 1983, was the inclusion in the curriculum of a required course that combined the critical consideration of major texts organized thematically with a focus on developing critical writing skills. These courses, required of all incoming first-year students and initially called freshman seminars, were to be taught by regular faculty drawn from throughout the college and in a seminar-like format, with enrollment limited to sixteen students. (This would be in addition to a two-semester writing course required for first-year students and taught by members of the English Department.) The seminars were introduced in the fall of 1984. With surprisingly little alteration, other than a change in title to First-Year Seminar and the inclusion in some of the seminars of a speaking component, the classes remain a feature of the Barnard curriculum today.[33]

A second curricular innovation coming out of the 1981–1982 comprehensive review was another required course: Quantitative Reasoning. Put in place to ensure that all Barnard students had an early exposure to analytical methods making use of numbers and statistics, it in turn encouraged several departments in the sciences and social sciences to develop courses that fulfilled this requirement because they introduced non- or prospective majors to a range of discipline-specific methodologies.[34]

A third initiative was the Centennial Scholars Program, funded by an anonymous donor and designed to attract top applicants to Barnard, regardless of their financial circumstances. The program underwrote special seminars that Centennial Scholars would take alongside their regular coursework and provided stipends for summer research. Throughout its twenty-five-year existence, the program was successively co-chaired by several of Barnard's leading scholars and most innovative teachers, among them Barbara S. Miller, class of 1962; Les Lessenger; and Helene Foley. In 2015, it was merged with the Athena Scholars Program, and in 2017, it was revived through the generosity of trustee Ruth Ellen Horowitz (class of 1983) as the Scholars of Distinction Program.[35]

Other curricular initiatives substantially increased Barnard's involvement in the arts. Successive directors of theater, Paul Berman and Denny Partridge, gave Barnard's stage presentations a more professional character, even as they expanded the nonacting components of the theater offerings. Dance was similarly strengthened by expanding its offerings and promoting one member of its staff, Sandra Genter, to a tenured position. In English, the appointment of the writer Mary Gordon, class of 1971, to a chaired professorship marked another breakthrough, giving full recognition to writing in a department largely devoted to literary analysis and signaling Barnard's full embrace of the arts as an integral part of its liberal arts curriculum. These initiatives were first clustered in a composite Program in the Arts and more recently as freestanding departments of music, theater, and dance.[36]

Barnard in the 1980s also took the lead on Morningside Heights in introducing (and hosting) interdisciplinary undergraduate majors in urban studies, environmental science, and architecture. These programs all attracted Columbia students, and they contributed significantly to containing the imbalance in cross-registrations and assuring that Barnard's role in the Barnard-Columbia curricular relationship was that of provider as well as consumer. Each year between 1988 and 1992, the number of Columbia students taking Barnard courses rose and the imbalance narrowed, prompting Columbia in 1993 to agree to a change in the annual cross-registration payments from the original per capita basis to one where registrations fell within broad bands from which a predetermined

FIGURE 10.2 Mary Gordon, class of 1971, McIntosh Professor of English (1990–2020), teaching at head of seminar table. Barnard Archives.

charge would be set. This both facilitated planning and allowed Barnard to predict cross-registration costs more precisely.[37]

Back in the era of creative retrenchment, board chair Eleanor Elliott was heard to complain that "Barnard keeps its light under a basket." In the new competitive environment in which Barnard found itself, it became crucial to increase Barnard's visibility both in the New York region and nationally. Responsibility for this challenge with respect to high schoolers and their parents fell principally to Director of Admissions Christine Royer. New publications and putting more recruiters on the road visiting schools and attending college fairs all followed. The results were impressive, especially given the national drop in eighteen- to twenty-four-year-olds, with applications to Barnard holding steady at around 2,000 through the 1980s.[38]

But the job of horn tooting fell principally to President Futter. "I chose to use the crisis to get the Barnard quality story out," she later said. A good example of turning a problem into an asset: Barnard's public commitment to "need-blind" admissions, whereby the financial staus of an applicant does not enter into the admission decision. Even while recognizing that

such a policy put a real if unpredictable strain on the budget and complicated planning, the *New York Times* hailed Barnard for remaining
true to its commitment to first-generation-to-college clientele. A second
instance of Barnard securing national attention in the 1980s was through
the research and writings of M. Elizabeth Tidball on the outsized role that
women's colleges, and singularly Barnard, played in sending its graduates on to PhD studies and medical school. A third instance of national
attention focused on Barnard occurred in 1992, when Barnard hosted a
conference of college leaders and later published a report underwritten by
the Mellon Foundation to promote the idea of college faculty having a real
role in their scholarly disciplines—and staying better teachers for having
one. Thanks to these efforts and to President Futter's many public appear-
ances in person and in print, Barnard caught the interest and attention of
potential students; revived alumnae support; and gave physical substance
to her brave assertion, "We're here to stay."[39]

BETTING THE RANCH

Barnard's financial situation five years into the Futter presidency remained
precarious. The return to pre-Mattfeld lower enrollments meant a decline
in tuition revenues, while economies expected with the cap on tenure
were slow to be realized. Student recruitment of academically qualified
students not requiring financial aid remained a challenge. The 2,000 applications received for the entering class in 1983, the first year that Columbia
College admitted women, represented a 15 percent drop from the year
before. Early head-to-head competition with Columbia for acceptances
from applicants admitted to both schools heavily favored Columbia. Of
the 126 applicants accepted at both colleges, seventy-eight enrolled at
Columbia, eight enrolled at Barnard, and the remaining forty went elsewhere. Barnard that year also had nine students transfer to Columbia. The
cost of sustaining an academically qualified student body by maintaining
its commitment to need-blind admissions was high. Nearly half of those
(47 percent) who came to Barnard received financial assistance with their
tuition and, but only those coming from outside New York City received
financial assistance for room and board.[40]

The admissions picture improved later in the decade, but given the demographic headwind, not markedly. Admission rates remained in the 60 percent range, with yields around 50 percent. Financial aid costs were at the upper limit of Barnard's capacity to provide and required modest departures from need-blind in cases of transfers and wait-listed applicants. Financial necessity—and transparency—also mandated the short-term creation of a new financial aid category for admitted students: aid-eligible-but-not-assured. Even so, as a Barnard financial staffer later described the situation, "We were buying students more so than the other Sisters."[41]

With the opening of the South Campus dormitories, Columbia could now offer all admitted students housing, but Barnard still had on-campus housing for only about half of an incoming class, and the chances of those wanting but not getting housing their first year then getting housing as sophomores or juniors still something of a crapshoot. In 1980, when the trustees again looked into the possibility of borrowing $20,000,000 to build a dormitory with funds from the issuance of bonds on the commercial market backed by the federal agency HUD, they were informed that Barnard's long-term debt, which amounted to some $6,000,000, for a college with a modest endowment of $28,000,000, ($87 million in 2020 dollars) made it ineligible for inclusion in the federal program. Members of the Finance Committee had suspected as much.[42]

In 1983, Arthur Altschul stepped down as board chair, a post he had held for seven years. He was succeeded by Helene L. Kaplan, class of 1953, who had joined the board a decade earlier. The following year, the continuing need for a new dormitory again became the top priority, and one that at least one trustee was prepared "to bet the ranch." Another later recalled the prevailing sentiment to go ahead with the dorm without the funds to pay for it less apocalyptically: "We thought it essential."[43]

The opportunity to do so came in the form of a last call to apply to a program managed by the New York State Dormitory Authority, which was prepared to put its "full moral authority"—as opposed to its more binding "full legal authority"—behind bonds that private "distressed" New York colleges could issue to underwrite dormitory construction. Such bonds were a device designed by bond lawyer (and later Nixon attorney general) John Mitchell in the 1960s to circumvent the constitutional requirement that all New York State "legal obligation" bond issues secure two successive referenda approvals before issuance. "Full moral authority" bonds could be bought by investors for less than "full legal authority" bonds because they were a riskier investment.[44]

In 1986, Barnard requested and secured permission to issue $40 million of these bonds to underwrite construction of what came to be called Centennial Hall while it awaited a naming gift. Barnard's bonds found a sufficiency of ready buyers, some likely operating under the assumption that they were getting Columbia quality bonds. By the late 1980s, Columbia's bonds earned the university an AAA bond rating, on the cheap, after its sale of the land under Rockefeller Center in 1986 for $500 million. The two other New York colleges who issued bonds under this same "distressed colleges" program subsequently closed before paying off their bondholders, leaving it to the state of New York to do so.[45]

On May 20, 1985, the trustees announced plans for the new dorm as part of a three-year $100 million capital campaign to mark the college's centenary in 1989. Unlike Barnard fundraising campaigns before and since, and diverging from accepted fundraising practice, this campaign was launched backward, that is, without the usual pre-campaign gifts in hand to assure future would-be donors that the campaign was already well along toward its goal. Rather, more like the land speculators of the trans-Mississippi arid West after the Civil War, they hoped with the settlers would come the rain.[46]

And rain it did. Centennial Hall opened in the fall of 1988, allowing the college to make good on its promise to provide housing for every incoming student seeking it. Meanwhile, the Centennial campaign, highlighted by a series of events spanning eighteen months marking the college's founding in 1889, met its goal on schedule. In 1991, a combined gift of $5 million from members of the Sulzberger family helped pay for the new dormitory by covering its carrying costs for the first five years and led to the building being named in honor of Iphigene Ochs Sulzberger, class of 1914.[47]

FACULTY EMPOWERED

Any curricular reform effort undertaken was constrained by the financial uncertainties under which Barnard existed in the first years following coeducation at Columbia. President Futter's first two budgets imposed cuts in almost every expense area except student recruitment and communications. In 1984, the board directed the president to develop a faculty planning profile that limited the proportion of tenured faculty to a maximum of 50 percent of the full-time faculty. When the proportion was applied at the level of individual departments, the profile proved even more restrictive and brought the proportion of entire tenured faculty below 40 percent. The proportion of tenured faculty at most colleges comparable to Barnard at the time was 60 percent, with several as high as 70 percent.[48]

Some of this trimming was accomplished through attrition, leaving empty positions vacated by retirement. But it also required informing assistant professors upon hiring that, in the absence of demonstrated institutional need, even well-received publications and effective teaching would not secure them tenure. Of the forty-eight assistant professors on the Barnard faculty in 1980, thirty-three (69 percent) left without receiving tenure. The short-term effect of this policy was to make tenure at Barnard seem to faculty, tenured and untenured alike, subject to the law of infinite regression. One bright spot, however, was the introduction in 1987 of five Ann Whitney Olin Term Professorships (for three to five years), funded with a $500,000 gift.[49]

The change in expectations with regard to junior faculty members and their tenure prospects did not occur without personal distress and career repercussions. Three cases in point involved promising female assistant professors of economics, each of whom joined the Barnard faculty in the mid-1970s and came up for tenure consideration in the early 1980s. The first was Sylvia Hewlett, an English economist trained at Cambridge University and the University of London, who joined the Barnard Economics Department in 1974. She inaugurated the department's track in political economy and was a successful classroom teacher and an active feminist on campus. When her senior colleagues evaluated her prospects in 1980, they enthusiastically supported her nomination for tenure. The college wide Committee on Appointments and Tenure Promotion (ATP) was equally positive, sending the nomination to the university-based ad hoc committee for its final consideration. There, however, the process ended, with the committee and the university provost declining to approve Hewlett's nomination, purportedly because many of her publications were directed at other than professional peers and did not adhere to the then-dominant neoclassical paradigm. Barnard considered appealing the outcome but did not do so. She too considered suing the university for gender discrimination but, rather than seek another academic position, retooled to become a handsomely paid industrial consultant and commentator on gender and workplace issues. Not getting tenure at Barnard, she later concluded, was the best thing that ever happened to her![50]

A second case involved Alice Amsden: she was Brooklyn-born, received an AB from Cornell and a PhD from the London School of Economics, and joined the Economics Department in 1974 as its developmental economist. She quickly developed an ambitious research program that had her doing original work on Korean industrialization. Unlike Hewlett, however, Amsden received mixed student reviews as a classroom teacher, some complaining about her unwillingness to "hold students' hands" (as she herself put it), and a tendency to reschedule classes to attend professional conferences and pursue her research. Although her senior colleagues recommended her for tenure in the fall of 1982, the ATP committee declined to do so the following spring. Amsden publicly disputed the decision.

"I think they judged me by established standards, and every time those standards are challenged it makes them uncomfortable. There was something in the whole way I think, in the whole way I act, in the whole way I dress." Five months after Barnard confirmed Amsden's termination, she received an offer from the Harvard Business School, which she accepted. It proved a better fit. There, and later at the New School and for two decades as the Barton L. Weller Professor of Political Economy at Massachusetts Institute of Technology (MIT), her work was widely heralded as pathbreaking. She died in 2012, and she was recognized by Barnard colleague Duncan Foley as "one of a handful of the most influential development economists of her generation."[51]

A third case involved Bettina Berch, a Barnard graduate, class of 1971, who had gone on to the University of Wisconsin, where she earned a PhD in economics before returning to Barnard in 1975 as an assistant professor of economics. A self-described rebel in her student days but one who earned President Peterson's respect for her feistiness, she quickly made her presence known as a junior faculty member, both by her success in the classroom and her involvement with feminist activities on campus. She taught in both the women's studies and American studies programs as well as courses in economics, and in 1980, she organized a Women's Center–sponsored Conference on Women and Technology. Finding no suitable secondary materials for a course she developed on women in the workforce, she wrote and secured publication for the widely adopted text-book/reader, *The Endless Day: The Political Economy of Women and Work* (Harcourt Brace, 1982).

In 1984, when it came time for the Economics Department to consider Berch for tenure, its two senior members declined to nominate her. The likely reason was the relative absence of publications in the field's standard journals, her text being viewed as part of her teaching credentials. Berch and some of her supporters suspected another factor, pointing to the simultaneous promotion to tenure of a male colleague, although a grievance committee found no evidence of gender discrimination. Nor did a subsequent lawsuit change the outcome. After two decades living abroad and publishing two biographies of feminists, Berch returned to New York and to a faculty position at the Borough of Manhattan Community College, where she teaches economics and writing. "I did a lot for Barnard. And most of it counted against me," she recalled thirty-five years later after her termination, "because I identified myself with things which Barnard was not ready to embrace, one of them was feminism. I think Barnard took more from me than Barnard gave."[52]

The 1982 modification of the composition of ad hoc committees that substituted an outside scholar in the candidate's field for one of the three Columbia members, however welcomed, did not alter the heightened expectations for scholarly production. The Barnard Faculty Planning Committee accordingly introduced a mandatory third-year review for all assistant professors eligible for tenure that, along with reviewing the candidate's teaching effectiveness, focused on her postdissertation scholarly activities.

To make clear that the expectation of continued publication did not end at tenure but applied to senior faculty members as well, three other reforms were introduced. Salary increases for faculty continuing in rank would no longer be automatic and across the board but would have some portion of any increase based on merit. Promotion from associate professor to full professor would no longer be as it had been in the past, mostly a matter of time served in rank, but would now be accelerated or delayed and even withheld as determined by a review of the associate professor's

teaching and ongoing scholarship. And third, in the absence of a suffi-
ciency of fully endowed permanent professorships (there were only four
in 1990), a series of three-year rotating Ann Whitney Olin Professorships
(later extended to five years) were established to recognize particularly
productive senior faculty members and to award them modest salary
supplements.[53]

Other related changes confirmed the thrust of the college's new scholar-teacher ethos. The dean of the faculty was authorized to respond to outside offers with counteroffers that typically involved adjustments in salary
and sometimes teaching programs. In 1989, the trustees approved the
Senior Faculty Research Program, which allowed senior faculty members
to apply for a paid semester's leave between their guaranteed seventh-year
sabbatical leaves. And finally, select departments were encouraged to consider filling leadership positions, as they opened up, with outside appointments. During the Futter presidency, this led to the appointments of Mary
Gordon in English, John Hawley in religion, Irene Bloom in Asian studies, and Jonathan Reider in sociology. Other senior hires who came and
then left for university appointments elsewhere included Nancy K. Miller
in women's studies, Benjamin Buchloh in art history, and Caryl Phillips
and Robert O'Meally in English. Still subject to periodic raiding, from
both Columbia and other Ivy League schools, Barnard was now doing a
little raiding of its own.[54]

Other gender-specific demographic changes were underway in the
composition of the Barnard faculty. Leaving Barnard was no longer a
characteristic possessed exclusively or even primarily by male faculty
members; women faculty members were now as likely or even more likely
to receive and accept outside offers. The loss of two recently tenured Black
women faculty members, the economists Cecelia Conrad in 1989 and
Maria Crummett in 1993, spoke both to this generational shift and to the
marketability of Barnard faculty. Into the 1970s, most women hired by
Barnard were the products of women's colleges; by the late 1980s, they
were more likely to come from Ivy or formerly men's colleges. And as
with their male colleagues, women new to the Barnard faculty were less
likely to have received their graduate training at Columbia than had faculty members in the past. And there were fewer native New Yorkers, too.[55]

Barnard now had a faculty composed of men and women self-identifying as scholar-teachers and open to the institutional changes over the

preceding two decades. Some of these actions were brought about by trustee fiat, others by the repeated judgments of faculty members until the ethos had been thoroughly internalized. With a heightened attentiveness to and expectation of scholarly productivity, teaching effectiveness did not cease to matter. Classroom prowess as directly observed by colleagues remained a necessary condition for promotion, but absent an impressive scholarly record, it was no longer sufficient. In 1989, the Barnard faculty adopted a standardized course evaluation system based on that pioneered by the First-Year Seminar Program. Since then, all considerations of promotion and merit increases include a consideration of teaching effectiveness as assessed by students.[56]

Differences remained between the work life of a Barnard College professor and a Columbia University professor, but less by gender than by field. Columbia faculty taught and continue to teach fewer courses than Barnard faculty and interact more frequently with graduate students. Otherwise, the life of a Barnard anthropologist or classicist was/is of a piece with their Columbia counterparts; however, differences persist in the sciences. Columbia scientists have greater access to graduate and postdoctoral students as well as to more extensive laboratory facilities, while the Barnard scientist relies primarily upon undergraduates. This differentiated their research agendas and the frequency with which their results reached print. But even among Barnard's relatively encumbered science faculty, the research ethos, once regularly disdained by faculty at even the best undergraduate colleges, and suspect in some quarters at Barnard within living memory, had been taken up by the early 1990s and, a generation later, looks very much like permanent residence.[57]

A TRANS-BROADWAY THAW

The relations between Barnard and Columbia throughout the 1970s had been strained, and in some departments, open and mutual hostility became the norm. The 1982 agreement did not immediately set matters right; it took work on both sides of Broadway to effect the discernible thaw in cross-Broadway relations that occurred in the 1980s and has persisted since. For Columbia officials, from President Sovern down through the administrative ranks, this largely meant focusing on improving the university's intellectual and financial standing among the nation's leading research universities, with occasional gestures of goodwill and cooperation addressed Barnard's way. Columbia's return to prosperity took Barnard off its action agenda. But for Barnard, putting matters right with Columbia remained an important order of business for trustees, administrators, faculty members, and students alike.[58]

An anecdote suggestive of this reconciliation effort occurred on the third day of Futter's acting presidency. A letter from the Columbia Dean of the Graduate Faculties George Fraenkel to Barnard Dean of the Faculty Charles Olton complaining about some matter had just arrived. Like others from Fraenkel, it was taken to be snarky in its language and tone, and seen to require a response in kind. When Futter met with her dean and was shown the proposed rejoinder, the following exchange ensued:

Futter: "What is this?"
Olton: "This is what George and I regularly do."
Futter: "Not anymore."

Olton's response after this exchange was, "Wow, a new style is being enforced," and prompted him to meet with Fraenkel "to let him know the world had turned. . . ."[59]

Other members of the Barnard administration have since described the new relationship in less Paul-on-the-road-to-Damascus terms. College counsel Kathryn Rodgers described the "new ethos" of dealings with university counsel Mason Harding and his staff during the Futter presidency as one "where we were no longer focused on prevailing in every disagreement, no matter how insignificant, but on finding mutually acceptable resolutions." Director of Finance Lewis Wyman remembers the period as one where "we moved from a complicated set of considerations to a series of cooperative understandings with less unpredictability, allowing for more confident planning."[60]

Much of the actual cooperation that led to the relationship coming to be seen as mutually beneficial occurred at the curricular and student services level. As a large research university, Columbia had been traditionally slow to engage in novel or experimental curricular undertakings. The Columbia College curriculum was seen as particularly resistant to change by admirers and critics alike, with the latter dismissively referring to its hallmark core as the "study of dead white men." Less bound by tradition, Barnard had always been more ready to experiment with new curricular offerings, such as in the late 1930s with its interdisciplinary programs in American and Medieval studies and even earlier with offerings in the performing arts that, into the early 1980s, still had no place in the Columbia College curriculum. Thus, Barnard could—and did—become the first Morningside home for an undergraduate theater program, an undergraduate urban studies major, and an undergraduate architecture program, all of which became occasions for Columbia College students making their way across Broadway. A similar migration occurred as Barnard pioneered in two other interdisciplinary majors that have since become Barnard mainstays: environmental studies and women's studies. The latter has since broadened to women's and gender studies.[61]

A specific instance of mutually but differently beneficial institutional cooperation involved intercollegiate athletics. With the admission of women in 1983, Columbia College found itself needing to field about a dozen women's teams (with more to follow) if it were to comply with Title IX as well as the requirements of the NCAA and the Ivy League. Meanwhile, since the 1960s, Barnard had been fielding several teams that participated in the Woman's Intercollegiate League. Both schools were alert to the admissions aspects of fielding credible NCAA-member teams to attract student-athlete applicants—and both to the expenses involved in doing so.

Barnard and Columbia senior administrators, with the active involvement of their respective athletic directors, proceeded in 1985 to create the Columbia-Barnard Athletic Consortium, by which Barnard student-athletes would be eligible to play on NCAA Division I Columbia teams. Some Barnard alumnae at the time lamented the end of a distinct Barnard presence in intercollegiate athletics—the uniforms would bear the name Columbia and the Barnard Bears would be no more—but incoming Barnard student-athletes have benefitted, by and large, from access to Columbia's athletic facilities, full-time coaches, and the opportunity to compete at a national level compared to the old Barnard Bears.[62]

The new state of Barnard-Columbia relations achieved during the Futter presidency fell short of peaceable. Reviewing the tenure of Barnard faculty members under the ad hoc system remained a source of tension, particularly in the rare instances where the university provost,

Jonathan Cole, exercised his authority to disregard a positive recommendation of his ad hoc committee and vetoed the tenure of a Barnard nominee. Barnard in turn was accused of rigging the cross-registration agreement by mounting new courses with exciting teachers designed to attract Columbia crossovers. Columbia College Dean Robert Pollack was sometimes seen from the Barnard side of Broadway to make too much of Columbia's success in competing with Barnard applicants admitted to both schools or in allowing the inference that Barnard admissions did less well academically than did Columbia's. (They did not.) And at the student level, there persisted a sense on the part of some Barnard students that their Columbia sisters took their acceptances as entitling them to local bragging rights.[63]

Both Barnard and Columbia benefitted significantly from the upswing in the fortunes of New York City. Widely deemed in the 1970s as politically ungovernable, financially bankrupt, and physically dangerous, the city a decade later showed signs of recovery on all three fronts. Perhaps of equal importance for Barnard's place in the city was to have a president who recognized its importance. Asked later about the New York connection, Futter declared, "We are absolutely tied to the City," and about the impact of its ongoing recovery: "It gave us wind at our back."[64]

EXIT ELLEN—*APOLOGIA PRO VITA SUA*

In May 1993, President Futter announced plans to leave at the end of the academic year to become president of the American Museum of Natural History (AMNH). Barnard trustee William Golden, who was also on the AMNH board, had recommended her for the position. (She was also a leading candidate that spring for the then-vacant presidency of the New York Public Library.) Plans for a smooth transition seem to have been underway for some time but closely guarded. Kathryn Rodgers, by virtue of her functioning first as college counsel, had her as a principal negotiator with Columbia officials, and later, when she was vice president for student affairs, she was in direct contact with students, so she was a logical choice for acting president. Sigmund Ginsburg, vice president for finance, left to join Futter at the museum a month later.[65]

Otherwise, Futter left behind a stable senior administrative staff, including myself as dean of the faculty; I stayed on through the transition and then returned to the History Department in 1994. Others, Dorothy Denburg, dean of the college; Carol Herring, vice president for development; and Doris Davis, director of admissions, stayed on well into the next administration. While some Barnard observers expressed surprise and disappointment at Futter's announcement, most agreed the time was propitious and, sensing the formidable challenges of her new job as head of another venerable but troubled West Side institution, understood her decision.

While taking a rightful measure of personal pride in her administration, Futter credited the Barnard board of trustees and singularly its chair Helene L. Kaplan with providing the support that made her own accomplishments possible. As for the board collectively, she praised it for "its ability to make tough decisions"—which I take to be chief among them the move to accede to Columbia's decision to admit women and to go ahead without funding on hand with the construction of the new dormitory—both of which have proved crucial to Barnard's future. As for Kaplan, Futter credits her with having a crucial role in the college's resurgence, including her active participation in the stressful negotiations with Columbia throughout the 1970s and into the early 1980s, her success as a fundraiser, and in leading the search for Barnard's next president. But even more singular was her management of a hyperactive board during the merger crisis and then easing it back into its traditional advisory role, with the day-to-day operation of the college left to the president and to the trusted staff she had put together. Here Kaplan's vast professional experience advising nonprofit boards proved invaluable. Not since Helen Rogers Reid had Barnard been so well served by its board and board chair.[66]

Futter had led Barnard for thirteen years, longer than her two predecessors combined, and, unlike them, departed under her own steam to take up another prestigious position in New York City. She left behind a decade of balanced budgets, an endowment twice the size of the one she inherited, and a second major campaign well underway. Problems remained, including a substantial debt burden incurred with the construction of Sulzberger Hall. Her success at winning the hearts of initially skeptical constituencies was more complete with some than others, but even those few faculty members still who pined for a scholar-president

FIGURE 10.3 Laurie Anderson, class of 1969, Joan Rivers, class of 1954, and Suzanne Vega, class of 1981 at the Barnard Centennial Celebration, 1989. Barnard Archives.

and had endured a decade of belt tightening acknowledged that their lawyer-president left the college in better shape, in just about every way, than she found it. Back in 1980, some of these same skeptics rightly worried whether Barnard would survive the coming decade; in 1993, there was every confidence that what Ellen V. Futter held out in 1982 as a doable proposition—an act of faith—might not be doable. Thanks in substantial part to her efforts, Barnard had become "now, more than ever, in charge of its own destiny."

11

"NEW YORK, NEW YORK"

I wouldn't trade Barnard's location for Wellesley's endowment.

—PRESIDENT JUDITH R. SHAPIRO, OFTEN[1]

The announcement in April 1993 of Ellen Futter's planned resignation after thirteen years as president of Barnard to accept the presidency of the American Museum of Natural History (AMNH) surprised some senior administrators and most faculty members, but apparently not the trustees. They promptly appointed Kathryn J. Rodgers, then vice president for student affairs, as acting president. A graduate of Smith College and Columbia Law School, Rodgers had been at Barnard since 1981 as one of acting president Futter's first outside appointees. They had known each other since law school and worked together early in their respective legal careers. As general counsel, Rodgers became responsible for the college's legal affairs and for community and government relations. Much of the negotiation that went on between Barnard and Columbia was conducted on the Barnard side by Rodgers; in the process, she became highly regarded by her university counterparts in Low Library. As vice president for student affairs, she was popular with students and she was innovative, especially in the provision of health services. Only the absence of professorial credentials led the presidential search committee to look further afield.[2]

This was an auspicious time for Barnard to be looking for a new leader, both because there were more qualified women administrators than in 1975 or 1980 and because of local circumstances. The person chosen as president would be the first in Barnard's 105-year history to commence her tenure as president with almost all the college's vital signs trending upward. Her predecessor had produced a turnaround in Barnard's fortunes, leaving the college in better shape than at any time since the transition from McIntosh to Park in 1962. But unlike Rosemary Park or Martha Peterson or Laura Drake Gill, all out-of-towners, and unlike Virginia Gildersleeve, a remnant of "Old New York," or Millicent McIntosh, a New Yorker by adoption, or even Futter, a child of the suburbs, the college's tenth leader and sixth president would personify Barnard's identity as a quintessential New York institution.

CHILD OF THE BOROUGHS

Judith Rae Shapiro was born in Jamaica, Queens, on January 24, 1942. Her family, which included a younger sister, later moved to the ethnically mixed but all-White neighborhood of Jamaica Estates North. "Upwardly mobile," she later allowed, "but not Jamaica Estates," where the Trumps lived. Shapiro's grandparents came from Belorussia, and her parents, while not very observant Reform Jews, were enough so that their daughter acknowledged, per Alfred Kazin, "I do feel like a New York Jew." Her father was an accountant for a meat company in the mornings and in the afternoons managed the books for Belmont, Aqueduct, and Jamaica race tracks. Her mother was a public school librarian and, unlike her husband, a college graduate. Judith attended Public School (PS) 26 (with Stephen Jay Gould and future Columbia provost, Jonathan Cole) and then went to Jamaica High School.[3]

Prospective colleges included a tour of Smith, where the pleated skirts, circle pins, and sweater sets (it was 1959) provoked the reaction, "Holy moly, get me out of here." (Barnard was not an option because she would have had to commute.) After giving serious thought to Carnegie Tech, she was encouraged by her mother to consider a liberal arts college with a strong theater program and settled on Brandeis. "I wanted to be an actress."[4]

Once at Brandeis, she quickly switched from theater to history to take advantage of that department's roster of academic notables, including Frank Manuel and Herbert Marcuse. Her interest in theater was sustained through performing in plays and folk-singing gigs in Cambridge and Provincetown, Massachusetts. At the time, Brandeis was divided into two student camps—"upwardly mobile Jewish kids headed for the professions" and "intellectuals/bohemians"—Shapiro aligned with the latter.[5]

Upon graduation in 1963, Shapiro accepted a fellowship in history at Berkeley, where she was hoping to work in European history with Carl Schorske. Two weeks into the program, she decided that "spending my life in an archive" was not for her and she returned to New York City. In the fall of 1965, she entered the Columbia doctoral program in cultural anthropology, having been awarded a National Institutes of Health (NIH) fellowship. In the summer of 1966, she undertook her first fieldwork with the Tapirape in Mato Grosso (central Brazil), where her mentor Charles Wagley had conducted fieldwork in 1939–1940. The people she encountered considered her Wagley's "niece." In 1967–1968, with her orals behind her, Shapiro lived among the Yanomami in what was then the northwestern territory and now the state of Roraima in Brazil. Her work there led to a completed dissertation published three years later as *Sex Roles and Social Structure among the Yanomami Indians of Northern Brazil* (1972).[6]

In 1970, Shapiro was appointed assistant professor at the University of Chicago, the first woman in its fabled Anthropology Department. She held that appointment for five years, during which she accepted a postdoctoral appointment at Berkeley in 1974–1975. From there, she went to Bryn Mawr College, receiving tenure shortly thereafter. She spent twelve years at Bryn Mawr as a member of its five-person Anthropology Department, becoming its chair in 1984. Mary Patterson McPherson, who became president of Bryn Mawr in 1978, and Mary Maples Dunn, the dean of the college, both made use of Shapiro in quasi-administrative tasks of increasing complexity. She in turn considered McPherson "an incarnational president, combining ego-strength with an absence of narcissism." Not least of her mentor's administrative skills was a capacity, when confronted with contentious issues, to "rise above" them in a manner that Shapiro later dubbed "the helium principle."[7]

In 1985, upon Dunn's departure to become president of Smith, McPherson made Shapiro dean of the college. A year later, she assumed the new position of provost. Her principal challenges were to work with the president and deans to close many of the college's once flourishing but now tiny graduate programs (including one in anthropology) without alienating the faculty members identified with them and to develop cooperative undergraduate programs with neighboring Haverford and Swarthmore. Her success in both undertakings, plus the active promoting by McPherson (who, by the late 1980s, had become recognized as head of the so-called Bryn Mawr Mafia, which specialized in the job placement of female administrative talent) led Shapiro to be mentioned as a candidate for the dean of faculty position at Amherst and the presidency of Williams. Neither struck McPherson or Shapiro as the right fit.[8]

The announcement of the Barnard search for a new president in the fall of 1993 sounded more promising. McPherson had served as chair of Barnard's Middle States Reaccreditation team in 1991 and was familiar with both its problems and its promise. "Barnard," the president of the more generously endowed Bryn Mawr wrote, "has always had to sail close to the wind," in a knowing reference to the college's comparatively straitened financial circumstances. McPherson had also served as an informal adviser to Futter at the outset of her presidency. Shapiro had her own friends at Barnard, among them the anthropologists Paula Rubel, Abraham Rosman, Morton Klass, and Joan Vincent, plus this author (I was the dean of the faculty and shared her company at several Seven Sister Conferences). Smitten with the search committee, which included three trustees, then trustee chair Helene Kaplan (class of 1953) and future chair Patricia Green (class of 1964), plus professor of Spanish Mirella Servodidio (class of 1955), Shapiro agreed to further discussions. Coming away from the interview, she later recalled her feelings: "I wanted this job, really wanted it."[9]

The search committee was equally enthusiastic. Shapiro was a native New Yorker (as were all search committee members save the journalist, author, and Hoboken resident Anna Quindlen), had administrative experience with women's colleges, and knew Columbia. Although the committee likely did not have it as a criterion, the faculty had made clear its desire that the next president be an academic. Although regretful to see her leave Bryn Mawr, McPherson became Shapiro's campaign manager for the presidency of Barnard.[10]

The trustees moved quickly and on March 21, 1994, announced the appointment of Judith R. Shapiro as Barnard's sixth president. The inauguration followed on October 27, a ceremony marked by the first-time inclusion of a thirty-four-year veteran of the college's support staff, Milton Elliott Tanis, among the official speakers. The recessional from Riverside Church included a recording of Frank Sinatra singing "New York, New York."[11]

THE FURTHER DOMESTICATION OF COLUMBIA

One task facing the new president in the fall of 1994 was finding a new dean of the faculty after my decision after seven years in the job to return to full-time teaching in the History Department. The political scientist Flora Davidson (class of 191969) served as acting dean from July 1994 until June 1995, and associate provost thereafter; she was then replaced by Elizabeth S. Boylan, who later also assumed the revived title of provost. Boylan, a Wellesley graduate and Cornell PhD in biology, had been a member of the Queens College faculty and its dean of faculty. Her credentials as a research scientist and professor added to the new administration's standing as one knowledgeable about academic folkways. Her appointment also broke with the nearly half-century practice of Barnard's chief academic officer being a male.[12]

One place where the president's and provost's prior experience as academic administrators was quickly put to use was in the college's ongoing dealings with Columbia, where a recent change in presidents made future relations again unclear. In 1993, after thirteen years, Michael I. Sovern retired as Columbia's president. His tenure was marked by the university's improving financial fortunes and the admission of women to Columbia College. His successor, George E. Rupp, while not a total stranger to Morningside Heights, came to it as an outsider. One thing that impressed the search committee was that, as president of Rice University and before that as dean of the experimental Johnston College at the University of Wisconsin, Green Bay, Rupp had demonstrated a keen interest in undergraduate education. What was not known was what, if anything, he thought about the Barnard connection.[13]

Rupp's first take on Barnard-Columbia relationship was hardly encouraging. At his introductory meeting with President Shapiro, he allowed the thought that Barnard should be folded into Columbia as Radcliffe had been into Harvard during his graduate school years in Cambridge, Massachusetts. He described Barnard's continued existence alongside a now coeducational Columbia College as "anomalous." When Shapiro offered "unique" as a more positive description, Rupp remained unpersuaded and continued to frame the Barnard-Columbia relationship as "a problem that needed solving."[14]

Yet in subsequent discussions, Rupp, whom Shapiro found "personally decent and constructive, and a good listener," proved open to evidence. This included the fact that Barnard grades matched those of Columbia students in both Barnard- and Columbia-taught classes, and that Barnard produced more science majors than Columbia, at a time when the push for more science, technology, engineering, and math (STEM) majors had become a national priority. Columbia Provost Jonathan Cole had been a classmate of Shapiro's at PS 26 and a fellow Columbia graduate student in the late 1960s. In their early official dealings, Cole advised Shapiro that the Barnard-Columbia relationship was "not that of Bryn Mawr and Haverford," by which he meant a relationship of equals. "Oh, Jonathan, I know that," she dependably responded. She "then proceeded to act as if it were."[15]

Good relations were quickly established and then maintained between Provost Boylan and her principal Columbia counterparts, university provosts Jonathan Cole and Alan Brinkley, and Dean of Columbia College Austin Quigley. Boylan remembers her dealings with Brinkley, as "especially cordial" and transacted with a "sense of collegiality." Relations with Dean Quigley were similarly amicable and perhaps made especially so by the fact that, as the Columbia English Department's leading specialist in dramatic literature, he had earlier advised Barnard on the setting up of its theater program. It also helped that his wife, Patricia Denison, was a member of the Barnard English Department. At the committee-of-instruction working level, Columbia College Dean of Academic Affairs Kathryn Yatrakis and Barnard Associate Provost Flora Davidson shared a friendship going back twenty years from their days as junior members of the Barnard Political Science Department.[16]

BUMPS ALONG THE WAY

Still, it was not all good times. Shapiro later recalled the on-again, off-again strike of the union representing Barnard's mostly female support staff in the spring of 1996 as "my one truly horrible experience at Barnard." The strike occurred early in her presidency and only weeks after the installation of a new provost; involved many of Barnard's lowest paid employees; and centered on Barnard's efforts to alter their healthcare benefits, making it especially stressful. The strikers won the vocal support of most students and many faculty members, who refused to cross picket lines and moved classes off campus. "The strike was traumatic for me," the president has since acknowledged. "I became depressed by it." Some observers worried she might decamp for Bryn Mawr, while Associate Dean Flora Davidson, hoping to take her mind off the strike, took her boss bowling. Outside mediation eventually convinced the union officials that they had won when Barnard withdrew its proposed cut in healthcare benefits and the college's other unions did not join the support staff in the strike. A settlement was reached in September and the campus returned to normal.[17]

The other personally taxing incident in the Shapiro presidency came near its close in 2007. It involved a tenure controversy. Unlike those that turned on a rejection of a Barnard nominee by an ad hoc committee or by the university provost, this one involved Nadia Abu El-Haj, a Bryn Mawr graduate, Duke PhD, and assistant professor of anthropology since 2002. She was nominated for tenure by her department and approved by Barnard's Appointments and Tenure Committee in 2006. At this point, her principal published work, *Facts on the Ground: Archaeological Practice and Territorial Self-Fashioning in Israeli Society*, published five years earlier in 2001, came under fire from critics who charged Abu El-Haj with a pro-Palestinian bias. Among those calling for her to be denied tenure were Barnard graduates, some living in Israel, who threatened to withhold funds from Barnard. They also included a senior member of the Barnard Religion Department and noted scholar of Jewish studies, Alan F. Segal, whose opposition distressed both the president and his many friends and admirers on the faculty.[18]

President Shapiro intervened to the extent that she defended the tenure process as "one of the linchpins of academic freedom and liberal arts education" that must be conducted "thoughtfully, comprehensively, systematically and confidentially." Rather than voice her personal opinion of the book's thesis or criticize angry alumnae, she called for the review process to run its course without "outside lobbying." Segal was allowed to testify before the Barnard tenure committee, which unanimously forwarded the nomination to Columbia. When the university ad hoc committee recommended Abu-Haj be granted tenure and the Columbia provost confirmed that decision, the Barnard trustees almost all agreed. "Not quite an instance of 'Profiles in Courage,' " Shapiro later acknowledged, although others following the case, including Jane Kramer in the *New Yorker* and the editorial board of the *New York Times*, applauded her stance.[19]

Another instance of Shapiro's prudence in the face of discord occurred in 2005 when the Columbia University senate, at President Lee Bollinger's urging, seemed about to recommend to the trustees that its 1969 ban on officer-training programs be lifted and a Naval Reserve Officer Corps program be reinstalled. This was in keeping with similar actions following 9/11 on other Ivy League campuses. Barnard's president, whose younger sister was a colonel in the Army Medical Reserves, was personally in favor of doing so, as were some Barnard students from military families or those contemplating military careers. But when the Barnard faculty took up the question, it was clear opponents greatly outnumbered supporters. Shapiro quietly acceded to a vote that put the Barnard faculty on record as overwhelmingly opposed to a return of the military to the Columbia campus. The university went ahead anyway restoring ties with the navy.[20]

Other challenges encountered during the Shapiro presidency were taken on by members of her administrative team. One involved the *US News & World Report* annual rankings of colleges in which Barnard consistently ranked in the middle twenties among national liberal arts colleges, below all the other sister colleges as well as some wealthier but less selective colleges. For several years, Barnard officials complained that the metrics used by the magazine penalized Barnard for the economies resulting from its sharing resources with Columbia. Barnard became part of a consortium of select liberal arts colleges, under the rubric of the Annapolis Group, which included Carleton and Davidson, that stopped providing data to *US News & World Report*. But still the rankings rankled. On one occasion, Shapiro addressed the members of the board's Educational Policy Committee and delivered a full-throated attack on the methodology used by the magazine to compile its rankings, not realizing that the trustees had already discounted their significance. When she finished, one of the trustees solicitously inquired of their hyperventilating president: "Feel better now?"[21]

"ASPIRING CROWDS" REDUX

Good times made it possible to correct past college policies long questioned but never rescinded. Making changes to those involving student financial aid fell primarily to two senior members of the Shapiro administrative team, Dean of the College Dorothy Denburg and Financial Aid Director Suzanne Guard. Since the introduction of residential scholarships in the first years of Virginia Gildersleeve's deanship in 1913, only non–New York City residents were deemed eligible. The official explanation for this policy was to use the residential scholarships to broaden the geographical reach of the college; others saw it as intended to limit the number of Jews at Barnard.

Whatever the reasoning, this exclusionary policy remained in force into the 1990s when Denburg and Guard set about to change it. Denburg, whose parents were Holocaust survivors, was properly sensitive to the policy's discriminatory history. However, both realized that the policy no longer affected primarily Jewish New Yorkers but all New Yorkers otherwise eligible for financial aid and who, without such aid but seeking a residential experience, went elsewhere. With the active support of President Shapiro, board chair Patricia Green and Finance Committee chair Dale Horowitz, the nine-decade policy was changed. Henceforth, New York City residents eligible for tuition assistance were also eligible for assistance for room and board. Admitted applicants from the city's top public schools who might have earlier gone off to Cornell or Stony Brook with full financial support now received it if they chose to come to Barnard. The five-decade-long slide in the percentage of New Yorkers attending Barnard has since stabilized, and they now regularly make up a quarter of entering classes.[22]

Another change affecting students and their tuition-paying parents made in the Shapiro presidency involved study abroad. Traditionally,

Barnard students who wished to spend a semester or a year studying abroad (usually in their junior year) did so by taking a leave of absence from Barnard and enrolling in a site-specific program administered by one of the American universities that maintained several programs in or near universities around the globe. (Syracuse and Boston universities were two of the larger providers.) The cost of studying abroad for a semester for a Barnard student was typically less than had she remained at Barnard, a fact not lost on tuition-paying parents. Thus, for students whose families were paying full ticket for their college education, study abroad could not only be culturally enriching but could also help them save money.[23]

Not so for Barnard students on financial aid. The long-standing college policy limited such assistance to when a student was attending Barnard, and the aid was not transferable should she enroll in a study abroad program. Thus, for her and her family, study abroad required an additional and very likely unavailable outlay. The upshot was that students with substantial financial aid packages into the 1990s seldom ventured abroad.

This was an equity problem for which no inexpensive solution seemed to exist, that is, until Dean of the College Denburg again joined forces with Director of Financial Aid Guard to come up with one that was both ingenious and income-neutral for Barnard if not for families who paid full fees. They proposed that students planning to study abroad continue to make tuition payments to Barnard, which would take responsibility for covering the costs of the particular study abroad provider. This meant that a Barnard student paying full tuition would no longer pocket any difference between Barnard's higher tuition and the study abroad provider's lower tuition. But it also meant that students on financial aid could now go abroad to study at no additional tuition cost. In this classic instance of downward wealth redistribution, Barnard found a way of doing good while doing well.[24]

These adjustments in residential policy and study abroad funding might seem minor in the larger scheme of things, just small adjustments at the margin made by responsible administrators doing their job. But together they formed part of a more comprehensive and president-led commitment to making Barnard more accessible and welcoming to those who, in an earlier day, would not have considered coming to Barnard and, once they were at Barnard, to make what the college earlier had to offer to some available now to all. No small ambition.

Meanwhile, efforts undertaken in the previous two presidencies to, as Futter put it, "get Barnard's story out there," along with the improving demographic picture brought about by the uptick in the number of college-age Americans, produced annual increases in applications, which in turn allowed Barnard to become increasingly selective. By 2000, Barnard had become the most selective of the remaining five sister colleges, admitting 33 percent of its applicants, down from 45 percent eight years earlier, when Doris Davis, Barnard's first black senior administrator, began as director of admissions. Davis's departure that year to become director of admissions at Cornell became the occasion for Barnard to appoint as her successor Jennifer Fondiller, class of 1988, previously admissions director at the New School's Eugene Lang College. Under Fondiller's direction, the volume of applications continued to rise, and the admission process became ever more selective. In the argot of college hunting, due in part from New York City's continued upswing, Barnard was "hot."[25]

FACULTY "JUST COMING AND GOING"

A more substantive challenge facing the college continued to be the tenure of Barnard faculty. To be sure, many of the difficulties that followed on the adoption of the Columbia ad hoc procedures in 1974 had been resolved by the late 1980s, mostly by Barnard becoming more insistent upon demonstrated scholarly performance by its inside candidates and more frequently hiring established scholars from outside. But what if an unintended consequence of this two-pronged strategy was that men were now more successful in securing tenure than women?

One particularly stressful case early in Boylan's provostship where gender, race, and interdisciplinarity intersected involved Judith Weisenfeld, an African American scholar of the Black religious experience in America. A Barnard graduate (1986) and Princeton PhD, Weisenfeld was appointed assistant professor of religion in 1991. At the time of her tenure review, she was one of the college's most popular teachers, the chair-designate of the African Studies Department, and the author of *African American Women and Christian Activism: New York's Black YWCA, 1905–1945* (1997). Recommended by her department and approved by

Barnard's tenure committee, she was rejected by the university provost after a divided vote of the Columbia ad hoc committee reviewing her case. She shortly thereafter returned to Princeton, was awarded tenure, and currently holds a chaired professorship in religion and African American studies. Although President Shapiro did not formally challenge the provost's decision, many at Barnard thought Columbia had not appreciated the importance to Barnard of securing tenure for one of its most promising faculty members of color.[26]

Faculty numbers for 1997–1998 suggested something else was amiss when women constituted 61 percent of the full-time faculty but less than 50 percent of the tenured faculty. Still more worrying, the percentage of tenured women faculty was trending downward. In 1998–1999, it dropped into the 40 percent range. Like the careful scientist she was, Provost Boylan sought out data to determine whether this was so, and if so, why.[27]

The data came in a study undertaken independently in the spring of 1999 by assistant professor of astronomy Laura Kay and assistant professor of sociology Kelly Moore, who tracked the career progress of all 111 assistant professors appointed at Barnard between 1981 and 1992. They found that the survival rate (i.e., promotion to tenure) among them was 23 percent, just under one in four. (This approximated that of Columbia assistant professors but was considerably lower than other sister colleges and most select liberal arts colleges.) Among male assistant professors, the survival rate was 29 percent; among female assistant professors, it was 17 percent. The study also confirmed anecdotal evidence that, while women made it through the Barnard tenure process at comparable rates to men, they experienced tougher going at the Columbia ad hoc level. As expected, preliminary analysis pointed to two contributing factors to the divergence: the recent success in the outside hiring of several senior men, and the persistent problems posed by the ad hoc system for junior women.[28]

Both Kay and Moore expected lower survival rates for scientists than for those in other fields given Barnard's chronic lack of laboratory space and access to postdoctoral and graduate students. Kay later described the situation in Altschul, the college's building housing most of the college's science faculty: "They were just coming and going." To Kay and Moore's surprise, they found that faculty in the humanities, of both genders, fared worse than did those in the sciences and social sciences. As for those in the sciences, they reported, to no one's surprise, "people who published more were more likely to get tenure."[29]

Out of these findings came a number of corrective actions, all pressed for by the provost, supported by President Shapiro, and approved by the board of trustees. They included a lifting of the 50 percent tenure cap on the percentage of tenured faculty that had been in place since the mid-1980s and that, when applied at the department level, resulted in an overall tenure level closer to 40 percent. Directly addressing the situation confronting women faculty, the leave policy was modified to allow faculty on maternal leave more time to advance their scholarly agendas. This benefit was later extended to male faculty with parental responsibilities. Again, with special reference to the sciences, start-up packages were increased substantially to provide more funds to get labs up and running without waiting for outside grants.[30]

Meanwhile, the trustee-imposed embargo on additional hires was lifted at the urging of President Shapiro and Provost Boylan, allowing the faculty to expand from 165 full-time officers of instruction in 1994 to 198 in 2008. This has made it possible to increase modestly faculty diversity through the use of a 2005 Ford Foundation Difficult Dialogues grant that led to a subsequent cluster hire (in 2010) of literary theorist Tina Campt, historian Celia Naylor, and poet/novelist Yvette Christianse, whose appointments assured senior staffing in Africana studies, English, history, and women's studies. Appointing and retaining minority faculty remained a challenge for Barnard in a fiercely competitive market, especially in the case of female minority faculty, but Barnard in the Shapiro era became more willing to commit the resources to do so.[31]

By the end of the Shapiro presidency, the gender gap in tenure rates had not only closed but women were now advancing to tenure at a higher rate than men, or so analysis of the fifty-two assistant professors hired between 1998 and 2006 would suggest. Of these, twenty-four have since been tenured for an overall survival rate of 46 percent. Of the thirty-two women, nineteen (59 percent) were promoted to tenured associate professorships, while of the twenty men, five (25 percent) were promoted.[32]

Two women hired during this period and subsequently tenured, the historian of science Deborah Coen and the political scientist Kimberly Johnson, have since moved on to Yale and New York University (NYU), respectively. Among those who came and went during the Shapiro presidency were the literary biographer Gretchen Gerzina, who went to Dartmouth after coming to Barnard from Vassar, and the philosopher/ archaeologist Alison Wylie, who went to the University of Washington. Such voluntary departures were (and still are) not limited to women scholars, as evidenced by the departures of Benjamin Buchloh, in art history, who went to Harvard, and the novelist Caryl Phillips, who went to Yale, but the number of voluntary departures for Barnard's female faculty reflects a professional mobility that was once limited to Barnard's male faculty.[33]

Another faculty development during the Shapiro presidency was the further internationalization of the curriculum. The case of the History Department, while Rosalind Rosenberg was chair, serves as a specific instance of a more general trend. In 1994, the department was comprised of a dozen faculty who focused their teaching and research on the United States and Western Europe, with some attention during the Cold War era having been paid to Russia and the Soviet Union. Asia, Africa, Latin America, and the Middle East were left almost entirely to Columbia historians. At Rosenberg's urging, it became the policy of the president and her provost to have the History Department develop competences in these neglected regions and provided the lines to do so. In 2001, two hires, one senior East Asian specialist, Dorothy Ko, and one junior appointment in South Asian history, Anupama Rao, broadened the department's global coverage. The junior appointment in 2004 of Nara Milanich followed a year later by the senior appointment of Jose Moya further extended departmental coverage to Latin America, with Milanich having a topical interest in family history and Moya in migration studies. In 2007, a junior appointment was made in African history with the hiring of Abosede George, who combines work in urban history and women's studies. All three junior appointees—Rao, Milanich, and George—have since been tenured. That five of the six self-identify as faculty of color (as does the 2008 appointee, Celia Naylor, an Americanist who works in African American and Native American history) had the additional benefit of transforming, in the space of a decade, a department earlier made up entirely of White faculty into one more ethnically and racially representative of both the world and Barnard students.[34]

While U.S. presidential scholar Richard Pious was chair and with the support of Professor Peter Juviler, the department's specialist in human rights, the Political Science Department made a similar transformation from a department focused primarily on American politics to one with strengths in comparative politics, international relations, and theory. The faculty and curriculum also became more international. These changes included the appointments of Xiaobo Lu in Chinese politics and comparative politics, Kimberly Marten in international security and Russia, and Alexander Cooley, a specialist on Central Asia. Such speedy departmental transformations do not occur in academic life without effective, carrot-and-stick administrative advocacy whereby a department is allowed to expand but in directions that serve the college.[35]

Elsewhere, faculty ranks were renewed and modestly expanded. This occurred through a combination of securing tenure for a growing number of junior hires whose scholarship and teaching earned them the recommendation of their departmental seniors, the support of the Barnard Committee on Appointments and Tenure, and the endorsement of a Columbia review board, and through targeted senior hires. Science departments, except for psychology, that in the two prior decades had an especially difficult time securing tenure for their junior members were now more successful in doing so. During the Shapiro presidency, Barnard's science faculty increased from 19 percent to 25 percent of the college's full-time faculty.[36]

Meanwhile, Barnard during the Shapiro years made seven senior appointments that provided departmental leadership upon arrival. Of these, four were women, none of whom had attended a women's college or did their graduate work at Columbia.[37]

"HOW'M I DOIN'?"

Gauging the overall institutional wellbeing of a college at a given point in its history is a tricky business and depends too often upon anecdotal evidence and surmise. This said, some measureable vital signs—metrics—do exist that collectively permit a cautious response to the question regularly posed by Edward Koch to his fellow New Yorkers during his eight years as mayor (1978–1986) and is equally applicable for college leaders: "How'm I doin'?" Available numbers for Barnard at the millennial turn allow the answer, "Pretty well."

STUDENT SELECTIVITY

In 1994, at the commencement of the Shapiro presidency, Barnard received 2,731 applications for admission; in 2007, the start of Shapiro's last year, it received 4,574, an increase of 67 percent. In 1994, Barnard admitted 43 percent of its applicants; in 2007, 29 percent, a decrease of 33 percent. Yield rates (admitted students who enrolled) remained in the 45 percent to 50 percent range throughout these years.[38]

STUDENT DIVERSITY

In 1994, 22 percent of the Barnard student body came from homes outside the Northeast; in 2007, 32 percent, with Californians second only to New Yorkers in state representation among Barnard students.[39]

ECONOMIC CIRCUMSTANCES

In 1994, 22 percent of Barnard incoming students were eligible for low-income Pell Grants; in 2008, the percentage had slipped slightly to 18 percent, but it was still substantially higher than any of the other sister colleges and was comparable to the percentage of Pell grantees at Columbia.[40]

RACE AND ETHNICITY

In 1995, 30 percent of the Barnard student body identified as students of color; in 2007, 40 percent did so, with most of the increase attributable to growing numbers of Hispanic students. Asian Americans continued to be the most represented and African Americans the eighth lowest represented.[41]

BUDGETARY MANAGEMENT

The financial situation at the start of the Shapiro presidency in 1994 was decidedly mixed. On the upside was the fact that the Futter administration had consistently operated with balanced budgets, even on occasion enjoying an end-of-year surplus, which Finance Committee chair Horowitz preferred calling "instances of income exceeding expenditures." It had also launched two capital campaigns, the first Centennial Campaign for $20 million to help underwrite the construction of the dormitory, and the second, for $40 million, in progress in 1994 when Shapiro arrived, and that she and the board promptly increased to $65 million.[42]

On the downside, most of the cost of Sulzberger Hall was financed by issuing thirty-year bonds that had to be paid back from operating income. The Sulzberger family naming gift of $5 million covered only the debt service for the first five years. Also of concern was that the costs of the capital campaigns were carried "off budget" and now needed to be included in 1995–1996 and 1996–1997 budgets, adding another $1.5 million to the expense side of each. Once this was accomplished, the Shapiro presidency thereafter also regularly experienced budgetary "instances of income exceeding expenditures."[43]

ENDOWMENT GROWTH

The endowment that the Shapiro presidency inherited had a market value of $60 million ($140 million in 2019 dollars), which represented a doubling in the thirteen-year Futter presidency; the endowment the Shapiro presidency turned over in 2008 had a market value of $220 million ($252 million in 2019 dollars), a near quadrupling. Favorable economic times certainly helped, but so did effective fundraising aimed at endowment enhancement. During the Shapiro presidency, the number of regularly endowed professorships swelled from eight at its outset to fifteen at its close. Olin term professorships grew from five in 1993 to ten in 2008.[44]

PLANT EXPANSION

The major planned capital project of the Shapiro presidency was an architecturally striking multi-use, four-story building fronting on Broadway for which construction began in 2004, replacing the four-decade-old and already bedraggled McIntosh Student Center. Originally given the placeholding name of "Nexus," it was renamed the Diana Center after the college received a naming gift of $15 million from Roy and Diana Vagelos, she a Barnard alumna (Diana Touliatou, class of 1955) and trustee.[45]

But even as this building was going up, the Barnard trustees received an out-of-the-blue offer: the chance to acquire the still-under-construction, fourteen-story Cathedral Gardens located on 110th Street, across from the southern limits of Morningside Park. Its unexpected availability followed on Columbia's deciding to offload the building upon redirecting its expansionary plans northward to Manhattanville. Despite not having a naming gift for one building but aware of the ongoing need for student and faculty housing, the trustees quickly decided that this was an offer they could not refuse and proceeded to vote to borrow the money to buy it. Provost Boylan, who was involved in the deliberations, later cited it as a prime instance of the ethos animating the board, its chair Anna Quindlen, and the Shapiro administration: "If we didn't take those risks it would never have happened."[46]

Other building projects included the 1997 renovation of the Altschul Science Tower to provide its faculty inhabitants with additional laboratory space; the refurbishing of a classroom on the fourth floor of Milbank, hereinafter the Kreuger Auditorium, named for longtime trustee Constance Kreuger (class of 1953); and construction of a new auditorium on the third floor of Barnard Hall, named in honor of the distinguished and beloved Barnard art historian, Julius Held. Not since the McIntosh era four decades earlier had so much of the Barnard campus been designated "Hard Hats Only."[47]

ADMINISTRATIVE CONTINUITY

Shapiro's fourteen-year tenure made her the third-longest serving administrative head in the college's history. Several members of her senior staff enjoyed comparably lengthy terms, which made for an impressively stable period in the college's administrative history. Dean of the College Dorothy Denburg was in place at the outset of Shapiro's presidency and stayed on into that of her successor;

Provost Boylan came at the start of Shapiro's second year in the presidency and stayed on three years after she left; two directors of admissions, Doris Davis (1992–2002) and Jennifer Gill Fondiller (2002–), served during the Shapiro presidency. More discontinuous was the position of chief financial officer, which was held successively by Sigmund Ginsburg (1985–1994), Barry Kaufman (1995–2001), Lew Wyman (2001–2005), and Gregory Brown (2006–2014), with Brown staying on into the next presidential administration. Overall, steady management marked the period.[48]

TRUSTEE OVERSIGHT

Three women headed the board of trustees during the Shapiro presidency. Patricia Green, class of 1962, educator and wife of former congressional representative William Green, served as chair from 1994 to 1998; the financial consultant Gayle Robinson, class of 1975, from 1998 to 2003; and the journalist/novelist Anna Quindlen, class of 1974, from 2003 to 2013. Robinson was the first African American woman elected to lead an elite college board.[49]

During the Shapiro presidency, the board became less New York City–centric and Northeast-bounded with the election of three members from Florida; another three from California; and one from Greeley, Colorado. Of the New Yorkers on the board, however, nearly all still lived on Manhattan's East Side. Other changes included the fact that parents of Barnard students began to be sought out as prospects for board membership; turnover increased somewhat, as did the percentage of women. Of the forty-six trustees appointed between 1994 and 2007, thirty-five (76 percent) were women, eleven were men (24 percent). Of these thirty-five women, two were of Latina heritage (Sally Hernandez and Rosa Alonso, class of 1982), three were of Asian heritage (Amy Lai, class of 1989; Nancy Tze-Chung Wong, class of 1962; and Eileen Ling Moy, class of 1973), and one was African American (Nina Shaw, class of 1976). Jews likely continued to constitute the board's largest group by religious affiliation, but Catholics, including Quindlen and a future board chair, Jolyne Caruso-Fitzgerald, class of 1981, retained a presence, while the number of self-identified mainline Protestants declined.[50]

The era when male lawyers dominated the board was over; it now drew more of its membership from the world of finance, where women had only recently become a presence in numbers. Among the eleven male

appointees, three—Harry Payne, Peter Stanley, and Ronald Liebowitz—
were or had been liberal arts college presidents.[51]

For all these shifts in the social makeup of the board, its relationship
with the college's administrative team remained cordial and effective.
All three chairs developed trusting relationships with President Shapiro;
Provost Boylan; Dean of the College Denburg; and, toward the close of the
Shapiro presidency, Chief Financial Officer Gregory Brown. To be sure,
good times make such relationships easier to establish and sustain. But
so, too, does a concerted effort of all involved to exploit fully the opportunities to make permanent improvements in an institution that has known
its share of bad times.

A PROFESSOR'S PRESIDENT

It is surely a simplification to identify Barnard deans and presidents by the
constituency they seemed most attuned to serving. But in some instances,
Dean Gildersleeve's compliant attentiveness to the policy wishes of
Columbia's President Butler, President Futter's to her board of trustees,
President Peterson's to her fractious students and (it was said by her critics) to her Columbia interlocutors, doing so provides a starting point for
comparative analysis. When this principal-constituency test is applied to
the presidency of Judith Shapiro, the call is easy to make: she was a "professor's president."

Of Barnard's first eleven administrative leaders, only four came to their
office with credentials as card-carrying professors: Virginia Gildersleeve,
Rosemary Park, Millicent McIntosh, and Judith Shapiro. In the first two
cases, their time in the classroom—Gildersleeve two years as a Columbia
assistant professor of English, McIntosh three years a Bryn Mawr assistant
professor of English—were neither protracted nor dispositive. Neither
thereafter published in their fields, although McIntosh occasionally taught
a section of English as president. Park had an early career as a professor
of German literature, teaching at Connecticut College for a decade before
becoming its president, but once she was out of the classroom, she never
looked back. By contrast, Shapiro's pre-administrative career as a professor extended over fifteen years at three different institutions, while her

publications record and professional activities during that period established her scholarly reputation among academic anthropologists. When she became a candidate for the Barnard presidency, it was Morningside's anthropologists who first sang her praises and applauded loudest when she took the job. It mattered to both the new president and to them that she be listed among the Anthropology Department's professors in the college catalog, just as it mattered to the rest of the faculty that, when she took sabbatical leave in 2001, she returned to scholarly writing that had been dutifully put aside while president.[52]

Comfortable in most public circumstances, Shapiro was particularly at home when participating in faculty meetings. Rather than preside at these monthly gatherings, this being the job of the provost, she operated as one among equals. Her comments were delivered in a style, and accompanied by the occasional scholarly reference or insider witticism, immediately recognizable to faculty (for better or worse) as their own. Unlike her predecessor, a lawyer by training and not given to sharing more information than required, especially with faculty, Shapiro was her least guarded and most transparent in her dealings with faculty. Both presidential strategies proved effective in their day, but it was Shapiro's that endeared.

EMBRACING NEW YORK CITY

If there is a single theme that suffused the Shapiro presidency it might be that of "Barnard College *in* and *of* the City of New York." At no previous point in its history had the college so eagerly celebrated its urban identity, its connectedness to New York City past and present, and its appreciation of the city's diversity. That it did so even as its students, faculty members, and trustees came from increasingly far-flung origins with less claim to being birthright New Yorkers than earlier generations of these groups is not without a certain irony. The irony is less, however, if what Nicholas Murray Butler and Virginia Gildersleeve disparaged back in 1913 as being "too New Yorky" is viewed not so much inborn as an acquired taste. It is this way of thinking that earlier allowed the Pennsylvania-born Margaret Mead to call herself a New Yorker and subsequently for the California-reared and future president Sian Beilock to do likewise.[53]

Every public occasion became an opportunity for President Shapiro to stress the college's embrace of New York's cosmopolitan ways. Whether joining in the mourning and resolve that attended the city's response to the terrorist attack on the World Trade Center on September 11, 2001, or celebrating Columbia's 250th anniversary in 2004, she used the occasion to display Barnard's bona fides as a civic presence. When alumnae returned for reunions, they could count on being serenaded by their president with a medley of Broadway show tunes from their college years. And how many times did she share with all within

FIGURE 11.1 Judith Shapiro, sixth president of Barnard College(1994–2008), Barnard Archives.

hearing her core conviction that "I would not trade Barnard's location for Wellesley's endowment"?[54]

To be sure, it helped that New York City at the millennial turn was on the upswing. During the administrations of mayors Rudolph Guiliani (1994–2001) and Michael Bloomberg (2001–2013), the recovery first discernible to inveterate civic optimists during David Dinkins's single term, and promised still earlier by the indefatigable Ed Koch, came to be. It also helped that Columbia during the presidency of George Rupp and, after 2003, Lee Bollinger continued the recovery begun under Michael Sovern from a work-in-progress to an accomplished fact. In the meantime, Manhattan's Upper West Side had become not only an appealing neighborhood for the city's upwardly mobile citizenry but a safe and exciting place for the best and brightest of the world's young people to attend college.[55]

This said, the success of the Shapiro presidency was more than an instance of being in the right place at the right time. It was also more than a local institutional affirmation of Robert Merton's (by way of the New Testament evangelist) "Matthew Effect": "To everyone who has been given will be given more." It required prudent stewardship by an engaged

FIGURE 11.2 Annual "Take Back the Night" student march around the Morningside Heights neighborhood, 1990s. Barnard Archives.

and generous board, a commitment to classroom excellence and scholarly enterprise by its faculty, and the presence of students multi-talented and (per Anna Quindlen's anthem) "unafraid." But it also required effective administrative advocacy, emanating from the top, that allowed Barnard in the opening years of the twenty-first century to seize the propitious moment to confront questionable elements of its past and put them right even as it settled into being the most selective women's college in America.[56]

Barnard's sixth president had signed on for two six-year terms and stayed for an additional two years. In May 2007, Judith R. Shapiro gave the board a year's notice of her intention to retire. She remained in place on June 30, 2008, to welcome her successor and ensure a smooth transition. After briefly trying retirement, she did some consulting and returned to the classroom as a practitioner in and promoter of Barnard historian Mark Carnes's nationally acclaimed Reacting to the Past participatory learning project. In 2013, she became president of the Teagle Foundation, having earlier served on its board. Shapiro continues to live both on Morning-side Heights and in the Philadelphia suburb of Rosemont. She maintains a lively interest in the college, along with a healthy appreciation of the prime rule of administrative succession: "One-president-at-a-time."[57]

12

GOING GLOBAL

*Your engagement with outside power brokers must continue and expand
so that Barnard will be better known and appreciated in the world.*

—ANNA QUINDLEN TO DEBORA L. SPAR, 2009[1]

I need to mention two disclaimers. The last four chapters trace a part of the history of Barnard in which I participated, having arrived on Morningside Heights as an assistant professor of history in the fall of 1969. My involvement over the subsequent four decades and four presidencies was as a faculty member active in committee, departmental, and university affairs, and, from 1987 to 1994, dean of the faculty. During the presidency of Judith Shapiro (1994–2008), I returned to full-time teaching and resumed earlier roles as a department chair and collegewide committee member. Second disclaimer: since that time, while continuing to teach, I have played a lesser role in college affairs during the presidency of Debora Spar. When this limited personal vantage point is combined with the general risks of extending an historical account to the very near present, interpretive caution is advised. A documentary record has yet to be collected or made available, and various decisions have yet to stand the test of time.[2]

GOING GLOBAL

Barnard's seventh president, Debora L. Spar, was similar to her two predecessors in many ways. Like Futter and Shapiro, Spar came from the New
York region, in her case, the Westchester County suburban town of Chappaqua. Just short of forty-five when chosen, she took up the presidency
when she was younger than Shapiro (fifty-one) and older than Futter
(thirty-one). Debora attended public schools in Chappaqua, and while
in graduate school at Harvard she met and married Miltos Catomeris, a
Greek-born architect with a practice in Boston.[3]

More significant for members of the presidential search committee and
subsequent observers were the differences with earlier presidents. First was
the absence of any prior experience with women's colleges. Weed, Smith,
Gill, Gildersleeve, McIntosh, Park, Mattfeld, and Futter were all graduates
of women's colleges, while Shapiro had been employed at one for eighteen

FIGURE 12.1 Debora L. Spar, seventh president of Barnard College (2008–2017), on the
left, and Barack Obama, forty-fourth president of the United States (2009–2017), at the
2012 Barnard commencement.

years. Only Peterson (and now Sian Leah Beilock) among Barnard's administrative leaders had no extended prior exposure to women's colleges.

Spar was also unusual in that most of her higher education and subsequent occupational experience occurred in a professional environment. Her undergraduate degree was from the Foreign Service School of Georgetown University, where she prepared for a career in diplomacy ("I wanted to be a spy"), and, following PhD training in political science at Harvard, her teaching and administrative career of eighteen years took place at the Harvard Business School. No previous Barnard president had as little prior institutional exposure to the liberal arts.[4]

So what did the search committee see in Spar's vita that prompted her apparently unanimous and enthusiastic selection? The confidential nature of such deliberations made any speculation just that. But the committee had little reason, with Barnard's vital signs being generally positive, to be looking for a crisis manager of the Peterson or Futter type. Nor did the faculty members, given their well-provided-for feelings under Shapiro, have a strong claim for back-to-back "professors' presidents." Because Barnard was already the most selective of all women's colleges and comfortable in its relationship with Columbia, trustees and student members more likely saw Barnard looking to global challenges—and a new kind of president to take them on. Such ambitions are consistent with a rare breach of the committee's cone of silence when the committee chair later cited the comment of two student members after "another smart, articulate academic left the room": "She was great. But she wasn't Debora Spar."[5]

At her appointment, Spar was the most prolific author of all Barnard's presidents. Her four books—*Beyond Globalism: The Remaking of American Foreign Economic Policy* (with Raymond Vernon) (1989); *Ruling the Waves: From the Compass to the Internet* (2001); *Pirates, Prophets and Pioneers: Business and Politics Along the Technological Frontier* (2001); *The Baby Business: How Money, Science and Politics Drive the Commerce of Conception* (2005)—and a score of articles placed her among the most published of all but a handful of contemporary college or university presidents. Unlike Rosemary Park and Judith Shapiro, whose publications were directed at fellow academics, Spar wrote for a global audience of policymakers, both public and corporate. All this seems to have been important to the search committee.Likely more than any other qualification it was Spar's promise as a communicator that secured her the committee's endorsement. That is what the candidate later said she took away from her interviews, a sense that the committee believed Barnard was "punching below its weight." "What Barnard needed," Spar understood, "was someone to elevate it. When you are a place that has been as good as Barnard, you want to be known for that. And I think that was a big part of my job." The charge from the trustees after her first year as president only reinforced this impression: "Your engagement with outside power brokers must continue and expand so that Barnard will be better known and appreciated in the world."[6]

BLINDSIDED

Whatever else can be said about the start of the Spar presidency, it lacked good timing. Between January 30, 2008, when trustee chair Anna Quindlen announced the selection of Spar to be Barnard's seventh president and eleventh leader, and her installation five weeks later in March, the United States slid into the most serious financial crisis since the Great Depression. Problems with the home mortgage market, first publicly acknowledged in the fall of 2007, had spread the following spring to major banks and other financial institutions holding suddenly toxic mortgage-backed securities, putting them at risk of runs by depositors/ creditors and ensuing bankruptcy. On September 29, 2008, the stock market experienced its sharpest single-day drop (to that point) of 770 points. The Dow Jones Industrial Average, at 14,000 during the early meetings of the search committee in October 2007, had fallen to 9,000 five months later, bottoming out at 6,400 in April 2009. The stock market—and investors in it—had lost 54 percent of its earlier value.[7]

Meanwhile, Barnard's endowment, $212 million at President Shapiro's departure in the spring of 2008, had dropped a year later to $164 million, a loss of 22 percent in market value. The only positive note struck at the time by chief operating officer (COO) Greg Brown was that, because Barnard's endowment was so much smaller than its peers, its operating budget was less dependent on endowment draws, and its investment strategy more risk-averse, the college had lost relatively less than other institutions.[8]

The national financial crisis that greeted Barnard's new president limited her immediate options but did not keep her from thinking big. Spar's inaugural address on October 28, 2008, was nothing if not ambitious. It contained three major proposals, each drawing on initiatives of her predecessors, that were to become hallmarks of her administration. The first was to make Barnard a significant player on the global scene, both as a voice for women the world over and as an educator of the world's women. Gildersleeve had earlier staked out an international role for Barnard with her travels and diplomatic labors, and more recently Shapiro had effected a modern-day "opening" to China by her 1999 visit. But Spar proposed a series of annual global forums that, over the next eight years, had her engaging the elites of London, Beijing, Dubai, Johannesburg, Mumbai, São Paulo, and Shanghai.[9]

Her second proposal, building on Shapiro's Student Leadership Initiative, had Barnard taking a larger public role in the training of women for leadership roles in business and politics. This effort was to be housed in the newly created Athena Center for Leadership Studies, a co-curricular undertaking that would involve faculty members, administrative personnel, and outside advisers from the worlds of commerce and politics, all under the direction of Kathryn Kolbert, a prominent civil rights attorney and feminist. The Athena Center went on to host an annual Women's Film Festival, a series of Power Talks delivered by women and open to the public, and courses for Barnard students on leadership (developed by the historian Rosalind Rosenberg), entrepreneurship, and coding.[10]

The targeted beneficiary of the incoming president's third inaugural proposal was the Barnard faculty. Spar used the occasion both to applaud their scholarly productivity and to announce the establishment of a Presidential Faculty Research Fund, which would annually dispense $100,000 to support promising faculty research projects that had yet to secure external support. Here, too, previous administrations back to President Mattfeld had recognized the need for more internal support for Barnard's faculty members in their roles as scholars, while those of Futter and Shapiro had successfully increased the avenues and amounts of that support. But Spar, coming from institutional academic circumstances where research and publications were the coin of the realm, promised to take such support to a still higher level. She also announced her intention to reduce the standard teaching program of Barnard faculty from five courses to four—a move made earlier by the much wealthier Amherst and Wellesley but resisted at Barnard by her two predecessors for financial reasons. This made her embrace of the scholar-teacher model complete.[11]

Financial exigencies, not least being the drop in endowment income going into the annual budgets of 2009–2010, 2010–2011, and 2011–2012, slowed but did not prevent implementation of these proposals. The global forums commenced in 2009 with a presidential trip to London, the Athena Center was up and running, and a reduction in teaching programs went into effect in the fall of 2011. This reduction in teaching programs won the president and provost almost universal praise from faculty members and surprisingly little critical comment from students and parents. A few instructors wondered how their windfall would not result in fewer courses being taught by regular faculty and more adjunct faculty being hired to teach them, but they mostly kept these possibilities to themselves. Ultimately, both happened.[12]

Several administrative changes occurred early on in the Spar presidency. Gregory Brown, one of Judith Shapiro's last senior administrative hires as vice president for finance in 2006, was elevated to COO in May 2009. This had him overseeing finance, human resources, campus services, Barnard College information technology, and the general counsel. He also led the financing and opening of the Diana Center, instituted improvements to Barnard's computing and administrative systems, and redesigned the performance evaluation process for administrators. He later chaired the 2012 academic-space planning process and the campuswide steering committee charged with the creation of the new academic building to replace Lehman Hall and Wollman Library. Brown left Barnard in early 2014 to become vice president for finance at Swarthmore College and was replaced by Robert Goldberg, who was previously with the State Department.[13]

Shapiro's 1995 appointee as provost and dean of the faculty, Elizabeth Boylan, stayed on until July 2011. During her tenure, she increased the college's science offerings, further diversified the racial composition of the faculty, and implemented the four-course teaching program. She left to join the Alfred P. Sloan Foundation as director for science, technology, engineering, and math (STEM) education. Paul E. Hertz, professor of biology and director of the Howard Hughes Pipeline Project at Barnard, became acting provost for fifteen months, until Linda A. Bell, an economist and provost at Haverford, arrived as provost and dean of the faculty in October 2012.[14]

In February 2011, longtime Dean of the College Dorothy Denburg, class of 1970, was named vice president for college relations and charged with strengthening alumnae ties to the college. Avis E. Hinkson, class of 1984, a student affairs administrator at the University of California, Berkeley, and before that Pomona College, became dean of the college. Her appointment, along with that of Vivian Taylor in 2009 as the president's chief of staff, placed two African American women in senior administrative positions. Denburg retired in 2013 after a distinguished career at Barnard that extended over forty-three years. Taylor left in 2011 and Hinkson, after serving five years as dean of the college, returned to Pomona in 2018. The pace of administrative turnover had quickened.[15]

One administrative area that retained its earlier leadership was admissions, where Jennifer Fondiller, class of 1988, who became director in 2002, stayed on through the Spar presidency and into that of Sian Beilock. For all but two of her eighteen years as director, Barnard applications increased annually, as did selectivity. In 1999, Barnard received 3,883 applicants and admitted 1,443, for a selectivity rate of 37 percent. Of these, 558 accepted, for a yield of 42 percent. In 2019, Barnard received 9,320 applicants (two and a half times as many as twenty years earlier), admitted 1,097, for a selectivity rate of 12 percent. Of these, 635 accepted, for a yield of 58 percent. Applications up, selectivity up, yield up: Life is good.[16]

To be sure, more than effective enrollment management was at work here. My own guess is that, with the overall decline in the number of women's colleges since the 1970s, and the even sharper decline in the number of women's colleges offering an intellectually challenging liberal arts curriculum taught by an approachable faculty of scholar-teachers, Barnard has benefitted from a variant of what economists call inelastic demand, where Barnard attracts a larger and more selective share of the smaller number of women still seeking or at least open to a liberal arts education at a women's college, as long as it offers other attractive—and in combination unique—features such as an affiliation with a major research university and a desirable location in New York City. It also bears noting that historically most Barnard students did not come to Barnard because it was a women's college. It is likely the combination of these value-added features that gives Barnard its current competitive edge over the other remaining sisters colleges.

MIDTERM INITIATIVES

By the spring of 2011, with the endowment back up to 2008 levels ($215,500,000 in June 2011) and financial aid expenditures, which had sharply increased after 2008, leveling off, the improved financial outlook allowed Spar and her senior administration to take up new challenges. Chief among them was the planning and launch of the quiet phase of the $400 million Bold Standard Capital Campaign, the centerpiece of which was to be the construction of a $150 million teaching and learning center on the site of the soon-to-be-demolished Lehman Hall/Wollman Library. Other components of the campaign included $175 million for endowment, $100 million of which was hallmarked for financial aid, and $75 million for endowed professorships. In charge of this effort was Bret Silver, previously a fundraiser at the Lincoln Center, who came to Barnard as vice president for development in February 2011. Five years later, at the start of the public campaign, Barnard announced gifts totaling $70 million from the families of three trustees—Cheryl Milstein, class of 1982, P. '14; Leonard Tow and daughter Emily Tow Jackson, class of 1987; Diana Vagelos, class of 1955—in support of the still-under-construction and soon-to-be-named Cheryl and Philip Milstein Teaching and Learning Center, which opened in the fall of 2018.[17]

Also getting underway in 2011 was a three-year review of the curriculum led by professor of astronomy Laura Kay. Building on the Nine Ways of Knowing curriculum implemented during the Shapiro presidency in 1999 and maintaining the first-year seminars that dated back to the mid-1980s, the Foundations curriculum approved by the faculty in 2015 broke new ground by adding technology, global inquiry, and social difference components to the general requirements, as well as encouraging more academic attention to New York City and its nonacademic educational venues.[18]

A third accomplishment of the Spar administration, although not part of its initial agenda, was devising a policy with regard to enrolling and retaining transgender students. The issue had been first broached during the Shapiro administration and managed on a case-by-case basis, but with no definitive policy pronouncement. In 2013, with Barnard hosting the sister college presidents, Spar asked recently appointed Barnard Writer in

Residence and advocate for transgender rights Jennifer Boylan to address the subject at dinner. A year later, after the other remaining sister colleges had all promulgated policies that welcomed applicants from biological males who now identified as women, the Barnard board of trustees, specifically the Committee on Campus Life and its co-chairs, Diana Vagelos, class of 1955, and Frances Sadler, class of 1972, took up the issue. Five town hall meetings allowed students, alumnae, faculty members, and trustees to consider various options, along with an online solicitation of views from interested parties unable to attend these meetings. On June 4, 2015, board chair Jolyne Caruso-Fitzgerald, class of 1981, after much discussion and little dissent, announced the new policy:

> Barnard would welcome the applications of and would admit otherwise qualified self-identified women whatever their gender designation at birth; Barnard would continue to enroll transitioning students (female to male) if they wished to remain at Barnard; Barnard would continue to use gendered language that reflects our identity as a women's college.

Barnard was not always in the vanguard of constructive social change, and it was the last of the remaining sisters to develop a transgender policy. In this instance, however, Barnard moved deliberately and consensually to achieve the right outcome.[19]

Two initiatives came later. In December 2015, Barnard's board of trustees authorized the formation of the Presidential Task Force to Examine Divestment. Here, too, a year of discussions among students, faculty members, administrators, and board members ensued about how the college should respond to calls to divest from companies in the fossil fuel industry that denied the existence of and human contribution to climate change. The Barnard board was the first among its peers to approve a policy that directed its financial advisers to divest. A related undertaking began in the fall of 2016, under the faculty leadership of professor of environmental science Stephanie Pfirman and associate professor of theater Sandra Goldmark, focused on consumption and waste, energy, the local environment, curricula and research, and the campus. Here, too, Barnard was later than some of its other peers to take up environmentalism, but by 2016, the thoroughly urban Barnard had embraced the cause.[20]

EXIT MEGRIMS

On November 16, 2016, the *New York Times* carried the story of Debora Spar's departure from the Barnard presidency to become president of the Lincoln Center, effective March 2017. Surprised by the announcement, the trustees moved quickly to appoint Robert Goldberg, the college's COO, as acting president, and to launch a search for a new president. Goldberg then served as acting president for five months, doing so with grace, self-deprecating humor, and administrative skill, until Sian Leah Beilock arrived on campus in May as Barnard's eighth president.[21]

When Spar moved to run Lincoln Center in February, she had served just under nine years as Barnard's seventh president and eleventh administrative head. The many accomplishments of her tenure—weathering the financial crisis, securing funding for a major capital project, curricular updating, increasing support for and recognition of faculty research, devising an effective and timely transgender policy, continuing Barnard's commitment to diversity, raising Barnard's national and global visibility— have been noted. To these should be added the maintenance of good relations with Columbia officials, from President Bollinger and University Provost John Coatsworth, to the deans of Columbia's undergraduate and professional schools. Indeed, trans-Broadway comity had become so much the norm over the previous three decades that the *Sturm und Drang* of the 1970s had all but faded from institutional memory.[22]

This is not to suggest that the Spar presidency was without conflict. Spar did little to hide her early annoyance with many of the long-standing administrative arrangements, especially those that limited her presidential authority and the need to obtain the approval of standing committees made up of faculty and students. For their part, most students remained well-disposed toward her. Those who had her as a teacher in a team-taught course, Science and Public Policy, wrote what a colleague described as "rapturous evaluations." Two student remembrances compiled at her leaving referred to her glowingly as "D-Spar the Rock Star."[23]

Other students took exception to specific actions of her administration. The student government association (SGA) leadership in 2010 faulted Spar for insufficient transparency during the budgetary cutbacks. The costly international forums continued, while some student services were curtailed and faculty department amenities reduced. In 2014, Barnard members of Students for Palestinian Justice complained that their divestment campaign against Israel had been subverted by new campus rules limiting postering when a "Stand for Justice in Palestine" banner on the front of Barnard Hall had been unilaterally removed at the president's direction. Still other students believed that Spar's acceptance of a highly compensated place on the board of directors of Goldman Sachs in 2011 was inappropriate and that the explanation that she did so to press women's issues was disingenuous. And last, some members of the class of 2017 took her abrupt departure four months prior to their graduation as a personal affront.[24]

Spar kept up an active publishing agenda throughout her presidency, with mixed results. Her *Wonder Women: Sex, Power, and the Quest for Perfection* (2013) addressed women of professional standing. Favorably disposed reviewers heralded it as an instance of second wave feminism, while critics saw it as a paean to corporate feminism. Spar being linked with Facebook COO Sheryl Sandberg, a friend whom she secured as Barnard's commencement speaker at the 2011 graduation ceremony, and *Wonder Women* being paired with Sandberg's best seller, *Lean In: Women, Work and Will to Lead*, did not meet with universal approval from Barnard students, faculty members, alumnae, and feminist commentators. Some saw her as an apologist for a Wall Street version of feminism or, as one reviewer described it, "elite white feminism" and at odds with earlier noncorporate varieties of feminism with which Barnard traditionally identified. Nor did her frequent references to her marriage and children, to meeting the demands of being well coifed and smartly dressed, and to operating successfully in transactional male settings win her feminist skeptics over.[25]

But it was Spar's 2016 op-ed, "Aging and My Beauty Dilemma," in the *New York Times* on the utility of cosmetic surgery that produced the most vocal reaction. Its opening sentence is nothing if not attention-grabbing: "When I was 21, I underwent breast reduction surgery, reducing my embarrassingly large chest to something that could at least fit inside a cardigan." "Appreciated" and "timely," declared some of the readers whose responses were provided by the *Times*; "shocked" and "appalled" said others, with both camps including self-identifying Barnard alumnae.[26]

There were also issues internal to the Spar administration that drew criticism. Some felt Dorothy Denburg's abrupt removal as dean of the college in 2011 encapsulated the president's determination, in sidelining the senior administrator whose loyalty to the college was legendary and who possessed the longest institutional memory, to make the college into the "Harvard Business School on the Hudson." Her commissioning McKinsey & Company to conduct a review of administrative procedures and then apparently acting on its recommendations (the report was never made public) only reinforced that impression. One of these changes, placing the Office of Alumnae Relations under the direction of the vice president for development and the accompanying downgrading of the alumnae director's responsibilities, was seen by some as relegating alumnae to fundraising targets rather than seeing them as vital parts of the college community. The change also cost Barnard the services of another alumna, Erin Frederick, class of 2001, who resigned as director of alumnae relations.

Faculty members also exercised their constitutional right—buttressed in some cases by tenure—to grouse. The presidential decision to move from a five-course to four-course teaching program in 2011 was hailed by instructors except those in departments—the sciences and economics—where four-course programs had been the norm since the 1990s. But the shift left the incoming provost, Linda A. Bell, and department chairs scrambling to staff the courses that remained a regular part of their offerings but that regular instructors no longer taught. Simply dropping those courses was not an option given departmental requirements and the ongoing need to attract numbers of Columbia students across Broadway to maintain a reasonable cross-registration balance and avoid a reverse migration. Increasing the size of the faculty in the wake of the 2008 financial crisis lacked the approval of an increasingly tenure-leery board.[27]

Several departments turned to hiring part-time instructors on a semester-to-semester basis as determined by student demand. Another response was to fill gaps created by retirements or resignations of tenured or tenure-ladder faculty members with three-year nonrenewable term assistant professorships. This category was not an invention of the Spar administration: comparable temporary appointments had been used sparingly in the past as financial exigencies dictated. But in 2012 and 2013, term assistant professorships accounted for most of the full-time faculty appointments.[28]

Assistant professors remained subject to the ticking tenure clock. In their case, however, prospects for securing tenure during the Spar presidency improved. Credit here must go in part to the work of Barnard faculty members. In 2002, they constituted the Tenure Process Review Committee and, after a thorough investigation of the workings of the ad hoc system, called for its replacement. This change occurred in 2011, with the support of then-provost at Columbia Alan Brinkley. The committee created procedures whereby the qualifications of Barnard nominees are reviewed by a selection of standing members of a provost-appointed Tenure Review Advisory Committee (TRAC).[29] This process produced fewer negative outcomes—and fewer occasions for intervention on the part of the provost. Reversals of Barnard nominees for tenure have since become increasingly rare and only occur at the same rate as at other Columbia schools. Between 2011 and 2017, of the twenty-five Barnard faculty nominees submitted to TRAC, twenty-three were approved and secured tenure. The high rate of success was a result of the rigorous vetting of departmental nominations by the Barnard Appointments and Tenure Committee, chaired by Provost Bell.[30]

Faculty diversity also improved during this period, led by an administrative initiative launched in 2012 with the creation of a committee on Faculty Diversity and Inclusion (FCDI), chaired successively by Janet Jacobsen in women's studies and Debra Minkoff in sociology. While its existence attests to the college's commitment to diversity as a goal, a survey commissioned by the committee in 2014 and published in 2016 revealed that many faculty members remained unhappy with the pace and scope of diversification. This was especially true among faculty respondents who self-identified as persons of color; as lesbian, gay, bisexual, transgender, or questioning (LGBTQ); or as coming from working-class or first-generation-to-go-college backgrounds. Women faculty were overall more critical of college efforts than men, and those in the humanities were somewhat more so than in the sciences. Associate professors numbered disproportionately among the dissatisfied.[31]

As one of the last acts of the Spar presidency, the committee in February 2017 identified three action areas to transform the college into a more representative, inclusive, and equitable campus:

- Develop and implement organizational structures and practices that promote diversity, inclusion, and equity across the college (structural changes).

- Build an inclusive campuswide culture and community based on shared principles of representation, inclusion, and social justice (community building and climate).
- Institutionalize structures of accountability at every level in order to ensure constant, sustained, and effective systemic change (assessment and accountability).

The committee's principal recommendation, since adopted by the board of trustees: hire, over and above those appointed by regularly authorized faculty searches, new faculty from underrepresented groups in the next five years.[32]

The current existence of four tiers of full-time faculty—tenured, tenure-eligible, term-and-tenure-ineligible, off-ladder—alongside growing numbers of part-time instructors, strains the notion of the Barnard faculty as a community of institutionally dedicated teachers and scholars. Those at the top of the occupational pyramid, tenured professors and associate professors, now constitute a privileged and shrinking minority. Included among them is a growing number who have stayed on beyond the retirement-eligible age of sixty-five.[33] Meanwhile, more of the actual classroom teaching falls to instructors whose ties to Barnard are transactional and contingent. These include full-time off-ladder instructors whose appointments are subject to periodic reviews and terminations based on economic exigencies.

It was perhaps inevitable that the bottom of the faculty pyramid would seek a measure of occupational security through unionization and collective bargaining. In 2014, a group of contingent faculty members moved to secure representation from the National Labor Relations Board (NLRB) as a bargaining unit under the organizational umbrella of the United Auto Workers (UAW). Barnard voluntarily recognized the union in October 2015. After threatening to strike, the Barnard Contingent Faculty-UAW Local 2110 (BCF-UAW), with 200 members, signed its first contract with the college in February 2017. Terms included an increase in wages, a measure of job continuity if not job security, and some healthcare coverage; all went into effect at the start of the 2017–2018 academic year.[34]

Other recorded complaints with the Spar presidency included the fact that the Athena Center for Leadership Studies represented a departure from the college's liberal arts focus. Others raised concerns that the occupational preponderance of trustees appointed during the Spar presidency were drawn mostly from Wall Street. This along with Spar's acceptance of the Goldman Sachs directorship and the pattern of invited guests to campus from the world of finance and management consulting reinforced the impression of Barnard as becoming the captive of the capitalistic ethos. Even Spar's touted prowess as a fundraiser was seen by some as overrated because the three principal donors to her capital campaign were already longtime benefactors of the college.[35]

Nearly all the substantive criticisms heard about the Spar presidency came accompanied with subjective misgivings that Spar's mix of gravitas and glamour favored the latter. But did it? And if it did, what impact did her "presidential glitz" or "diva turns," as her critics would call them, have on the long-term well-being of the college? My bet is that, for all the commentary generated by her style and the anger at the manner of her leaving, hers will be judged to have been a sustaining presidency that did not slow the momentum building over the previous two presidencies.

DO PRESIDENTS REALLY MATTER?

To be sure, some aspects of Barnard's recent history transcend individual presidencies. An example is admissions trends. Both the upward swing in applications and the accompanying increase in selectivity began in the last years of the Futter presidency, continued almost uninterrupted through both the Shapiro and Spar presidencies, and show no signs of flattening at the outset of Beilock's presidency. If all this is true, which president deserves credit for an admissions trend of this duration? All four or none? If and when the trend ends, we will likely have a president to blame, but might she be only the otherwise innocent victim of bad timing?[36]

It might also be argued that the actions or personalities of individual presidents are less determinative of institutional well-being than changes affecting the college's other major constituencies. In the case of the trustees, for example, these include the shortening of average terms of service and the resultant increased turnover, the occupational shift away from lawyers and clergy to Wall Streeters and professionals, and the geographical dispersion from the Upper East Side to the ends of the world. The board's first African American, Barbara Watson, class of 1939, was elected in 1969. By 2019, five more African Americans, three Asian Americans, and two Latinos have been elected to the board. In 2019 the thirty-two-person board included five trustees of color. All these changes can be viewed as part of a century-long "de-WASPification" and feminization of the board and likely have less to do with presidential agency than the globalization of New York's "very earnest, philanthropic, public-spirited class."[37]

With shorter tenures, trustees have less time to get to know each other or the workings of the college. They also have fewer sources of independent knowledge and are more dependent upon assessments provided by senior administrators. Yet these same administrators today are themselves less likely to have a long acquaintance with the college. Fewer went to Barnard or served on the faculty than administrators earlier, and they are less likely to see Barnard as their permanent place of employment and more as a moment in a non-institution-bounded career. Of the dozen senior administrators who make up the President's Council in the summer of 2019, only three have been at Barnard more than three years and only two are graduates of Barnard. None has prior experience as a Barnard faculty member.[38]

The growth of administrative staff focused on student services is another fact transcending presidencies. It began at Barnard in the 1950s, accelerated in the 1980s, and currently shows no signs of abating. This is especially true in the provision of psychiatric services to what some see as an increasingly fragile student body, while others see a problem that has always been there and is now being recognized, treated, and discussed.[39]

The problem with relieving college presidents of personal responsibility is that it also limits the possibility of their presidential agency. Again, this may apply in the histories of large and impersonal organizations, or even smaller ones in the "long run," accepting Keynes's cautionary point that "in the long run we are all dead." But I believe it does not apply in the case of the relatively short and personality-infused history of American liberal arts colleges, which have remained relatively small institutions, and, at their best, communities more than corporations. And so for Barnard, with its four foundational characteristics: a liberal arts college, for women, located in New York City, affiliated with Columbia University. The account in this book has argued for three other distinguishing attributes: chronically undercapitalized, possessing a singularly heterogeneous student and alumnae body, an early home to a college faculty of scholar-teachers.

Barnard's successful leaders have accepted and subscribed to all four of the first foundational characteristics, although not equally. Emily James Smith paid more heed to the Columbia connection than to the scholarly aspirations of Barnard's teachers; McIntosh attended more to improving the college's shaky finances than to its liberal arts curriculum; Futter made less of Barnard as a women's college than as a rigorous liberal arts college; Shapiro made more of its New York locale than its modest endowment; Spar focused on branding and visibility more than on its alumnae. All reasoned that doing so was in the best interest of the Barnard of their moment, while reflecting their own educational and intellectual vision.

Among Barnard's arguably less successful leaders, Gill and Peterson never felt at home in New York City, while Mattfeld never appreciated the Columbia affiliation. Gildersleeve and Park were made uncomfortable by the college's persistent heterogeneity. But taken in aggregate, all eleven leaders have served the college well throughout Barnard's 130 years, thus making effective administrative leadership by women yet another

FIGURE 12.2 Sian Leah Beilock, eighth president of Barnard College (2017–) at her inauguration, October 2017.

hallmark of Barnard's history: a bracing finding for all who hold Barnard dear and an emboldening one at the outset of a new and promising presidency of Sian Leah Beilock.

AN ONGOING COMMITMENT TO DIVERSITY:
THE INCLUSION CHALLENGE

Having thus backed away from a last-moment conversion to Barnard's history as the story of impersonal forces and returned to the belief that individual Barnard presidents can and have mattered, let me conclude with a specific and contemporary instance where I believe presidential agency is crucial to the college's future. It concerns Barnard's ongoing commitment to diversity and inclusion, which I consider an affirmation of Barnard at its heterogenous and cosmopolitan best. But I also believe recent progress to the goal of a fully inclusive Barnard has brought the college to a point in its history where it becomes important to stress not just our diversity but also what we share in common. This holds for Barnard trustees and students, administrators and alumnae, although most of my evidence focuses on its faculty members and students.

Those who make up the Barnard faculty in 2020 have fewer ties to Barnard, to Columbia, to New York City, to women's education and, to each other than Barnard's earlier faculties. That is, they have less in common than the faculty in 1990, and less still than the faculty in 1965. While today's faculty contains about the same proportion of women as those two earlier moments in the college's history, far fewer of these women attended a women's college, including Barnard; of the 232 women appointed to the Barnard faculty since 1990, only sixteen (7 percent) were Barnard graduates. In 1964, more than half the Barnard faculty of whatever gender pursued their graduate studies at Columbia; in 2020, only about one in seven had done so. Most of us now come "from somewhere else," whereas earlier most had lived either in New York or the Northeast prior to joining the faculty. Few of us today, by our place of rearing, educational sources, career trajectories, and time at Barnard qualify as "homebodies."[40]

When this demographic reality is combined with the ascendancy within the faculty of the scholar-teacher ethos and the specialization enforced by that ethos, the tendency toward social isolation is compounded. As specialized scholars, we look to fellow specialists on other campuses and even in other countries for collaboration rather than to Barnard colleagues. We communicate with them via the internet or by attending conferences, not by face-to-face interactions at lunch. Nor do we see department colleagues as engaged with us in a collective and institution-rooted pedagogical enterprise (teaching the sweep of English literature or the range of psychology) but rather each with our own designated patch—and our own allotment of students.

By pointing to the operative centrifugal and atomizing pressures affecting today's Barnard faculty, I am hardly breaking new ground. Every faculty member who has served as a department chair has had to reckon with them. Even as chairs bask in the glow that covers their departments when a member receives a prestigious research grant, it falls to them to find arrangements to cover the about-to-be-absent grantee's teaching and student-advising duties, typically by calling on one of the department's fewer and fewer homebodies to do so. Several ongoing efforts by Barnard's Provost Linda Bell, including sponsoring collegewide faculty lectures and discussions, have sought to mitigate the silo effect of departmental isolation. A still more recent and constructive initiative of the newly installed President Beilock has been to have faculty members meet and talk with trustees about their teaching and research. This dialogue gives promise of greater understanding across what has at times seemed to be an impermeable constituency border.[41]

Centrifugal forces are also at work among today's students. The class of 2023 contains a majority of women of color, with substantial numbers identifying as other than cis-female; fewer have ties to each other or, despite a modest uptick in legacies, to earlier Barnard student populations. As the college's public announcements regularly highlight, Barnard students now come from all across America and beyond, with West Coast residents second only to New Yorkers in sheer numbers. This newly acquired demographic cosmopolitanism is rightfully celebrated and makes most of us New Yorkers by conscious choice rather than by geographical circumstance.

Less commented upon has been the growing divergence in the economic circumstances from which current Barnard students come. A 2017 study on economic diversity among college students showed Barnard students to have among the highest median family income ($190,100) of any of the 300 colleges in the survey, substantially higher than any of the other remaining sister colleges and all but Brown ($204,000), Penn State ($195,000) and Yale ($192,000), but including Columbia ($150,900), among the Ivy League schools. Seventeen percent of Barnard students were reported to come from families from the top 1 percent of families (those making $630,000 or more per year), placing it twenty-first among sixty-five elite colleges, again above all of the remaining sister colleges: Wellesley (11 percent, forty-third), Bryn Mawr (7.9 percent, fifty-first), Mount Holyoke (5.2 percent, fifty-third), and Smith (4.4 percent, fifty-seventh). Barnard's endowment remains the smallest of its peers, barely a sixth of Wellesley's or Smith's, but its students are no longer the poorest. For an increasing number of Barnard students in the post-2008 economy coming from wealthy families with college-educated and professionally employed parents, the challenge is to maintain the privileged place from which they come, not to aspire to outdo them, as with most earlier Barnard students.[42]

The same 2017 study also reported Barnard's student body as having among the highest share of students from the bottom 20 percent (6.6 percent) of the median family income distribution, again higher than that of any of the remaining sister colleges and higher than Columbia (5.1 percent). Yet the percentage of incoming Barnard students eligible for Pell grants in 2019 (11 percent) is less than half the percentage back in the late 1980s (24 percent). The cumulative inference is of a bipolar Barnard student body with increasing numbers of members from wealthy families, a relatively substantial but decreasing number from economically strapped families, and a shrinking number in between. Contemporary Barnard provides a striking on-campus instance of the widely reported phenomenon of the "hollowing out of the middle class," which represents a dramatic departure from its historical character as the least "plutocratic" of the sister colleges and a magnet for New York City's "aspiring crowds."[43]

PEERING AHEAD

The principal challenge of the last quarter of the twentieth century for Barnard was to maintain the college's autonomy and its affiliation with Columbia University; both were successfully achieved primarily through the efforts of a committed board of trustees and savvy presidents, with help from adventurous students, loyal alumnae, and engaged faculty members. What, then, of the challenges today and the next quarter-century? Herewith are a half-dozen I foresee:

1. Meeting the educational needs of a share of the world's brightest young women, including some of limited financial means, from minority backgrounds, with uneven academic preparation and for whom college is a first for their family.
2. Recruiting and retaining a diverse faculty committed to providing Barnard students with inspiring and innovative classroom instruction even as they advance their own demanding scholarly agendas and academic careers.
3. Raising revenues beyond those derived from tuition and fees to meet the salary needs of its faculty and staff, the expenses of an evolving curriculum increasingly reliant upon digital technology, and the maintenance and updating of an environmentally responsible physical plant in a densely populated neighborhood.
4. Attracting a diverse body of trustees whose commitment, professional expertise, and financial support provide Barnard with the fiduciary oversight and leadership worthy of a world-class academic institution.
5. Securing an administrative team responsive to the rapidly changing character of American higher education in a global setting, as well as one appreciative of the college's legacy as a consummate New York institution with a tradition of serving the educational needs of young women for whom a Barnard degree opens doors that were otherwise closed to them.
6. Maintaining relations with Columbia that serve both Barnard's needs and recognize its contributions to the well-being of the university.

Each represents a formidable challenge, challenges not always met in the past. But none is insurmountable and I believe all can be achieved going forward with the wise use and careful expansion of resources already on hand, including the following:

Today's Barnard students are already the most racially diverse and academically selective in the college's history and are only likely to become more so.

Today's Barnard faculty members are as committed to their instructional roles as any that preceded them, and they are substantially more engaged in research and publishing than at any time in the past.

Today's financial situation is stronger than at any time since the college's founding, with the last four capital campaigns all exceeding their targets and with an in-place development team singularly alert to securing support for Barnard's academic programs and physical plant from foundations, alumnae and individual donors.

Today's board of trustees is a racially and ethnically diverse mix of Barnard alumnae; parents of current Barnard students and longer-term members of the Barnard community; with others knowledgeable in the ways of academic institutions, finance, and the law and stands committed to advancing the fiscal and ethical well-being of the college.

Today's alumnae consist of some 35,000 graduates and, while they are still concentrated in the New York metropolitan region, they are more geographically dispersed than classes predating the 1970s, are more likely to have experienced Barnard as residential students, and are more willing to support the college.

Today's administrative team is being renewed at the outset of a new presidency that is as promising as any in my five decades of Barnard watching.

Today's relations with Columbia, perhaps best described by Columbia's President Lee Bollinger, as he did at the inauguration of Sian Leah Beilock as Barnard's eighth president on February 9, 2018:

> First, on the relationship between Barnard and Columbia: I want to affirm the principle that Barnard is an integral part of Columbia University. It is indeed essential to defining Columbia's character. Columbia would not be Columbia without the presence of Barnard, its faculty and students, with its determined independence, deep sense of self, and world-altering ambitions. And, I hope it is also true that Barnard could only be Barnard by fusing its identity as one of the world's finest liberal arts colleges with a pride in being part of one of the world's great research universities.

Succeeding on all these fronts will require help from all these parties, but it is a cumulative challenge that the new president, the president as flywheel, as broker, joining together disparate parts of the community in a common enterprise, is uniquely positioned to guide. She need not have been "one of us" at her installation; indeed, an outsider may be better able to sense the need for the integration of Barnard's many disparate parts. But she must, in confronting the demands of the college's separate and, at times competing constituencies, be cognizant of the collective value of shared experiences.

One such common experience, whether for a semester or for half a century, is our connection with the arc of Barnard's history, which, I have tried to argue here, is an imperfect but improving one. Another is that we are all New Yorkers, by birthright, choice, or current happenstance. By connecting with Barnard's past, warts and all, critically as well as in celebration, and with our city, with its own distinctive integrative challenges, may we in the future connect more fruitfully with each other. And by so doing, may we ensure Barnard another century of beneficent educational endeavor for women in the city of New York.

NOTES

1. "WHAT'S A NEW YORK GIRL TO DO?"

1. Annie Nathan Meyer, *It's Been Fun: An Autobiography* (New York: Henry Schuman, 1951), 5.

2. The standard accounts are Mabel Newcomer, *A Century of Higher Education for American Women* (New York: Harper, 1959); Thomas Woody, *A History of Women's Education in the United States*, 2 vols. (New York: Science Press, 1929), 2: 137–223.For lively recent histories of women's higher education in the United States, see Barbara Miller Solomon, *In the Company of Educated Women: A History of Women and Higher Education in America* (New Haven, CT: Yale University Press, 1985); Roger L. Geiger, "The Superior Instruction of Women, 1836–1890," in *The American College in the Nineteenth Century*, ed. Roger L Geiger (Nashville, TN: Vanderbilt University Press, 2000), 183–195.

3. Dorothy A. Plum and George B. Dowell, *The Magnificent Enterprise: A Chronicle of Vassar College* (Poughkeepsie, NY: Vassar College, 1961).

4. Carl Becker, *Cornell University: Founders and the Founding* (Ithaca, NY: Cornell University Press, 1943).

5. Elizabeth Deering and Helen French Greene, *Sophia Smith and the Beginnings of Smith College* (Northampton, MA: Smith College, 1925); Jean Glascock, ed., *Wellesley College, 1875–1975: A Century of Women* (Wellesley College, 1975); Patricia Palmeri, *In Adamless Eden: The Community of Women Faculty at Wellesley* (New Haven, CT: Yale University Press, 1975).

6. On Bryn Mawr, see Cornelia Meigs, *What Makes a College? A History of Bryn Mawr* (New York: Macmillan, 1956); Helen Lefkowitz Horowitz, *The Power and Passion of M. Carey Thomas* (New York: Knopf, 1984).

7. Woody, *History of Women's Education*, 2: 160–223.

8. Lawrence A. Cremin, *American Education: The Metropolitan Experience, 1876–1980* (New York: Harper & Row, 1988), 580–585.

9. Samuel White Patterson, *Hunter College: Eighty-Five Years of Service* (New York: Lantern Press, 1955).

10. Rosalind Rosenberg, *Changing the Subject: How the Women of Columbia Shaped the Way We Think About Sex and Politics* (New York: Columbia University Press, 2004), 13–16; Allan Nevins and Milton Halsey Thomas, eds., *The Diary of George Templeton Strong*, vol. 4 (New York: Macmillan, 1952), 497.

11. Robert A. McCaughey, *Stand, Columbia: A History of Columbia University in the City of New York, 1754–2004* (New York: Columbia University Press, 2003), 148–150.

12. McCaughey, *Stand, Columbia*, 146–152.

13. William J. Chute, *Damn Yankee! The First Career of Frederick A.P. Barnard* (Port Washington, NY: National University Publishers, 1978), 4–11; John Fulton, *Memoirs of Frederick A. P. Barnard, 10th President of Columbia College in the City of New York* (New York: Macmillan, 1896); Robert A. McCaughey, "Barnard, Frederick Augustus Porter," *American National Biography* (1999), https://doi.org/10.1093/anb/9780198606697.article.0900058.

14. McCaughey, *Stand, Columbia*, 150.

15. Robert McCaughey, *A Lever Long Enough: A History of Columbia's School of Engineering and Applied Science Since 1864* (New York: Columbia University Press, 2014), 28–31; John W. Burgess, *Reminiscences of an American Scholar: The Beginnings of Columbia University* (New York: Columbia University Press, 1934).

16. Morgan Dix, "Diary," January 30, 1883, Columbia University Archives; Rosenberg, *Changing the Subject*, 21–43.

17. McCaughey, *Stand, Columbia*, 155–160, 166.

18. Laurel T. Ulrich, ed., *Yards and Gates: Gender in Harvard and Radcliffe History* (Cambridge, MA: Harvard University Press, 2004).

19. For Barnard's presidential reports, William F. Russell, ed., *The Rise of a University: The Later Days of Columbia College*, Part Two ["Education of Women"] (New York: Columbia University Press, 1937), 249–284.

20. Russell, *Rise of a University*, 249–259.

21. Russell, *Rise of a University*, 257.

22. Russell, *Rise of a University*, 259–271.

23. Burgess, *Reminiscences of an American Scholar*, 241–242.

24. Russell, Rise of a University, 281 Barnard, *President Report* (1881), 281.

25. Rosenberg, *Changing the Subject*, 38–41.

26. Rosenberg, *Changing the Subject*, 32–34; Columbia College Board of Trustees, Minutes, June 8, 1883, Columbia University Archives.

27. Rosenberg, *Changing the Subject*, 35

28. On Columbia's short-lived "Collegiate Course for Women," Rosenberg, *Changing the Subject*, 41–45; McCaughey, *Stand, Columbia*, 167.

29. On Annie Nathan Meyer, see Meyer, *It's Been Fun: An Autobiography* (New York: Henry Schuman, 1951); Lynn D. Gordon, "Annie Nathan Meyer and Barnard College: Mission and Identity in Women's Higher Education, 1889–1950," *History of Education Quarterly* 26, no. 4 (Winter 1986): 503–522; Linda Kerber, "Annie Nathan Meyer," *Notable American Women:The Modern Period* (Cambridge, MA: Harvard University Press, 1980), 510,

473–474; Myrna Goldenberg, "Annie Nathan Meyer: Barnard Godmother and Gotham Gadfly," PhD diss., University of Maryland, 1987.

30. Meyer, *It's Been Fun*, 10–13.

31. Stephen Birmingham, *The Grandees: America's Sephardic Elite* (New York: Harper & Row, 1971).

32. Stephen Birmingham, *"Our Crowd": The Great Jewish Families of New York* (New York: Harper & Row, 1967); Annie Nathan Meyer to Laura Drake Gill, [1902?], Laura Drake Gill Correspondence, Barnard College Archives.

33. Goldenberg, "Annie Nathan Meyer," 153.

34. Meyer, *It's Been Fun*, 121.

35. "Chief Founder and Trustee of Barnard College," *New York Times*, September 24, 1951, 27.

36. Goldenberg, "Annie Nathan Meyer," 202.

37. Morgan Dix, "Diary," January 30, 1883, Columbia University Archives.

38. Annie Nathan Meyer, *Barnard Beginnings* (Boston: Houghton Mifflin, 1935), 30.

39. Meyer, *It's Been Fun*, 5.

40. Annie Nathan Meyer to Nicholas Murray Butler, January 10, 1910, Biographical Files, Columbia University Archives.

41. Annie Nathan Meyer, "The Higher Education for Women in New York," *The Nation*, January 21, 1888; reprinted in *Barnard Beginnings*, Appendix C, 167–174.

42. Meyer, "The Higher Education for Women in New York," 169.

43. Meyer, "The Higher Education for Women in New York," 168–169.

44. Meyer, "The Higher Education for Women in New York," 173.

45. Meyer, *Barnard Beginnings*, 50.

46. Meyer, *Barnard Beginnings*, 49, 62–68; Meyer, *It's Been Fun*, 5; Morgan Dix, "Diary," February 2, 1888, Columbia University Archives.

47. Meyer, *Barnard Beginnings*, 68.

48. Columbia College Board of Trustees, Minutes, March 5, 1888.

49. Meyer, *Barnard Beginnings*, 120–121.

50. On "Old New York," see Edith Wharton, *Old New York* (New York: Appleton, 1924); Clifton Hood, *In Pursuit of Privilege: A History of New York City's Upper Class and the Making of a Metropolis* (New York: Columbia University Press, 2017); David C. Hammack, *Power and Society: Greater New York at the Turn of the Century* (New York: Columbia University Press, 1987); Susie J. Pak, *Gentlemen Bankers: The World of J. P. Morgan* (Cambridge, MA: Harvard University Press, 2013); Sven Beckert, *The Monied Metropolis: New York City and the Consolidation of the American Bourgeoisie, 1850–1896* (Cambridge: Cambridge University Press, 2003), 265–267. Charles Philips Trevelyan, *The Great New People: Letters from North America and the Pacific* (New York: Doubleday, 1971), 12.

51. Meyer, *Barnard Beginnings*, 84–115. For original trustees, see Table T.2., Trustee Statistical Appendix," http://blogs.cuit.columbia.edu/ram31/appendices/appendices-index-page /trustees-appendix/original-barnard-college-board-of-trustees/.

52. Meyer, *Barnard Beginnings*, 109. See also website "Making Barnard History, "Original Trustees," http://blogs.cuit.columbia.edu/ram31/appendices/appendices-index-page/trustees -appendix/original-barnard-college-board-of-trustees/.

53. "Original Trustees," .http://blogs.cuit.columbia.edu/ram31/appendices/appendices-index
-page/trustees-appendix/original-barnard-college-board-of-trustees/.
54. Ibid.
55. Meyer, *Barnard Beginnings*, 150–151. The Meyers pledged $100 annually for five years; they were eventually listed among the founders sometime after 1898 for having made subsequent gifts totaling $5,000.
56. On Barnard's early instructional staff, see chapter 2. In addition to those included in the Faculty Listings, the part-time instructors in 1889 included Edward B. Wasson in English, Guillaume A. Scribner in French, and Bernard O'Connor in German.
57. On founders of late-nineteenth-century colleges and universities, see Laurence R. Veysey, *The Emergence of the American University* (Chicago: University of Chicago Press, 1965).
58. Daniel A. Wren, "American Business Philanthropy and Higher Education in the Nineteenth Century," *The Business History Review* 57, no. 3 (Autumn 1983): 321–346; Edward Chase Kirkland, *Dream and Thought in the Business Community, 1860–1900* (Ithaca, NY: Cornell University Press, 1956), chapter IV ("The Higher Learning").
59. George M. Marsden, *The Soul of the American University: From Protestant Establishment to Established Nonbelief* (New York: Oxford University Press, 1994).
60. Wren, "American Business Philanthropy," 326–334. Meyer later explained the financial arrangements: "It is usually said that Barnard was started on five thousand dollars a year pledged for four years. But the Truth is that the amount was far less than that. Thirty-six pledges of one hundred dollars each for four years were received. . . . Thus Barnard College, at the beginning, could depend only on thirty-seven hundred and fifty dollars pledged annually for four years, another fifty dollars pledged for two years, and it possessed in outright gifts five thousand and fifty dollars." Meyer, *Barnard Beginnings*, 140; Marian Churchill White, *A History of Barnard College* (New York: Columbia University Press, 1954), 139.

2. EAST SIDE, WEST SIDE: A TALE OF TWO CITIES

1. Arthur Brooks, "The Constituency of Barnard College," *Barnard Annual*, vol. 1 (May 1894), 10.
2. Virginia S. Brownell, "Ella Weed—In Memoriam," *Barnard Annual*, vol. 1 (May, 1894); "Ella Weed," *Vassar College Encyclopedia*, vcencyclopedia.vassar.edu/alumni/ella.weed.html.
3. George A. Plimpton to Ella Weed, March 11, 1893, Plimpton Papers, Barnard College Archives.
4. Annie Nathan Meyer, *Barnard Beginnings*, (Boston: Houghton Mifflin, 1935), 84–90.
5. Marilyn Ogilvie, "Emily L. Gregory," *Biographical Dictionary of Women in Science*, vol. 1 (London: Rutledge, 2001): 528.
6. http://blogs.cuit.columbia.edu/ram31/appendices/appendices-index-page/faculty
-appendix/barnard-faculty-by-appointment-year-1889-2019/

7. Annette K. Baxter, "Emily James Smith Putnam," *Notable American Women, 1607–1950*, vol. 3, 106–108.

8. Robert A. McCaughey, *Stand, Columbia: A History of Columbia University in the City of New York, 1754–2004* (New York: Columbia University Press, 2003), 189.

9. McCaughey, *Stand, Columbia*, 189.

10. "Agreement between the Trustees of Columbia College in the City of New York and Barnard College, New York City," January 19, 1900. Reprinted in Meyer, *Barnard Beginnings*, 185–189.

11. Emily James Smith Putnam to George A. Plimpton, February 26, 1901, Plimpton Papers, Barnard Archives; [James Harvey Robinson] Acting Dean's Report, 1900–1901.

12. George A. Plimpton, "Early Barnard Finances," *Bulletin of the Associate Alumnae of Barnard College*, vol. 4, no. 2 (June 1915): 10–14.

13. Meyer, *Barnard Beginnings*, 141–142.

14. Cyrus Adler, *Jacob H. Schiff*, 2 vols. (Garden City, NY: Doubleday, 1929); Naomi Cohen, *Jacob H. Schiff: A Study in American Jewish Leadership* (Waltham, MA: Brandeis University Press, 1999); Meyer, *Barnard Beginnings*, 176–177.

15. Frederick S. Wait to Seth Low, March 22, 1893, Special Collections, Columbia University Archives, Box 664; Barnard Board of Trustees, Minutes, May 12, 1893; Barnard College Financial Appendix, http://making-barnard-history.com/finances/.

16. George A. Plimpton to Ella Weed, March 11, 1893; Plimpton, "The Financial History of Barnard College," *Bulletin of the Associate Alumnae of Barnard College*, vol. 4, no. 2 (June 1915): 10–14.

17. George A. Plimpton to Ella Weed, March 11, 1893, 13.

18. George Plimpton to Ella Weed, "Proofs of the statement of finances for four complete years," November 1, 1893, Barnard College Archives; Barnard Board of Trustees, Minutes, May 11, 1894; Mrs. F. P. Olcott to George A. Plimpton, May 12, 1896, Plimpton Papers, Barnard College Archives.

19. George A. Plimpton to Mrs. Joseph H. Choate, April 26, 1894, Plimpton Papers, Barnard College Archives.

20. $140,000 gift from Mrs. Josiah M. Fiske announced at Barnard College Board of Trustees meeting of May 7, 1897. John William Robson, ed., *A Guide to Columbia University* (New York: Columbia University Press, 1937), 125–136.

21. Rockefeller challenge gift of $10,000, made in letter of June 25, 1898, to George A. Plimpton, announced at board's meeting of October 12, 1898.

22. "Memorial of Rev Arthur Brooks," *New York Times*, January 20, 1896.

23. http://blogs.cuit.columbia.edu/ram31/appendices/appendices-index-page/trustees -appendix/barnard-trustees-by-appointment-year-1889-2019/.

24. http://blogs.cuit.columbia.edu/ram31/appendices/appendices-index-page/trustees -appendix/barnard-trustees-by-era-and-occupational-field/.

25. http://blogs.cuit.columbia.edu/ram31/appendices/appendices-index-page/trustees -appendix/1646-2/.

26. Meyer, *Barnard Beginnings*, 110.

27. http://blogs.cuit.columbia.edu/ram31/appendices/appendices-index-page/trustees -appendix/barnard-trustees-by-appointment-year-1889-2019.

28. "500 Honor Memory of Mrs. H. F. Osborn," *New York Times*, November 11, 1930, 26.
29. David C. Hammack, *Power and Society: Greater New York at the Turn of the Century* (New York: Columbia University Press, 1982), 65–78; Sven Beckert, *The Monied Metropolis: New York City and the Consolidation of the American Bourgeoisie, 1850–1896* (Cambridge: Cambridge University Press, 2001), 237–272.
30. http://blogs.cuit.columbia.edu/ram31/appendices/appendices-index-page/trustees-appendix/1646-2/ history.com/people/trustees/.
31. Manhattan's East Side defined here as encompassing the blocks south of Central Park over to Sixth Avenue and east of the park to Third Avenue, with the southern limit at about Twenty-Ninth Street and the northern limits at the time around Eighty-Ninth Street..
32. Barnard Board of Trustees, Minutes, December 1, 1898, Barnard College Archives.
33. Clifton Hood, *In Pursuit of Privilege: A History of New York City's Upper Class and the Making of a Metropolis* (New York: Columbia University Press, 2017), 207–250.
34. Hood, *In Pursuit of Privilege*, 207–250.
35. Sven Beckert, *The Monied Metropolis: New York City and the Consolidation of the American Bourgeoisie, 1850–1896* (Cambridge: Cambridge University Press, 2001), 265–267.
36. Annie Nathan Meyer letter to *The Nation*, January 21, 1888, reprinted in *Barnard Beginnings*, Appendix C., 167–174.
37. On Meyer not being an advocate of Barnard as a melting pot, Myrna Goldenberg, "Annie Nathan Meyer," Michael Berenbaum and Fred Skolnik, eds., *Encyclopedia Judaica*, vol. 14 (Detroit: Macmillan, 2007): 146.
38. Rev. Arthur Brooks, "The Constituency of Barnard College," *Barnard Annual*, vol. 1 (May 1894): 10–12.
39. Helen Dawes Brown, "Report of the Students' Committee," in Barnard Board of Trustees, Minutes, November 11, 1891. On the establishment of the college's first scholarships, *The Barnard Dean's Annual Report, 1898–1899*.
40. http://making-barnard-history.com/people/trustees/.
41. In 1900, five Brearley graduates and two Spence graduates were candidates for admission to Barnard. Meanwhile, six New York City public high schools sent twenty-two candidates. Early Academic Records, Box 12, Barnard College Archives. Elizabeth Man Sarcka, class of 1917, Centennial Oral History Interview by Arline Winer, Barnard College Archives.
42. http://making-barnard-history.com/people/students/.
43. Virginia C. Gildersleeve, "I Move Out of the Back Row," *Many a Good Crusade* (New York: Macmillan, 1954), 34–48.
44. Gildersleeve, "A Victorian Childhood," *Many a Good Crusade*, 17–33.
45. Gildersleeve, *Many a Good Crusade*, 23.
46. Gildersleeve, *Many a Good Crusade*, 3–16.
47. Gildersleeve, *Many a Good Crusade*, 13–16, photograph facing 20.
48. Gildersleeve, *Many a Good Crusade*, 34–39.
49. Gildersleeve, *Many a Good Crusade*, 40.
50. Virginia Crocheron Gildersleeve's mother listed as honorary member of the class of 1899 in 1896 *Barnard Mortarboard*.

51. On Grace Goodale, who later became a Barnard instructor of classics, Edith Striker, and Alte Stilwell, see Gildersleeve, *Many a Good Crusade*, 41.

52. Gildersleeve, *Many a Good Crusade*, 41.

53. Gildersleeve, *Many a Good Crusade*, 41–42.

54. Gildersleeve, *Many a Good Crusade*, 42. For Virginia Crocheron Gildersleeve's Jewish classmates, http://making-barnard-history.com/people/students/social-profile-of-class-of-1899/.

55. On Alpha Omicron Pi's founding at Barnard, https://en.wikipedia.org/wiki/Alpha_Omi-cron_Pi. A Jewish member of the class of 1909 later recalled the operative situation: "We knew that Kappa Kappa was 'the sorority.' And we knew we weren't going to be asked there." Hannah Falk Hofheimer, class of 1909, Barnard Centennial Oral History Interview by Arline Winer, 1986, Barnard College Archives.

56. Virginia Crocheron Gildersleeve, "The Changing College Population," April 25, 1899; reprinted in Nancy Woloch, ed., *Early American Women: A Documentary History, 1600–1900* (Belmont, CA: Wadsworth, 1992), 466–468.

57. In 1900, of the ninety-four candidates applying to Barnard, the three schools that catered to New York City's German Jewish community sent at least seventeen candidates. Early Academic Records, Box 12, Barnard College Archives.

58. Myrna Goldenberg, "Annie Nathan Meyer," Michael Berenbaum and Fred Skolnik, eds., *Encyclopedia Judaica*, vol.14 (Detroit: Macmillan, 2007), 146.

59. N. W. Liggett to Laura Drake Gill, July 20, 1901, Laura Gill Correspondence, Box 2, Barnard College Archives.

60. Florence Samet Rothschild, class of 1908, Barnard Centennial Oral Histories, 1988, Barnard College Archives.

61. *King's Handbook of New York City*, vol. 1. (Boston, 1893; reissued 1972), 274.

62. Moses Rischin, *The Promised City: New York's Jews: 1870–1914* (Cambridge, MA: Harvard University Press, 1977); Morris Horowitz and Lawrence J. Kaplan, *The Jewish Population of the New York Area* (New York: Federation of Jewish Philanthropies of New York, 1979).

63. History of the University of the State of New York and the State Education Department, 1784–1996, http://www.nysl.nysed.gov/edocs/education/sedhist.htm#boces; Joseph King Van Denburg, *Causes of Elimination of Students in Public Secondary Schools in New York City* (New York: Teachers College,1911), 38; Diane Ravitch, *The Great School Wars: A History of the New York City Public Schools* (New York: Basic Books, 1988).

64. Van Denburg, *Causes of Elimination of Students*, 127.

65. Van Denburg, *Causes of Elimination of Students*, 54–57.

66. Van Denburg, *Causes of Elimination of Students*, 98.

67. Gildersleeve, *Many a Good Crusade*, 44.

68. Nicholas Lemon, *The Big Test: The Secret History of the American Meritocracy* (New York: Farrar, Straus, 1999), 17–18, 112; Michael Rosenthal, *Nicholas Miraculous: The Amazing Career of the Redoubtable Dr. Nicholas Murray Butler* (New York: Farrar, Straus, 2006), 93–94.

3. BECOMING BARNARD: A PLACE IN THE CITY

1. Charles Knapp, "The Growth of Barnard College," *The Mortarboard*, vol. 14 (1910): 26–32.
2. Joseph Choate, *The Life of Joseph Hodges Choate as Gathered Chiefly from His Letters* (New York: Scribner's, 1927), 1:453.
3. http://making-barnard-history.com/people/students/.
4. Iphigene Ochs Sulzberger, *Iphigene: Memoirs of Iphigene Ochs Sulzberger of the New York Times Family as Told to Her Granddaughter Susan W. Dryfoos* (New York: Dodd, Mead, 1981), 67–68.
5. Marian Churchill White, *A History of Barnard College* (New York: Columbia University Press, 1954), 39–44.
6. George A. Plimpton to E. J. Smith, November 22, 1898, Plimpton papers, Barnard College Archives; Annie Nathan Meyer to George A. Plimpton, December 2, 1904, Plimpton Papers, Barnard College Archives. For photograph of a Fiske dorm room, White, *A History of Barnard College*, 106.
7. Helen Lefkowitz Horowitz, *Alma Mater: Design and Experience in Women's Colleges from Their Nineteenth Century Beginnings to the 1930s* (New York: Alfred A. Knopf, 1984), 134–142, 247–261.
8. Horowitz, *Alma Mater*, 251.
9. Horowitz, *Alma Mater*.
10. Virginia C. Gildersleeve, *Barnard Dean's Report, 1911*, Box No. 2, BC 11.5, Barnard College Archives.
11. On commuting to Barnard from Queens, see Mollie Galchus, class of 2015, http://blogs.cuit.columbia.edu/ram31/barnard-book-of-numbers/iii-studentalumna-numbers/students-student-life/commuting-to-barnard-mollie-galchus/.
12. Andrew S. Dolkart, *Morningside Heights: A History of its Architecture and Development* (New York: Columbia University Press, 1999), 13–36.
13. Florence L. Sanvile, BC1901, at installation of Dean Laura Drake Gill, May 1, 1901, Laura Gill Correspondence, 1901–1904, Barnard College Archives.
14. Silas Brownell to Seth Low, January 16, 1900, Central Files, Box 659, Columbia University Archives.
15. Laura D. Gill, *Annual Report of the Dean of Barnard College*, 1901–1902, 183.
16. Nicholas Murray Butler to Laura Drake Gill, December 8, December 12, December 15,1904; Laura Drake Gill to Nicholas Murray Butler, December 10, December 14, 1904, Box 660, Central Files, Columbia University Archives. For a later round of acrimonious correspondence in 1906, see the LDG-NMB exchanges in Folder 25, Gill Correspondence, Barnard College Archives.
17. Bette Weneck, "Social and Cultural Stratification in Women's Higher Education: Barnard College and Teachers College, 1898–1912," *History of Education Quarterly*, vol. 31, no.1 (Spring 1991): 1–25.
18. Nicholas Murray Butler to Annie Nathan Meyer, March 1, 1905, Central Files, Columbia University Archives; Alice Duer Miller and eight other Barnard alumnae signatories to Nicholas Murray Butler, December 21, 1905, Gill Correspondence, Barnard College Archives.

19. Virginia Gildersleeve, *Many a Good Crusade* (New York: Macmillan, 1954), 64.

20. Margaret W. Rossiter, *Woman Scientists in America: Struggles and Strategies to 1940* (Baltimore, MD: Johns Hopkins University, 1982), 15–16.

21. Annie Nathan Meyer to Laura Drake Gill, 1902, Laura Drake Gill Correspondence, 1901–1904, Barnard College Archives.

22. Robert A. McCaughey, *Stand, Columbia: A History of Columbia University in the City of New York, 1754–2004* (New York: Columbia University Press, 2003), 257.

23. Harold S. Wechsler, "The Selective Function of American College Admissions Policies, 1870–1970," PhD diss., Columbia University, 2 vols., 1974; McCaughey, *Stand, Columbia*, 256–276.

24. George A. Plimpton to Horace W. Carpentier, August 18, 1910, Plimpton Papers, Barnard College Archives.

25. McCaughey, *Stand, Columbia*, 268.

26. McCaughey, *Stand, Columbia*, 260–61.

27. Frederick P. Keppel, *Columbia* (New York: Oxford University Press, 1914), 179–180

28. [Francis S. Bangs], Report of the Committee on Education, Columbia University Trustee Minutes, May 5, 1913, Columbia University Archives; Frederick Keppel to Nicholas Murray Butler, May 13, 1913, Keppel Papers, Columbia University Archives.

29. As late as the 1950s, it was not unheard of at Barnard for some of its more clubbable students to wonder aloud about a socially suspect classmate, "Why didn't she go to Hunter?" Joseph G. Brennan, *The Education of a Prejudiced Man* (New York: Scribners, 1976), 170.

30. Bursar N. W. Liggett to George A. Plimpton, June 20, 1906, Plimpton papers, Barnard College Archives.

31. Bursar N. W. Liggett to George A. Plimpton, June 20, 1906. Of the 164 applicants in 1906 who completed entrance exams, sixty-nine (42 percent) were marked by Liggett being "Hebrews."

32. Bursar N. W. Liggett to George A. Plimpton, June 20, 1906.

33. Bursar N. W. Liggett to George A. Plimpton, June 20, 1906.

34. At least two admitted students Liggett identified as Jewish later became members of Barnard fraternities supposedly limited to Christians.

35. http://making-banrd-histoy.com/people/students/social-profile-of-barnard-class-of-1910/.

36. [Virgil Prettyman], Report of Columbia College Special Committee, December 11, 1908, Columbia University Archives.

37. Roberta Frankfurt, *Collegiate Women: Domesticity and Career in Turn-of-the-Century America* (New York: New York University Press, 1977), 50.

38. Frankfurt, *Collegiate Women*, 76; Mary E. Cookingham, "Bluestockings, Spinsters and Pedagogues: Women College Graduates, 1865–1910," *Population Studies*, vol. 38, no.3 (November 1984): 349–364.

39. George A. Plimpton to Mrs. Russell Sage, June 17, 1909, Plimpton Papers, Barnard College Archives.

40. Laura Drake Gill, *Annual Report of the Dean of Barnard College*, 1901–1902, 143.

41. Elizabeth Man Sarcka, class of 1917, Barnard Centennial Oral History conducted in 1988 by Arline Winer, Barnard College Archives.

42. Hannah Falk Hofheimer, class of 1909, Centennial Oral History Interview in 1986, Barnard College Archives. Maybe not "much of a college experience," but enough to later secure for the college the financial support of Hannah Falk Hofheimer and her family, as well as the service of her son Joseph Hofheimer as a loyal trustee (1981–1994) in trying times.

4. WHO'S AFRAID OF VIRGINIA GILDERSLEEVE?

1. Nicholas Murray Butler, "Induction of the Dean," *Bulletin of the Associate Alumnae of Barnard College*, vol. 4., no. 2 (June 1914): 8.

2. George A. Plimpton to Daniel Coit Gilman, February 19, 1894; Plimpton to George Smith, August 11, 1896; Plimpton to Wallace Buttrick, January 8, 1909, Barnard College Archives.

3. George A. Plimpton, "Early Barnard Finances," *Bulletin of the Associate Alumnae of Barnard College*, vol. 4, no. 2 (June 1915): 10–14.

4. George A. Plimpton to Mrs. Francis A. Hackley, February 15, 1899, Plimpton Papers, Barnard College Archives. Archives.

5. "George Plimpton, Publisher, Is Dead," *New York Times*, July 21, 1936, 21; Annie Nathan Meyer, *Barnard Beginnings* (Boston: Houghton-Mifflin Company, 1937), 132.

6. George A. Plimpton, "Financial History of Barnard College," *Bulletin of the Associate Alumnae of Barnard College*, vol. 4, no. 2 (June 1915), 10–14.

7. http://blogs.cuit.columbia.edu/ram31/appendices/appendices-index-page/students-alumnae-appendix/barnard-collge-annual-enrollments-1889-90-to-2018-19/.

8. Nicholas Murray Butler to Annie Nathan Meyer, May 26, 1905, Central Records, Biographical File, Columbia University Archives.

9. Nicholas Murray Butler to Laura Gill, December 15, 1902; George A. Plimpton to Elizabeth Milbank Anderson, October 27, 1904, Plimpton Papers, Barnard College Archives.

10. Nicholas Murray Butler to William Tenney Brewster, January 14, 1908, Central Records, Biographical File, Columbia University Archives.

11. Consolidating admissions operations followed on the recommendation of the Prettyman Committee's Report of 1908, in which the headmaster of the Columbia-owned Horace Mann School reported that less than half of the school's graduates going on to college chose to attend Columbia College or Barnard. See Harold S. Wechsler, "The Selective Function of American College Admissions Policies, 1870–1970," PhD diss., Columbia University, 2 vols., 1974, 2:232–236.

12. William T. Brewster, *Barnard College Acting Dean's Report, 1907–08*, 116.

13. George A. Plimpton to Elizabeth Milbank Anderson, June 16, 1910, Plimpton Papers, Barnard College Archives.

14. Nicholas Murray Butler to George A. Plimpton, August 11, 1910, Plimpton Papers, Barnard College Archives.

15. Nicholas Murray Butler to George A. Plimpton, November 18, 1910, Plimpton Papers, Barnard College Archives.

16. Butler to George A. Plimpton, November 18, 1910, Plimpton Papers.

17. Silas Brown Brownell to Nicholas Murray Butler, December 31, 1907, Brownell Folder, Biographical File, Columbia university Archives. A later affirmation of his desire for consolidation, December 22, 1909, Silas Brown Brownell Folder # 659, Biographical Folders, Central Files, Columbia University Archives.

18. Nicholas Murray Butler, "Induction of the Dean," *The Installation of Virginia Crocheron Gildersleeve . . . as Dean of Barnard College, Columbia University in the City of New York.* February 16, 1911.

19. Virginia C. Gildersleeve, *Many a Good Crusade* (New York: Macmillan, 1954), 51–53. Generally on Gildersleeve's professional life, Stephen Turner, "When Empathy Fails: Some Problematic 'Progressives' and Expertise: Crystal Eastman and Virginia Gildersleeve" http://usf.academia.edu/Stephen Turner; Robert A. McCaughey, "Gildersleeve, Virginia Crocheron," *Dictionary of American Biography*, Supplement Seven (New York: Scribner's, 1981), 288–289; Rosalind Rosenberg, "Virginia Gildersleeve: Opening the Gates," in William Theodore de Bary, ed., *Living Legacies at Columbia* (New York: Columbia University, 2006), 465–480; Patrick Dilley, *The Transformation of Women's Collegiate Education: The Legacy of Virginia Gildersleeve* (Cham, Switzerland: Palgrave Macmillan, 2017); an unfinished biography by Dorothea Seltzer, photocopy in Barnard College Archives; Nancy Woloch, conversations with the author about her forthcoming biography of Virginia Gildersleeve.

20. Gildersleeve, *Many a Good Crusade*, 53–56.

21. Gildersleeve, *Many a Good Crusade*, 59.

22. Gildersleeve, *Many a Good Crusade*, 63–66.

23. Nicholas Murray Butler, "Induction of the Dean," *The Installation of Virginia Crocheron Gildersleeve ... as Dean of Barnard College, Columbia University in the City of New York.* February 16, 1911, 26.

24. Albert G. Milbank to George A. Plimpton, December 19, 1910, Plimpton Papers, Barnard College Archives.

25. Nicholas Murray Butler, "Induction of the Dean," *Bulletin of the Associate Alumnae of Barnard College*, vol. 4., no. 2 (June 1914): 8.

26. Virginia C. Gildersleeve to George A. Plimpton, November 26, 1912, Plimpton Papers, Barnard College Archives.

27. Gildersleeve to George A. Plimpton, November 26, 1912, Plimpton Papers.

28. George A. Plimpton to Virginia C. Gildersleeve, November 27, 1912, Plimpton Papers, Barnard College Archives.

29. Hannah Falk Hofheimer, class of 1909, Centennial Oral History Interview, 1986, Barnard College Archives.

30. George A. Plimpton to Mrs. Adolph S. Ochs, January 15, 1912, Plimpton Papers, Barnard College Archives.

31. Marian Churchill White, *A History of Barnard College* (New York: Columbia University Press, 1954), 89–91.

32. Freda Kirchwey, "Observations and Discussion: Fraternities *versus* Democracy," *Barnard Bear*, vol. 8 (1912–1913): 3–6; "Fraternities Are Reactionary, Useless and Democracy's Enemy, Says Miss Kirchwey at Barnard," *New York Times*, October 20, 1912, 10.

33. Virginia Gildersleeve, "The Fraternity Question," *Bulletin of the Associate Alumnae of Barnard College*," vol. 1, no. 2 (December 1913): 3–4.

34. "Barnard Secret Societies to Stop," *New York Times*, May 29, 1913, 11.

35. "Frats at Barnard Missed by the Dean," *New York Times*, October 31, 1915, 1.

36. Gildersleeve, *Many a Good Crusade*, 42.

37. [Virginia Gildersleeve] *Barnard Dean's Report, 1911*, http://making-barnard-history /people/students/.

38. "Lucille Pulitzer Residence Scholarships," *Bulletin of Associate Alumnae of Barnard College*, vol. 1, no.1. (May, 1912): 1–2.

39. *Barnard Bulletin of Associate Alumnae*, vol. 8, no. 1 (December 1918): 1–2.

40. "Cooperative Dorm," *Bulletin of the Associate Alumnae Barnard College*, vol. 6, no.1 (December 1916): 3. In 1917, there were two alumnae-sponsored rented apartments at 99 Claremont Avenue accommodating forty-two students. *Barnard College Dean Report*, 1917. See Maya Garfinkel, class of 2019, "The Ideal Home for the Embryonic New Woman: Barnard College and the Housing Imperative," Barnard College Senior Thesis in History, Spring 2019.

41. Report of the Dean of Barnard College for the Year Ending June 30, 1920, 11.

42. Margaret Mead, *Blackberry Winter: My Earlier Years* (New York: Washington Square Press, 1972), 109–125; "Dormitory Life," *Bulletin of Associate Alumnae Barnard College*, vol.16, no. 2 (May 1927): 3–4.

43. Silas Brown Brownell to Virginia C. Gildersleeve, January 14, 1914, Plimpton Papers, Barnard College Archives.

44. Virginia C. Gildersleeve, *Barnard College Dean's Report, 1913–14*, 6. During the first year when Regents scholarships were awarded, seventy-two holders of these scholarships went to Barnard students.

45. Frances Siegel Rosenman, class of 1917, transcript of her oral history memoir. Copy provided author by Toni Coffee, class of 1945.

46. Barnard College Board of Trustees, Minutes, January 14, 1914.

47. Silas B. Brownell to Virginia C. Gildersleeve, January 29, 1914, copy in Plimpton Papers, Barnard College Archives.

48. Board action confirming tuition hike to $200 taken at its meeting on February 10, 1914.

49. Quarter Century Fund," *Bulletin of Associate Alumnae of Barnard College*, vol. 1., no. 2. (April 1913): 1–2.

50. Gildersleeve, *Many a Good Crusade*, 86–88.

51. George A. Plimpton to Horace W. Carpentier, August 18, 1910, Plimpton Papers, Box #2, Barnard College Archives.

52. Jacob H. Schiff, to George A. Plimpton, May 24, 1910; Plimpton to Schiff, March 5, 1912, Plimpton Papers, Rare Book and Manuscript Library, Columbia University; Plimpton to Gildersleeve, July 8, 1915, Plimpton Papers, Barnard College Archives.

53. George A. Plimpton to Virginia Gildersleeve, July 30, 1915, Plimpton Papers, Barnard College Archives.

54. Silas Brown Brownell to George A. Plimpton, September 15, 1915, Plimpton Papers, Barnard College Archives.

55. "Carpentier Leaves Columbia a Million," *New York Times*, February 21, 1918.

56. Gildersleeve, *Many a Good Crusade*, 87–88.

57. Horace W. Carpentier to George A. Plimpton, October 27, 1915; Plimpton to Carpentier, October 29, 1915, Plimpton Papers, Barnard College Archives.

58. "Carpentier Leaves Columbia a Million," *New York Times*, February 21, 1918.

59. *Annual Report of the Dean* (1914), 3.

60. William Summerscales, *Affirmation and Dissent: Columbia's Response to the Crisis of World War One* (New York: Teachers College Press, 1970); Alan Ryan, *John Dewey and the High Tide of American Liberalism* (New York: Norton, 1995), 156–157.

61. On Butler's change of position on the war in Europe, Robert A. McCaughey, *Stand, Columbia: A History of Columbia University in the City of New York, 1754–2004* (New York: Columbia University Press, 2003), 246–247; Michael Rosenthal, *"Nicholas Miraculous": The Amazing Career of the Redoubtable Dr. Nicolas Murray Butler* (New York: Farrar, Straus & Giroux, 2006), Chapter 10.

62. Virginia Gildersleeve, *Many a Good Crusade*, 114–118; Carol S. Gruber, *Mars and Minerva: World War I and the Uses of the Higher Learning in America* (Baton Rouge, LA: Louisiana State University Press, 1975).

63. David Saville Muzzey, "Professor James Harvey Robinson at Barnard," *Barnard College Alumnae Monthly*, vol. 25, no. 7 (April 1936): 7. Muzzey resignation letter to Butler in Barnard Committee on Instruction Minutes, November 26, 1917.

64. Beard was never a member of the Barnard faculty but taught a class in American history required for admission to the School of Journalism at Barnard from 1912 to 1917.

65. McCaughey, *Stand, Columbia*, 250–254.

66. McCaughey, *Stand, Columbia*, 250–254; On Montague, Gruber, *Mars and Minerva*, 205; Huttman resolution in Barnard College Committee on Instruction, Minutes, December 10, 1917.

67. George A. Plimpton to James Harvey Robinson, May 20, 1918, Plimpton Papers, Barnard College Archives.

68. Barnard's wartime efforts detailed in "Barnard College and War Relief," and "Alumnae Notes—War," *The Barnard Bulletin of the Associate Alumnae*, respectively, vol. 6 (June 1917): 1–2; vol. 7 (December 1917): 16–17.

69. "War Service Number," *The Bulletin of the Associate Alumnae of Barnard College*, vol. 8, no. 1 (December 1918), 6–39. This article includes a section devoted to "Letters from Our Alumnae in France."

70. Rosalind Rosenberg, *Changing the Subject: How the Women of Columbia Shaped the Way We Think about Sex and Politics* (New York: Columbia University Press, 2004), 127–129.

5. GOOD TIMES: BARNARD IN THE TWENTIES

1. Margaret Mead, *Blackberry Winter* (New York: Washington Square Press, 1972), 97.

2. Virginia C. Gildersleeve, *Many a Good Crusade*, (New York: Macmillan, 1954), 113–123.

3. Gildersleeve, *Many a Good Crusade*, 133–142.

4. Gildersleeve, *Many a Good Crusade*, 188–196.

5. Gildersleeve, *Many a Good Crusade*, 117, 120.

6. Michel Rosenthal, *"Nicholas Miraculous": The Amazing Career of the Redoubtable Dr. Nicolas Murray Butler* (New York: Farrar, Straus & Giroux, 2006).

7. Gildersleeve, *Many a Good Crusade*, 171–187.

8. http://making-barnard-history.com/trustees/barnard-trustees-by-appointment-year -1921–1945/.

9. Gildersleeve, *Many a Good Crusade*, 97–99; Barbara Aronstein Black, "In Commemoration—The 75th Anniversary of Women at Columbia Law School," *Columbia Law Review*, vol. 102, no. 6 (October 2002): 1451–1468.

10. http://making-barnard-histoty.com/people/faculty/.

11. James McKeen Cattell, *American Men of Science* (New York: Science Press, 1910); on Reimer and Maltby, Marilyn Ogilvie, *Biographical Dictionary of Women in Science* (New York: Rutledge, 2000), vol. 2, 835, 1088.

12. Margaret W. Rossiter, *Woman Scientists in America: Struggles and Strategies to 1940* (Baltimore, MD: Johns Hopkins University Press, 1982), 144–146; Jessie Bernard, *Academic Women* (University Park: Penn State University Press, 1964)

13. http://blogs.cuit.columbia.edu/ram31/appendices/appendices-index-page/faculty -appendix/.

14. Gildersleeve, *Many a Good Crusade*, 78–79.

15. On Margaret Bieber appointment, William Bell Dinsmoor, "The Department of Fine Arts and Archeology," John Herman Randall Jr., ed., *A History of the Faculty of Philosophy, Columbia University* (New York: Columbia University Press, 1957), 263. Other sister colleges, with the exception of Wellesley, which had a virtually all-female faculty through World War II, similarly privileged its male faculty members.

16. http://blogs.cuit.columbia.edu/ram31/appendices/appendices-index-page/faculty -appendix/.

17. http://blogs.cuit.columbia.edu/ram31/appendices/appendices-index-page/faculty -appendix/.

18. Eric Pace, "Mirra Komarovsky. Authority on Women's Studies, dies at 93," *New York Times*, February 1, 1999.

19. Moore was hired with funds from the 1925 Adrian Joline family bequest, which established Barnard's first endowed professorship.

20. Most of the interwar Barnard male faculty members were married; a majority of the female faculty members were not.

21. Rosalind Rosenberg, *Changing the Subject: How the Women of Columbia Shaped the Way We Think about Sex and Politics* (New York: Columbia University Press, 2004), 255–257.

22. Robert A. McCaughey, *Stand, Columbia: A History of Columbia University in the City of New York, 1754–2004* (New York: Columbia University Press, 2003), 286–288

23. Timothy P. Cross, *An Oasis of Order: The Core Curriculum at Columbia College* (New York: Columbia University Press, 1995), 39–53.

24. Gildersleeve, *Many a Good Crusade*, 83;

25. M. Elizabeth Tidball and Vera Kistiakowsky, "Baccalaureate Origins of American Scientists and Scholars," *Science*, vol. 193, no. 4254 (August 20, 1976): 646–652; "Statistics of Alumnae of Barnard College Table of Postgraduate and Professional Study," no cited author or compiler, *Register of the Associate Alumnae of Barnard College* (1925), 145–149.

26. "Proposed New Curriculum at Barnard College," *School and Society*, vol. 22, no. 558 (September 5, 1925): 299–300; "New Curriculum," *Bulletin of Associate Alumnae of Barnard College*, vol. 15, no. 2 (May 1926): 14

27. William E. Weld and Kathryn W. Sewry, *Herbert E. Hawkes, Dean of Columbia College, 1918–1943* (New York: Columbia University Press, 1958), 48.

28. Gildersleeve, *Many a Good Crusade*, 82.

29. Harold S. Wechsler, "The Selective Function of American College Admissions Policies, 1870–1970," PhD diss., Columbia University, 2 vols., 1974, 248.

30. Weld and Sewry, *Herbert E. Hawkes*, 48; Nicholas Murray Butler to Frederick P. Keppel, January 27, 1914, Keppel Papers, Columbia University Archives.

31. Wechsler, "The Selective Function of American College Admissions Practices," 260–267.

32. Herbert E. Hawkes to Frederick P. Keppel, October 2, 1919, Keppel Papers, Columbia University Archives.

33. Herbert E. Hawkes to Edwin B. Wilson, June 16, 1922, Herbert E. Hawkes Papers, Columbia University Archives.

34. Hawkes to Edwin B. Wilson, June 16, 1922, Herbert E. Hawkes Papers.

35. Heywood Broun and George Britt, *Christians Only: A Study in Prejudice* (New York: Vanguard Press, 1931). Broun and Britt gave the percentage of Jewish students at Barnard as "slightly lower than Columbia College," which they pegged at 22.5 percent.

36. Virginia Gildersleeve to Nicholas Murray Butler, November 12, 1920; 1926 Columbia College/Barnard College comparisons on public schoolers in *School and Society* vol. 22 (December 19, 1925), 791.

37. Wechlser, "The Selective Function of American College Admissions Practices," 229.

38. Eli Ginzberg, *My Brother's Keeper* (New Brunswick, NJ: Transaction Publishers, 1989), 33.

39. [Freda Kirchwey], *The Nation*, vol. 115 (July 26, 1922): 94–95.

40. Rebecca Grecht, "Anti-Semitism at Barnard, *The Nation*, vol. 115 (October 4, 1922): 337

41. Virginia C. Gildersleeve, "Class and Creed at Barnard," *The Nation*, vol. 115 (December 6, 1922): 607.

42. Gildersleeve, *Many a Good Crusade*, 74.

43. Virginia C. Gildersleeve, "The Barnard Admissions Policy," *Barnard College Alumnae Monthly*, vol. 27, no. 8 (May 1939): 4–5.

44. Gildersleeve, *Many a Good Crusade*, 72.

45. George Barry Ford, *A Degree of Difference* (New York: Farrar, Straus, 1969); McCaughey, *Stand, Columbia*, 274–276.

46. On Anne Anastasi, https://www.intelltheory.com/anastasi.html.

47. Esther Biederman, 1931, Barnard Centennial Oral History interview by Arline Winer, December 13, 1988, Barnard College Archives.

48. Eric Pace, "Mirra Komarovsky, Authority on Women's Studies, Dies at 93," *New York Times*, February 1, 1999.

49. Eleanor Rosenberg, class of 1929, Oral History Interview by Julie Marsteller, May 1, 1973, Barnard College Archives.

50. Margaret Mead, *Blackberry Winter: My Earlier Years* (New York: Washington Square Press, 1972), 97.

51. Mead, *Blackberry Winter*, 109–125.

52. Zora Neale Hurston, *Dust Tracks on a Road: An Autobiography* (Philadelphia: Lippincott, 1942), 52. The year Hurston was admitted, Barnard also enrolled fourteen foreign students (seven Asians and seven Europeans), as well as two residents of Puerto Rico. *Bulletin of the Associate Alumnae of Barnard College*, vol. 15, no. 1 (January 1926): 15.

53. Linda M. Perkins, "The African American Female Elite: The Early History of African American Women in the Seven Sister Colleges, 1880–1960," *Harvard Educational Review*, vol. 67, no. 4 (Winter 1997): 740–744, 741.

54. On Gildersleeve's campaign to reduce New Yorkers to 50 percent of the student body, "Barnard Becomes a National College," *New York Times*, October 2, 1921.

55. John William Robson, ed., *A Guide to Columbia University* (New York: Columbia University Press, 1937), 135; Andrew S. Dolkart, *Morningside Heights: A History of Its Architecture and Development* (New York: Columbia University Press, 1998), 222–223.

56. Andrew S. Dolkart, "In on the Ground Floor: The Building of Barnard College," *Barnard* (Summer 1999): 22–25.

57. *Barnard College Dean's Report* (1925); http://making-barnard-history.com/finances/.

58. Elaine Kendall, *"Peculiar Institutions": An Informal History of the Seven Sister Colleges* (New York: G.P. Putnam's Sons, 1975), 29.

59. Gildersleeve, *Many a Good Crusade*, 89–91.

60. "The Question of the Women's Colleges," *Atlantic Monthly* (November, 27, 1927).

61. http://blogs.cuit.columbia.edu/ram31/appendices/appendices-index-page/finances -appendix/.

62. Virginia C. Gildersleeve, *Annual Report of the Dean of Barnard College*, 1929, 10.

63. Emilie J. Hutchinson, "The Barnard School for Women Workers in Industry," *Bulletin of the Associate Alumnae of Barnard College*, vol. 17, no. 1 (January 1928): 7–8; Marian Churchill White, *A History of Barnard College* (New York: Columbia University Press, 1954), 102–103.

64. Gildersleeve, *Many a Good Crusade*, 88.

65. McCaughey, *Stand, Columbia*, 301–303.

66. Scott M. Cutlip, *Fund Raising in the United States* (New Brunswick, NJ: Rutgers University Press, 1969).

6. TOUGH TIMES: DEPRESSION, WAR AND OTHER DISTRACTIONS

1. Elizabeth Hall Janeway, statement made while concluding term as alumnae trustee in 1982. Barnard Board of Trustees Minutes, May 26, 1982.

2. Virginia C. Gildersleeve, *Many a Good Crusade* (New York: Macmillan, 1954), 216.

3. Robert Cohen, *When the Old Left Was Young: Student Radicals and America's First Mass Student Movement, 1929–1941* (New York: Oxford University Press, 1997), 11–12.

4. [George W. Mullins, Acting Dean] *Report of the Barnard College Dean, 1930*; "Notes from Dean Gildersleeve's Office," *Barnard College Alumnae Bulletin*, vol. 20, no. 1 (December 1930): 12.

5. *Bulletin of the Associate Alumnae of Barnard College*, vol. 22, no.1 (October, 1932), 11; http:// blogs.cuit.columbia.edu/ram31/appendices/appendices-index-page/students-alumnae -appendix/.

6. Virginia Gildersleeve, "From the Dean's Office, *The Barnard College Alumnae Bulletin*, vol. 22, no. 1 (October 1932): 11; *Report of the Dean of Barnard College for Period Ending June 30, 1932*, 6.

7. Helen Phelps Bailey, Oral History interview conducted by Darlene Levy, April 1979, OHRO #1269, Rare Book and Manuscript Library, Butler Library, Columbia University.

8. Bailey, Oral History interview conducted by Darlene Levy, April 1979.

9. *Report of the Dean of Barnard College, 1935–1936*, 7–8.

10. Caroline Agger Fortas, class of 1931, Oral History Interview conducted by Arline Winer, March 13, 1989, Barnard College Archives; Nathalie Woodbury, class of 1939, Oral History Interview conducted by Arline Winer, 1989, Barnard College Archives; On Juliet Points/Poyntz, class of 1907, Agnes E. Meyer, *Out of These Roots: The Autobiography of an American Woman* (Boston: Little, Brown and Company, 1953), 54–57; Cohen, *When the Old Left Was Young* (New York: Oxford University Press, 1997), 63, 153, 198, 250, 262.

11. Mary Dublin Keyserling, Oral History Interview conducted by Arline Winer, 1986, Barnard College Archives.

12. "Students Well Diversified," *Barnard College Alumnae Monthly*, vol. 24, no. 4 (January 1935): 8; Miriam Lichtenberg, class of 2019, interview with Shirley Adelson Siegel, November 29; 2018; http://blogs.cuit.columbia.edu/ram31/appendices/appendices-index -page/students-alumnae-appendix/.

13. Frank Bowles to Nicholas Murray Butler, January 31, 1935, Frank Bowles Papers, Columbia University Archives; Robert A. McCaughey, *Stand, Columbia: A History of Columbia University in the City of New York, 1754–2004* (New York: Columbia University Press, 2003), 272–273.

14. "Dr. Gregory, Associate Dean," *Barnard College Alumnae Quarterly*, vol. 22, no. 1 (October 1932), 3.

15. http://blogs.cuit.columbia.edu/ram31/appendices/appendices-index-page/faculty -appendix/barnard-faculty-by-appointment-year-1915-1939/.

16. http://blogs.cuit.columbia.edu/ram31/appendices/appendices-index-page/faculty -appendix/barnard-faculty-by-appointment-year-1915-1939/.

17. The psychologist Anne Anastasi, class of 1928, PhD, Columbia 1930, served nine years as an instructor before leaving to become an assistant professor at Queens College and later chair of the Fordham Psychology Department. She was later a Science Medal of Distinction awardee.

18. http://blogs.cuit.columbia.edu/ram31/appendices/appendices-index-page/faculty -appendix/barnard-faculty-by-appointment-year-1915-1939/.

19. http://blogs.cuit.columbia.edu/ram31/appendices/appendices-index-page/faculty -appendix/barnard-faculty-by-appointment-year-1915-1939/.

20. Eli Ginzberg, *My Brother's Keeper* (New Brunswick, NJ: Transaction Publishers, 1989), 35.

21. Helen Phelps Bailey, class of 1933, Oral History Interview conducted by Darlene Levy (April 1979), Oral History Research Office #1269, Rare Book and Manuscript Library, Butler Library, Columbia University. It was only in 1950 that Columbia waived the requirement that all dissertations had to be published before the degree was conferred, a stipulation that carried with it a considerable price tag.

22. Bailey, Oral History interview conducted by Darlene Levy, April 1979.

23. http://making-barnard-history.com/people/faculty/.

24. Francis T. P. Plimpton Papers, Box #2, Barnard College Archives.

25. *Barnard College Dean Report*, 1936, 11–12, on receipt of a $255,000 gift from the Rockefeller-funded General Educational Board to permit the purchase of the Claremont property for $500,000.

26. Virginia C. Gildersleeve, "What Are They Going To Do?," *Barnard College Alumnae Quarterly*, vol. 24, no. 9 (June 1935): 14.

27. Dorothy Wololf, "As We Turn the Corner: An Interview with Dean Gildersleeve," *Barnard College Alumnae Monthly*, vol. 24, no. 5 (February 1935): 15.

28. Wololf, "As We Turn the Corner," 15–16.

29. Gildersleeve, *Many a Good Crusade*, 86.

30. Marian Churchill White, "Interview with Sara Straus Hess," *Barnard College Alumnae Monthly*, vol. 25 (January 1936): 12–13.

31. "New Name for Students Hall," *Bulletin of the Associate Alumnae of Barnard College*, vol. 15, no. 1, 1; Andrew S. Dolkart, *Morningside Heights: A History of Its Architecture and Development* (New York: Columbia University Press, 1998), 220–222; Myrna Goldenberg, *Annie Nathan Meyer: Barnard Godmother and Gotham Gadfly*, PhD diss., University of Maryland, 1987, 227; Annie Nathan Meyer to George A. Plimpton, February 14, 1934, George A. Plimpton papers, Barnard College Archives.

32. Annie Nathan Meyer, *Barnard Beginnings* (Boston: Houghton-Mifflin Company, 1935).

33. Unsigned, "Review of *Barnard Beginnings*, by Annie Nathan Meyer," *Barnard College Alumnae*, vol. 25, no. 2 (November 1935): 13–14

34. Unsigned, "Review of *Barnard Beginnings*, by Annie Nathan Meyer."

35. Unsigned, "Review of *Barnard Beginnings*, by Annie Nathan Meyer," 14.

36. Alice Duer Miller, class of 1899, and Susan Myers, class of 1998, *Barnard College: The First Fifty Years* (New York: Columbia University Press, 1939); Goldenberg, *Annie Nathan Meyer*, 301.

37. Stephen Norwood, *The Third Reich in the Ivory Tower: Complicity and Conflict on American Campuses* (Cambridge: Cambridge University Press, 2009), 93. For Gildersleeve's interview where she seems to defend German policies keeping Jews from attending universities, "Dean Gildersleeve Back from Europe," *New York Times*, September 11, 1935. On Butler's flirtation with Fascism, Michael Rosenthal, *Nicholas Miraculous: The Amazing Career of the Redoubtable Dr. Nicholas Murray Butler* (New York: Farrar, Straus, 2006), Chapter 16.

38. Virginia Gildersleeve, "Sabbatical Travels," *Bulletin of Associate Alumnae of Barnard College*, vol 20, no. 1 (December 1930): 4.

39. Gildersleeve, *Many a Good Crusade*, 217–219, 221–222, 277.

40. Alice Duer Miller, "White Cliffs of Dover," http://famouspoetsandpoems.com/poets/alice _duer_miller/poems/1942.

41. Gildersleeve, *Many a Good Crusade*, 247–392.

42. Millicent McIntosh, "Reminiscences," Oral History Interview, conducted by Isabel Grossner in 1966, Oral History Research Office, no. 626, vol. 2: 256.

43. Linda M. Perkins, "The African American Female Elite: The Early History of African American Women in the Seven Sister Colleges, 1880–1960," *Harvard Educational Review*, vol. 67, no. 4 (Winter 1997): 718–756. These numbers are estimates and are based on visual identifications. A more complete accounting has been generously provided to the author by Corinth Jackson, Barnard College, class of 2020.

44. Virginia Gildersleeve to the Rev. James H. Robinson, n.d., reprinted in the *Barnard Bulletin*, March 1, 1943.

45. Perkins, "The African American Female Elite," 718–756, 740–744. These numbers are estimates and are based on visual identifications. A somewhat more complete accounting has been generously provided to the author by Corinth Jackson, Barnard College, class of 2020.

46. Virginia C. Gildersleeve, "Havens for Homeless Jews," Letter to the *New York Times*, October 9, 1945; reprinted in *Many a Good Crusade*, 185–186; Stephen H. Norwood, *The Third Reich in the Ivory Tower* (Cambridge: Cambridge University Press, 2009), 130.

47. Harold S. Wechsler, "The Selective Function of the American College Admissions Policies, 1870–1970," PhD diss., Columbia University, 1974, vol. 2: 295–311.

48. McIntosh, "Reminiscences," vol. 2: 326.

49. Gildersleeve, *Many a Good Crusade*, 416–419.

50. McIntosh, "Reminiscences," vol 2: 319

51. Emma Stecher, Oral History Interview, June 2, 1971; John Kouwenhoven, Oral History Interview, April 22, 1975; Eleanor Rosenberg, Oral History Interview, May 1, 1973; Julius held, Oral History Interview, Julius Held, Oral History Interview, May 21, 1970, Barnard College Archives.

52. [Gildersleeve], Report of the Dean of Barnard College for Year Ending June 30, 1932, 11; http://blogs.cuit.columbia.edu/ram31/appendices/appendices-index-page/administrative -appendix/.

7. AGAINST NOSTALGIA: THE McINTOSH ERA

1. Frances Hamermesh, class of 1965, Interview with author, September 27, 2017.

2. Biographical information from Millicent McIntosh, "Reminiscences," Oral History Interview, 1966, conducted by Isabel Grossner, OHRO 626, Rare Book and Manuscript Library, Columbia University, 328.

3. McIntosh, "Reminiscences," 121–127.

4. McIntosh, "Reminiscences," 179.

5. McIntosh, "Reminiscences," 260.

6. McIntosh, "Reminiscences," http://making-barnard-history.com/finances/.

7. McIntosh, "Reminiscences," 320.

8. Andrew Dolkart, *Morningside Heights: A History of Its Architecture and Development* (New York: Columbia University Press, 1998), 325–340.

9. Dorothea Setzer, Biographical Notes, Gildersleeve Papers, Box No. 2, Folder 64, Barnard College Archives

10. Agnes E. Meyer, *Out of These Roots* (Boston: Atlantic-Little Brown, 1953), 49.

11. McIntosh, "Reminiscences," on Jean Palmer Barnard Dean's Report, 1949–1950.

12. McIntosh, "Reminiscences," 408.

13. *Barnard President's Report, 1949–1950*; McIintosh, "Reminiscences," 399–402.

14. McIntosh, "Reminiscences," 409–410.

15. "McIntosh Chair Announced," *Barnard Alumnae Magazine*, vol. 45, no. 1 (November 1955): 14.

16. McIntosh, "Reminiscences," Dean to president.

17. http://making-barnard-history.com/people/students/.

18. http://blogs.cuit.columbia.edu/ram31/appendices/appendices-index-page/students -alumnae-appendix/.

19. Millicent McIntosh, "Inaugural Address," MCM on students as varied and interesting as New York itself."

20. McIntosh memo, February 10, 1949, Millicent McIntosh Papers, Barnard College Archives.

21. Educational Testing Service, "Seven College Conference Study [Confidential]," Table II, 1952. Copy in Barnard Archives, McIntosh Papers. Dorothy Denburg, class of 1970, interview with author, 2015; Paula Franzese, class of 1980, interview with Elizabeth Moye, class of 2015.

22. "Seven College Conference Study," 14. Radcliffe was the only other Sister located in a major city; [Jeremiah Finch], "Evaluation of Barnard College for the Middle States Accreditation, March 6–9, 1960," Barnard College Archives.

23. McIntosh, "Reminiscences," 344; http://blogs.cuit.columbia.edu/ram31/appendices/appendices -index-page/administrative-appendix/.

24. McCann quoted in "The Big Admissions Question," *Barnard Alumnae Magazine*, vol. 46, no. 5 (November 1957): 3–7, 20. The 275-member Barnard class entering in 1955 had seven daughters of alumnae; http://making-barnard-history/peple/students/.

25. For general discussion of admissions in the 1950s, Elizabeth A. Duffy and Idana Goldberg, *Crafting a Class: College Admissions and Financial Aid, 1955–1994* (Princeton, NJ: Princeton University Press, 1998), 3–11.

26. On New York City's public colleges in the post–World War II period, see William G. Bowen and Eugene M. Tobin, *Locus of Authority: The Evolution of Faculty Roles in the Governance of Higher Education* (Princeton, NJ: Princeton University Press, 2015), 315–360; Sheila C. Gordon, "The Transformation of the City University of New York, 1945–1970, PhD diss., Columbia University, 1975.

27. https://www.suny.edu/about/history/.

28. Dorothy Denburg, correspondence with the author, 2017.

29. Joseph Gerald Brennan, *The Education of a Prejudiced Man* (New York: Charles Scribner's Sons, 1977), 169–170.

30. Hazel Schizer, class of 1956, communication with author, March 5, 2017.

31. "Atlanta U. Professor [Dr. William Boyd] Becomes First Negro Lecturer at Barnard College," "Three Black Admits to Barnard," *New York Times*, November 12, 1949, October 2, 1951. Of the three students enrolled, Janet Moorhead graduated in 1954. See Corinth Jackson, class of 2020, list of black students prior to 1968, Barnard College Archives.

32. *Barnard Alumnae Magazine*, vol. 46, no.2 (January 1956).

33. http://blogs.cuit.columbia.edu/ram31/appendices/appendices-index-page/students -alumnae-appendix/barnard-college-graduating-classes-by-hometowns/.

34. Joseph Brennan, "The Younger Generation," *Barnard Alumnae Magazine*, vol.49 (February 1960): 3–4.

35. Audrey Weinberg, ""Is College Compatible with Marriage?," *Barnard Alumnae Magazine* (Spring 1960): 4–6; John Updike, "When Everyone Was Pregnant," *Museums and Women, and Other Stories* (New York: Alfred Knopf, 1972). On earning PhDs in the 1950s, see M. Elizabeth Tidball, *Taking Women Seriously: Lessons and Legacies for Educating the Majority* (Phoenix, AZ: American Council of Education, 1999).

36. Anne Bernays and Justin Kaplan, *Back Then: Two Lives in 1950s New York* (New York: HarperCollins, 2002), 43–48. On alumnae identifying McIntosh as a feminist, Vivian R. Gruder, class of 1959, correspondence with author, July 18, 2018; Louise Bernikow, class of 1959, correspondence with the author.

37. John Erskine, *My Life as a Teacher* (New York: 1948), 38.

38. http://blogs.cuit.columbia.edu/ram31/appendices/appendices-index-page/faculty -appendix/barnard-faculty-by-appointment-year-1915-1939/.

39. http://blogs.cuit.columbia.edu/ram31/appendices/appendices-index-page/faculty -appendix/barnard-faculty-by-appointment-year-1915-1939/.

40. http://blogs.cuit.columbia.edu/ram31/appendices/appendices-index-page/faculty -appendix/barnard-faculty-by-appointment-year-1915-1939/.

41. http://blogs.cuit.columbia.edu/ram31/appendices/appendices-index-page/faculty -appendix/barnard-faculty-by-appointment-year-1915-1939/.

42. McIntosh, "Reminiscences," 360.

43. Morton Keller and Phyllis Keller, *Making Harvard Modern: The Rise of America's University* (New York: Oxford University Press, 2001), 22–31; McIntosh, "Reminiscences," 518.

44. McIntosh, "Reminiscences," 511.

45. McIntosh, "Reminiscences," 516.

46. McIntosh, "Reminiscences," 352.

47. Brennan, *The Education of a Prejudiced Man*, 118–129; Gladys Meyer, interview with Julie Marsteller, November 18, 1974, Julius Held, interview with Julie Marsteller, May 21, 1970, Barnard College Archives.

48. Brennan, *The Education of a Prejudiced Man*, 121; Fred M. Hechinger, "Plain Talk about Teaching," *Barnard Alumnae Magazine*, vol. 48, no. 4 (July 1959), 3–6: The class of 1959 included thirty-nine graduates of the Education Program.

49. Ursula Niebuhr, "Religion on Campus," *Barnard Alumnae Magazine*, vol. 45, No. 5 (July 1956), 2-4,14; McIntosh, "Reminiscences," 326–328.

50. Bernays and Kaplan, *Back Then*, 45.

51. Renee Fox, *In the Field, A Sociologist's Journey* (New Brunswick, NJ: Transaction Publishers, 2011); http://blogs.cuit.columbia.edu/ram31/appendices/appendices-index-page/faculty-appendix/barnard-faculty-1940-1964/.

52. Gladys Meyer, interview with Julie Marsteller, November 18, 1974, Barnard College Archives.

53. http://blogs.cuit.columbia.edu/ram31/appendices/appendices-index-page/faculty-appendix/barnard-faculty-1940-1964/.

54. David Robertson, Jr., correspondence with author, 1974; Middle States Evaluation, 1960; John Kouwenhoven, interview with Julie Marsteller, April 22, 1975, Barnard College Archives

55. McIntosh, "Reminiscences," 478; Ellen W. Schrecker, *No Ivory Tower: McCarthyism & the Universities* (New York: Oxford University Press, 1986), 236–240, 255–257.

56. Iphigene Ochs Sulzberger and Susan W. Dryfoos, *Iphigene: Memoirs of Iphigene Ochs Sulzberger of the New York Times Family, as told to Susan W. Dryfooos* (New York: Dodd, Mead, 1981); Agnes E. Meyer, *Out of These Roots: The Autobiography of an American Woman* (Boston: Little, Brown and Company, 1953).

57. Schrecker, *No Ivory Tower*, 236–240.; Brennan, *The Education of a Prejudiced Man*, 126–128.

58. Dolkart, *Morningside Heights*, 427, note 84; Robert A. M. Stern, Thomas Mellins, and David Fishman, *Architecture and Urbanism Between the Second World War and the Bicentennial* (New York: Monacelli Press, 1995), 740.

59. Dolkart, *Morningside Heights*, 427, note 84.

60. Dolkart, *Morningside Heights*, 427, note 86..

61. McIntosh, "Reminiscences," 596

62. McIntosh, "Reminiscences," 512.

63. McIntosh, "Reminiscences," 492, 496.

64. Karen Arenson, "Millicent McIntosh, 102, Dies: Taught Barnard Women to Balance Career and Family," *New York Times*, January 5, 2001.

65. McIntosh, "Reminiscences," 605.

66. http://blogs.cuit.columbia.edu/ram31/appendices/appendices-index-page/finances-appendix/.

67. Barbara Schmitter, interview with author, July 28, 2014; Christine Royer, interview with author, July 21, 2014.

68. McIntosh, "Reminiscences," 590–600.

69. Gladys Meyer, Interview with Julie Marsteller, November 18, 1974, Barnard College Archives.

70. Karen Arenson, "Rosemary Park, 97, Dies: Force in Educating Women," *New York Times*, April 26, 2004.

8. INTO THE STORM

1. Susan Slyomovics, "A Sense of Rightness," in Paul Cronin, ed., *A Time to Stir: Columbia '68* (New York: Columbia University Press, 2018), 330–332.

2. Martha Peterson Papers, Kansas Collection, RH MS 953, Kenneth Spencer Research Library, University of Kansas

3. Dennis Hevesi, "Martha Peterson, 90, Barnard President in Vietnam Era, Dies," *New York Times*, July 20, 2006.

4. Robert A. McCaughey, *Stand, Columbia: A History of Columbia University in the City of New York, 1754–2004* (New York: Columbia University Press, 2003), 391–422.

5. Travis Beal Jacobs, *Eisenhower at Columbia* (New Brunswick, NJ: Transaction Publishers, 2001), 139–175; Millicent McIntosh, "Reminiscences," Oral History Interview, Columbia Oral History Office, 1966.

6. McCaughey, *Stand, Columbia*, 341–351, 356.

7. McCaughey, *Stand, Columbia*, 411–413; Allan M. Cartter, *An Assessment of Quality in Graduate Education* (Washington, DC: American Council on Education, 1966).

8. McCaughey, *Stand, Columbia*, 376.

9. Paul Cronin, ed., *A Time to Stir: Columbia '68* (New York: Columbia University Press, 2018), 51–72; McCaughey, *Stand, Columbia*, 427–441.

10. Rosalind Rosenberg, *Changing the Subject: How the Women of Columbia Shaped the Way We Think about Sex and Politics* (New York: Columbia University Press, 2004), 235–238.

11. Cronin, *A Time to Stir*, 51–72.

12. McCaughey, *Stand, Columbia*, 427–441.

13. Barbara S. Schmitter, interview with author, June 28, 2014.

14. Cronin, *A Time to Stir*, 1–7, 94–98, 147–154, 277–280, 330–332, 341–348; Mary Gordon, interview with author, December 23, 2017.

15. Karla Spurlock-Evans, "Forming Community, Forging Commitment: A Hamilton Hall Story," in Paul Cronin, ed., *A Time to Stir: Columbia '68* (New York: Columbia University Press, 2018), 341–348.

16. "Peterson Becomes President," *Barnard Bulletin*, May 1, 1968.

17. McCaughey, *Stand, Columbia*, 456–459.

18. "Barnard Students Arrested," *Barnard Bulletin*, May 1, 1968, list of names of 107 Barnard students arraigned at 14th Precinct included in Columbia'68 Collection, Rare Book and Manuscript Library, Columbia University.

19. Barbara S. Schmitter, interview with author, June 28, 2014; Barnard Board of Trustees, Minutes, May 7, 1968, Barnard College Archives.

20. McCaughey, *Stand, Columbia*, 490–496.

21. "616 Residents Vote to Abolish Curfews," *Barnard Bulletin*, October 30, 1968.

22. "Barnard Trustees to Discuss Student Vote," *Barnard Bulletin*, December 2, 1971.

23. http://making-barnard-history.com/people/faculty.

24. "Minority Suites to Continue, Appeal Made for Black Floor," *Barnard Bulletin*, March 28, 1974; "BOSS Appeals of Regents Ruling," *Barnard Bulletin*, September 19, 1974.

25. "Experimental College on 107th St.," *Barnard Bulletin* September 18, 1970; "Magazine Features on the EC Embarrass College PR Office," *Barnard Bulletin*, January 13, 1971. The two publications were the *New York Post* and *New Yorker*. For a more favorable retrospective, Peter Balsalm, interview with author, March 27, 2018.

26. "[Faculty] Form Barnard AAUP," *Barnard Bulletin*, March 3, 1971; "Faculty Finance Committee," *Barnard Bulletin*, March 9, 1972.

27. "Barnard Opens Women's Center," *Barnard Bulletin*, March 3, 1971; "Gould to Head Women's Center," *Barnard Bulletin*, September 7, 1972; Jane S. Gould, *Juggling: A Memoir of Work, Family, and Feminism* (New York: Feminist Press at the City University of New York, 1997), 156–172.

28. McCaughey, *Stand, Columbia*, 496–502.

29. "Agreement Reached," *Barnard Bulletin*, February 8, 1973. The projected payments included a back payment of $910,365.74 for 1971–1973, plus an agreement to make ongoing annual payments estimated to be between $350,000 to $500,000.

30. George K. Fraenkel, oral history interviews with author, 1997–1999.

31. Barnard Board of Trustees, Minutes, BC board with CU.

32. Paul Carter to William McGill, November 16, 1972, Central Files, Box 707 (1972–73), Columbia University Archives.

33. "Agreement Reached," *Barnard Bulletin*, February 8, 1973.

34. http://blogs.cuit.columbia.edu/ram31/appendices/appendices-index-page/finances-appendix/.

35. Barnard Board of Trustees, Minutes, June 6, 1973.

36. Bernard Friedman to Peter Kenen, September 17, 1970, Box 109, Central Files, Columbia University Archives.

37. George K. Fraenkel to William J. McGill, November 1971 to January 1972, Central Files, Folder 21, Box 683, Columbia University Archives.

38. "Junior Faculty on Proposed Ad Hoc Procedures," *Barnard Bulletin*, May 11, 1972.

39. Barnard Board of Trustees, Minutes, February 5, 1973, June 6, 1973.

40. Eleanor L. Elliott, interview with Rosalind Rosenberg, July 8, 1999.

41. Elliott, interview with Rosalind Rosenberg, July 8, 1999; Ellen V. Futter, interview with author, June 25, 2015.

42. Christine Royer, interview with author, July 21, 2014.

43. Barnard Board of Trustees, Minutes, April 16, 1975; Gedale Horowitz, interview with author, March 8, 2016.

44. "Peterson Resigns to Head Beloit; Search Committee Seeks Replacement," *Barnard Bulletin*, September 15, 1975.

45. Helen Bacon to Wallace Jones, Barnard Board of Trustees, July 2, 1975; Helen Bacon to William J. McGill, Central Files, Box 768, Columbia University Archives.

46. Joseph Gerald Brennan, *The Education of a Prejudiced Man* (New York: Charles Scribner's Sons, 1977), 244.

47. Karla Jay, *Tales of the Lavender Menace: A Memoir of Liberation* (New York: Basic Books, 2000), 6–7, 11.

48. "Heroin in BHR?" *Barnard Bulletin*, October 28, 1970; "Faculty Alarmed at Drug Situation," *Barnard Bulletin*, November 4, 1970; "Administration's Role on Drugs Debated," *Barnard Bulletin*, November 18, 1970. Barbara Bernstein, class of 1971, Class of 1971 Oral History Interviews.

49. On BOSS, Karla Spurlock-Evans, class of 1971, Class of 1971 Oral History Interview., BOSS; Frances Sadler, class of 1972, interview with Lee Beaty, class of 2018, May 1, 2018.

50. Carla Santaniello, class of 1971, Class of 1971 Oral History Interview: "I had an abortion at the end of my freshman year." Procedure performed in Philadelphia for $300.

51. Class of 1971 Oral History Project transcripts, Barnard College Archives.

52. Class of 1971 interviews with Ruth Stuart Bell, Katherine Brewster, Carol Santanello Spencer, Fay Chew Matsuda, Karla Spurlock-Evans, Barnard College Archives.

53. Christine Royer, Interview with author, July 21, 2014; http://blogs.cuit.columbia.edu/ram31/appendices/appendices-index-page/students-alumnae-appendix/1660-2/.

54. Ellen V. Futter, class of 1971; Dorothy Denburg, class of 1970; Mary Gordon, class of 1971, Constance Brown, class of 1971, Interviews with author.

55. *Barnard-Columbia Course Guide* began publication in 1963.

56. http://blogs.cuit.columbia.edu/ram31/appendices/appendices-index-page/students-alumnae-appendix/.

9. SAYING NO TO ZEUS

1. Anne L. Prescott, class of 1959, interview with Elizabeth Moye, class of 2015, April 8, 2015.

2. "President Search Committee," Box 768, Corporate Files, Barnard College I, Folder 16 (1975), Columbia University Archives; Barnard Board of Trustees, Minutes, July 2, 1975.

3. "Trustees Formally Appoint Mattfeld," *Columbia Spectator*, November 13, 1975; "Trustees Vote Mattfeld New Barnard President," *Barnard Bulletin*, November 13, 1975.

4. Barnard Board of Trustees, Minutes, November 12, 1975, December 10, 1975

5. Nina McCain, "Jacquelyn Mattfeld at Brown," *Change* (Summer 1973): 19–21.

6. McCain, "Jacquelyn Mattfeld at Brown," 20–21. Felicity Laboy [daughter of Jacquelyn Mattfeld], correspondence with author, April 14, April 30, and May 6, 2019. HEW is the Department of Health, Education, and Welfare.

7. Barnard Board of Trustees, Minutes, December 10, 1975.

8. Jacquelyn A. Mattfeld to William J. McGill, April 14, 1976; *Columbia Spectator*, April 19, 1976.

9. "Low Library Is Divided on CU-Barnard Relations," *Columbia Spectator*, March 19, 1976; William T. deBary, Oral History Interview, 1989, Oral History Research Office, Rare Book and Manuscript Library, Columbia University, 371.

10. Barnard Board of Trustees resolution, May 11, 1976; "Mattfeld's Letter to Barnard," *Barnard Bulletin*, September 13, 1976.

11. Edward Fiske, "Barnard, Columbia in a Merger Struggle," *New York Times*, May 14, 1976

12. "Barnard President Inaugurated at Lavish Ceremony," *Columbia Spectator*, November 8, 1976; "Special Inauguration Supplement," *Barnard Bulletin*, November 9, 1976; Christine Royer, interview with author, New York City, July 21, 2014.

13. " 'Sisterhood Is Powerful': Mattfeld Traces Life and Times," *Columbia Spectator*, November 17, 1976.

14. Helene L. Kaplan, interview with Rosalind Rosenberg, New York City, March 22, 2000; Royer, interview with author, July 21, 2014.

15. Kaplan interview with Rosalind Rosenberg, March 22, 2000; Gedale Horowitz, interview with author, New York City, March 8, 2016.

16. Royer, interview with author, July 21, 2014.

17. Charles S. Olton, interview with author, Shelter Island, NY, June 10, 2014; Joanne Blauer, interview with author, New York City, September 11, 2014.

18. Author's recollections. Not surprisingly, her spirited advocacy of faculty salary parity with Columbia won her the enthusiastic endorsement of the Faculty Finance Committee.

19. Barnard Board of Trustees, Minutes, October 13, 1970.

20. Annual publication by the American Association of University Professors (AAUP) of by-rank median salary statistics of both Barnard and Columbia, and their republication in the *Columbia Spectator*, made the gap painfully obvious. See "Report Confirms Disparity in Barnard, Columbia Pay," *Columbia Spectator*, November 6, 1975.

21. Horowitz, interview with author, March 8, 2016. The 1980 Middle States Accreditation Report reported Barnard running deficits for seven straight years (1971–1977), with first in-balance budget ending June 30, 1978. That year, tuition accounted for 72 percent of all income.

22. Royer, interview with author, July 21, 2014; http://making-barnard-history.com/people /students/. For contemporary comparisons with other liberal arts colleges, see Elizabeth A. Duffy and Idana Goldberg, *Crafting a Class: College Admissions and Financial Aid* (Princeton, NJ, Princeton University Press, 1998), 12–24.

23. "Albers to Leave Barnard," *Barnard Bulletin*, October 17, 1977. For Albers statement, *Columbia Spectator*, December 8, 1977; Horowitz interview with author, March 8, 2016; Lewis Wyman, interview with author, New York City, April 15, 2015.

24. http://making-barnard-history.com/people/students/.

25. Room squeeze and rent hikes extensively covered by *Barnard Bulletin*; see March 21, 1978; March 30, 1987; April 26, 1979; July 25, 1979; September 6, 1979. Meanwhile, the plant conditions, as reported by a 1978 commissioned review conducting by the architectural consultants, were characterized as follows: "Quality of academic buildings seriously and desperately deficient; dormitories still more deficient."

26. *Barnard Bulletin*, April 15, 1980; Paul Franzese, class of 1980, interview with Elizabeth Moye, class of 2015, March 10, 2015.

27. Franzese, interview with Moye, March 10, 2015; Marcia Sells, class of 1981, interview with author, New York City, October 2, 2014. See also [David A. Robertson] *Report of the Self-Study for Commission on Higher Education of Middle States Association* (1981).

28. For imposition of energy surcharge, *Barnard Bulletin*, November 30, 1979; for repeal, *Barnard Bulletin*, January 20, 1980.

29. Author's recollection of faculty concerns.

30. Barnard Faculty Meeting, Minutes, April 2, 1980, and Barnard Board of Trustees, Minutes, April 16, 1980.

31. [David A. Robertson] *Report of the Self-Study for Commission on Higher Education of Middle States Association* (1981), 22.

32. By 1979, the gap between Barnard and Columbia faculty salaries for assistant professors had been eliminated, that between associate professors had narrowed to $4,000, while that between full professors remained a matter of dispute. For progress toward her goal of salary parity, see Jacquelyn Mattfeld, *President's Report, 1976–1979* "Without Peer," July 1979.

33. Personal recollection of the author, then regularly teaching graduate courses and a member of the Columbia history department.

34. Michael Alexander, interview with author, August 28, 2014; Blauer, interview with author, September 11, 2014. The author had one telephone conversation with Jacquelyn Mattfeld in 2015, initiated by her from her home in Evanston, Illinois, after I had posted a brief biography on a blog maintained for my undergraduate seminar, "Making Barnard History." A more substantive correspondence later occurred in the spring of 2019 between the author and Felicity Laboy, one of Mattfeld's two daughters.

35. Olton, interview with author, June 10, 2014.

36. Olton, interview with author, June 10, 2014.

37. Kaplan, interview with Rosalind Rosenberg, March 22, 2000.

38. Alexander, interview with author, August 28, 2014.

39. Royer, interview with author, July 21, 2014; Sells, interview with author, October 2, 2014.

40. Robert A. McCaughey, *Stand, Columbia: A History of Columbia University in the City of New York, 1754–2004* (New York: Columbia University Press, 2003), 533–535.

41. Blauer, interview with author, September 11, 2014; Michael I. Sovern, *An Improbable Life: My Sixty Years at Columbia and Other Adventures* (New York: Columbia University Press, 2014), 158–159.

42. Olton, interview with author, June 10, 2014; Blauer, interview with author, September 11, 2014.

43. Felicity Laboy, correspondence with the author, April 14, April 30, and May 6, 2019.

44. http://blogs.cuit.columbia.edu/ram31/appendices/appendices-index-page/students-alumnae-appendix/1660-2/.

45. Based on author's experiences as Barnard faculty member (1969–2020), as founding member of the Faculty Finance Committee (1973–1980), chair of the history department (1983–1987; 1996–1999); dean of the faculty (1987–1994), and member of the Faculty Appointments and Tenure Committee (1997–2000).

46. Trilling to *Columbia Spectator*, May 23, 1968, quoted in McCaughey, *Stand, Columbia*, 462.

47. Author's direct experience.

48. Author's direct experience.

49. Author's direct experience.

50. A particularly critical take on the scholarly accomplishments of the Barnard faculty in the early 1970s was that of Columbia's dean of graduate studies, George K. Fraenkel. See

McCaughey, *Stand, Columbia*, 503–504. The two Columbia departments were history and Spanish.

51. "Faculty on Proposed Ad Hoc Procedures," *Barnard Bulletin*, May 11, 1972.

52. Prescott, interview with Elizabeth Moye, April 8, 2015.

53. Barnard Board of Trustees, Minutes, April 8, 1974. The other three other members of the Barnard faculty tenured under the new provisions were Elaine Pagels in religion, Jonathan Cole in sociology, and the author in history.

54. The survey, funded by the Dorothy Spivack Faculty Research Fund, went to 144 of the 152 full-time officers of academic instruction (the eight instructors in physical education were not polled). Of these recipients, 102 returned surveys; ninety-five (66 percent) contained scalable responses to all the questions posed. The respondents were representative of the faculty in terms of field, rank, and gender, the three independent variables used in the analysis. See Robert A. McCaughey, "A Statistical Profile of the Barnard College Faculty, 1900–1974" (Barnard College, mimeograph, Spring 1975).

55. McCaughey, "A Statistical Profile of the Barnard College Faculty," 63, 84–91, 101, 102.

56. Robert A. McCaughey, *Scholars & Teachers: The Faculties of Select Liberal Arts Colleges and Their Place in American Higher Learning* (New York: Andrew W. Mellon Foundation, 1994). One last surmise on the evolution of the Barnard scholar-teacher: In occurring concurrently with post-1968 Columbia coming to focus more on its undergraduates and, since the 1990s, requiring all its faculty to provide undergraduate instruction, the respective professional identities of Barnard and Columbia faculty, once diverging, have since converged.

10. BARNARD RISING

1. Ellen V. Futter, interview with author, American Museum of Natural History, June 15, 2015.

2. Michael I. Sovern, *An Improbable Life: My 60 Years at Columbia and Other Adventures* (New York: Columbia University, 2014), 158; "Columbia Asks Barnard for Rise in Coeducation," *New York Times*, May 27, 1981.

3. "Plimpton Area Muggings Continue," *Barnard Bulletin*, October 20, 1980.

4. *Columbia Spectator*, October 31, 1979; Gedale Horowitz, interview with author, March 8, 2016.

5. [Ruth Adams, chair] Middle States Evaluation Report, May 1981; http://making-barnard-history.com/finances/.

6. "Ellen Futter Appointed Barnard's Acting Head," *New York Times*, July 11, 1980. Faculty members James Harvey Robinson served as acting dean in 1900–1901; George Mullins served as acting dean, 1930–1932; Henry Boorse served as acting president, 1968; and Leroy Breunig served as acting president, 1975–1976.

7. Ellen V. Futter, interview with author, New York City, June 25, 2015.

8. Charles S. Olton, interview with author, June 10, 2014.

9. Paula Franzese, class of 1981, interview with Elizabeth Moye, class of 2015, March 10, 2015.

10. Futter interview with author, June 25, 2015.

11. Futter interview with author, June 25, 2015.

12. Futter interview with author, June 25, 2015. In a September 1980 Columbia College Survey on Coeducation, 84 percent of respondents declared e BC/CC cooperation not satisfactory, while 74 percent favored admitting women.

13. Dean of Studies Roger Lehecka, quoted in *Columbia Spectator*, September 30, 1980.

14. "Women Against Merger, *Columbia Spectator*, October 8, 1980.

15. Futter, interview by author, June 25, 2015; author's recollections.

16. Barnard Board of Trustees, Minutes, July 9, 1980; *Columbia Spectator*, July 16, 1980.

17. "Columbia College Report Urges Co-Ed College by 1981," *Columbia Spectator*, October 23, 1980.

18. [Ronald Breslow], *Report of Select Committee for the Study of Coeducation in Columbia College* (April 16, 1981).

19. [Breslow], *Report of Select Committee.*

20. [Jacquelyn A. Mattfeld], *President's Report, 1976–1979 ["Without Peer"]*; Breslow, Committee Report,

21. Barbara S. Schmitter, interview with author, New York City, July 28, 2014.

22. On Peat, Marwick scenarios, Lewis Wyman, interview with author, April 15, 2015.

23. Ellen V. Futter to Michael I. Sovern, November 16, 1981, Office of Columbia Provost Records, Box 109, Columbia University Archives; Futter, interview with author, June 25, 2015.

24. Futter, interview with author, June 25, 2015; Peter Likins account in *Columbia Spectator*, January 23, 1981.

25. Futter, interview with author, June 15, 2015; Wyman interview with author, April 15, 2015.

26. *Columbia Spectator*, January 23, 1982.

27. Helene Kaplan, interview with Rosalind Rosenberg, March 22, 2000; Ellen V. Futter to Barnard faculty, January 25, 1982, quoted in *Columbia Spectator*, January 26, 1982.

28. Futter, quoted in *Columbia Spectator*, January 23, 1982.

29. "Futter Sells Students on Barnard's Future," *Columbia Spectator*, January 26, 1982. Ratification of the new agreement, to run until 1989, was signed by Barnard trustees on June 8, 1982.

30. Futter, interview with author, June 15, 2015.

31. Rachel Corbman, "The Scholars and the Feminists: The Barnard Sex Conference and the History of the Institutionalization of Feminism," *Feminist Formulations*, vol. 27, no. 3 (2015): 49–80; http://blogs.cuit.columbia.edu/ram31/appendices/appendices-index-page /faculty-appendix/survival-rates-among-assistant-professors-1980-2003/; Elizabeth Wilson, "The Context of 'Between Pleasure and Danger': The Barnard Conference on Sexuality," *Feminist Review*, no. 13 (Spring, 1983), 35–41:, Iona Forrester, class of 2019, "The Barnard Sex Conference," December 4, 2019, Making Barnard History Seminar (Fall 2019); https://courseworks2.columbia.edu/courses/92600/discussion_topics/412925.

32. On the Barnard curriculum, Olton, interview with the author, June 10, 2014; on the formation of the Curriculum Committee, *Columbia Spectator*, February 23, 1982. The author served on the committee.

33. "Faculty to Vote on Two New Courses for 1983 Freshmen," *Barnard Bulletin*, December 8, 1982; "New Curriculum Nears Vote," *Barnard Bulletin*, February 2, 1983.

34. "New Curriculum Nears Vote," *Barnard Bulletin*, February 2, 1983.

35. Gedale Horowitz, interview with author, March 8, 2016.

36. "The Re-evaluation of Program in the Arts: Proposed Changes in Barnard's Arts Curriculum," *Barnard Bulletin*, April 15, 1987.

37. Interdisciplinary studies programs were either started or expanded while the author was dean of the faculty; the change in payments from a per capita charge to a fixed charge was primarily the accomplishment of college counsel and Barnard's chief negotiator with Columbia, Kathryrn J. Rodgers.

38. Christine Royer, interview with author, July 21, 2014; http://making-barnard-history.com/people/students/

39. Futter, interview with author, June 25, 2015; M. Elizabeth Tidball and Vera Kistiakowsky, "Baccalaureate Origins of American Scientists and Scholars," *Science*, vol. 193 (August 20, 1976): 646–652; M. E. Tidball, "To Nourish What Is Strong Already," *Barnard Alumnae Magazine*, vol. 50 (1979): 7–11; "Conference of Select Liberal Arts Colleges," January 23 and 24, 1992, organized by the author, twenty-one colleges were represented.

40. "Number of Barnard College Accepts Falls but Quality Rises," *Columbia Spectator*, April 14, 1983; "Co-education: Little Effect on Barnard College," *Barnard Bulletin*, January 7, 1983.

41. Lewis Wyman, interview with author, April 15, 2015.

42. Gedale Horowitz, interview with author, March 18, 2016.

43. Gedale Horowitz, interview with author, March 18, 2016, Futter Interview, June 25, 2015.

44. Gedale Horowitz, interview with author, March 18, 2016.

45. Gedale Horowitz, interview with author, March 18, 2016.

46. On running a fundraising campaign in reverse, Futter, interview with author, June 25, 2015.

47. "Sulzberger Family Gives $5 Million—Centennial to Become Sulzberger Hall," *Columbia Spectator*, January 16, 1991.

48. http://blogs.cuit.columbia.edu/ram31/appendices/appendices-index-page/faculty-appendix/survival-rates-among-assistant-professors-1980-2003/.

49. "Why Professors Are Here Today and Gone Tomorrow," *Barnard Bulletin*, February 12, 1979.

50. "Futter May Appeal Hewlett Tenure Denial," *Columbia Spectator*, October 8, 1981; Charles S. Olton, interview with author, June 10, 2014.

51. "Amsden Blasts Tenure Panel for Intolerance to 'Deviation,'" *Columbia Spectator*, February 25, 1983; Duncan Foley, correspondence with author September 21, 2019; "Development Economist Alice Amsden Dies at 68," *MIT News*, March 16, 2012.

52. Bettina Berch, interview with Frances Garrett Connell, Barnard College class of 1971, Oral History Collection, May 22, 2015. Other Barnard departments involved in these disputed tenure cases included history and psychology. See "Why Professors Are Here Today and Gone Tomorrow," *Barnard Bulletin*, February 12, 1979; "Chambers Denied Tenure; History Department Crippled," *Barnard Bulletin*, April 6, 1981.

53. Three- and five-year Ann Whitney Olin Term Professorships funded with $500,000 gift, were first introduced in November 1987. Their number has since been increased, with 27 faculty members holding Olin professorships in 2020. Currently, the number of fully endowed professorships has increased to 41. At its inception, the Senior Faculty Research Program was by application; in 2014, it became available to all senior faculty.

54. http://blogs.cuit.columbia.edu/ram31/appendices/appendices-index-page/faculty-appendix/barnard-college-faculty-1965-1989/.

55. http://blogs.cuit.columbia.edu/ram31/appendices/appendices-index-page/faculty-appendix/barnard-college-faculty-1965-1989/.

56. Course evaluations became a required element in faculty tenure and promotion deliberations by a vote of the faculty in April 1989.

57. On the research ethos becoming firmly established, see Robert A. McCaughey, *Scholars & Teachers: The Faculties of Select Liberal Arts College and Their Place in American Higher Learning* (New York: Andrew W. Mellon Foundation, 1994).

58. Robert A. McCaughey, *Stand, Columbia: A History of Columbia University in the City of New York, 1754–2004* (New York: Columbia University Press, 2003), 562–568.

59. Charles S. Olton, interview with author, June 10, 2014.

60. Kathryn J. Rodgers, interview with author, April 7, 2015; Wyman, interview with author, April 15, 2015.

61. "Dean: Dismantling of PIA a Commitment to BC Arts," *Columbia Spectator*, February 2, 1989

62. "Barnard & Columbia Form Athletic Consortium," *Barnard Bulletin*, March 2, 1983. Celebrations in the spring of 2019 for the thirty-fifth anniversary of the athletics consortium agreement speak to its ongoing utility.

63. "Prof. Sues for Settlement from Discrimination," *Columbia Spectator*, February 5, 2003; Hannah McCaughey, class of 1989, interview with the author, December 24, 2018.

64. Futter, interview with author, June 25, 2015.

65. "Barnard's President to Head Museum of Natural History," *New York Times*, June 29, 1993.

66. Futter, interview with author, June 25, 2015.

11. "NEW YORK, NEW YORK"

1. Judith R. Shapiro, interview with author, June 22, 2015.

2. Kathryn J. Rodgers, interview with author, April 7, 2015.

3. Shapiro, interview with author, June 22, 2015. Alfred Kazin, *New York Jew* (New York: Vintage, 1979).

4. Shapiro, interview with author, June 22, 2015.

5. Shapiro, interview with author, June 22, 2015.

6. Shapiro, interview with author, June 22, 2015.

7. Shapiro, interview with author, June 22, 2015.

8. Shapiro, interview with author, June 22, 2015.; "Mary Patterson McPherson, Sixth President of Bryn Mawr College (1978–1997)," *Leading Bryn Mawr: An Exhibition in Honor of Nancy J. Vickers. Bryn Mawr College* (Bryn Mawr, PA: Bryn Mawr, 1998).

9. [Mary Patterson McPherson], Middle States Accreditation Report (1991); Paula Rubel and Abraham Rosman, interview with author, July 8, 2014; Shapiro, interview with author, June 22, 2015.

10. Richard Pious, correspondence with author, June 3, 2014.

11. "With the Greatest Pride and Confidence" [videorecording], The inauguration of Judith R. Shapiro, Barnard College, October 27, 1994 (David Gordon Production, 1994).

12. Elizabeth Boylan, interview with author, Alfred P. Sloan Foundation, New York City, November 3, 2016.

13. Robert A. McCaughey, *Stand, Columbia: A History of Columbia University in the City of New York, 1754–2004* (New York: Columbia University Press, 2003), 557–561; George E. Rupp, "The Rupp Presidency," a talk given at the University Seminar on the History of Columbia University, May 1, 2019.

14. Shapiro, interview with author, June 22, 2015.

15. Shapiro, interview with author, June 22, 2015.

16. Boylan, interview with author, November 3, 2016; author's personal knowledge.

17. Barnard Board of Trustees Minutes, June 19, 1996; Lisa Tolin, "Local 2110 Strike Continues into Fall," *Columbia Spectator*, September 3, 1996.

18. "Alums Question Barnard Prof's Legitimacy," *Columbia Spectator*, September 10, 2007.

19. "Professor Protests Abu El-Haj's Claims," *Columbia Spectator*, September 25, 2007; Karen Arenson, "Fracas Erupts over Book on Mideast by a Barnard Professor Seeking Tenure," *New York Times*, September 10, 2007; Alan Finder, "Embattled Barnard Anthropologist Is Awarded Tenure," *New York Times*, November 3, 2007.

20. Barnard Faculty Meeting Minutes, ROTC.

21. "Barnard No Change in USNWR Rankings," *Columbia Spectator*, September 14, 2007; Boylan, interview with author, November 3, 2016.

22. Jennifer Fondiller, interview with author, January 4, 2017; Flora Davidson, correspondence with author, 2015; Gedale Horowitz, interview with author, March 8, 2016; http://blogs.cuit.columbia.edu/ram31/appendices/appendices-index-page/students-alumnae-appendix/barnard-college-graduating-classes-by-hometowns/.

23. Lewis Wyman, interview with author, April 15, 2015.

24. Dorothy Denburg, correspondence with author, 2017.

25. Jennifer Fondiller, interview with author, January 4, 2017.

26. Yojairy Sanchez, "Rejection of Prof's Tenure Criticized," *Columbia Spectator*, February 12, 1993; Barnard Board of Trustees Minutes, June 23, 1993; Lesley Sharpe, interview with author, April 15, 2015.

27. Boylan, interview with author, November 3, 2016.

28. http://blogs.cuit.columbia.edu/ram31/appendices/appendices-index-page/faculty-appendix/survival-rates-among-assistant-professors-1980-2003/

29. Laura Kay, interview with author, March 16, 2017.

30. Kay, interview with author, March 16, 2017; Boylan, interview with author, November 3, 2016.

31. Boylan interview.

32. Barnard Board of Trustees, Minutes, December 3, 1997; Boylan, interview with author, November 3, 2016.

33. logs.cuit.columbia.edu/ram31/appendices/appendices-index-page/faculty-appendix/barnard-college-faculty-appointees-1990-2018/

34. Rosalind Rosenberg, correspondence with author, 2018, and author's direct knowledge.

35. Pious, correspondence with author, June 3, 2014.

36. http://blogs.cuit.columbia.edu/ram31/appendices/appendices-index-page/faculty-appendix/barnard-faculty-by-field-selected-years/; Kay, interview with author, March 16, 2017. These appointments included Reshmi Mukherjee (1997) and Jenna Levin (2004) in physics/astronomy; Christian Rojas (1997) and Dina Merrer (2001) in chemistry; Brian Morton (1995), Hilary Callahan (1995), John Glendenning (1996), and Jennifer Mansfield (2006) in biology. All have since been promoted to tenure.

37. Senior appointments included Walter Neumann, mathematics (2000); Anne Higonnet, art history (2000); Janet Jakobsen, women's studies (2001); David Weiman, economics (2001); Frederick Neuhouser, philosophy (2003); Kim Hall, English and Africana studies (2006); and Dusa McDuff, mathematics (2007).

38. http://blogs.cuit.columbia.edu/ram31/appendices/appendices-index-page/students-alumnae-appendix/1660-2/.

39. http://blogs.cuit.columbia.edu/ram31/appendices/appendices-index-page/students-alumnae-appendix/1660-2/.

40. http://blogs.cuit.columbia.edu/ram31/appendices/appendices-index-page/students-alumnae-appendix/barnard-students-with-pell-grants/.

41. http://blogs.cuit.columbia.edu/ram31/appendices/appendices-index-page/students-alumnae-appendix/barnard-students-by-racial-ethnic-composition/.

42. Gedale Horowitz, interview with author, March 8, 2016; Lewis Wyman, interview with author, April 15, 2015.

43. Barnard Board of Trustees, Minutes, December 4, 1996, April 25, 2003.

44. Boylan, interview with author, November 3, 2016.

45. "BC Names Nexus Donor Vagelos Family Donates $15 Million for Completion of New Student Center," *Columbia Daily Spectator*, April 16, 2008.

46. Tess Bernstein, "New Dorm to Open for Barnard Profs," *Columbia Daily Spectator*, December 8, 2005; Horowitz, interview with author, March 8, 2016; Boylan, interview with author, November 3, 2016.

47. Boylan interview.

48. http://blogs.cuit.columbia.edu/ram31/appendices/appendices-index-page/administrative-appendix/.

49. Gayle F. Robinson, interview with author, February 2, 2017; Jolyne Caruso-Fitzgerald, interview with author, April 11, 2019.

50. http://blogs.cuit.columbia.edu/ram31/appendices/appendices-index-page/trustees-appendix/barnard-trustees-by-appointment-year-1889-2019/.

51. http://blogs.cuit.columbia.edu/ram31/appendices/appendices-index-page/trustees-appendix/barnard-trustees-by-appointment-year-1889-2019/.

52. Shapiro, interview with author, June 22, 2015; Paula Rubel and Abraham Rosman, interview with author, July 8, 2014.

53. Thomas Bender, *New York Intellect: A History of the Intellectual Life in New York City, from 1750 to the Beginning of Our Own Time* (New York: Knopf, 1987), 269–271. Although raised in California, President Sian Leah Beilock was born in New York City.

54. Shapiro, interview with author, June 22, 2015.

55. The safety of the neighborhood was challenged after this paragraph was written by the brutal killing of a Barnard first-year student, Tessa Majors, class of 2023, in Morningside Park in the early evening of December 11, 2019. Ed Shanahan and Matthew Sedacca, "Student, 18, Is Fatally Stabbed Near Barnard Campus," *New York Times*, December 13, 2019, https://www.nytimes.com/2019/12/11/nyregion/barnard-student-fatal-stabbing.html.

56. Robert K. Merton, "The Matthew Effect in Science," *Science*, vol. 159 (1968): 56–63; Fondiller, interview with author, January 4, 2017.

57. Shapiro, interview with author, June 22, 2015.

12. GOING GLOBAL

1. Anna Quindlen, "The Making of DSpar," *Barnard Magazine*, vol. 105, no. 2 (Spring 2017), 27.

2. This chapter was written without access to the Minutes of the Barnard Trustees, which are closed for twenty-five years. Access to the minutes encompassing the Shapiro presidency through 2008 was granted with special permission of President emerita Shapiro and president Sian Leah Beilock. My thanks to both.

3. Karen W. Arenson, "Professor from Harvard to Be Barnard President," *New York Times*, January 8, 2008; Joy Resmovitz and Jacob Schneider, "Debora Spar Named Barnard President," *Columbia Daily Spectator*, January 29, 2008.

4. "An Inspirational Legacy—Debora Spar in a Conversation with Jennifer Finney Boylan," *Barnard Magazine*, vol. 105, no. 2, 18–26.

5. Anna Quindlen, "The Making of DSpar," 27.

6. https://en.wikipedia.org/wiki/Debora_Spar; "An Inspirational Legacy – Debora Spar in a Conversation with Jennifer Finney Boylan," 23; Anna Quindlen, "The Making of DSpar," 27.

7. www.investopedia.com/terms/f/financial-crisis.asp.

8. Robert Goldberg and Eileen DeBenedetto, joint interview with author, fall 2018; Jolyne Caruso-Fitzgerald, correspondence with author, April 5, 2019.

9. Spar's Inaugural Address, October 28, 2008.

10. Madina Toure, "Barnard to Launch Athena Center," *Columbia Spectator*, March 27, 2013.

11. Elizabeth Boylan, interview with author, November 3, 2016.

12. Boylan interview.

13. "Early Retirement for Barnard Administrators," *Columbia Daily Spectator*, November 19, 2012; "BC Finance Head Gregory Brown Leaving for Swarthmore," *Columbia Daily Spectator*, January 22, 2014.

14. Paul Hertz, interview with author.

15. Dorothy Urman Denburg, "It Never Felt Like Work," *Barnard Magazine* (Summer 2013).

16. Jennifer Fondiller, interview with author, January 4, 2017; http://blogs.cuit.columbia
.edu/ram31/appendices/appendices-index-page/students-alumnae-appendix/1660-2/.

17. "Building Barnard—Three Families," *Barnard Magazine*, vol. 104 (Winter 2016). The
author is currently ensconced on the ninth floor of the Milstein center, with a command-
ing west view of the Hudson River.

18. Laura Kay, interview and correspondence with the author, March 16, 2017, July 30, 2018.

19. Jolyne Caruso-Fitzgerald and Debora Spar, "Barnard Announces Transgender Admissions Policy – Letter to Members of the Barnard Community," June 4, 2015; Jolyne
Caruso-Fitzgerald, correspondence with author, April 5, 2019.

20. On Presidential Task Force to Examine Divestment, Jolyne Caruso-Fitzgerald to author,
April 4, 2019.

21. "Spar to Lead Lincoln Center," *New York Times*, November 16, 2016.

22. One moment of cross-Broadway tension did occur in 2012 when President Barack
Obama, class of 1983, spoke at the Barnard College commencement. This required
changing the regularly assigned on-campus venues to maximize security for the Barnard
ceremony, inconveniencing several Columbia schools. The following year, Barnard
moved its commencement ceremony to Radio City Music Hall, where the ceremony continues be held as of 2019. Richard Perez-Pena, "After Barnard Gets Obama for Speech,
Tensions with Columbia Bubble Up," *New York Times*, March 12, 2012.

23. On Spar as teacher, Philip Ammirato, interview with author, fall 2017; for other positive student sentiments, "Students on Spar," *Barnard Magazine*, vol. 105, no. 2 (Spring
2017).

24. "Barnard Reverses New Posting Policy after Complaints from SGA," *Columbia Daily
Spectator*, October 25, 2012; Madina Toure, "President Spar to Serve on Board of Goldman Sachs," *Columbia Daily Spectator*, January 29, 2013.

25. Jodi Kantor, "Finding Satisfaction in Second Best," *New York Times*, September 15, 2013;
Patricia Cohen, "Striving to Have It All, and Then Recalculating," *New York Times*,
September 24, 2013; Lori Leibovich, "Debora Spar, Barnard President, Says Women Can't
Have It All—And Shouldn't Even Try," *Huffington Post*, September 30, 2013; Ying Chang,
"Wonder Woman: An Interview with Debora Spar," *The Eye*, January 30, 2014. Sheryl
Sandberg was Barnard's commencement speaker in 2013.

26. Debora Spar, "Aging and My Beauty Dilemma," *New York Times*, September 24, 2016; for
reader responses, *New York Times*, September 29, 2016.

27. Staffing for interdepartmental programs such as first-year seminars became increasingly
difficult to secure from the ranks of the full-time faculty, resulting in an increased reliance on part-timers and adjuncts. Personal knowledge.

28. The presence of term appointees on the faculty jumped from fifteen in 2013–2014 to
thirty-one in 2014–2015, to thirty-five in 2015–2016. http://making-barnard-history.com
/people/faculty.

29. http://blogs.cuit.columbia.edu/ram31/appendices/appendices-index-page/faculty-appendix
/barnard-college-faculty-appointees-1990-2018/.

30. For Tenure Review Advisory Committee (TRAC) and its success rate for Barnard faculty nominated for tenure since 2011, see https://provost.columbia.edu/content/tenure-review -guidelines http://making-barnrad-history.com/people/faculty.

31. [Debra Minkoff and Rebecca Friedkin], Barnard College Committee on Faculty Diversity and Development, *Report on the 2015–16 Faculty Diversity Survey* (June 2016).

32. https://barnard.edu/diversity-inclusion/council/.

33. Full disclosure: the author is one of these superannuated miscreants.

34. On contingent faculty and their 2017 contract, https://barnard.edu/academics-library /provost-dean-faculty/resources/contingent-faculty.

35. These and similar grousings were regularly voiced in my interviews with faculty members, trustees, and administrators, as well as by my students in successive years of my undergraduate seminar, Making Barnard History, although those of one constituency often said complaints from other constituencies were unmerited. Interviewed trustees and students, although disappointed by the abruptness of Spar's departure, were on balance more favorably disposed toward her presidency than were faculty members and older alumnae interviewees. No claims are made for this sampling's representativeness.

36. http://blogs.cuit.columbia.edu/ram31/appendices/appendices-index-page/students -alumnae-appendix/1660-2/.

37. http://blogs.cuit.columbia.edu/ram31/appendices/appendices-index-page/trustees -appendix/barnard-trustees-by-appointment-year-1889-2019/.

38. Rapidly rising administrative costs are also associated with student mental health issues and the elaboration of student services more generally. In 2019, one-quarter of the Barnard student body self-identified as having a disability. Jolyne Caruso-Fitzgerald, interview with author, April 5, 2019.

39. http://blogs.cuit.columbia.edu/ram31/appendices/appendices-index-page/faculty -appendix/; http://blogs.cuit.columbia.edu/ram31/appendices/appendices-index-page/faculty -appendix/faculty-homebody-index-by-eras/; Alvin Gouldner, "Cosmopolitans and Locals: Toward an Analysis of Latent Social Roles, II," *Administrative Science Quarterly*, vol. 2, no.4 (March 1958): 444–480.

40. Office of Provost faculty research dinners

41. https://barnard.edu/first-year-class-profile.

42. "Some Colleges Have More Students Coming from the Top 1 Percent," *New York Times*, January 18, 2017; https://www.nytimes.com/interactive/2017/01/18/upshot/some-colleges-have -more-students-from-the-top-1-percent-than-the-bottom-60.html.

43. Raj Chetty, "Mobility Report Cards: The Role of Colleges in Intergenerational Mobility," https://www.nber.org/papers/w23618.

SELECTED BIBLIOGRAPHY

PRIMARY SOURCES

The Barnard Annual, 1894–1897; Barnard *Mortarboard*, 1898–2019, http://digitalcollections .barnard.edu/yearbook.

Barnard Bulletin, 1901–2002, Barnard College Charter, By-Laws and Reports and Pamphlets Relating to the Education of Women, 1882–1898.

Barnard College Board of Trustees, Minutes, 1889–2008.

Barnard College Committee on Instruction, Minutes, 1900–2017.

Barnard College Dean's Reports, 1891–1952, Barnard College Archives (BCA).

Barnard College Faculty, Meeting Minutes, 1900–2017.

Barnard College Financial Records, 1890–1979.

Barnard College Office of Communications Records, 1934–2016.

Barnard College President's Reports, 1952–2002.

Bulletin of the Associate Alumnae of Barnard College, Barnard College Alumnae Bulletin, Barnard College Alumnae Monthly, Barnard Magazine, 1912–2019, http://digitalcollections.barnard .edu/barnard-magazine.

Middle States Reaccreditation Reports, 1961, 1971, 1981, 1991, 2001, 2001.

Register of the Associate Alumnae of Barnard College, 1905, 1910, 1915, 1925.

BARNARD RELATED PAPERS/COLLECTIONS IN BARNARD COLLEGE ARCHIVES (BCA)

Gildersleeve, Virginia C., Paper, 1901–1964.

Gill, Laura, Correspondence, 1910–1908.

Meyer, Annie Nathan, Papers, 1890–1950.

Plimpton, Francis T. P., Papers,1936–1981.

Plimpton, George A., Papers, 1889–1936, BCA and Columbia University Archives (CUA).

Setzer, Dorothea, "Biography Notes, Gildersleeve Papers, No. 64, Box #2, BCA.S.

BARNARD-RELATED PAPERS/COLLECTIONS IN COLUMBIA UNIVERSITY ARCHIVES (CUA)/COLUMBIANA

Brewster, William Tenney, Central Files, Box 317, CUA.

Brownell, Silas Brown, Papers, Central Files, Box 659, CUA.

Clark, John Bates, Papers, Central Files, Box 659, CUA.

Dix, Morgan, Diary 1856–1899.

Gill, Laura D., Central Files, Box 660, CUA.

Hewitt, Abram S., Papers, Central Files, Box 661, CUA.

Liggett, N. W., Central Files, Box 661, CUA.

Myer, Anne E. H., Papers, Central Files, Box 662, CUA.

Smith, Emily James {Putnam), Papers, Central Files, Box 663, CUA.

NEWSPAPERS

Barnard Bulletin, 1910–2019, http://digitalcollections.barnard.edu/bulletin.

Columbia Daily Spectator, 1889–2019, http://spectatorarchive.library.columbia.edu/.

New York Times, 1889–2019.

INTERVIEW AND CORRESPONDENCE ROSTER

Alexander, Michael, special assistant to President Mattfeld, 1978–1981, interview with author, August 28, 2014.

Alperstein, Janet, class of 1992, interview with Miriam Lichtenberg, class of 2019, November 29, 2018.

Ammirato, Philip, Biology Department (1974–2000), correspondence with author, fall 2018.

Bailey, Helen Phelps, class of 1933, French Department (1933–1953), dean of studies (1953–1976), interview with Darlene Levy, Columbia University Oral History Office, April 1979.

Balsalm, Peter, Psychology Department (1975–), interview with author, March 27, 2018.

Berch, Bettina, class of 1971, Economics Department (1975–1981), interview with Columbia University Oral History Office, 1983; interview with Frances Connell, Class of 1971 Interview, May 22, 2015.

Bernstein, Barbara, class of 1971, Class of 1971 Interview, February 2011.

Biederman, Esther Gebelsky, class of 1931, interview with Arline Winer, class of 1954, Barnard Centennial Oral Histories, December 13, 1988.

Blauer, Joanne, college counsel (1978–1981), interview with author, September 11, 2014.

Boylan, Elizabeth S., provost (1995–2011), interview with author, November 3, 2016.

Brewster, Katherine, Barnard student 1967–1968, Class of 1971 Interview, February 5, 2011.

Callahan, Hilary, Biology Department (1998–), interview with Sloane Pick, class of 2019, April 10, 2018.

Carter, Dona Summers, class of 1971, Class of 1971 Interviews, January 2011.

Caruso-Fitzgerald, Jolyne, class of 1981; trustee (2000-_), trustee chair (2008–2013), interview with Maddie Harrison, class of 2015, and Bridget Harrison, class of 2018, April 4, 2015; interview with author, April 5, 2019.

Coffee, Toni, class of 1956, editor of *Barnard Alumnae* (1979–), interview with author, January 4, 2017.

DeBary, William T., Columbia provost (1971–1978), Columbia University Oral History Interview, 1983.

Di Benedetti, Eileen, vice president for finance, interview with author, fall 2018.

Elliott, Eleanor Thomas, class of 1948; trustee (1959–2007), trustee chair (1973–1976), interview with Rosalind Rosenberg, July 8, 1999.

Foley, Duncan, Economics Department (1977–1995), correspondence with author, fall 2018.

Fondiller, Jennifer, class of 1988; admissions director (2000–), interview with Jenna Davis, class of 2015, April 25, 2015; interview with author, January 4, 2017.

Fortas, Carolyn Ager, class of 1931, interview with Arline Winer, class of 1954, Centennial Oral History Interviews, March 13, 1989.

Fredrick, Erin, class of 2001; alumnae director (2005–2014), interview with Jenna Davis, class of 2016, April 30, 2015.

Futter, Ellen V., class of 1971; trustee (1972–1996); president (1980–1993), interview with author, June 25, 2015.

Gavronsky, Serge, French Department (1960–2012), interview with author, 2017.

Goldberg, Robert, chief financial officer (2014–2019), interview with author, fall 2018.

Gruder, Vivian, class of 1957, interview with author, September 17, 2015.

Hawes, Candace, class of 1971; Class of 1971 Interviews, March 5, 2011.

Held, Julius, Art History Department (1937–1980), interview with Julie Marsteller, May 21, 1970.

Hertz, Barbara Valentine, class of 1943, development officer, interview with Arline Winer, class of 1954, 1989.

Hofheimer, Hannah Falk. class of 1909, interview with Arlene Winer, class of 1954, Centennial Oral History Interviews, 18896

Horowitz, Gedale, trustee (1977–2002), chair of finance committee (1977–1999), interview with author, March 8, 2016.

Kaplan, Helene L., class of 1953; trustee (1974–2013); trustee chair (1984–1994), interview with Rosalind Rosenberg, March 22, 2000.

Kay, Laura, Physics and Astronomy Department (1991–), interviews with author, March 16, 2017, July 30, 2018.

Keyserling, Mary Dublin, class of 1930; interview with Arlene Winer, class of 1954, Barnard Centennial Oral Histories, 1989.

Kouwenhoven, John, English Department (1946–1975), interview with Julie Marsteller, April 22, 1975.

Kurze, Heather, class of 1971; Class of 1971 Interviews, February 2011.

Laboy, Felicity, daughter of President Mattfeld, correspondence with author, spring 2018.

Lofromento, Mary Ann, class of 1977, trustee (2011–2013), interview with author, September 10, 2015.

Matsuda, Fay Chew, class of 1971; Class of 1971 Interviews, December 2011.

McIntosh, Millicent C., dean (1947–1953); president (1953–1962), interview with Isabel Grossner, Columbia University Oral History Office, 1966; interview with Arline Winer, January 30, 1989.

Meyer, Gladys, Sociology Department (1949–1975), interview with Julie Marsteller, November 18, 1974.

Milstein, Cheryl, class of 1982, trustee (2000–) and trustee chair (2018–), correspondence with author, 2018.

Olton, Charles S., dean of faculty (1977–1987), interview with author, June 10, 2014.

Pious, Richard, Political Science Department (1975–2014), correspondence with author, 2015.

Prescott, Anne Lake, class of 1959; English Department (1961–1994), interview with Elizabeth Moye, class of 2017, April 8, 2015.

Quindlen, Anna, class of 1974, trustee and trustee chair (1998–2008), correspondence with author, fall 2018.

Ricci, Carla, class of 1971; Class of 1971 Interviews, February 18, 2011.

Robinson, Gayle F. class of 1975; trustee (1995–2013), trustee chair (1998–2003), interview with author, February 2, 2017.

Rodgers, Kathryn J., college counsel, vice president for student affairs, acting president (1981–1995), interview with author, April 7, 2015.

Rosenberg, Eleanor, class of 1929; English Department (1953–1978), interview with Julie Marsteller, May 1, 1973.

Rosenman, Francis Siegel, class of 1917; self-reported memoir, May 20, 1983, provided to author by Toni Coffee, Barnard College Archives.

Rosman, Abraham, Anthropology Department (1965–1998), interview with author, July 28, 2014.

Rothschild, Florence Samet, class of 1908, interview with Arlene Winer, class of 1954, Barnard Centennial Oral Histories,

Royer, Christiner, English Department (1965–1977); admissions director (1977–1987); vice president for public affairs (1987–1999), interview with author, July 21, 2014.

Rubel, Paula, Anthropology Department (1966–1998), interview with author, July 28, 2014.

Sadler, Francis, class of 1972, trustee (2009–), interview with Lee Beaty May 1, 2018.

Saidel, Beth, special assistant to President Shapiro and Spar, staff writer (2002–2020), interview with author, July 16, 2018.

Schmitter, Barbara, Psychology Department (1957–1962), associate dean of studies (1955–1965); dean of studies (1965–1999), interview with author, July 28, 2014.

Sells, Marcia, class of 1981, trustee (2015–), interview with author, October 2, 2014.

Shapiro, Judith R., president (1994–2008), interview with author, June 22, 2015; correspondence, 2018.

Sharpe, Lesley, Anthropology Department (1994–), interview with author, spring 2018.

Siegel, Shirley Adelson, class of 1937, interview with Liz Galst, *Barnard Magazine*, Spring 2018.

Spar, Debora, president (2018–2017), correspondence with author, fall 2018.

Spencer, Carol Santinello, class of 1971; Class of 1971 Interviews, February 12, 2011.

Spurlock-Evans, Karla, class of 1971; Class of 1971 Interview, February 12, 2011.

Stecher, Emma, class of 1925; Chemistry Department (1945–1975), interview with Julie Marsteller, June 2, 1971.

Vagelos, Diana T., class of 1955; trustee (2000–), interview with Alyssa Choo, class of 2020, April 10, 2018.

Wallis, Lila Amdurska, class of 1947, interview with Arlene Winer, Barnard Centennial Oral Histories.

Woodbury, Nathalie, class of 1939; interview with Arlene Winer,1986.

Wyman, Lewis, budget director (1979–1995); vice president for finance (2001–2005), interview with author, April 15. 2015.

SECONDARY SOURCES

Alperstein, Janet F. The Influence of Boards of Trustees, Senior Administrators and Faculty on the Decision of Women's Colleges to Remain Single Sex in the 1980s. Teachers College, EDD 2001.

Beckert, Sven. The Monied Metropolis: New York City and the Consolidation of the American Bourgeoisie, 1850–1896. New York: Cambridge University Press, 2001.

Birmingham, Stephen. The Grandees: America's Sephardic Elite. New York: Harper and Row, 1971

——. Our Crowd: The Great Jewish Families of New York. Syracuse, NY: Syracuse University Press, 1967.

Carter, Susan B. "Academic Women Revisited: An Empirical Study of Changing Patterns in Women's Employment as College and University Faculty," Journal of Social History 14, no. 4 (1981): 675–699.

Cohen, Robert. When the Old Left Was Young: Student Radicals and America's First Mass Student Movement, 1929–1941. Oxford: Oxford University Press, 1997.

Cookingham, Mary E. "Bluestockings, Spinsters and Pedagogues: Women College Graduates, 1865–1910." Population Studies 38 (1984): 349–364.

Cutlip, Scott M. Fund Raising in the United States. New Brunswick, NJ: Transaction Publishers, 1969.

Dolkart, Andrew S. Morningside Heights: A History of Its Architecture & Development. New York: Columbia University Press, 1998.

Frankfort, Roberta. Collegiate Women: Domesticity and Career in Turn-of-the-Century America. New York: New York University Press, 1977.

Goldenberg, Myrna G. and Annie Nathan Meyer. "Barnard Godmother and Gotham Gadfly." Phd diss., University of Maryland, 1987.

Gouldner, Alvin W. "Cosmopolitans and Locals: Toward an Analysis of Latent Social Roles," Administrative Science Quarterly, 2 (March 1958): 444–480.

Gruber, Carol S. Mars and Minerva: World War I and the Uses of the Higher Learning in America. Baton Rouge, LA: Louisiana State University Press, 1975.

Hammack, David C. Power and Society: Greater New York at the Turn of the Century. New York: Russell Sage Foundation, 1987.

Hood, Clifton. In Pursuit of Privilege: A History of New York's Upper Class & the Making of a Metropolis. New York: Columbia University Press, 2017.

Horowitz, Helen Lefkowitz. Alma Mater: Design & Experience in Women's Colleges from the Nineteenth Century Beginnings to the 1930s. Amherst, MA: University of Massachusetts Press, 1985.

Komarovsky, Mirra. *Women in College: Shaping New Feminine Identities*. New York: Basic Books, 1985.

Leman. Nicholas. *The Big Test: The Secret History of the American Meritocracy*. New York: Farrar, Straus and Giroux, 1999.

McCaughey, Robert A. *Scholars and Teachers: The Faculties of Select Liberal Arts Colleges and Their Place in American Higher Learning*. New York: Columbia University Press, 1994.

Newcomer, Mabel, and Evelyn S. Gibson. "Vital Statistics from Vassar College." *American Journal of Sociology*, 29 (January 1924): 430–444.

Norwood, Stephen H. *The Third Reich in the Ivory Tower*. New York: Cambridge University Press, 2009.

Pak, Susie J. *Gentleman Bankers: The World of J. P. Morgan*. Cambridge, MA: Harvard University Press, 2014.

Perkins, Linda M. "The African American Female Elite: The Early History of African American Women in the Seven Sisters Colleges, 1880–1960," *Harvard Educational Review*, 67 (Winter 1997): 718–756.

Rischin, Moses. *The Promised City: New York's Jews: 1870–1914*. Cambridge, MA: Harvard University Press, 1977.

Rosenberg, Rosalind. *Changing the Subject: How the Women of Columbia Shaped the Way We Think about Sex and Politics*. New York: Columbia University Press, 2004.

Rossiter, Margaret. *Women Scientists in America; Struggles and Strategies to 1940*. Baltimore: Johns Hopkins University Press, 1982.

Schreker, Ellen W. *No Ivory Tower: McCarthyism & the Universities*. New York: Oxford University Press, 1986.

Solomon, Barbara Miller. *In the Company of Educated Women*. New Haven, CT: Yale University Press, 1985.

Tidball, M. Elizabeth. "Baccalaureate Origins of American Scientists and Scholars." *Science*, 193 (August 20, 1976): 646–652.

Van Denburg, John King. *Cause of the Elimination of Students in Public High Schools of New York City*. New York: Teachers College, Columbia University, 1911.

Walton, Andrea. "Achieving a Voice and Institutionalizing a Vision for Women: The Barnard Deanship for Women at Columbia University, 1884–1917." *Historical Studies in Education* 13, no. (Fall 2001): 113–146.

Wechsler, Harold S. "The Selective Function of American College Admissions Policies, 1870–1970." PhD diss., Columbia University, 1974.

Woody, Thomas. *A History of Women's Education in the United States*. New York: Science Press, 1929.

Wren, Daniel A. "Business Philanthropy and Higher Education in the Nineteenth Century." *The Business History Review*, 57 (Autumn 1983): 321–346.

BARNARD-RELATED BIOGRAPHIES AND AUTOBIOGRAPHIES

Bernays, Anne, and Justin Kaplan. *Back Then: Two Lives in 1950s New York*. New York: William Morrow, 2002.

Brennan, Joseph G. *The Education of a Prejudiced Man*. New York: Scribner, 1977.

Chute, William J. *Damn Yankee! The First Career of Frederick A. P. Barnard*. Port Washington, NY: Kennikat Press, 1978.

Cohen, Naomi. *Jacob H. Schiff: A Study in American Jewish Leadership*. Lebanon, NH: University Press of New England, 1999.

Dilley, Patrick. *The Transformation of Women's Collegiate Education: The Legacy of Virginia Gildersleeve*. London: Palgrave Macmillan, 2017.

Gildersleeve, Virginia. *Many a Good Crusade*. New York: Macmillan, 1954.

Ginzberg, Eli. *My Brother's Keeper*. New Brunswick, NJ: Transaction Publishers, 1991.

Goldin, Claudia, and Lawrence F. Katz. "The Shaping of Higher Education: The Formative Years in the United States, 1890–1940." *Journal of Economic Perspectives*, 13 (Winter 1999): 37–62.

Gordon, Lynn D. "Annie Nathan Meyer and Barnard College: Mission and Identity in Women's Higher Education, 1889–1950." *History of Education Quarterly*, 26 (Winter 1986): 503–522.

Gould, Jane S. *Juggling: A Memoir of Work, Family and Feminism*. New York: Feminist Press at the City University of New York, 1997.

Hirst, Gertrude M. *From a Yorkshire Town to Morningside Heights: Early Recollections*. New York: Barnard College, 1957.

Horowitz, Helen Lefkowitz. *The Power and Passion of M. Carey Thomas*. Champaign, IL: University of Illinois Press, 1984.

Jay, Karla. *Tales of the Lavender Menace: A Memoir of Liberation*. New York: Basic Books, 1999.

Mead, Margaret. *Blackberry Winter: My Earlier Years*. New York: Simon and Schuster, 1972.

Meyer, Agnes Ernst. *Out of These Roots*. New York: Atlantic Monthly Press, 1953.

Meyer, Annie Nathan. *It's Been Fun*. New York: Schuman, 1951.

Rosenthal, Michael. *Nicholas Miraculous: The Amazing Career of the Redoubtable Dr. Nicholas Murray Butler*. New York: Farrar, Straus and Giroux, 2006.

Sovern, Michael I. *An Improbable Life: My 60 Years at Columbia and Other Adventures*. New York: Columbia University Press, 2014.

Sulzberger, Iphigene. *Iphigene: Memoirs of Iphigene Ochs Sulzberger*. New York: Dodd, Mead, 1981.

INSTITUTIONAL HISTORIES OF BARNARD

Brewster, William Tenney. "Barnard College, 1889–1909." *Columbia University Quarterly*, 12 (March 1910): 151–171.

[Dobkin, Marjorie]. *A History of Barnard College*. New York, 1964

Knapp, Charles. "The Growth of Barnard College;" *Mortarboard* (1910): 26–32.

McCaughey, Robert A. *A Statistical Profile of the Barnard College Faculty, 1900–1974*. New York, 1974.

Meyer, Annie Nathan. *Barnard Beginnings*. Boston: Houghton Mifflin, 1935.

Miller, Alice Duer, and Susan Myers. *Barnard College: The First Fifty Years*. New York: Columbia University Press, 1939.

Rosenberg, Rosalind. *Changing the Subject: How the Women of Columbia Shaped the Way We Think about Sex and Politics*. New York: Columbia University Press, 2004.

Weneck, Bette. "Social and Cultural Stratification in Women's Higher Education: Barnard College and Teachers College, 1898–1912." *History of Education Quarterly*, 31 (Spring 1991): 1–25.

White, Marian Churchill. *A History of Barnard College*. New York: Columbia University Press,1954.

OTHER RELEVANT ACADEMIC INSTITUTIONAL HISTORIES

Cronin, Paul, ed. *A Time to Stir: Columbia '68*. New York: Columbia University Press, 2018.

Cross, Timothy P. *An Oasis of Order: The Core Curriculum at Columbia College*. New York: Office of the Dean, Columbia College, 1995.

Duffy, Elizabeth A., and Idana Goldberg. *Crafting a Class: College Admissions and Financial Aid*. Princeton, NJ: Princeton University Press, 1998.

Geiger, Roger L., ed. *The American College in the Nineteen Century*. Nashville, TN: Vanderbilt University Press, 2000.

Glascock, Jean, ed. *Wellesley College: 1875–1975: A Century of Women*. Wellesley, MA: Wellesley College, 1975.

Jacobs, Travis Beal. *Eisenhower at Columbia*. New Brunswick, NJ: Transaction Publishers, 2001.

Keller, Morton, and Phyllis Keller. *Making Harvard Modern: The Rise of America's University*. New York: Oxford University Press, 2001.

Kendall, Elaine. *"Peculiar Institutions": An Informal History of the Seven Sisters Colleges*. New York: Putnam, 1975.

King, Stanley. *A History of the Endowment of Amherst College*. Amherst, MA: Amherst College Press, 1950.

McCaughey, Robert A. *Stand, Columbia: A History of Columbia University in the City of New York, 1754–2004*. New York: Columbia University Press, 2003.

Newcomer, Mabel. *A Century of Higher Education for American Women*. New York: Harper, 1959.

Palmeri, Patricia. *In Adamless Eden: The Community of Women Faculty at Wellesley*. New Haven, CT: Yale University Press, 1975.

Patterson, Samuel W. *Hunter College: Eighty-Five Years of Service*. New York: Lantern Press, 1955.

Plum, Dorothy A., and George B. Dowell. *The Magnificent Enterprise: A Chronicle of Vassar College*. Poughkeepsie, NY: Vassar College, 1961.

Ulrich, Laurel T., ed. *Yards and Gates: Gender in Harvard and Radcliffe History*. Cambridge: Palgrave Macmillan, 2004.

Veysey, Laurence R. *The Emergence of the American University*. Chicago: University of Chicago Press, 1965.

Weld, William, and Kathryn Sewry. *Herbert E. Hawkes, Dean of Columbia College, 1918–1943*. New York: Columbia University Press, 1958.

INDEX

GPSR Authorized Representative: Easy Access System Europe, Mustamäe tee
50, 10621 Tallinn, Estonia, gpsr.requests@easproject.com